MCSE Guide to
Microsoft Exchange Server 2003 Administration

Larry Chambers
Byron Wright
Dan DiNicolo

THOMSON

COURSE TECHNOLOGY

Australia • Canada • Mexico • Singapore • Spain • United Kingdom • United States

THOMSON
COURSE TECHNOLOGY

MCSE Guide to Microsoft Exchange Server 2003 Administration

by Larry Chambers, Byron Wright, and Dan DiNicolo

Managing Editor:
Will Pitkin III

Developmental Editor:
Jim Markham

Text Designer/Compositor:
GEX Publishing Services

Product Manager:
Nick Lombardi

Associate Product Manager:
Sarah Santoro

Cover Design:
Steve Deschene

Production Editor:
Jill Klaffky

Editorial Assistant:
Jenny Smith

Copy Editors:
Karen Annett, Mark Goodin

Technical Edit/Quality Assurance:
Green Pen Quality Assurance, LLC
Christian Kunciw
Serge Palladino

Manufacturing Coordinator:
Melissa Hulse

Marketing Manager:
Guy Baskaran

Proofreaders:
Nancy Lamm, Harold Johnson

Indexer:
Rich Carlson

BRIEF
Contents

TABLE OF
Contents

Introduction

Welcome to *MSCE Guide to Microsoft Exchange Server 2003 Administration*. This book provides information about and experience working with Microsoft Exchange Server 2003. The book's pedagogical approach – combining theoretical information with hands-on practice – will help readers gain both the knowledge and skills they need to prepare for the Microsoft Certification Exam 70-284: *Implementing and Managing Microsoft Exchange Server 2003*. For the network professional who will be administering an actual Exchange installation, the book provides ample coverage of the various tasks with which an Exchange administrator must be intimately familiar. Coverage includes pre-installation planning and server preparation; installation and configuration; routine administrative tasks such as creating and managing recipient objects; security issues; client access; uninstallation; upgrading; and advanced configuration.

The Intended Audience

This book was written for network professionals and would-be network professionals alike. No previous experience with Exchange is assumed; however, readers should have experience with and understand the concepts involved in administering a Windows server. Knowledge of basic networking issues is required, as is familiarity with Active Directory 'infrastructure, permissions, and so on.

To reap maximum benefit from the activities in this book, you should read all instructions closely and follow the steps in the activities carefully. So that readers are exposed to all aspects of Exchange administration – from installation; through configuration, maintenance, and troubleshooting; to uninstallation – each chapter must, by necessity, build upon previous chapters. This means that all steps and chapters should be completed fully and in the order in which they appear in the book. Skipping steps or going through chapters out of order will prevent you from completing the activities in later chapters.

Chapter Descriptions

Chapter 1, "Introduction to Exchange Server 2003," provides an overview of messaging systems in general, introduces Exchange Server 2003 and its new features, and discusses those features that were present in Exchange 2000 Server but that were not included in Exchange Server 2003. The chapter also walks students through the Windows Server 2003 installation process.

Chapter 2, "Installing and Configuring Exchange Server 2003," first compares the Standard and Enterprise editions of Exchange Server 2003. After discussing the necessary planning and server preparation tasks that should be carried out before installing Exchange, the chapter walks students through the Exchange installation and configuration process.

Chapter 3, "Managing Recipients," explores how to create and manage user, group, and contact recipient objects and how to create and apply recipient policies.

Chapter 4, "Configuring Outlook and Outlook Web Access," discusses the various client access methods through which users can connect to Exchange Server 2003. The chapter also shows students how to configure an Outlook client to access Exchange and how to enable and configure Outlook Web Access through a web browser.

Chapter 5, "Managing Addresses," explains the different types of address lists used by Exchange Server 2003, demonstrates the use of recipient policies, and discusses the Recipient Update Service.

Chapter 6, "Public Folders," explains the use and purpose of public folders in Exchange Server 2003, and demonstrates how to create, configure, manage, and troubleshoot public folders. The chapter also explores public folder replication and public folder referrals.

Chapter 7, "Configuring and Managing Exchange Server," takes a close look at the configuration and administration of Exchange through the use of multiple administrative and routing groups. In this chapter, students work in pairs to uninstall Exchange and then reinstall it into a front-end/back-end configuration, which is used for the rest of the book.

Chapter 8, "Managing Routing and Internet Connectivity," provides an overview of SMTP and how it is used by Exchange Server 2003. This chapter explains message routing and Exchange's use of connectors, and details how the link state algorithm is used to route mail both internally and externally.

Chapter 9, "Managing Data Storage and Hardware Resources," discusses Exchange's data storage architecture, explains the Extensible Storage Engine and the use of transaction logging and content indexing, and outlines some general considerations to bear in mind when designing a data storage subsystem for Exchange Server 2003.

Chapter 10, "Securing Exchange Server 2003," delves into the security features of Exchange Server 2003 on several different levels. In addition to demonstrating how to administer permissions and delegate authority in Active Directory and Exchange, the chapter provides an overview of public key-based cryptography and Exchange's use of the Windows 2003 PKI. The chapter also demonstrates how to configure end-to-end security using S/MIME.

Chapter 11, "Backup and Recovery of Exchange Server 2003," covers the various methods of backing up an Exchange Server 2003 installation and provides information about the steps necessary to prepare for disaster recovery.

Chapter 12, "Troubleshooting Connectivity," provides an overview of several different tools available for troubleshooting transport issues, explains the use and content of non-delivery reports, and discusses the types of issues that often lead to transport errors.

Chapter 13, "Monitoring and Troubleshooting the Server," discusses some of the tools available for monitoring the status of Exchange Server 2003 environment. The chapter also surveys some of the tools and techniques used for server maintenance and troubleshooting.

Chapter 14, "Upgrading to Exchange Server 2003" discusses various upgrade paths to Exchange Server 2003 and how each type of upgrade is implemented.

Features and Approach

To ensure a successful learning experience, *MSCE Guide to Microsoft Exchange Server 2003 Administration* includes the following pedagogical features:

- **Chapter Objectives**—Each chapter begins with a detailed list of the concepts to be mastered. This list gives you a quick reference to the chapter's contents and is a useful study aid.

- **Activities**—Activities are incorporated throughout the text, giving you practice in setting up, managing, and troubleshooting network security. The activities give you a strong foundation for carrying out network administration tasks in the real world. As noted, because of this book's progressive nature, completing the activities is essential before moving on to the end-of-chapter case projects and subsequent chapters.

- **Chapter Summary**—Each chapter's text is followed by a summary of the concepts introduced in that chapter. These summaries provide a helpful way to recap and revisit the ideas covered in each chapter.

- **Key Terms**—All of the terms within the chapter that were introduced with boldfaced text are gathered together in the Key Terms list at the end of the chapter. This provides you with a method of checking your understanding of all the terms introduced.

- **Review Questions**—The end-of-chapter assessment begins with a set of review questions that reinforce the ideas introduced in each chapter. Answering these questions will ensure that you have mastered the important concepts.

- **Case Projects**—Each chapter closes with a section that proposes certain situations. You are asked to evaluate the situations and decide upon the course of action to be taken to remedy the problems described. This valuable tool will help you sharpen your decision-making and troubleshooting skills, which are important aspects of network administration.

- **Lab Manual**—The CD-ROM that accompanies this text contains includes **Lab Manual** exercises in PDF format. There are several lab exercises for each chapter and they are designed to provide additional hands-on experience that complements the content covered in the main text. The projects in each Lab Manual chapter are intended to be completed after you have finished the corresponding chapter in the main text.

- **Test Preparation Software**—The CD-ROM that accompanies this text also includes CoursePrep® test preparation software, which provides sample MCSE exam questions mirroring the look and feel of the MCSE exams.

Text and Graphic Conventions

Additional information and exercises have been added to this book to help you better understand what is being discussed in the chapter. Icons throughout the text alert you to additional materials. The icons used in this textbook are as follows:

Tips offer extra information on resources, how to attack problems, and time-saving shortcuts.

Notes present additional helpful material related to the subject being discussed.

The Caution icon identifies important information about potential mistakes or hazards.

Each Activity in this book is preceded by the Activity icon.

Case Project icons mark the end-of-chapter case projects, which are scenario-based assignments that ask you to independently apply what you have learned in the chapter.

Instructor's Resources

The following supplemental materials are available when this book is used in a classroom setting. All of the supplements available with this book are provided to the instructor on a single CD-ROM.

Electronic Instructor's Manual. The Instructor's Manual that accompanies this textbook includes additional instructional material to assist in class preparation, including suggestions for classroom activities, discussion topics, and additional activities.

Solutions. Solutions are provided for the end-of-chapter material, including Review Questions, and, where applicable, Case Projects.

ExamView®. This textbook is accompanied by ExamView, a powerful testing software package that allows instructors to create and administer printed, computer (LAN-based), and Internet exams. ExamView includes hundreds of questions that correspond to the topics covered in this text, enabling students to generate detailed study guides that include page references for further review. The computer-based and Internet testing components allow students to take exams at their computers and also save the instructor time by grading each exam automatically.

PowerPoint presentations. This book comes with Microsoft PowerPoint slides for each chapter. These are included as a teaching aid for classroom presentation, to make available to students on the network for chapter review, or to be printed for classroom distribution. Instructors, please feel at liberty to add your own slides for additional topics you introduce to the class.

Figure files. All of the figures and tables in the book are reproduced on the Instructor's Resource CD, in bitmap format. Similar to the PowerPoint presentations, these are included as a teaching aid for classroom presentation, to make available to students for review, or to be printed for classroom distribution

Minimum Lab Requirements

- **Hardware:**

  One computer capable of running Windows Server 2003, Enterprise Edition with Exchange Server 2003, Enterprise Edition is required for each student. Chapter 1 walks students through the installation and configuration of Windows Server 2003. As part of this installation the student is instructed to delete any partitions existing on the machine. Chapter 2 walks students through the installation of Exchange Server 2003. The Exchange Server 2003 installation is configured throughout the rest of the book. Be aware that the activities in Chapters 7-14 require each student to have access to two servers. Staring with Chapter 7 it is assumed that students are working in pairs.

  In addition, starting with Chapter 5, a Windows XP client workstation is needed for various optional activities.

  All hardware should be listed on Microsoft's Hardware Compatibility List for Windows Server and should meet the following hardware requirements.

Hardware Component	Server
CPU	Intel Pentium or compatible 133 MHz or higher (733 MHz recommended)
Memory	256 MB RAM (512 MB RAM recommended)
Disk Space	Minimum of one 4 GB partition (C), with all partitions available for deletion
Drives	CD-ROM (or DVD-ROM)
Networking	All lab computers should be networked. A connection to the Internet is assumed.

Hardware Component	Client workstation (optional)
CPU	Intel Pentium or compatible 233 MHz or higher (300 MHz recommended)
Memory	128 MB RAM (512 MB RAM recommended)
Disk Space	Minimum of one 4-GB partition (C), with 150 MB of available hard disk space
Drives	CD-ROM (or DVD-ROM)
Networking	All lab computers should have the ability to be networked. A connection to the Internet is assumed.

- **Software:**

  The following software should be available to students on CD:

  - Windows Server 2003, Enterprise Edition

  - Exchange Server 2003, Enterprise Edition

  The following software should be available to students at the network location \\serverinst\office:

  - Microsoft Office 2003 (any edition)

  Please note if the Microsoft Office 2003 installation files are available from a different location, Step 2 in Chapter 4's Activity 4-1 should be modified appropriately.

- **Set Up Instructions:**

  As mentioned, Chapters 1 and 2 walk the students through the installation of Windows Server 2003 and Exchange Server 2003. No set up is required in advance.

  The Windows XP client workstation (necessary for various optional activities stating with Chapter 5) should be set up as follows:

  - Windows XP Home or Professional installed in either the domain created by the student in Chapter 1 or a workgroup

  - Outlook 2003 installed and configured for at least one account in the student's Exchange organization

1

INTRODUCTION TO EXCHANGE SERVER 2003

After reading this chapter you will be able to:

♦ Describe different types of messaging systems

♦ Understand the features available in Exchange Server 2003

♦ List the new features available in Exchange Server 2003

♦ List the features removed from Exchange Server 2003

Exchange Server 2003 is the latest version of the Microsoft Exchange **messaging system** and is one of the most popular messaging systems in the world. Early versions suffered from a lack of scalability, but the latest versions have an exceptional range of features and massive scalability.

To better appreciate the benefits of Exchange Server 2003, it is important to understand which features of Exchange Server 2003 are new. Knowing the new features helps you understand when upgrading older versions is required or desirable.

This chapter begins by describing the two generic types of messaging systems. Next, the overall features of Exchange Server 2003 are discussed followed by an examination of its new features. Finally, this chapter discusses the features not present in Exchange Server 2003 that were present in Exchange 2000 Server.

TYPES OF MESSAGING SYSTEMS

Messaging systems have become a standard part of almost every company. They allow easy communication between all levels of staff in an organization. They are a much faster method of disseminating information than traditional paper memos. Many messaging systems also support workflow for certain tasks. For instance, in a hospital three people might be required to grant approval before a patient is released. Messaging systems can be used to route the request for approval between the proper three people without requiring paper to be passed between them.

Today, a messaging system goes well beyond just an e-mail system. Messaging users expect to be able to use new technologies, such as cellular phones and personal digital assistants, to access their information and respond in real time. The choice of a messaging system is a strategic choice that can offer companies great advantages. For instance, a messaging system that easily integrates with the existing infrastructure of a company can allow overdue notices to be automatically sent to customers rather than requiring expensive custom programming to achieve the same goal. Regardless of the functionality available in messaging systems, they can be divided into two categories: **shared file messaging systems** and **database messaging systems**.

Shared File Messaging Systems

In a shared file messaging system, a central server is used to store messages in files, but the client software is responsible for performing most of the work. The early messaging systems designed for corporate use, such as Microsoft Mail, were shared file messaging systems because they were relatively easy for programmers to implement. Microsoft Mail required a post office to be created. The post office was a shared folder structure stored on a network server. When the user Bob sent mail to the user Alice, Bob's client software connected to the central post office and put the mail message into Alice's folder. The server was merely a repository for the messages. It didn't do any active processing. Most UNIX mail servers used by Internet service providers (ISPs) are shared file messaging systems.

The fact that the client software performs all the work makes a shared file messaging system inefficient. The client software cannot possibly understand the overall system when a message is sent to many users. Therefore, when a single message is sent to 10 users, that message is stored 10 times—once in the folder of each user to whom it was addressed. In addition, without centralized software, the messages cannot be indexed for efficient searching.

Scalability is a concern with shared file messaging systems. Many shared file messaging systems are unstable when many users attempted to access them at the same time. In some cases, the way the messages are stored causes stability problems; in other cases, the client software causes large amounts of network traffic as messages are processed.

Database Messaging Systems

Database messaging systems use a central database to store the messages for all users. In these systems, the client software does not access the database directly because the overall messaging system is too complex for the client software to reliably handle. All messages are stored in and retrieved from the database by a service running on the e-mail server. The server actively processes each message. Current messaging systems, such as Microsoft Exchange, Lotus Notes, and Novell GroupWise, are database messaging systems.

Message storage is much more efficient in a database messaging system than in a shared file messaging system. If a message is sent to 10 users, it is stored in the database only once. In the database, a pointer is created to that message for each user to whom it is addressed. This means a message sent to the entire company takes up no more space in the database than one sent to a single user. In larger organizations, this saves large amounts of storage space.

Modern databases are very scalable. They can be accessed reliably by thousands of users at the same time. This makes database messaging systems much more scalable and reliable than shared file messaging systems. In addition, databases are designed to be indexed for fast searching.

EXCHANGE SERVER 2003

Many features of Exchange Server 2003 make it a compelling messaging solution. These include the following features:

- Active Directory integration
- Cluster capable
- Policy-based management
- Recipient management flexibility
- Excellent client software
- Address book manageability
- Public folders
- Scalability
- Security
- Disaster recovery
- Flexible upgrade options

Active Directory Integration

Early versions of Exchange Server included their own directory service for tracking user characteristics and system configuration. **Active Directory**, which was released by Microsoft as part of Windows 2000 Server, is based on those early versions of the directory service.

Exchange Server 2003 can be installed on Windows 2000 Server with Service Pack 3 or Windows Server 2003. It can also use Active Directory installed on either platform. However, for full functionality, Exchange Server 2003 must be installed on Windows Server 2003. More information about installation requirements is found in Chapter 2, "Installing Exchange Server 2003."

Activity 1-1: Installing Windows Server 2003

Time Required: 60 to 90 minutes

Objective: Install Windows Server 2003.

Description: Exchange Server 2003 requires either Windows 2000 Service Pack 3 or Windows Server 2003. In this activity, you install Windows Server 2003. This allows you to do Web research and install Exchange Server 2003 in future activities.

1. Insert the **Windows Server 2003, Enterprise Edition CD-ROM** in your computer and reboot the system.

2. When the message "Press any key to boot from CD" appears, press any key on the keyboard. A blue screen appears and begins loading drivers. The drivers being loaded are shown in the white bar at the bottom of the screen.

3. When the "Welcome to Setup" message appears on the screen, shown in Figure 1-1, press **Enter** to begin installing Windows Server 2003, Enterprise Edition.

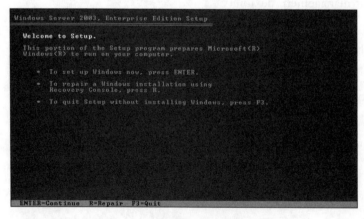

Figure 1-1   Welcome to Setup screen

4. Press **F8** to accept the license agreement.

5. If your server has a previous installation of Windows Server 2003, you are prompted to repair the existing installation. Press **Esc** to install a new copy of Windows without repairing the old one.

6. Before installing the software, delete all existing partitions on your system. If only unpartitioned space is shown, skip to Step 7. Otherwise, for each existing partition, complete the following steps.

   a. Use the arrow keys to highlight the partition you want to delete.

   b. Press **D** to delete the selected partition.

   c. Press **Enter** to confirm the deletion of this partition, if necessary.

   d. Press **L** to reconfirm the deletion of this partition.

   e. Repeat these steps for each remaining partition.

7. Press **C** to create a new partition.

8. In the Create partition of size (in MB) text box, type **4096**, and press **Enter**. This creates a 4-GB partition for Windows Server 2003.

9. Select **C: Partition1[New (Raw)]** and press **Enter** to install Windows Server 2003 on that partition.

10. Select **Format the partition using the NTFS file system**, and press **Enter**. Formatting the partition takes about 5 minutes. After the partition is formatted, the installation files are copied to the hard drive. Copying the installation files takes 5 to 10 minutes.

11. When the system reboots, the Regional Language and Options screen appears. Click **Next** to accept the default language setting of English (United States), the default text input language, and the U.S. keyboard layout.

12. In the Name text box, type your name. In the Organization text box, type **Security Financial**, and click **Next**.

13. In the Product Key text box, enter the product key that came with your copy of Windows Server 2003. Click **Next** to continue.

14. If necessary, select the **Per server** option button. In the Number of concurrent connections text box, type **20**, and then click **Next**.

15. In the Computer name text box, type **SERVER***xx*, where *xx* is a student number assigned to you by your instructor, as shown in Figure 1-2. If you are not in a classroom environment, you can use any two-digit number.

16. Type **Password!** in the Administrator password text box and the Confirm password text box, and then click **Next**.

17. Ensure that the date, time, and time zone are correct, and then click **Next**.

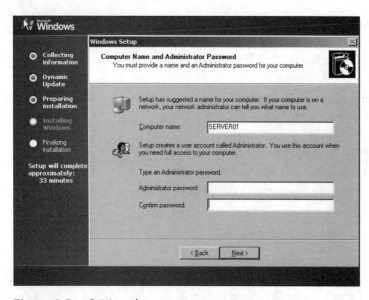

Figure 1-2   Setting the computer name

18. On the Network Settings screen, ensure that Typical settings is selected. This automatically detects and installs the network drivers for your network card. The card will be configured to obtain an IP address automatically. You configure the card in a later activity. Click **Next** to continue.

19. If necessary, on the Workgroup or Computer Domain screen, select **No, this computer is not on a network, or is on a network without a domain**. Click **Next** to continue. The remainder of the installation takes 20 to 40 minutes, depending on the speed of your server.

20. At the end of the installation, your server reboots automatically. After your server reboots, log on as **Administrator** with a password of **Password!**.

21. The Manage Your Server window appears by default on first logon. To stop this behavior, check the **Don't display this page at logon** check box and close the Manage Your Server window.

ACTIVITY

Activity 1-2: Configuring a Static IP Address

Time Required: 5 minutes

Objective: Configure your server with a static IP address.

Description: It is a standard practice to configure servers with static IP addresses. This makes it easier for clients to find services. A server running Exchange Server 2003 should also be configured with a static IP address. In this activity, you configure your server with a static IP address.

1. If necessary, log on to your computer as Administrator with a password of Password!.

2. Click **Start**, point to **Control Panel**, and double-click **Network Connections**. The Network Connections window opens.

3. Right-click **Local Area Connection**, click **Rename**, type **Classroom**, and press **Enter**.

4. Right-click **Classroom** and click **Properties**. This opens the Classroom Properties dialog box shown in Figure 1-3.

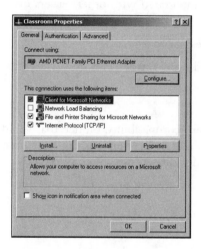

Figure 1-3   Classroom Properties dialog box

5. Click **Internet Protocol (TCP/IP)** and click the **Properties** button.

6. Click the **Use the following IP address** option button.

7. In the IP address text box, type **192.168.0.xx**, where *xx* is the student number assigned to you by your instructor. This is a network that can connect to the Internet. If your environment is different, change the IP address accordingly.

8. In the Subnet mask text box, type **255.255.255.0**.

9. In the Default gateway text box, type **192.168.0.254**, unless given an alternative gateway by your instructor. This might vary depending on how your classroom accesses the Internet. Click **OK**.

10. Click **Close**.

11. Close the **Network Connections** window.

ACTIVITY

Activity 1-3: Installing Active Directory

Time Required: 20 minutes

Objective: Install Active Directory.

Description: Exchange Server 2003 requires Active Directory to store configuration information. Running Dcpromo configures your server as a domain controller with a copy of Active Directory. In this activity, you configure your server as a domain controller.

1. If necessary, log on to your computer as Administrator with a password of Password!.

2. Click **Start**, right-click **My Computer**, and then click **Properties**.

3. Click the **Computer Name** tab and read the information on this tab. The information shows that this computer is part of a workgroup. This indicates that it is a stand-alone server and its security database is not integrated with other servers or workstations.

4. Click **Cancel** to close the System Properties dialog box.

5. Click **Start**, click **Run**, type **dcpromo**, and press **Enter**. This starts the Active Directory Installation Wizard.

6. Click **Next** to begin.

7. Read the information about operating system compatibility. Notice that Windows 95 and Windows NT 4.0 Service Pack 3 (SP3) and earlier versions cannot communicate with Windows Server 2003 domains using default settings. Click **Next**.

8. If necessary, click the **Domain controller for a new domain** option button, as shown in Figure 1-4, and click **Next**.

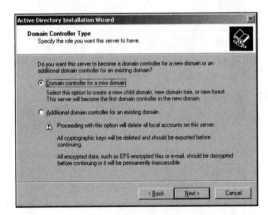

Figure 1-4   Active Directory Installation Wizard

9. If necessary, click the **Domain in a new forest** option button, and click **Next**.

10. In the Full DNS name for new domain text box, type **securexx.local**, where *xx* is your student number, and click **Next**.

11. Accept the default Domain NetBIOS name of SECURE*xx*, where *xx* is your student number, and click **Next**.

12. Accept the default Database folder and Log folder locations, and click **Next**.

1

13. Accept the default Share System Volume location, and click **Next**.

14. Click the **Install and configure DNS server on this computer, and set this computer to use this DNS server as its preferred DNS server** option button, and click **Next**.

15. On the Permission screen, if necessary, click the **Permissions compatible only with Windows 2000 or Windows Server 2003 operating systems** option button, and click **Next**.

16. Type **Password!** in the Restore Mode Password text box and the Confirm password text box, and then click **Next**.

17. On the Summary screen, click **Next**.

18. If prompted for the Windows Server 2003 CD-ROM, place it in the CD-ROM drive, and the installation continues. If a dialog box opens requesting that you select an action, click **Take no action**, check the **Always do the selected action** check box, and then click **OK**.

19. When the wizard is complete, click **Finish**.

20. Click **Restart Now** to reboot your server and complete the installation of Active Directory.

21. Log on to your server as **Administrator** with a password of **Password!**.

22. Click **Start**, right-click **My Computer**, and then click **Properties**.

23. Click the **Computer Name** tab. Read the information on this tab. The information shows that this computer is part of a domain. This indicates that it is no longer a standalone server and that its security database can now be integrated with other servers or workstations.

24. Click **Cancel** to close the System Properties dialog box.

Cluster Capable

Windows **clustering** allows applications to be installed on multiple servers but running on only one at a time. If an application fails on one server, a second server takes over. Exchange Server 2003 is compatible with Windows clustering. This is important for systems that must be highly available. With Windows clustering, an entire Exchange server can fail and users will have minimal, if any, disruption.

ACTIVITY

Activity 1-4: Modifying Microsoft Internet Explorer Default Security

Time Required: 5 minutes

Objective: Modify the default security settings of Internet Explorer.

Description: The default security settings of Internet Explorer block many Web sites. To perform Web research using your server, you must reduce the security settings on your server. In this activity, you lower the security settings in Internet Explorer.

1. If necessary, log on to your computer as Administrator with a password of Password!.

2. Click **Start**, point to **All Programs**, and then click **Internet Explorer**.

3. Read the warning dialog box that opens. Click the **Learn more about Internet Explorer's Enhanced Security Configuration** link.

4. Click **OK** on the new warning dialog box that opens, and read the Web page that appears. Pay particular attention to the section Browser Security – Best Practices.

5. Close the **Internet Explorer** window with the security configuration information.

6. In the Internet Explorer dialog box, shown in Figure 1-5, check the **In the future, do not show this message** check box, and then click **OK**.

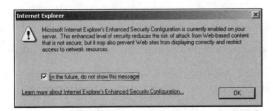

Figure 1-5   Internet Explorer dialog box

7. In the Address Bar, type **http://www.google.com** and press **Enter**.

8. If the New Connection Wizard appears, then perform the following steps:

   a. Click **Next** on the Welcome to the New Connection Wizard screen.

   b. If necessary, click the **Connect to the Internet** option button, and click **Next**.

   c. Click the **Connect using a broadband connection that is always on** option button, and click **Next**.

   d. Click **Finish**.

9. You receive a warning dialog box indicating that some content on this Web site is blocked by the current security settings. Click the **Close** button.

10. Click the **Tools** menu and click **Internet Options**.

11. Click the **Security** tab and click **Internet**.

12. In the Security level for this zone area, slide the bar down to **Medium-low**, as shown in Figure 1-6. When the warning dialog box opens, read it and click **Yes**.

13. Click **OK** to close the Internet Options dialog box and save the settings.

14. Close **Internet Explorer**.

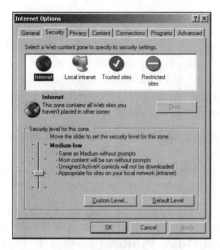

Figure 1-6   Security tab

15. Click **Start**, point to **All Programs**, and then click **Internet Explorer**.

16. In the Address Bar, type **http://www.google.com** and press **Enter**. Notice that there was no warning about blocked content this time.

17. Close **Internet Explorer**.

Policy-Based Management

To enhance manageability, policies can be used to manage Exchange **recipients** and servers. Recipient policies allow administrators to define criteria for groups of users to be managed. For example, a recipient policy can be configured to give a different e-mail address for users in a particular department.

Server policies are used to manage groups of servers. A server policy can apply settings for many servers at once. This is very efficient in larger organizations that have many Exchange servers. One setting that can be configured is mailbox size limits.

Recipient Management Flexibility

Users are the most common type of recipient in an organization, but Exchange Server 2003 has many more potential recipients. Exchange Server 2003 can use both security groups and distribution groups as recipients. This makes it easy to take advantage of groups based on workgroups or departments that have already been created for security purposes. Other potential recipients include contacts and **public folders**. The details of creating and maintaining recipients are in Chapter 3, "Managing Recipients."

Excellent Client Software

Exchange Server 2003 is capable of acting as a server for many different e-mail clients. However, Microsoft Outlook is the best client software to use. Many advanced features in Exchange Server 2003 are available only when using Outlook as the client software. Many organizations already own Outlook as part of the Microsoft Office suite of applications. It can also be purchased as a bundle with Exchange Server 2003.

A Web-based version of Outlook called **Outlook Web Access (OWA)** is included with Exchange Server 2003. Having a Web interface is excellent for mobile users such as salespeople who need to access their mail messages and calendar from remote sites like hotels.

Any standard Internet e-mail client, such as Outlook Express or Eudora, can also be used to access Exchange Server 2003. Exchange Server 2003 supports **Simple Mail Transfer Protocol (SMTP)** for mail delivery and **Post Office Protocol version 3 (POP3)** and **Internet Message Access Protocol (IMAP)** for reading e-mail. POP3 is a simple protocol for reading e-mail that allows users to store messages in a single Inbox. IMAP is more flexible because it allows users to store messages in multiple folders and choose from multiple synchronization options. Many advanced features of Exchange Server 2003, such as calendaring and Inbox rules, are not available through Internet e-mail clients.

More information about client software configuration is available in Chapter 4, "Configuring Outlook and Outlook Web Access."

ACTIVITY

Activity 1-5: Installing Internet Information Services

Time Required: 10 minutes

Objective: Install Internet Information Services (IIS).

Description: IIS is required for Outlook Web Access. In this activity, you install IIS to ensure that OWA is functional after installing Exchange Server 2003 in Chapter 2.

1. If necessary, log on to your computer as Administrator with a password of Password!.

2. If necessary, insert the Windows Server 2003 CD-ROM into your CD-ROM drive.

3. Click **Start**, point to **Control Panel**, and click **Add or Remove Programs**.

4. Click **Add/Remove Windows Components**.

5. Check the **Application Server** check box, as shown in Figure 1-7, and click **Next**.

6. Click **Finish**.

7. Close the **Add or Remove Programs** window.

8. Click **Start**, point to **Administrative Tools**, and then click **Internet Information Services (IIS) Manager**.

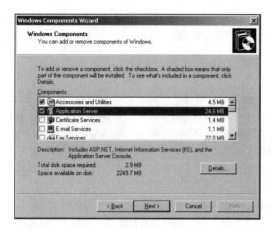

Figure 1-7   Windows Components Wizard

9. Click the **Web Sites** folder. A single Web site named Default Web Site is created and is running. This is the Web site that will host OWA.

10. Close **Internet Information Services (IIS) Manager**.

Address Book Manageability

Several types of address books can be made available to users. The **Global Address List (GAL)** is always available to users. Typically, the GAL is a list of all users in an organization. However, administrators can modify this to provide different GALs to different groups of users. This is useful when Exchange hosting has been outsourced to an **application service provider (ASP)**. The ASP can ensure that each customer only has his own employees in the GAL that they use. Address book management is covered in Chapter 5, "Managing Addresses."

Public Folders

Public folders are used by Exchange Server 2003 to support shared calendars, discussion groups, shared mailboxes, and messaging applications. Shared calendars can be created in a public folder to support booking resources or time tracking for consultants. A discussion group can be used to facilitate topic-based communication in an organization and keep a long-term record of what was said. Departments can use shared mailboxes to have a single e-mail address by which users can make contact with them. Messaging applications use public folders as their repository for information.

Public folders can store more than just messages. A public folder can also store files that are shared. Within a public folder, security can be controlled. Some users can be given permissions to create new content and change existing content, whereas others can be given permission only to view content. Security can be controlled separately for each public folder.

The content stored in public folders can be replicated to multiple servers. This makes access to public folder information more efficient across the network.

Scalability

Exchange Server 2003 supports **scaling out**. Scaling out is when a single application is installed on multiple servers and those servers communicate to operate as a single system. Exchange Server 2003 can be installed on more than one server with each server acting as part of a larger system. This means that larger organizations can have many servers instead of being limited by the capacity of a single server. Scaling out by adding multiple servers is generally less expensive than scaling up, which increases the capacity of a single server.

When multiple servers are part of a single Exchange organization, they can be organized into routing groups. Routing groups control how messages are transferred in the organization. Administrators can control the cost to move messages from one routing group to another.

Security

The security built in to Exchange Server 2003 is very flexible. Administrative tasks can be delegated to certain parts of the Exchange organization. This allows the administrative workload to be spread among multiple administrators. For example, one administrator can be granted permissions to manage a group of servers in a single location.

Security is also supported when users are sending messages. The protocol **Secure Multipurpose Internet Mail Extension (S/MIME)** is used to encrypt Internet e-mail messages and is supported by Outlook and Exchange Server 2003. In addition, access to OWA can be encrypted using **Secure Sockets Layer (SSL)**. SSL is used to encrypt communication between Web servers and Web clients.

Finally, when combined with third-party software, Exchange Server 2003 can effectively block e-mail viruses before they are delivered to users. Because Exchange Server 2003 is extremely popular, many vendors, such as Symantec and McAfee, produce virus and spam blocking software for it.

Disaster Recovery

If your implementation of Exchange Server 2003 encounters a problem, tools are available to repair the Exchange databases. This enhances the chances of recovering all the information on the Exchange server.

Databases cannot be backed up while they are in use without special software. When Exchange Server 2003 is installed, a new version of NT Backup is also installed. This new version of NT Backup is capable of backing up the Exchange databases while users are accessing it. Third-party vendors of backup software also sell agents for backing up Exchange while it is running.

NT Backup can back up and restore only entire Exchange databases. Third-party backup software can restore individual messages.

NOTE

Flexible Upgrade Options

A key factor in deciding whether to upgrade from an older product to a new one is the difficulty of the upgrade. Both Exchange Server 5.5 and Exchange 2000 Server can be upgraded to Exchange Server 2003 fairly easily. Tools are included with Exchange Server 2003 to migrate information from the older server to the new and maintain connectivity between them during the migration. Exchange 2000 Server can be upgraded with a simple in-place upgrade, whereas Exchange Server 2003 is installed over an existing Exchange 2000 server.

Exchange Server also includes tools for upgrading and connecting to messaging systems from other vendors. This makes it easier to migrate from older messaging systems to Exchange Server 2003. Tools are included to migrate from both Novell GroupWise and Lotus Notes.

NEW FEATURES OF EXCHANGE SERVER 2003

To justify migrating users to a new version of Exchange Server, there must be compelling new features. In the late 1990s, corporations might have upgraded just because a new version was available, but since the year 2000, a quantifiable benefit to the organization must exist. Buying new software has to add value to the company by decreasing costs, increasing revenue, or providing some other qualitative benefit.

The following new features in Exchange Server 2003 add value to an organization:

- Improved OWA
- Kerberos authentication
- RPC over HTTP
- Mobile Services for Exchange
- Query-based distribution groups
- Recovery storage group
- Enhanced clustering
- Internet Mail Wizard
- Connection filtering

Improved OWA

OWA has been significantly improved since Exchange 2000 Server. The new version of OWA has almost the complete functionality of the full Outlook client. This makes it realistic to have a group of users that uses only OWA and not the full client. OWA can be used in remote locations, such as field sales offices, where a technology staff is not available to support the full client.

The new version of OWA has a much improved user interface that even looks like Outlook 2003. It supports rule editing so mobile users can create rules for forwarding and managing their mail.

Other changes seem cosmetic but add significant increases to productivity, such as a spelling checker and signature files. The spelling checker saves users time proofreading. Support for signature files reduces time spent typing contact information into each message.

A major new feature of OWA is **attachment blocking** and **junk e-mail filtering**. Attachment blocking automatically stops attachments with certain file extensions. This can greatly reduce the number of viruses entering an organization through e-mail. Junk e-mail filtering enhances productivity by automatically moving junk mail out of the main Inbox and into a junk mail folder.

Finally, the new OWA supports S/MIME. This allows OWA users to send encrypted e-mail.

Kerberos Authentication

Exchange Server 2003 supports using Kerberos as its authentication protocol when communicating with Outlook 2003. Previous versions of Outlook and Exchange Server were not capable of using Kerberos. Kerberos is the standard authentication protocol for all versions of Windows starting with Windows 2000 Server and Professional. It provides enhanced security over the older NTLM authentication used by previous versions of Exchange Server and older versions of Windows.

RPC over HTTP

Remote procedure call (RPC) over Hypertext Transfer Protocol (HTTP) is a huge advance for mobile users who want to use the full Outlook client. RPC over HTTP allows the full Outlook client to connect over the Internet via HTTP and have full access to all Outlook features.

Before RPC over HTTP, users wanting to use the full Outlook client remotely were required to use a **virtual private network (VPN)** connection. Only after the VPN connection was up and running could Outlook connect to the Exchange server. This extra level of complexity led to many frustrated users and administrators.

NOTE RPC over HTTP is only possible when Outlook 2003 is used for the client software, Windows XP is used for the client operating systems, and Windows Server 2003 is used for the server operating system.

Mobile Services for Exchange

Millions of people use mobile devices, such as cellular phones and pocket PCs. Mobile Services for Exchange allows these users to access their information stored on Exchange Server 2003. Mobile Services for Exchange reformats the normal output of OWA in a format that renders properly on smaller devices.

Query-Based Distribution Groups

One of the headaches when managing a messaging system is managing the membership of distribution groups. In large organizations, this can become a full-time job. For example, a company with 20,000 users might be required to add several hundred changes to distribution group memberships each day as new employees are hired and others move between departments and workgroups.

A query-based distribution group dynamically defines the membership of a group based on a Lightweight Directory Access Protocol (LDAP) query. By searching for a particular user attribute, such as department, group membership is automatically kept up-to-date. This reduces administrative time spent maintaining the memberships and makes them more accurate.

Recovery Storage Group

Previous versions of Exchange Server required you to keep a spare server if you wanted to recover individual mail messages. A backed-up version of the information store was restored to the spare server. Then, any required message could be exported to a .pst file and imported by the client. It was difficult to configure the server for this operation and it was cumbersome to recover the messages required.

Exchange Server 2003 uses a new feature called the **recovery storage group** to recover individual messages instead. The backed-up version of the information store is restored to the recovery storage group. Then, users are able to retrieve their messages from it. This is a much simpler process and does not require the maintenance of extra hardware.

Enhanced Clustering

The clustering support in Exchange 2000 Server only allowed for two servers in a cluster. This limit forced companies either to double the amount of hardware they used or limit their use of clustering to only critical servers.

Exchange Server 2003 supports using up to eight servers in a cluster. This allows up to seven servers in a cluster to be active as Exchange servers with one server passively waiting for an active server to fail. This is a much more effective use of hardware as only one of seven servers is idle.

Internet Mail Wizard

The Internet Mail Wizard makes it much easier for administrators with fairly simple environments to configure their Exchange servers to connect with the Internet. A variety of functions, such as e-mail domains, relaying, and rules for outbound messages, can be controlled through the Internet Mail Wizard. A simplified process reduces the likelihood of configuration errors that can result in downtime.

Connection Filtering

Exchange Server 2003 is capable of using block lists for **connection filtering**. Connection filtering restricts which servers are allowed to send e-mail messages to an Exchange server. Block lists provide data about IP addresses based on rules that can be configured to block incoming mail from the IP addresses. For example, when a mail server attempts to deliver an e-mail message to an Exchange server, the Exchange server queries the block list to find out more about it. The block list might report back that this IP address is an open relay. Based on this information, the Exchange server can filter the connection because the message is unlikely to be legitimate.

 Block lists are maintained by third parties and are accessible over the Internet.

NOTE

FEATURES REMOVED IN EXCHANGE SERVER 2003

The following features that were present in Exchange 2000 Server have been removed from Exchange Server 2003 because they were no longer required or redundant with other Microsoft products:

- Connectors for Lotus ccMail and Microsoft Mail
- Real-time collaboration features
- M: drive
- Key Management Service

Connectors for Lotus ccMail and Microsoft Mail

Lotus ccMail and Microsoft Mail are very old e-mail products. They have not been commonly used since the late 1990s. Microsoft has made the decision that it is no longer relevant to offer ongoing connectivity between Lotus ccMail and Microsoft Mail. If you require ongoing connectivity to either Lotus ccMail or Microsoft Mail, you should ensure that there is at least one Exchange 2000 server in your organization.

Real-Time Collaboration Features

Exchange 2000 Server provided real-time collaboration for instant messaging. In addition, when used with Exchange Conferencing Server, it supported multiuser conferences with text chat, sound, white boards, and video. None of these features is available in Exchange Server 2003. These features are now found in a separate product called Live Communications Server 2003.

M: Drive

In previous versions of Exchange Server, the drive letter M was created on the server to provide access to the information store. In theory, this allowed users to access their message through the file system across the network. Some applications were written to use this. However, unless a custom application was written to use this, there was little if any benefit to average users.

In many cases, the M: drive allowed the information store to be corrupted by antivirus software and other automated file maintenance routines. Most file maintenance software did not exclude the M: drive by default and many administrators did not configure software to avoid it. These software utilities did not realize that the M: drive was a virtual drive.

 The M: drive is disabled by default in Exchange Server 2003, but can be enabled if it is required for a software application.

NOTE

Key Management Service

The Key Management Service has been removed from Exchange Server 2003 because it is no longer required. Both Windows 2000 Server and Windows Server 2003 include Certificate Services, which replaces the functionality of the Key Management Service.

Chapter Summary

- The two generic types of messaging systems are shared file messaging systems and database messaging systems. Shared file messaging systems rely on the client software to manage the messages and are not very scalable. Database messaging systems use services running on a server to manage the messages and are highly scalable. Exchange Server is a database messaging system.

- Features of Exchange Server 2003 include Active Directory integration, cluster capable, policy-based management, recipient management flexibility, excellent client software, address book manageability, public folders, scalability, security, disaster recovery, and flexible upgrade options.

- New features of Exchange Server 2003 include improved OWA, Kerberos authentication, RPC over HTTP, Mobile Services for Exchange, query-based distribution groups, recovery storage group, enhanced clustering, Internet Mail Wizard, and connection filtering.

- Features removed from Exchange Server 2003 are the connectors for Lotus ccMail and Microsoft Mail, real-time collaboration features, M: drive, and Key Management Service.

Key Terms

Active Directory — The directory service included with Windows 2000 Server and Windows Server 2003.

application service provider (ASP) — A company that provides outsourced access to an application running at a remote location for a subscription fee.

attachment blocking — A feature that automatically blocks e-mail attachments with certain file extensions such as .exe or .vbs.

clustering — A system in which a service or application is installed on two or more servers, and if the application fails on one server, another takes over its role. Clustering enhances availability of services and applications.

connection filtering — A feature that restricts which servers are allowed to send messages to Exchange Server 2003. Servers can be blocked based on block lists that identify open relay servers.

database messaging system — A messaging system in which a service on the server manages the central database of messages. These messaging systems are very scalable.

Global Address List (GAL) — An address list generated by Exchange Server 2003. By default, this list contains all recipients in the Exchange organization.

Internet Message Access Protocol (IMAP) — A protocol that is used by e-mail clients to retrieve messages from mail servers. It can manage multiple folders for message storage.

junk e-mail filtering — A feature that automatically moves messages deemed likely to be junk mail to a junk mail folder.

messaging system — At a minimum, a method to send text messages from one computer user to another. More sophisticated systems also include features such as calendaring.

Outlook Web Access (OWA) — A Web-based version of the Outlook client software. The Exchange Server 2003 version of OWA has almost the complete functionality of the standard Outlook client.

Post Office Protocol version 3 (POP3) — A protocol that is used by e-mail clients to retrieve messages from mail servers. It can manage only a single folder, usually named Inbox, for message storage.

public folder — A storage location in Exchange Server 2003 for shared calendars, discussion groups, shared mailboxes, and messaging applications.

recipient — An object in Active Directory that Exchange Server 2003 recognizes as having the ability to send or receive messages. These include users, distribution groups, and public folders.

recovery storage group — A special storage group that can be used to restore backed-up versions of Exchange databases to assist in recovering individual mail messages.

remote procedure call (RPC) over Hypertext Transfer Protocol (HTTP) — A protocol that lets the full Outlook client communicate with Exchange Server 2003 over the Internet by tunneling remote procedure call commands inside HTTP packets.

scaling out — The process of installing an application on multiple servers to enhance performance.

Secure Multipurpose Internet Mail Extension (S/MIME) — A protocol that is used to encrypt and digitally sign e-mail messages.

Secure Sockets Layer (SSL) — A protocol used between Web browsers and Web servers to encrypt communication.

shared file messaging system — A messaging system in which client software performs the work of managing messages. These messaging systems are not very scalable.

Simple Mail Transfer Protocol (SMTP) — A standard for the set of commands used for communication between Internet mail servers. It was created in 1982.

virtual private network (VPN) — A remote access connection that encrypts information as it is transmitted across the Internet to keep it private.

REVIEW QUESTIONS

1. Which protocol is used to send messages between Internet mail servers?

   a. POP3

   b. SMTP

   c. IMAP

   d. HTTP

2. Most messaging systems used by corporations today are shared file messaging systems. True or False?

3. Which of the following are new features of Exchange Server 2003? (Choose all that apply.)

   a. Active Directory integration

   b. improved OWA

   c. scalability

   d. RPC over HTTP

   e. query-based distribution groups

4. Which of the following can be used as recipients in Windows Server 2003? (Choose all that apply.)

   a. contacts

   b. security groups

   c. distribution groups

   d. servers

   e. public folder

5. Which feature of Exchange Server 2003 allows roaming users to use the full Outlook client without using a VPN connection?

   a. RPC over HTTP

   b. clustering

   c. OWA

   d. Mobile Services for Exchange

   e. Kerberos authentication

6. Which feature of Exchange Server 2003 allows roaming users to access their messages with a cellular phone?

   a. RPC over HTTP

   b. clustering

   c. OWA

   d. Mobile Services for Exchange

   e. Kerberos authentication

7. Which new feature of OWA removes files from e-mail messages based on their file extension?

   a. junk e-mail filtering

   b. connection filtering

   c. attachment blocking

   d. GAL

   e. RPC over HTTP

8. List two database messaging systems.

9. Which feature of Exchange Server 2003 can be used to stop incoming messages from open relay servers?

   a. junk e-mail filtering

   b. connection filtering

   c. attachment blocking

   d. GAL

   e. RPC over HTTP

10. Which feature of Exchange Server 2003 makes it easier to restore mail messages for a user?

    a. clustering

    b. Internet Mail Wizard

    c. Kerberos authentication

    d. recovery storage group

    e. connection filtering

11. A new version of which utility is required to back up Exchange databases while they are running?

    a. NT Backup

    b. Exchange Backup

    c. Windows Server 2003 Backup

    d. third-party backup software

    e. Active Directory Users and Computers

12. A database messaging system uses less storage space than a shared file messaging system. True or False?

13. Which feature was removed from Exchange Server 2003 because it often caused database corruption when used with antivirus software?

    a. the connector for Lotus ccMail

    b. the connector for Microsoft Mail

    c. the real-time collaboration features

    d. the M: drive

    e. the Key Management Service

14. A shared file messaging system is more scalable than a database messaging system. True or False?

15. Which feature allows Exchange Server 2003 to fail over from one server to another?

16. Which feature was removed from Exchange Server 2003 because it has been replaced by Certificate Services?

    a. the connector for Lotus ccMail

    b. the connector for Microsoft Mail

    c. the real-time collaboration features

    d. the M: drive

    e. the Key Management Service

17. Which Exchange Server 2003 feature allows group memberships to change dynamically?

18. The fact that Exchange Server is widely used is a benefit because many third-party products, such as antivirus software, are available for it. True or False?

19. On which platforms can Exchange Server 2003 be installed? (Choose all that apply.)

    a. Windows NT 3.51

    b. Windows NT 4 with Service Pack 6a

    c. Windows XP

    d. Windows 2000 Server with Service Pack 3 or higher

    e. Windows Server 2003

20. How many servers can be in an Exchange Server 2003 cluster?

    a. 2

    b. 4

    c. 8

    d. 16

    e. 32

Case Projects

Case Project 1-1: Choosing a Messaging System

Gigantic Life Insurance has over 4,000 users and offices in five cities throughout North America. You have been called in as a consultant to give advice about what type of messaging system they should implement. An ISP has suggested using POP3 accounts that access a shared file messaging system. One of the internal staff has suggested using Exchange Server 2003, which is a database messaging system. What are the differences between a shared file messaging system and a database messaging system?

Case Project 1-2: Features for Roaming Users

Hyperactive Media Sales has 10 sales representatives who travel on a regular basis. These sales representatives require daily access to their e-mail and calendar. Which features of Exchange Server 2003 can they use to access their e-mail and calendar?

Case Project 1-3: Disaster Recovery

Helping Hand Social Services provides a wide variety of services such as counseling to clients in need. Approximately 150 staff members have e-mail accounts. Many internal systems have been converted to run on Exchange Server 2003. Exchange Server 2003 is not considered an essential service in the organization. Which features of Exchange Server 2003 enhance reliability and disaster recovery?

Case Project 1-4: Internet Mail Concerns

Buddy's Machine Shop has 30 staff, each with e-mail accounts. They are currently using POP3 mail accounts with their ISP but have been having problems. Some days, they are going over their limit on the number of messages that can be transferred. In addition, the ISP does not allow for more than 30 e-mail accounts, which will be a problem if a new staff person is added.

Buddy is concerned that if they get their own mail server, they will be vulnerable to spam and viruses. Spam filtering and antivirus scanning is currently provided by the ISP. What features of Exchange Server 2003 should put Buddy's mind at ease?

2

INSTALLING AND CONFIGURING EXCHANGE SERVER 2003

After reading this chapter, you will be able to:

♦ Differentiate between editions of Exchange Server 2003

♦ Prepare a Windows Server 2003 and an Active Directory environment for the installation of Exchange Server 2003

♦ Install Exchange Server 2003

♦ Identify and access Exchange Server 2003 administration and management tools

♦ Configure Exchange Server 2003 modes, global settings, and policies

♦ Configure server properties for an Exchange Server 2003 system

♦ Configure DNS to support Exchange Server 2003

Much like the Windows Server 2003 family, Exchange Server 2003 is offered in different editions. To best meet the needs of a particular environment, it's important to choose the edition that will not only meet current needs, but also meet future ones. The decision as to which edition of Exchange Server 2003 to select is not only impacted by needs, but also by the Windows Server version or edition on which it will be installed, and its specifications.

Prior to installing the first Exchange Server 2003 system, both the Windows Server operating system and Active Directory must first be "prepared." This involves ensuring that certain services are installed on the Windows server, and then running tools included with Exchange Server 2003 to prepare the Active Directory forest and domains for the installation process.

After Exchange Server 2003 has been installed, two main tools are used to manage and configure related settings. The first is **Exchange System Manager**, which is used to manage everything from an organization-wide setting to message queues. The second is a tool with which you are probably already familiar—**Active Directory Users and Computers**. Over the course of this and future chapters, you will become extremely familiar (and hopefully proficient) with these tools.

The initial configuration of an Exchange organization involves managing a range of global and server settings. This chapter introduces you to some of the more basic Exchange configuration settings that apply to both the Exchange organization and server objects.

EXCHANGE SERVER 2003 EDITIONS

To meet the needs of different customers, Exchange Server 2003 is offered in two different editions—Standard Edition and Enterprise Edition. The following sections outline the capabilities of each edition, including details on minimum and recommended server requirements.

Exchange Server 2003, Standard Edition

Exchange Server 2003, Standard Edition is the Microsoft Exchange Server solution aimed at meeting the messaging and collaboration needs of small- to medium-sized businesses. In some situations, Standard Edition is also a suitable solution for larger businesses, though it largely depends on the customer's need for scalability.

The main limitations of Exchange Server 2003, Standard Edition include:

- Support for a maximum of one storage group
- Support for a maximum of one mailbox store and one public folder store per storage group
- A maximum per-database size of 16 GB
- No clustering support
- The X.400 connector is not included

Table 2-1 outlines the minimum requirements and Microsoft recommendations for servers running Exchange Server 2003, Standard Edition.

Table 2-1   Exchange Server 2003, Standard Edition hardware requirements

Component	Minimum Requirement	Microsoft Recommendation
CPU	Intel Pentium (or compatible) 133 MHz or higher	Intel Pentium (or compatible) 550 MHz or higher
Memory	256 MB RAM	512 MB RAM
Operating system	Windows 2000 Server or Advanced Server with SP3 or higher Windows Server 2003, Standard Edition or Enterprise Edition	Windows Server 2003, Standard Edition or Enterprise Edition

Table 2-1 Exchange Server 2003, Standard Edition hardware requirements (continued)

Component	Minimum Requirement	Microsoft Recommendation
Free hard disk space	500 MB on the installation drive 200 MB on the system drive	500 MB on the installation drive 200 MB on the system drive
Additional drives	CD-ROM drive	CD-ROM drive
Display settings	VGA resolution or higher	VGA resolution or higher
File system settings	The following partitions must use the NTFS file system: - System partition - Partition storing Exchange Server binaries - Partitions containing transaction log files - Partitions containing database files - Partitions containing other Exchange Server files	The following partitions must use the NTFS file system: - System partition - Partition storing Exchange Server binaries - Partitions containing transaction log files - Partitions containing database files - Partitions containing other Exchange Server files

Exchange Server 2003, Enterprise Edition

Exchange Server 2003, Enterprise Edition is the Microsoft Exchange Server solution aimed at meeting the messaging and collaboration needs of large enterprise customers. It offers a range of scalability features that allow it to support much larger network environments, with room to expand as needs dictate.

The primary features that make Exchange Server 2003, Enterprise Edition a better choice for large organizations include:

- Support for up to four storage groups
- Support for up to five databases
- A maximum database size of 8 TB, limited only by server hardware
- Support for clustering implementations of up to eight nodes
- Built-in X.400 connector

Table 2-2 outlines the minimum requirements and Microsoft recommendations for servers running Exchange Server 2003, Enterprise Edition.

Table 2-2   Exchange Server 2003, Enterprise Edition hardware requirements

Component	Minimum Requirement	Microsoft Recommendation
CPU	Intel Pentium (or compatible) 133 MHz or higher	Intel Pentium (or compatible) 733 MHz or higher
Memory	256 MB RAM	512 MB RAM
Operating system	Windows 2000 Server, Advanced Server, or Datacenter Server with SP3 or higher Windows Server 2003, Standard Edition, Enterprise Edition, or Datacenter Edition	Windows Server 2003, Standard Edition, Enterprise Edition, or Datacenter Edition
Free hard disk space	500 MB on the installation drive 200 MB on the system drive	500 MB on the installation drive 200 MB on the system drive
Additional drives	CD-ROM drive	CD-ROM drive
Display settings	VGA resolution or higher	VGA resolution or higher
File system settings	The following partitions must use the NTFS file system: - System partition - Partition storing Exchange Server binaries - Partitions containing transaction log files - Partitions containing database files - Partitions containing other Exchange Server files	The following partitions must use the NTFS file system: - System partition - Partition storing Exchange Server binaries - Partitions containing transaction log files - Partitions containing database files - Partitions containing other Exchange Server files

PREPARING TO INSTALL EXCHANGE SERVER 2003

Installing Exchange Server 2003 involves more than simply running the Exchange setup program. A number of services first must be added to the Windows Server 2003 system on which you will complete the installation, and Active Directory forests and domains also must be prepared to support Exchange.

The basic processes that must be completed prior to installing Exchange Server 2003 include:

- Installing the Windows Server 2003 services required by Exchange
- Running the ForestPrep tool to prepare the Active Directory forest for the creation of the first Exchange organization

■ Running the DomainPrep tool to prepare each Active Directory domain for the installation or use of Exchange Server in that domain

In the following sections, you prepare your Windows Server 2003 system and Active Directory environment for the installation of Exchange Server 2003.

Installing Windows Server 2003 Services

To install Exchange Server 2003, a number of Windows Server 2003 services first must be installed. These include:

■ .NET Framework

■ ASP.NET

■ Internet Information Services (IIS)

■ World Wide Web Publishing service

■ Simple Mail Transfer Protocol (SMTP) service

■ Network News Transfer Protocol (NNTP) service

NOTE

When installing Exchange Server 2003 on a Windows 2000 server, the Exchange installation process adds and installs the .NET Framework and ASP. NET automatically.

Some of these services were installed along with IIS in Chapter 1, "Introduction to Exchange Server 2003."

ACTIVITY

Activity 2-1: Installing Windows Server 2003 Services Required for Exchange Server 2003

Time Required: 10–15 minutes

Objective: Install Windows Server 2003 services required to install Exchange Server 2003.

Description: In this activity, you install the Windows Server 2003 services required to install Exchange Server 2003.

1. Log on to your Windows Server 2003 system with the user name **Administrator** and the password **Password!**.

2. Click **Start**, click **Control Panel**, and then click **Add or Remove Programs**.

3. In the Add or Remove Programs window, click **Add/Remove Windows Components**.

4. At the Windows Components screen, click **Application Server**, and then click **Details**.

5. In the Application Server window, select the **ASP.NET** check box, as shown in Figure 2-1.

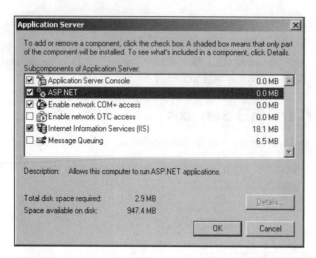

Figure 2-1   Adding the ASP.NET component from the Application Server screen

6. Click **Internet Information Services (IIS)** and then click **Details**.

7. In the Internet Information Services window, select the **NNTP Service** and **SMTP Service** check boxes, as shown in Figure 2-2. Click **OK** twice to return to the Windows Components screen.

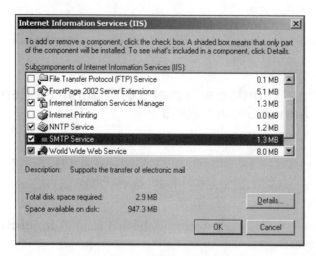

Figure 2-2   Adding the NNTP Service and SMTP Service components from the Internet Information Services (IIS) screen

8. Click **Next** to begin the installation process for these components. If prompted, insert your Windows Server 2003 CD, and click **OK**.

9. When the Windows Component Wizard completes, click **Finish** and then close the Add or Remove Programs window.

NOTE If you're unsure whether your Windows network is configured correctly to support Exchange Server 2003, you might want to consider installing the Windows Server 2003 Support Tools found in the Support Tools folder on the Windows Server 2003 CD. Once installed, you can use the DCDIAG and NETDIAG tools to determine whether any network- or Active Directory-related issues currently exist on your network.

Running ForestPrep

Prior to installing the first Exchange server in an Active Directory forest, the Exchange Server 2003 **ForestPrep** tool must be run to prepare the environment. ForestPrep must be run in the Active Directory domain where the **domain controller** holding the role of **schema** master resides. By default, the schema master role is held by the first domain controller installed in the Active Directory forest, although it can be changed.

To run ForestPrep, you must be a member of both the Enterprise Administrators and Schema Administrators group. The Administrator account in the first domain in an Active Directory forest is part of both of these groups by default.

The main functions carried out by ForestPrep include:

- Extending the Active Directory schema to include classes and attributes required by Exchange Server 2003

- Creating the Exchange organization container object in Active Directory

- Designating a user or group account that will have the Exchange Full Administrator permissions to the Exchange organization object

ACTIVITY

Activity 2-2: Preparing an Active Directory Forest for Exchange Using ForestPrep

Time Required: 20–30 minutes

Objective: Run ForestPrep to prepare your Active Directory forest for the installation of Exchange Server 2003.

Description: Prior to installing the first Exchange Server 2003 system in an Active Directory forest, the forest first must be prepared by running the ForestPrep tool. In this activity, you run the ForestPrep tool on your Windows Server 2003 domain controller.

1. Insert the Exchange Server 2003 CD into your CD-ROM drive.

2. Click **Start**, and then click **Run**. In the Open text box, type **D:\setup\i386\setup /ForestPrep**, where D represents your CD-ROM drive letter. Click **OK**.

3. At the Welcome to the Microsoft Exchange Installation Wizard screen, click **Next**.

4. At the License Agreement screen, click **I agree**, and then click **Next**.

5. At the Component Selection screen, ensure that the Action column is set to Forest-Prep, as shown in Figure 2-3, and then click **Next**.

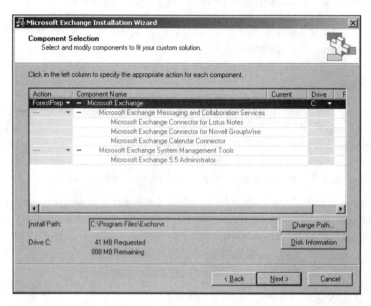

Figure 2-3 Ensuring that ForestPrep is selected in the Action column at the Component Selection screen

6. At the Microsoft Exchange Server Administration Account screen, ensure that your domain name and Administrator account are listed, and then click **Next**.

7. The Component Progress screen provides details about the progress of the Forest-Prep process, and can take a significant amount of time depending upon the specifications of your server. After the Completing the Microsoft Exchange Wizard screen appears, click **Finish**.

Running DomainPrep

After the ForestPrep process has completed, individual domains need to be prepared for Exchange Server 2003 by running **DomainPrep**. DomainPrep needs to be run in each of the following domains:

- The Active Directory **forest root domain**

- Any domains that will contain Exchange Server 2003 systems

- Any domain that will contain Exchange Server 2003 mail-enabled objects, even if no Exchange Server 2003 system will be present in those domains

- Any domains that include domain controllers configured as **global catalog servers**

■ Any domains that include user or group accounts that will manage the Exchange Server 2003 organization

To run DomainPrep, you must have administrator privileges in the domain in which the command is being issued.

The main functions carried out by DomainPrep include:

■ Creating the Exchange Domain Servers global group and Exchange Enterprise Servers local group in Active Directory

■ Making the Exchange Domain Servers global group a member of both the Exchange Enterprise Servers and the Pre-Windows 2000 Compatible Access local groups

■ Creating the Exchange System Objects container

■ Configuring permissions for the Exchange Enterprise Servers group

■ Modifying the AdminSdHolder template that sets permissions for the Administrators local group

■ Performing preinstallation checks prior to installing Exchange Server 2003

ACTIVITY

Activity 2-3: Preparing an Active Directory Domain for Exchange Using DomainPrep

Time Required: 5–10 minutes

Objective: Run DomainPrep to prepare your Active Directory domain for the installation of Exchange Server 2003.

Description: Prior to installing the first Exchange Server 2003 system in an Active Directory domain, the domain first must be prepared by running the DomainPrep tool. In this activity, you run the DomainPrep tool on your Windows Server 2003 domain controller.

1. Click **Start**, and then click **Run**. In the Open text box, type **D:\setup\i386\setup /DomainPrep**, where D represents your CD-ROM drive letter. Click **OK**.

2. At the Welcome to the Microsoft Exchange Installation Wizard screen, click **Next**.

3. At the License Agreement screen, click **I agree**, and then click **Next**.

4. At the Component Selection screen, ensure that the Action column is set to DomainPrep, as shown in Figure 2-4, and then click **Next**.

5. When the Microsoft Exchange Installation Wizard dialog box appears, read the contents of the message, and click **OK**.

6. The Component Progress screen provides details about the progress of the Domain-Prep process. After the Completing the Microsoft Exchange Wizard screen appears, click **Finish**.

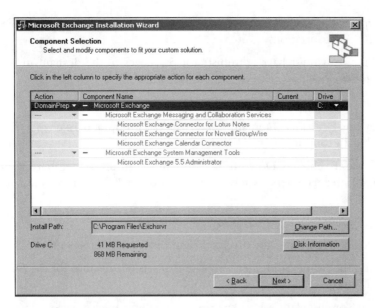

Figure 2-4   Ensuring that DomainPrep is selected in the Action column at the Component Selection screen

---

INSTALLING EXCHANGE SERVER 2003

After the necessary steps have been taken to prepare Active Directory for the installation of Exchange Server 2003, it's time to begin the server installation process. To install the first Exchange Server 2003 system in a forest, you must use an account that has the Exchange Full Administrator permission at the organization level, and is a member of the local Administrators Group on the Windows server on which the installation will be completed.

Activity 2-4: Installing Exchange Server 2003, Enterprise Edition

Time Required: 40–50 minutes

Objective: Install Exchange Server 2003 on your Windows Server 2003 system.

Description: With the necessary Windows Server 2003 services installed, and having run ForestPrep and DomainPrep to prepare the forest and domain respectively, you are ready to install Exchange Server 2003. In this activity, you install Exchange Server 2003, Enterprise Edition on your server.

1. Insert your Microsoft Exchange Server 2003 CD in your CD-ROM drive if necessary. Click **Start**, and then click **Run**. In the Open text box, type **D:\setup\i386\setup**, where D represents your CD-ROM drive letter. Click **OK**.

2. At the Welcome to the Microsoft Exchange Installation Wizard screen, click **Next**.

3. At the License Agreement screen, click **I agree**, and then click **Next**.

4. At the Component Selection screen, ensure that the Action column next to both Microsoft Exchange Messaging and Collaboration Services and Microsoft Exchange System Management Tools are set to **Install**, as shown in Figure 2-5. Click **Next**.

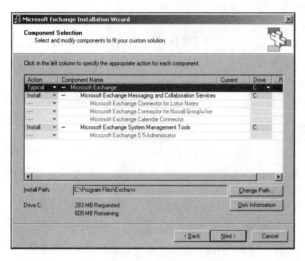

Figure 2-5 The Component Selection screen when installing Exchange Server 2003

5. At the Installation Type screen, ensure that **Create a new Exchange Organization** is selected, and click **Next**.

6. At the Organization Name screen, type **BLATHERCONSULTINGXX** in the Organization Name text box (as shown in Figure 2-6), where XX is your assigned student number. Click **Next**.

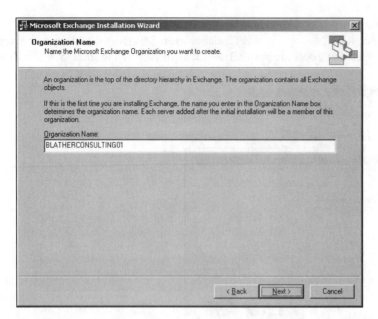

Figure 2-6   Specifying a name for your Exchange organization

7. At the License Agreement screen, click **I agree that I have read and will be bound by the license agreements for this product**, and then click **Next**.

8. At the Installation Summary screen, review the selected components, and click **Next**.

9. The Component Progress screen provides details about the progress of the Exchange Server 2003 installation process. After the Completing the Microsoft Exchange Wizard screen appears, click **Finish**.

Unattended Installations of Exchange Server 2003

Although small organizations might install only a single Exchange server, large organizations often need to install many Exchange servers to meet their needs. For cases in which Exchange needs to be installed on multiple servers, Exchange Server 2003 supports the ability to automate the process using unattended setups.

The unattended installation process can be used to install all but the first Exchange server in an organization. Unattended installations can be used for the following tasks:

- Installing Exchange Server 2003 on all but the first Exchange server in the organization

- Installing the Exchange Server 2003 System Management tools

- Running DomainPrep in all but the first domain

2

NOTE

Unattended setups cannot be used to install the first Exchange server in an organization, install Exchange on a Windows cluster, or install Exchange in a mixed mode environment (for example, one that includes Exchange Server 5.5 and Exchange Server 2003 systems). Unattended setups also cannot be used to perform Exchange maintenance tasks, such as adding or removing programs, reinstalling Exchange, or upgrading from a previous version of Exchange.

To perform an unattended setup, an administrator first needs to create an answer file that contains the information that would typically be supplied during a normal, manual installation. An answer file can be created on any system that meets the specifications for installing Exchange Server 2003 by inserting the Exchange CD, opening the Run command, and issuing the following command:

```
D:\setup\i386\setup /createunattend c:\answers.ini
```

When the /createunattend switch is used, the Exchange setup process appears to proceed just like any normal installation. However, rather than actually installing Exchange, the setup creates a file named answers.ini on drive C. All of the options selected during this mock installation process are added to the answers.ini file to be used for unattended installations of Exchange on subsequent servers. For example, with the answer file completed, an administrator could copy it to the C drive of another server, insert the Exchange CD, and issue the following command:

```
D:\setup\i386\setup /unattendfile c:\answers.ini
```

After being issued, this command completes the entire installation process using the answers found in the answers.ini file, rather than prompting for information to be entered manually. Ultimately, unattended installations can save administrators a great deal of time and effort, especially in larger network environments in which many Exchange servers need to be installed.

Deploying Exchange Server 2003 in a Cluster

In environments in which high levels of reliability and fault tolerance are critical, Exchange Server 2003, Enterprise Edition can be deployed as part of a cluster. In simple terms, a **cluster** is a group of independent servers (commonly referred to as nodes) that work together to ensure system availability. Should a single Exchange server that is part of a cluster fail, another server in the cluster can take on its roles to ensure that the server's resources continue to be accessible to users.

NOTE

Clustering is not supported with Exchange Server 2003, Standard Edition.

The clustering capabilities of Exchange Server 2003, Enterprise Edition relies on the Windows Clustering service to function. The maximum number of nodes supported in an Exchange Server 2003 cluster is eight, although this capacity depends on the Windows Server version in use. Table 2-3 outlines the clustering capabilities of Exchange Server 2003, Enterprise Edition, according to the version/edition of Windows Server on which it will be installed.

Table 2-3   Clustering capabilities of Exchange Server 2003, Enterprise Edition by Windows Server version/edition

Windows Server Version/Edition	Maximum Cluster Nodes
Windows 2000 Server, Windows Server 2003, Standard Edition	0 (Windows clustering is not supported on these operating systems)
Windows 2000 Advanced Server	2
Windows 2000 Datacenter Server	4
Windows Server 2003, Enterprise Edition	8
Windows Server 2003, Datacenter Edition	8

NOTE

You learn more about the clustering capabilities of Exchange Server 2003 in Chapter 7, "Configuring and Managing Exchange Server."

EXCHANGE SERVER 2003 ADMINISTRATION TOOLS

After Exchange Server 2003 is installed, a new program group called Microsoft Exchange is added under All Programs on the Start menu. The two primary tools used to manage an Exchange organization are found in this group—Exchange System Manager and Active Directory Users and Computers. In the following sections, you learn more about each of these tools and their roles in administering Exchange-related settings.

Exchange System Manager

Exchange System Manager is the primary administrative tool used to manage an Exchange Server environment and related system settings. After Exchange Server 2003 is installed, this tool can be accessed from Start, All Programs, Microsoft Exchange, System Manager. As a **Microsoft Management Console (MMC)** snap-in, the tool can also be added to custom consoles that include other administrative tools.

Examples of common administrative tasks that can be carried out with Exchange System Manager include:

   ■ The configuration of global settings, such as message formats, message delivery options, and mobile service settings

- The configuration of recipient settings, including templates, address lists, update services, and policies

- The configuration and management of administrative groups and routing groups

- The configuration and management of server settings, including message queues, storage groups, and protocols

- The configuration of connectors between Exchange and other messaging systems

- The delegation of Exchange administrative roles

- The configuration of server and recipient policies

Activity 2-5: Exploring Exchange System Manager

Time Required: 10 minutes

Objective: Access and explore the Exchange System Manager tool.

Description: Exchange System Manager is one of the primary administrative tools used to manage an Exchange organization. In this activity, you open and explore Exchange System Manager for the first time.

1. Click **Start**, point to **All Programs**, point to **Microsoft Exchange**, and then click **System Manager**. The Exchange System Manager tool opens, as shown in Figure 2-7.

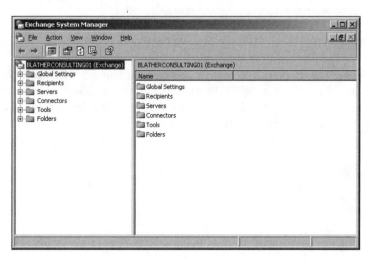

Figure 2-7   The Exchange System Manager tool

2. Click the **plus sign (+)** next to Global Settings to expand it. Global settings that can be configured include Internet Message Format, Message Delivery, and Mobile Services.

3. Click the **plus sign (+)** next to Recipients to expand it. Recipient settings that can be viewed or configured with Exchange System Manager include template settings, address lists, update services, and policies.

4. Click on Servers, as shown in Figure 2-8. Click the **plus sign (+)** next to Servers to expand it, and then click **ServerXX**, where XX is your assigned student number. Elements found directly beneath your server name include Queues, First Storage Group, and Protocols. Expand additional items below each to get a better sense of settings and elements available in this section, but do not change any settings.

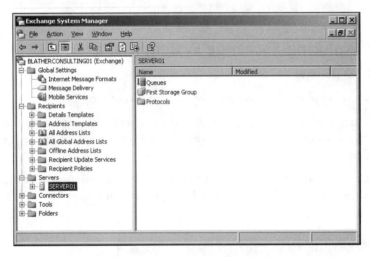

Figure 2-8   Expanding a server in Exchange System Manager

5. Right-click **ServerXX** (where XX is your assigned student number), and click **Properties**. This opens the ServerXX Properties window to the General tab, as shown in Figure 2-9. Click **Cancel** to close the window. You learn more about the configuration of server properties later in this chapter.

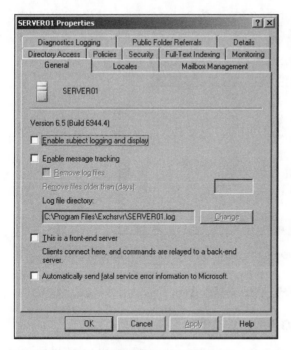

Figure 2-9   Viewing the properties of a server in Exchange System Manager

6. Click the **Connectors** folder to view its contents. Because no connectors were installed with Exchange Server 2003, the Connectors window should be empty.

7. Click the **Tools** folder. Tools found here include Site Replication Services, Monitoring and Status, Message Tracking Center, and Mailbox Recovery Center.

8. Click the **plus sign (+)** next to Folders to expand it. Click **Public Folders** to view its contents. By default, only the Internet Newsgroups folder is listed, as shown in Figure 2-10.

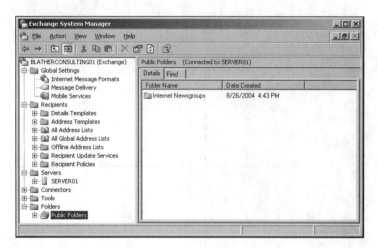

Figure 2-10   Viewing Public Folders in Exchange System Manager

9. Close the **Exchange System Manager** window.

Active Directory Users and Computers

Active Directory Users and Computers is the main administrative tool used to manage user, group, and computer account objects in a Windows Server 2003 Active Directory environment. After Exchange Server 2003 is installed, Active Directory Users and Computers can be accessed from the main Administrative Tools menu, or by clicking Start, All Programs, Microsoft Exchange, Active Directory Users and Computers.

The installation of Microsoft Exchange Server 2003 (specifically running ForestPrep) extends the Active Directory schema to include additional objects and attributes required for integrated Exchange messaging. These changes add many additional configurable settings to the properties of objects such as users and groups in Active Directory Users and Computers. Specifically, installing Exchange Server 2003 adds the following tabs to the properties of a user account:

- Exchange General
- Exchange Addresses
- Exchange Features
- Exchange Advanced

In addition, installing Exchange also extends the commands available from the Active Directory Users and Computers shortcut menus, such as Exchange Tasks, which opens a wizard to perform e-mail-related functions on an object.

The primary Exchange-related administrative tasks carried out with Active Directory Users and Computers include:

- Configuring e-mail addresses for users and groups
- Enabling or disabling user access to Exchange features
- Configuring user delivery options, delivery restrictions, and storage limits
- Configuring mailbox rights
- Creating and managing distribution groups

Activity 2-6: Exploring Exchange-Related Changes to Active Directory Users and Computers

Time Required: 10 minutes

Objective: Access and explore changes to Active Directory Users and Computers after Exchange Server 2003 has been installed.

Description: Active Directory Users and Computers is another administrative tool used to manage Exchange settings related to users and groups. In this activity, you open and explore Active Directory Users and Computers for the first time.

1. Click **Start**, point to **All Programs**, point to **Microsoft Exchange**, and then click **Active Directory Users and Computers**. The Active Directory Users and Computers tool opens, as shown in Figure 2-11.

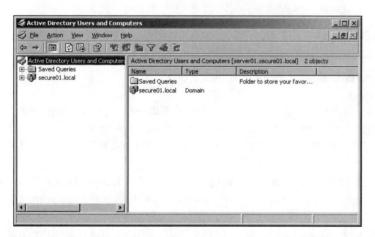

Figure 2-11   The Active Directory Users and Computers tool

2. Click the **plus sign (+)** next to secureXX.local to expand its contents, where XX is your assigned student number.

3. Click the **Users** folder to view its contents. The Users folder is actually a built-in Active Directory container that is used to store user and group objects.

4. Right-click the **Administrator** user, and view the options available on the shortcut menu. Click **Properties**. The Administrator Properties dialog box opens, as shown in Figure 2-12.

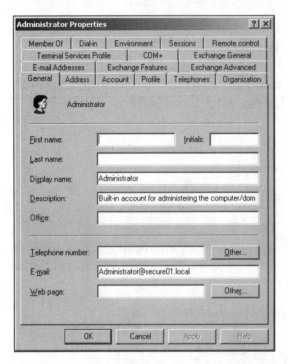

Figure 2-12   The Administrator Properties dialog box

5. Click each of the **Exchange General**, **E-mail Addresses**, **Exchange Features**, and **Exchange Advanced** tabs to view their configurable settings. These tabs are added to the properties of a user account when Exchange Server 2003 is installed. Do not make any changes to existing settings. Click **Cancel**.

6. Right-click the **Domain Admins** group, and click **Exchange Tasks**. This opens the Exchange Task Wizard, a tool to help administrators complete common Exchange-related tasks. Click **Next**.

7. At the Available Tasks screen, review the options available, as shown in Figure 2-13. Do not make any changes, as the configuration of user and group settings is looked at in detail in Chapter 3, "Managing Recipients." Click **Cancel**.

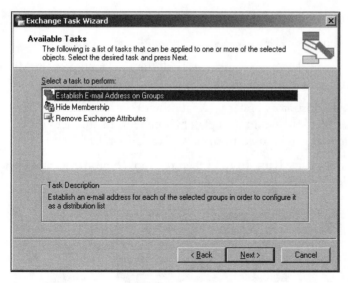

Figure 2-13 The Available Tasks screen of the Exchange Task Wizard

8. Close **Active Directory Users and Computers**.

You learn more about configuring user and groups with Active Directory Users and Computers in Chapter 3.

NOTE

Customized Consoles

Although both Active Directory Users and Computers and Exchange System Manager are both easily accessible from the Microsoft Exchange menu under All Programs, many administrators prefer to work with both tools from a single, consolidated management console. Windows Server 2003 allows you to create customized MMCs that include the specific snap-ins that you work with on a regular basis. These custom consoles can then be saved with a suitable name to a convenient location, such as your desktop.

Managing an Exchange server and e-mail users most frequently involves working with Active Directory Users and Computers and Exchange System Manager.

Activity 2-7: Creating a Custom MMC

Time Required: 10 minutes

Objective: Create a custom MMC that includes both the Exchange System Manager and Active Directory Users and Computers tools.

Description: Many administrators prefer to create their own custom MMCs as a way to consolidate administrative tools within a single environment. In this activity, you create a custom MMC console that can be used to manage Exchange-related settings.

1. Click **Start**, and then click **Run**. In the Open text box, type **mmc**, and click **OK**. An empty console opens, as shown in Figure 2-14.

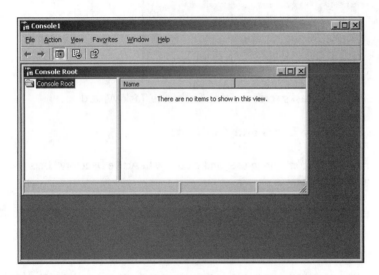

Figure 2-14   An empty MMC

2. Click **File** and then click **Add/Remove Snap-in**.

3. At the Add/Remove Snap-in window, click **Add**.

4. At the Add Standalone Snap-in window, click **Active Directory Users and Computers**, and click **Add**.

5. Scroll down, click the **Exchange System** icon, as shown in Figure 2-15, and click **Add**.

Figure 2-15 Adding the Exchange System snap-in to a custom console

6. At the Change Domain Controller window, accept the default value of Any Write-able Domain Controller by clicking **OK**.

7. Click **Close** to close the Add Standalone Snap-in window.

8. Click **OK** to close the Add/Remove Snap-in window. The console now includes both the Active Directory Users and Computers and Exchange System Manager snap-ins, as shown in Figure 2-16.

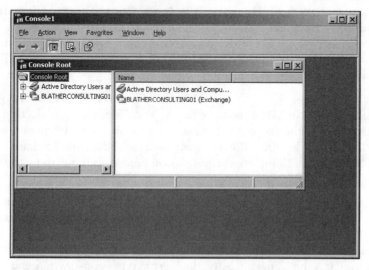

Figure 2-16 The custom console that includes both Active Directory Users and Computers and Exchange System Manager

9. Click **File** and then click **Save As**. Select **Desktop** from the Save in drop-down menu. In the File name text box, type **MyConsole**, and click **Save**. Close the MyConsole window.

10. When you are finished, an icon for MyConsole.msc appears on your desktop. Double-click **MyConsole.msc** to open your custom console, and then close it after you've confirmed that it works. When prompted as to whether you want to save changes to the console, click **No**.

Picking a Server Management Location

After Exchange Server 2003 is installed on a Windows server, it can be administered in many different ways. Some administrators prefer to handle all administration tasks directly from the server console, whereas others opt to use tools such as Terminal Services to remotely connect to the server's desktop from their workstation. Although both methods are valid, it is generally preferable to install the required server tools on a management workstation instead, such as an administrator's desktop system.

The administrative tools required to manage both a Windows server and Exchange Server 2003 can both be installed on a Windows XP Professional system running Service Pack 1 or higher. To install all of the necessary tools to manage an Exchange server, including Active Directory Users and Computers and Exchange System Manager, follow these steps:

1. Insert the Windows Server installation CD in the Windows XP Professional system, and install the adminpak.msi file found in the i386 directory. This installs the Windows server management tools found on the server's Administrative Tools menu.

2. Open **Add or Remove Programs** in Control Panel on the Windows XP system, and click **Add/Remove Windows Components**. Click **Internet Information Services (IIS)** and then click **Details**. Check the **SMTP Service** check box, click **OK**, click **Next**, and supply your Windows XP Professional CD to complete the installation if prompted. The SMTP service must be present to install Exchange System Manager.

3. Insert the Exchange Server 2003 CD in the Windows XP system and issue the command **D:\setup\i386\setup.exe**. At the Component Selection screen, click **Custom** in the drop-down menu next to Microsoft Exchange, and then select **Install** in the drop-down menu next to Microsoft Exchange System Management Tools. Complete the installation process to install these tools on the Windows XP Professional system.

4. After the Exchange setup process is complete, click **Start**, and click **Run** to open the Run dialog box on Windows XP Professional, type **services.msc** in the Open text box, and click **OK**. In the Services MMC, scroll down until you find the **Simple Mail Transfer Protocol (SMTP)**, right-click it, and select **Properties**. On the General tab, use the Startup type drop-down menu to disable the service, as it is no longer required after the Exchange System Management Tools are installed.

MANAGING EXCHANGE SERVER 2003

Managing an Exchange organization consists of a variety of tasks ranging from policy and server configuration through to mailbox and user management. Although you will become familiar with a wide variety of management tasks through this text, this chapter introduces you to some of the more common initial management tasks carried out after the first Exchange Server 2003 system is installed in a new environment.

Management-related tasks to be explored in this section include:

- Switching an Exchange organization from mixed mode to native mode
- Configuring Exchange global settings
- Configuring Exchange server property settings
- Working with system policies

Switching from Mixed Mode to Native Mode

After Exchange Server 2003 is installed, the Exchange organization runs in **mixed mode** by default. When running in mixed mode, an organization can support and coexist with Exchange servers running previous versions, such as Exchange Server 5.5. If your Exchange organization does not need to support interoperability with Exchange Server 5.5 systems, you should change the organization to **native mode**.

NOTE

Switching to native mode is a one-way process and cannot be reversed, so it's important to ensure that Exchange Server 5.5 systems won't need to be added to the organization in the future prior to completing the process.

The benefits of switching an organization to Exchange Server 2003 native mode include:

- The ability to create query-based distribution groups
- Bandwidth savings, because bridgehead servers will use 8BITMIME data transfers rather than the 7-bit exchanges used in Exchange Server 5.5 environments
- The ability for routing groups to contain servers for different administrative groups
- The ability to move Exchange Server 2003 systems between routing groups
- The ability to move mailboxes between administrative groups
- SMTP is used as the default routing protocol

After an Exchange organization has been switched to native mode, the Microsoft Exchange Information Store service should be restarted on all Exchange servers for them to be able to take advantage of native mode features. This can be accomplished by rebooting each server, although restarting the service using the Services MMC is generally preferable.

Activity 2-8: Switching Exchange Server 2003 to Native Mode

Time Required: 10 minutes

Objective: Switch Exchange Server 2003 from mixed mode to native mode.

Description: Many Exchange Server 2003 features are not available until an Exchange organization is promoted from mixed mode to native mode. In this activity, you promote your Exchange organization from mixed mode to native mode.

1. Click **Start**, point to **All Programs**, point to **Microsoft Exchange**, and then click **System Manager**.

2. Right-click **BLATHERCONSULTINGXX (Exchange)**, where XX is your assigned student number. Click **Properties**. The BLATHERCONSULTINGXX Properties window to the General tab opens, as shown in Figure 2-17.

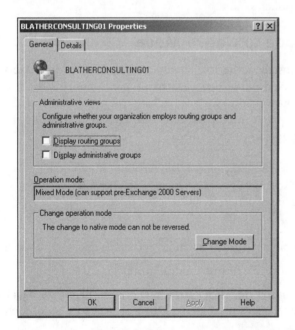

Figure 2-17 Reviewing the current organization mode

3. Note that the current Operation mode is set to Mixed Mode by default, a mode in which pre-Exchange 2000 servers are also supported. In the Change operation mode section, click the **Change Mode** button.

4. After the Change Mode button is clicked, you are presented with the Exchange System Manager dialog box. Click **Yes** after you've read the message.

5. After the switch to native mode is complete, check both the **Display routing groups** and **Display administrative groups** check boxes in the Administrative views section, and click **OK**. This reorganizes the way Exchange System Manager

2

displays information for a native mode environment. When the Exchange System Manager dialog box appears, click **OK**. Close Exchange System Manager.

6. Click **Start**, click **Run**, type **services.msc** in the Open text box, and click **OK**. This opens the Services MMC.

7. Scroll down until you reach Microsoft Exchange Information Store. Right-click **Microsoft Exchange Information Store**, and click **Restart**. After the Microsoft Exchange Information Store service has restarted, close the **Services MMC**.

Configuring Global Settings

The Global Settings node in Exchange System Manager allows you to configure systemwide settings for your Exchange organization. Ultimately, the settings that you configure in this section will apply to all of your Exchange servers as well as all recipients. The Global Settings node consists of three main configuration areas:

- Internet Message Formats
- Message Delivery
- Mobile Services

In the following sections, you learn more about the configuration of Internet Message Formats and Message Delivery settings. The configuration of Mobile Services settings is beyond the scope of this text.

Internet Message Formats

Internet Message Formats control how e-mail messages are formatted when sent to or received from Internet clients. When a message is sent from a Messaging Application Programming Interface (MAPI) e-mail client such as Microsoft Outlook to an Internet client such as Outlook Express or Eudora, SMTP converts the message from Microsoft Rich Text Format (RTF) to **Multipurpose Internet Mail Extensions (MIME)** format.

MIME message formatting information is included in messages so that the receiving client can determine which "helper" applications might be necessary to read the message or access attachments. For example, if you send an Internet user a message that includes an Apple QuickTime movie as an attachment, MIME information about the attachment is included in the message header. In this case, the MIME information added is Content-Type: movie\quicktime.

In most cases, the default MIME types and associations created automatically for the Exchange organization should be sufficient. However, additional MIME content types can be defined and managed if necessary by right-clicking on Internet Message Formats and clicking Properties, as shown in Figure 2-18.

When you click on the Internet Message Formats node, you'll notice an entry named Default. This is actually the default SMTP policy, used to control the formatting of all messages sent to Internet domains. Beyond message formatting, the settings found within an

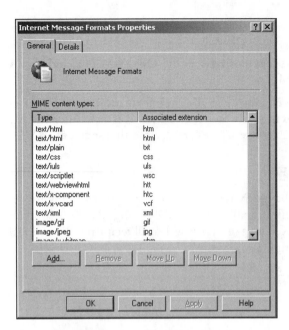

Figure 2-18   Viewing MIME content types

SMTP policy also allow you to control items such as whether your organization allows nondelivery reports, out-of-office messages, and automatic replies. You can also define different settings for other domains through the creation of additional SMTP policies. For example, if you create a policy for the course.com domain, messages sent to the course.com domain are subject to that policy's settings, whereas messages to all other domains still fall under the scope of the default policy.

To configure the Default SMTP policy, right-click on it, and click Properties. The window that opens includes four tabs: General, Message Format, Advanced, and Details, as shown in Figure 2-19.

SMTP policy settings are configured from the Message Format and Advanced tabs. Settings found on the Message Format tab include:

- *Message encoding*—These settings allow you to configure the encoding type to be used with messages. Set to MIME by default, you also control whether outgoing messages are sent as plain text or Hypertext Markup Language (HTML). Plain text messages use less storage space, but lack formatting such as italic, hyperlinks, and so forth. It's worth noting that not all e-mail clients support HTML formatting.

- *Character sets*—These settings allow you to specify a character set to be used for both MIME and non-MIME messages. Be careful not to choose an incorrect character set, as it might stop recipients from being able to read sent messages.

Settings configured from the Advanced tab include:

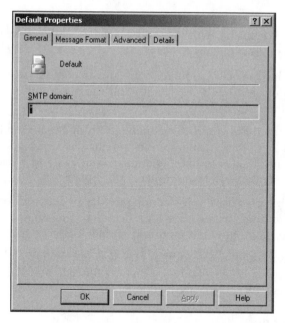

Figure 2-19   Properties of the Default SMTP policy

- *Exchange rich-text format*—These options allow you to specify whether Exchange rich-text format should always be used, never be used, or controlled by user settings. If the Always use option is selected, the recipient's e-mail client must support Exchange rich-text format or she will not be able to open the attachment.

- *Message text word wrap*—These options control whether word wrap is used for messages. Set to Never use by default, this ensures that a recipient sees the message exactly the way the sender typed it. However, some older e-mail clients cannot display messages that do not use word wrap. In most cases, the default setting suffices. If word wrap is required for a specific domain, consider creating a policy dedicated to that domain that implements this feature.

- *Automatic reply settings*—The lower portion of the Advanced tab consists of check boxes that control whether automatic replies are permitted in response to messages received. For example, if the Allow out of office responses check box is checked, these replies can be sent to Internet users. If left unchecked, all out of office responses are blocked.

Message Delivery

The Global Settings Message Delivery node allows you to configure message delivery options for your Exchange organization. Examples of settings configured here include maximum message size restrictions, maximum number of recipients per message, and message filtering features used to help reduce exposure to unsolicited (SPAM) e-mail messages.

The Message Delivery Properties dialog box consists of six tabs: General, Defaults, Sender Filtering, Connection Filtering, Recipient Filtering, and Details. Configurable message delivery settings are found on the following tabs:

- *Defaults*—Settings on this tab allow you to configure maximum sending and receiving message sizes (each 10 MB by default) and the maximum number of recipients per message (5000 by default).

- *Sender Filtering*—This tab allows you to filter messages from certain senders. If a sender's e-mail address or display name appears on this tab, messages are not delivered to the recipient. Wildcards like *@domain.com can also be added to block messages from all senders at a given domain.

- *Connection Filtering*—This tab allows you to configure the IP addresses of SMTP servers with which Exchange server allows or denies connections, as well as configure rules that determine how servers found on block lists are handled.

- *Recipient Filtering*—This tab allows you to filter messages to certain recipients. If a recipient's e-mail address or display name appears on this tab, messages are not delivered to that recipient. Wildcards like *@domain.com can also be added to block messages to all recipients at a given domain. Authenticated users are not subject to recipient filtering.

Activity 2-9: Configuring Exchange Global Settings

Time Required: 15 minutes

Objective: Configure global settings on an Exchange Server 2003 system.

Description: Configurable Global Settings in Exchange System Manager include Internet Message Formats and Message Delivery settings. In this activity, you configure these settings and explore the contents of the Default SMTP policy.

1. Click **Start**, point to **All Programs**, point to **Microsoft Exchange**, and then click **System Manager**.

2. Click the **plus sign (+)** next to Global Settings to expand it.

3. Right-click **Internet Message Formats** and click **Properties**.

4. Review the MIME content types list, and then click **Cancel**.

5. Click **Internet Message Formats**. The Default policy is listed, as shown in Figure 2-20.

6. Right-click **Default** and click **Properties**.

7. Click the **Message Format** tab to explore its settings, but do not make any changes.

8. Click the **Advanced** tab. Check the **Allow out of office responses** check box, as shown in Figure 2-21. Click **OK**.

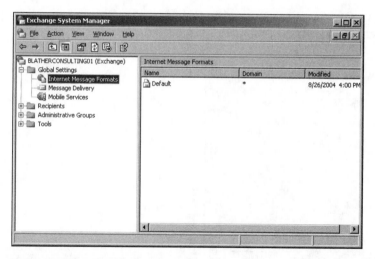

Figure 2-20   The Default SMTP policy listed in Internet Message Formats

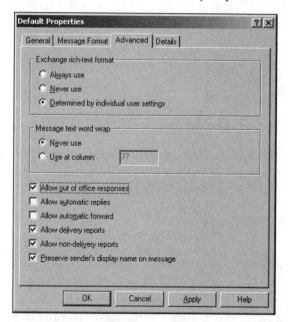

Figure 2-21   Configuring Advanced settings to allow out of office responses

9. Right-click **Message Delivery** and click **Properties**.

10. Click the **Defaults** tab. In the Sending message size text box, type **5120**. This limits the maximum sent message size to 5 MB.

11. In the Receiving message size text box, type **5120**. This limits the maximum received message size to 5 MB as well.

12. In the Recipient limits text box, type **2000**. This limits any message to a maximum of 2000 recipients, as shown in Figure 2-22.

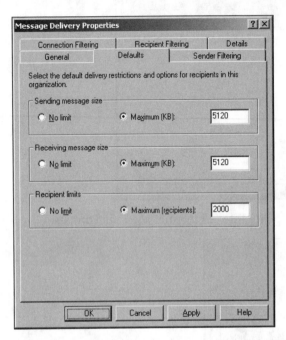

Figure 2-22   Changing maximum message sizes and recipient limits

13. Click the **Sender Filtering**, **Recipient Filtering**, and **Connection Filtering** tabs to view their configurable settings, but do not make any changes. When you are finished, click **OK**, and close **Exchange System Manager**.

Configuring Server Property Settings

Whereas global settings impact an entire Exchange organization, server-specific settings are used to control the functions of a particular Exchange Server 2003 system. Server settings are configured from the Properties pages of a server in Exchange System Manager. After an Exchange organization has been promoted to native mode, the server object for the first server installed can be found under the Administrative Groups, First Administrative Group node, as shown in Figure 2-23.

To access the configurable settings for a server object, right-click on the server's name, and click Properties. The Server Properties dialog box consists of 11 tabs, as outlined in the following list:

- *General*—This tab allows you to configure e-mail subject and message tracking, a feature that allows the contents and subject fields of e-mail messages to be searched by administrators using tools such as Message Tracking Center. Other options available on this tab include the ability to designate the Exchange server as a

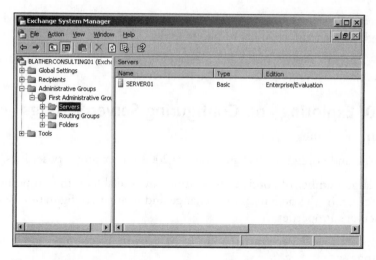

Figure 2-23 Viewing the contents of the Servers node

front-end server and to control whether fatal service error information should be forwarded to Microsoft.

- *Locales*—This tab allows you to configure locale settings that determine how elements such as currency, time, and date settings are displayed to clients of the server.

- *Mailbox Management*—This tab allows you to start the mailbox management process that is used to create reports about recipient policies that set age and size limits for messages. You also use this tab to schedule when the mailbox management process should run, and specify the mailbox to which reports should be delivered.

- *Directory Access*—This tab allows you to view and manipulate information about the domain controllers in the Directory Access topology.

- *Policies*—This tab allows you to view any system policies that currently apply to the server. System policies are looked at later in this chapter.

- *Security*—This tab allows you to view the user and group permissions applied to the server object.

- *Full-Text Indexing*—This tab allows you to control the server resource usage levels to be applied to indexing Exchange databases for the purpose of conducting searches.

- *Monitoring*—This tab allows you to define which resources on the server (such as CPU threshold, free disk space, and so on) should be actively monitored.

- *Diagnostics Logging*—This tab allows you to configure the levels of diagnostic logging for different Exchange services. Messages about Exchange services are ultimately logged to the application log in Event Viewer.

- *Public Folder Referrals*—This tab allows you to configure the manner in which the Exchange server redirects users to public folders.

- *Details*—This tab allows you to add messages or notes about the configuration of the server object that might be helpful to other users.

Activity 2-10: Exploring and Configuring Server Settings

Time Required: 15 minutes

Objective: Explore and configure Exchange Server 2003 server property settings.

Description: A large number of configurable settings are available in the Properties pages of an Exchange server. In this activity, you exchange and change configuration settings in your Exchange server's Properties.

1. Click **Start**, point to **All Programs**, point to **Microsoft Exchange**, and then click **System Manager**.

2. Click the **plus sign (+)** next to Administrative Groups to expand it.

3. Click the **plus sign (+)** next to First Administrative Group to expand it.

4. Click the **Servers** folder to view its contents.

5. Right-click **ServerXX**, where XX is your assigned student number, and click **Properties**.

6. On the General tab, check the **Enable subject logging and display** check box.

7. Check the **Enable message tracking** check box. When the Exchange System Manager dialog box appears, read the message, and click **OK**.

8. Click the **Locales** tab to view its current settings.

9. Click the **Mailbox Management** tab to view its current settings.

10. Click the **Directory Access** tab to view its current settings.

11. Click the **Policies** tab. No policies are currently applied to this server, but a policy will be created and applied in Activity 2-11.

12. Click the **Security** tab. This tab lists user and group security permissions to this Exchange server object, as shown in Figure 2-24.

13. Click the **Full-Text Indexing** tab to view its current settings.

14. Click the **Monitoring** tab to view its current settings.

15. Click the **Diagnostics Logging** tab to view its current settings.

16. Click the **Public Folders Referrals** tab to view its current settings.

17. Click **OK** and close **Exchange System Manager**.

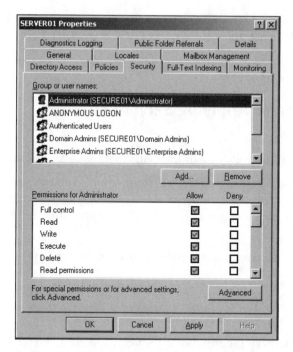

Figure 2-24   The Security tab in the properties of an Exchange server object

Working with System Policies

To help simplify the administration of groups of servers, mailbox stores, and public folder stores, Exchange supports the configuration of system policies. A **system policy** is simply a collection of settings that can be applied to these objects once, rather than individually on each and every object. For example, rather than configure message tracking on each and every Exchange server in an administrative group, you could instead create a system policy that enables this setting and apply it to Exchange servers in the group. Then, if you ever want to change the setting, you only need to reconfigure it once in the applied system policy.

When system policy settings are applied to an object (such as a server), those settings can no longer be configured manually for the object to which the policy is applied. Furthermore, only one system policy can be applied to an object at any given point in time. If you attempt to apply a new policy to an object that already has a policy applied, you are prompted to verify whether you want to remove the object from the control of the current policy.

Exchange Server 2003 supports three kinds of system policies:

- Mailbox store policies
- Public folder store policies
- Server policies

NOTE

Mailbox store policies are looked at in more detail in Chapter 3, "Managing Recipients," whereas public folder store policies are looked at in more detail in Chapter 6, "Public Folders."

ACTIVITY

Activity 2-11: Creating and Applying Server Policies

Time Required: 15 minutes

Objective: Create and apply a server policy to an Exchange Server 2003 system.

Description: Server system policies help administrators to apply and enforce configuration settings on multiple servers simultaneously, without the need to configure each server individually. In this activity, you create a server policy and then apply it to your Exchange server.

1. Click **Start**, point to **All Programs**, point to **Microsoft Exchange**, and then click **System Manager**.

2. Click the **plus sign (+)** next to Administrative Groups to expand it.

3. Click the **plus sign (+)** next to First Administrative Group to expand it.

4. Right-click **First Administrative Group**, point to **New**, and click **System Policy Container**. This adds the System Policies node to the First Administrative Group, as shown in Figure 2-25.

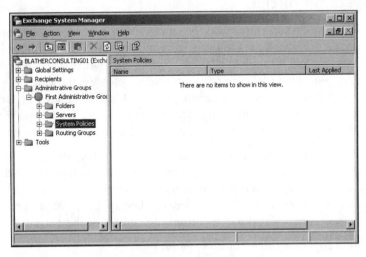

Figure 2-25   Viewing the System Policies node

5. Right-click **System Policies**, point to **New**, and click **Server policy**.

6. In the New Policy window, check the **General** check box, and click **OK**.

7. At the Properties window for the new policy, type **Tracking** in the Name text box.

8. Click the **General (Policy)** tab. Check both the **Enable subject logging and display** and **Enable message tracking** check boxes, as shown in Figure 2-26.

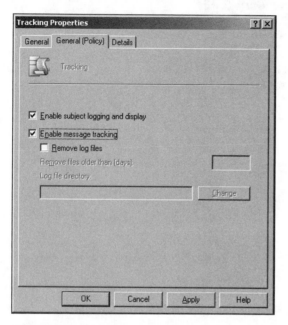

Figure 2-26   Configuring system policy settings

9. Click **OK**. The new Tracking policy appears in System Policies.

10. Right-click **Tracking** and click **Add server**. In the Select the items to place under the control of this policy window, type **ServerXX** in the Enter the object names to select text box, where XX is your assigned student number. Click **OK**. When the Exchange System Manager dialog box appears, click **Yes**.

11. Click the **plus sign (+)** next to Servers to expand it. Right-click **ServerXX** (where XX is your assigned student number), and click **Properties**.

12. On the General tab, notice that both options configured in Step 8 are grayed out, designating that these settings have been overridden by a system policy setting.

13. Click the **Policies** tab. The Tracking policy is now listed, as shown in Figure 2-27.

14. Click **OK** and then close **Exchange System Manager**.

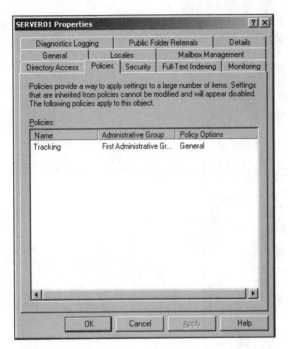

Figure 2-27   Viewing the policy applied to an Exchange server object

---

CONFIGURING DNS TO SUPPORT EXCHANGE SERVER 2003 INTERNET E-MAIL

In Chapter 1, you installed Windows Server 2003 as well as Active Directory. As part of the Active Directory installation process, you selected the option to have DNS automatically configured. When this option is selected, the Active Directory installation process installs the **Domain Name Service (DNS)** and creates what is known as an Active Directory integrated DNS zone. When installed in this manner, DNS information is stored as a group of objects in Active Directory.

The primary purpose of DNS is to provide name resolution services on a Transmission Control Protocol/Internet Protocol (TCP/IP) network. For example, when a client system needs to obtain the IP address associated with a fully qualified domain name (FQDN) like server01.secure01.local, it queries a DNS server in an attempt to gather the address. After the client has the IP address associated with the FQDN, it can communicate with that server over a TCP/IP network.

In the world of Internet e-mail, mail servers exchange messages over a TCP/IP network. When a mail server needs to deliver messages to a certain Internet domain, it must query DNS to attempt to find the IP address of a mail server in the recipient's domain. Mail servers are listed in DNS using a special type of resource record known as a **Mail Exchanger**

2

(MX). When a sending mail server is attempting to contact the mail server of the message's recipient, it queries a DNS server that is authoritative for that domain to find the associated MX record.

The MX record associated with a mail server does not list the mail server's IP address. Instead, MX records act as a pointer to the mail server's fully qualified name. After a sending mail server has found the MX record associated with a recipient's domain, it queries DNS again for the IP address associated with that name. After it has the server's IP address, the sending mail server can attempt to forward e-mail messages to the recipient's mail server. This process is outlined in Figure 2-28.

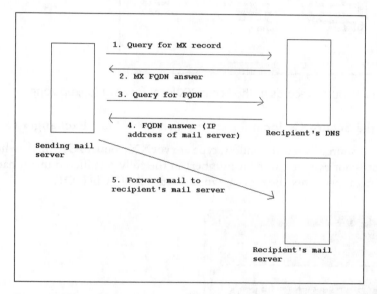

Figure 2-28   The DNS query process used by a sending mail server to find and exchange messages with a recipient's mail server over the Internet

ACTIVITY

Activity 2-12: Configuring DNS to Support Exchange Server 2003 Internet E-Mail

Time Required: 5 minutes

Objective: Configure DNS with an MX record to support Exchange Server 2003 as an Internet-based SMTP server.

Description: DNS MX records are used to designate mail servers within the DNS infrastructure on the Internet. In this activity, you add an MX record for your server in DNS.

1. Click **Start**, select **Administrative Tools**, and click **DNS**.

2. Click the **plus sign (+)** next to **ServerXX** to expand it, where XX is your assigned student number.

3. Click the **plus sign (+)** next to **Forward Lookup Zones** to expand it.

4. Click **SecureXX.local**, where XX is your assigned student number. The records in this zone are displayed as shown in Figure 2-29.

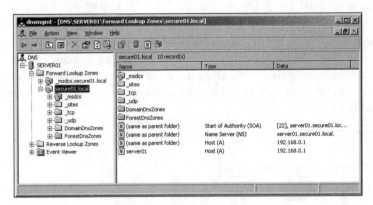

Figure 2-29   DNS resource records in the SecureXX.local forward lookup zone

5. Right-click the **SecureXX.local** folder and click **New Mail Exchanger (MX)**.

6. In the New Resource Record window, type **serverXX.secureXX.local** (where XX represents your assigned student number) in the fully qualified domain name (FQDN) of mail server text box, as shown in Figure 2-30. Click **OK**.

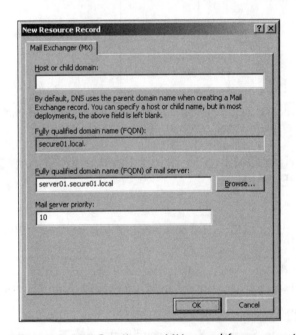

Figure 2-30   Creating an MX record for your mail server in the SecureXX.local forward lookup zone

7. Close all open windows.

CHAPTER SUMMARY

- Two editions of Exchange Server 2003 exist—Exchange Server 2003, Standard Edition and Exchange Server 2003, Enterprise Edition.

- Prior to installing Exchange Server 2003 on the first server in an Active Directory environment, both ForestPrep and DomainPrep must be run. ForestPrep is run once for the entire forest, whereas DomainPrep should be run in each Active Directory domain in which Exchange servers will be located, or Exchange-related capabilities will be required.

- The primary tools used to manage an Exchange Server 2003 organization are Exchange System Manager and Active Directory Users and Computers.

- When first installed, Exchange organizations run in mixed mode to support environments that include Exchange 5.5 servers. Organizations without Exchange 5.5 servers should switch to native mode to be able to take advantage of all Exchange Server 2003 features.

- Exchange Server 2003 supports the use of system policies to enforce consistent settings across one or more Exchange servers without the need to configure each individually.

- DNS MX records are used by sending mail servers to find a recipient's mail server when messages need to be transferred over the Internet.

KEY TERMS

Active Directory Users and Computers—The primary user and group administrative tool in Active Directory environments.

cluster—A group of independent servers (commonly referred to as nodes) that work together to ensure system availability.

domain controller—A Windows server that stores a copy of the Active Directory database.

Domain Name Service (DNS)—The distributed database system that provides name resolution services on TCP/IP networks.

DomainPrep—The tool used to prepare each Active Directory domain prior to the installation of Microsoft Exchange Server 2003.

Exchange System Manager—The primary Exchange management tool installed with Exchange Server 2003.

forest root domain—The first domain created in an Active Directory forest.

ForestPrep—The tool used to prepare an Active Directory forest prior to the installation of Microsoft Exchange Server 2003.

global catalog server—An Active Directory domain controller that stores information about all objects in a forest.

Mail Exchanger (MX)—The DNS resource record used to designate a mail server.

Microsoft Management Console (MMC)—The management environment into which different snap-in tools can be added for the purpose of managing system and application settings.

mixed mode—The default Exchange Server 2003 organizational mode that supports environments running Exchange 5.5 servers.

Multipurpose Internet Mail Extensions (MIME)—A message formatting method that includes information in messages such that the receiving client can determine which "helper" applications might be necessary to read the message or access attachments.

native mode—The primary Exchange Server 2003 organizational mode for environments that do not include Exchange 5.5 servers that makes it possible to take advantage of all Exchange Server 2003 features.

schema—The group of all defined object classes and attributes supported by Active Directory. The Active Directory schema must be extended (via ForestPrep) to support Exchange Server 2003.

system policy—The settings that simplify the administration of groups of servers, mailbox stores, and public folder stores by centralizing the configuration of multiple objects.

REVIEW QUESTIONS

1. On which of the following operating systems can Exchange Server 2003, Enterprise Edition be installed? (Choose all that apply.)

   a. Windows Server 2003, Standard Edition

   b. Windows 2000 Advanced Server, SP2

   c. Windows 2000 Advanced Server, SP3

   d. Windows Server 2003, Web Edition

2. On which of the following operating systems can Exchange Server 2003, Standard Edition be installed? (Choose all that apply.)

   a. Windows Server 2003, Datacenter Edition

   b. Windows Server 2003, Web Edition

   c. Windows Server 2003, Standard Edition

   d. Windows Server 2003, Enterprise Edition

3. What is the Microsoft recommended amount of RAM that should be available to install Exchange Server 2003 on a Windows Server 2003 system?

   a. 256 MB

   b. 512 MB

   c. 1 GB

   d. 4 GB

4. How much free disk space is required on the installation drive to install Exchange Server 2003?

   a. 200 MB

   b. 1 GB

   c. 500 MB

   d. 750 MB

5. ForestPrep needs to be run on every Exchange Server 2003 system installed in the same Active Directory forest. True or False?

6. Which of the following processes creates the Exchange Enterprise Servers group?

   a. Exchange installation

   b. DomainPrep

   c. ForestPrep

   d. none of the above

7. Which of the following processes modifies the Active Directory schema?

   a. DomainPrep

   b. ForestPrep

   c. Exchange installation

   d. none of the above

8. Which of the following file systems is required for the system partition on an Exchange Server 2003 system?

   a. NTFS

   b. FAT

   c. FAT32

   d. any of the above

9. Which of the following groups must you be a member of in order to run ForestPrep? (Choose all that apply.)

   a. Schema Administrators

   b. Enterprise Administrators

   c. Forest Administrators

   d. Domain Administrators

10. Which of the following groups must you be a member of in order to run DomainPrep? (Choose all that apply.)

   a. Enterprise Admins

   b. Domain Admins

   c. Exchange Admins

   d. Server Admins

11. Which of the following tasks are carried out as part of the ForestPrep process? (Choose all that apply.)

    a. extending the Active Directory schema

    b. creating the Exchange organization object container

    c. installing Exchange Server 2003

    d. designating a user or group account that will have the Exchange Full Administrator permissions to the Exchange organization object

12. Which of the following tasks are carried out as part of the DomainPrep process? (Choose all that apply.)

    a. configuring permissions for the Exchange Enterprise Servers group

    b. creating the Exchange System Objects container

    c. performing preinstallation checks prior to installing Exchange Server 2003

    d. installing Exchange Server 2003

13. Which of the following statements about unattended Exchange Server 2003 setups are true? (Choose all that apply.)

    a. An unattended setup can be performed on the first Exchange Server 2003 system installed in a forest.

    b. An unattended setup cannot be performed on the first Exchange Server 2003 system installed in a forest.

    c. Unattended setups can be used to run ForestPrep.

    d. Unattended setups cannot be used to run ForestPrep.

14. Which of the following switches is used with the Exchange Server 2003 setup program to create the answer file to be used in conjunction with an unattended setup? (Choose all that apply.)

    a. /createanswer

    b. /createunattend

    c. /unattendfile

    d. /unattend

15. Which of the following groups are created during the DomainPrep process? (Choose all that apply.)

    a. Exchange Domain Servers

    b. Exchange Administrators

    c. Exchange Enterprise Servers

    d. Exchange Servers

2

16. What type of DNS resource record is used to identify an e-mail server?
    a. MAIL
    b. MX
    c. A
    d. HOST

17. Exchange Server 2003, Standard Edition can be installed in a Windows cluster configuration. True or False?

18. A user granted Exchange Administrator permissions at the Exchange organization level has the ability to change permissions for all Exchange objects. True or False?

19. Which of the following pieces of information is returned by a DNS server in response to a query for an MX record?
    a. IP address
    b. FQDN
    c. mail server port number
    d. none of the above

20. An Exchange organization running in native mode cannot be switched back to mixed mode. True or False?

CASE PROJECTS

Case Project 2-1: Choosing an Exchange Server 2003 Edition

Super Siding Corporation is planning to deploy Exchange Server 2003 in their only office, located in Las Vegas, Nevada. The company currently has 200 PC users who need access to e-mail and does not expect more than 5% annual growth in the number of PC users that it employs. Last year, Super Siding deployed two Windows Server 2003, Standard Edition systems along with Active Directory. One of these servers will be used for the installation of Exchange Server 2003. Which edition of Exchange Server 2003 is the best choice for Super Siding, and why?

Case Project 2-2: Preparing a Network for Exchange Server 2003

The network administrator at Maple Sugar Systems is planning to install Exchange Server 2003 on a Windows 2000 Server system. The network at Sugar Maple Systems has Active Directory installed. What steps will the network administrator need to take prior to installing the first Exchange Server 2003 system to prepare the environment?

Case Project 2-3: Selecting a Windows Server Version and Edition

Magnetawan Industries is planning to move from their current NetWare 4.x environment to a Windows Server platform running Active Directory. The company has 3500 users across 20 locations, and is planning to use Exchange Server 2003, Enterprise Edition as their messaging and collaboration solution. Which versions or editions of Windows Server could the company use if they eventually plan to deploy Exchange Server 2003 in clusters of four or more servers?

3

MANAGING RECIPIENTS

> **After reading this chapter, you will be able to:**
>
> ◆ Understand the different types of recipients supported by Exchange Server 2003
>
> ◆ Create new user, group, and contact recipient objects
>
> ◆ Mailbox-enable existing user objects and mail-enabled existing group objects
>
> ◆ Discuss query-based distribution groups
>
> ◆ Understand and configure Exchange-related recipient object settings
>
> ◆ Understand, configure, and apply recipient policies

After Exchange Server 2003 is installed and the initial server configuration tasks are complete, the most common day-to-day administration tasks involve managing recipients.

Exchange Server 2003 supports a number of different recipient types. Although recipients might typically be associated with users, other valid recipients include groups, contacts, and even public folders.

To extend the functionality associated with sending messages to groups, Exchange Server 2003 introduces a new recipient type known as a query-based distribution group. These groups have their membership determined dynamically based on the results of a query against the Active Directory database. Ultimately, they make it possible for administrators to define groups in ways more powerful and flexible than with any previous version of Exchange Server.

Beyond simply creating recipients, it's also important to be familiar with the concept of recipient policies. Recipient policies can be used to create rules that dictate user e-mail addresses and control the mailbox management process.

This chapter introduces you to the core concepts associated with creating and managing recipients, including the process of creating and applying recipient policies.

UNDERSTANDING RECIPIENTS

In simple terms, an Exchange **recipient** is an object that can receive e-mail messages. In most cases, these "objects" are Active Directory users or groups. However, Exchange supports many different types of recipients to meet different organizational needs.

Examples of recipient objects supported in Exchange Server 2003 native mode environments include the following:

- Users
- InetOrgPerson objects
- Contacts
- Security groups
- Distribution groups
- Query-based distribution groups
- Public folders

Although the term *recipient* generically describes an object that can receive e-mail messages, Exchange Server 2003 actually supports two types of recipients, known as mailbox-enabled and mail-enabled.

A **mailbox-enabled recipient** is a recipient object that has a mailbox located on an Exchange server, such as a user. A **mail-enabled recipient** is a recipient object that can be sent e-mail messages, but does not have its own Exchange mailbox. A good example of a mail-enabled recipient is a security group. When an e-mail message is sent to a mail-enabled security group, the message is not stored in a mailbox allocated to that group. Instead, the message is sent to all members of the group. Some of these are mailbox-enabled recipients such as Active Directory users, whereas others could be mail-enabled recipients such as contact objects. In the case of the contact object, the message sent to the security group is ultimately sent to that user's external e-mail address.

Some recipient objects can only be mail-enabled, whereas others can be either mail-enabled or mailbox-enabled. Table 3-1 outlines each Exchange receipt object, and whether it can be mailbox-enabled or mail-enabled.

Table 3-1   Exchange recipient objects and recipient types

Object	Supported Recipient Types
User	Mailbox-enabled and mail-enabled
InetOrgPerson	Mailbox-enabled and mail-enabled
Contact	Mail-enabled only
Security group	Mail-enabled only
Distribution group	Mail-enabled only
Query-based distribution group	Mail-enabled only
Public folder	Mail-enabled only

Each of the recipient objects listed in Table 3-1 are looked at in more detail in the following sections.

Users

User objects are the most common type of recipient created in an Exchange organization. When a user account is mailbox-enabled, the associated user can send and receive messages, as well as store them in a personal mailbox located on an Exchange server.

Although most users in an Exchange organization are usually mailbox-enabled, user objects can also be mail-enabled only. When a user object is mail-enabled, an external e-mail address is associated with the user account, and no mailbox is configured on the Exchange server. As such, a mail-enabled user can receive e-mail messages, but can neither send messages via nor store messages on an Exchange server.

The Exchange Task Wizard allows you to both mailbox-enable and mail-enable user objects. To mailbox-enable a user, you select the wizard's Create Mailbox option. Conversely, to mail-enable a user object, the Establish E-mail Address option should be used. Both options are illustrated in Figure 3-1. You learn more about creating mailbox-enabled and mail-enabled user recipients later in this chapter.

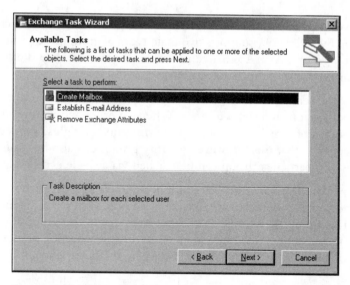

Figure 3-1   User objects can be mail-enabled or mailbox-enabled

InetOrgPerson

InetOrgPerson is a user object that includes an extended set of properties to improve compatibility with other directory services, such as Novell's eDirectory. InetOrgPerson objects in Active Directory can be both mailbox-enabled and mail-enabled in much the same way as a regular user object, but restrictions do apply. Specifically, mailbox-enabling or mail-enabling an InetOrgPerson object is only supported in environments that use Exchange Server 2003 only. In addition, a Windows Server 2003 system functioning as a domain controller is required.

Contacts

Unlike user objects, **contacts** are objects that represent people external to a particular company or organization. Contact objects include information about a particular person, such as their mailing address, phone number, and so forth. In Exchange environments, recipient contact objects can only be mail-enabled and not mailbox-enabled.

When a contact is mail-enabled, the e-mail address associated with the object is an external address. For example, a contact might be created for an important supplier or contract employee, and include their personal SMTP address. The benefits of adding contacts to Active Directory is that it keeps information about people external to the organization close at hand. In addition, contacts are added to the Exchange **Global Address List (GAL)**—although they can be hidden from address lists if necessary—and can even be added to Active Directory distribution groups.

Groups

At the most basic level, a **group** is a collection of objects, such as users, contacts, other groups, and so forth. Active Directory supports two main types of groups, known as security groups and distribution groups. After Exchange is installed, both security and distribution groups can be mail-enabled, but not mailbox-enabled.

In most Active Directory environments, **security groups** are created for the explicit purpose of assigning permissions and rights to users. When a user (or another group for that matter) is made a member of a security group, any permissions or rights assigned to the group automatically apply to that user. However, security groups can also be mail-enabled such that all members of a particular group can be reached via a single e-mail address.

Unlike Security groups, **distribution groups** cannot be assigned rights or permissions, and exist for use with messaging programs like Exchange. When a user is a member of a mail-enabled distribution group, the user receives all messages sent to that group. If your goal is to create groups for the purpose of sending e-mail messages to a collection of users (rather than assigning permissions or rights), distribution groups are the better choice.

Query-Based Distribution Groups

A new feature in Exchange Server 2003, **query-based distribution groups** are objects that can only be created when an Exchange organization is running in native mode. Unlike a traditional distribution group, query-based distribution groups have their member lists updated dynamically as the result of a **Lightweight Directory Access Protocol (LDAP)** query. For example, an administrator could create a query-based distribution group by defining a query that locates all objects in Active Directory with their State/Province attribute set to New York. Once created, messages could be sent to all users who meet the query criteria without the need to specify individual users or create new static distribution groups.

Much like standard distribution groups, query-based distribution groups can be mail-enabled. You learn more about query-based distribution groups later in this chapter.

Public Folders

Public folders are storage areas for e-mail messages and other files in an Exchange organization that can be configured as mail-enabled recipients. You learn more about all aspects of public folders in Chapter 6, "Public Folders."

CREATING USER, GROUP, AND CONTACT RECIPIENTS

The most common task associated with managing recipients include the following:

- Creating new mailbox-enabled users
- Mailbox-enabling existing users
- Creating new mail-enabled groups
- Mail-enabling existing groups
- Creating new mail-enabled contacts

The following sections outline each of these tasks in more detail.

Creating New Mailbox-Enabled Users

After Exchange Server 2003 is added to an Active Directory environment, the Active Directory Users and Computers tool is "extended" to include the ability to perform Exchange-related tasks, such as assigning e-mail addresses and creating user mailboxes. When you create a new user object with Active Directory Users and Computers, the account creation wizard gives you the option of creating an associated Exchange mailbox as part of the process.

In most cases, you will create Exchange mailboxes for all new users as part of creating their user account object. User recipients can be mailbox-enabled, meaning that they have a personal mailbox stored on the Exchange server that allows them to send and receive messages.

Activity 3-1: Creating Mailbox-Enabled Users

Time Required: 15 minutes

Objective: Create new mailbox-enabled user objects.

Description: One of the most common tasks associated with managing an Exchange organization is creating new mailbox-enabled recipients during the user object creation process. In this activity, you create a number of new mailbox-enabled user accounts.

1. Log on to your server with the user name **Administrator** and the password **Password!**.

2. Click **Start**, point to **All Programs**, point to **Microsoft Exchange**, and then click **Active Directory Users and Computers**.

3. Click the **plus sign (+)** next to secureXX.local to expand it, where XX is your assigned student number.

4. Click the **Users** container to view its contents.

5. Right-click the **Users** container, point to **New**, and then click **User**.

6. In the First name text box, type **Mike**.

7. In the Last name text box, type **Jones**. This automatically fills in the Full name text box, as shown in Figure 3-2.

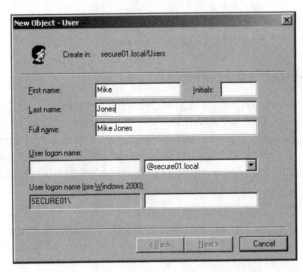

Figure 3-2   Configuring a new user account

8. In the User logon name text box, type **mjones**. This automatically fills in the User logon name (pre-Windows 2000) text box, as shown in Figure 3-3. Click **Next**.

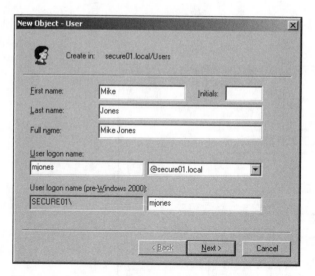

Figure 3-3   Configuring a user logon name

9. In the Password and Confirm password text boxes, type **Password!**. Uncheck the
    User must change password at next logon check box. Click **Next**.

10. Ensure that the **Create an Exchange mailbox** check box is checked, as shown in
    Figure 3-4. The wizard automatically checks this box when creating new user
    objects. Click **Next**.

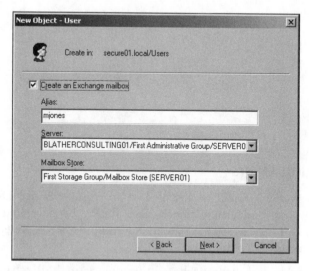

Figure 3-4   Choosing to mailbox-enable a new user account

11. Review the information provided about the new user account, and click

Finish. After the new user object is created, it is stored in the Users container, as shown in Figure 3-5.

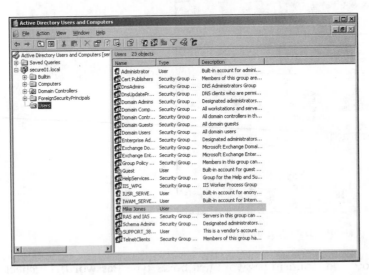

Figure 3-5   Contents of the Users container

12. Repeat Steps 6 through 11 to create the following user objects. This list includes first name, last name, and user logon name information (in parentheses) for each account.

   ■ Bob Smiley (bsmiley)

   ■ Susan Adams (sadams)

   ■ Elliot Lane (elane)

   ■ Wendy Messier (wmessier)

   ■ Jack Snider (jsnider)

13. Leave Active Directory Users and Computers open.

Mailbox-Enabling Existing Users

In many cases, Exchange Server 2003 will be installed in an existing Active Directory environment in which many user and group objects have already been created. When Exchange is installed into an existing environment, user and group objects will need to be mailbox-enabled (or mail-enabled).

The tool used to mailbox-enable and mail-enable existing objects is the Exchange Task Wizard in Active Directory Users and Computers. This tool can be used to mailbox-enable or mail-enable individual user objects, or multiple user objects simultaneously. To mailbox-enable a number of objects at once, simply select multiple objects in the Active Directory

Users and Computers interface, right-click, and select Exchange Tasks. The selected task (such as Create Mailbox) is then performed on all selected objects.

ACTIVITY

Activity 3-2: Mailbox-Enabling an Existing User Object

3

Time Required: 15 minutes

Objective: Mailbox-enable an existing user object.

Description: Existing user objects might have been created prior to Exchange being installed, whereas others might have originally been added without creating an associated mailbox. In this activity, you mailbox-enable an existing user object using the Exchange Task Wizard.

1. In Active Directory Users and Computers, right-click the **Users** container, point to **New**, and then click **User**.

2. In the First name text box, type **Mark**.

3. In the Last name text box, type **Majors**.

4. In the User logon name text box, type **mmajors**, and click **Next**.

5. In the Password and Confirm password text boxes, type **Password!**. Uncheck the **User must change password at next logon** check box. Click **Next**.

6. Ensure that the **Create an Exchange mailbox** check box is unchecked, as shown in Figure 3-6. Click **Next**.

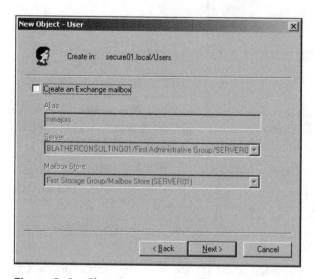

Figure 3-6   Choosing not to mailbox-enable a new user account

7. Review the information provided about the new user account, and click **Finish**.

8. Right-click the **Mike Jones** user object created in Activity 3-1, and click **Properties**. Notice that the account includes Exchange-related tabs, such as E-mail Addresses, Exchange Features, Exchange General, and Exchange Advanced, as shown in Figure 3-7. Click **OK**.

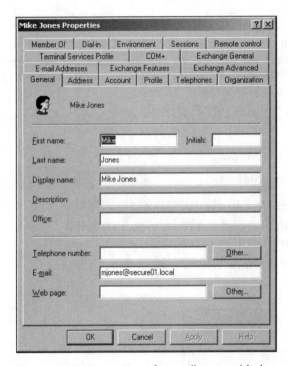

Figure 3-7   Properties of a mailbox-enabled user object

9. Right-click the **Mark Majors** user object, and click **Properties**. Notice that the account does not include Exchange-related tabs (as shown in Figure 3-8) because an Exchange mailbox was not created for this user account. Click **OK**.

10. Right-click the **Mark Majors** user object, and click **Exchange Tasks**.

11. At the Welcome to the Exchange Task Wizard screen, check the **Do not show this Welcome page again** check box, and click **Next**.

12. At the Available Tasks screen, ensure that **Create Mailbox** is selected, as shown in Figure 3-9, and click **Next**.

13. Review the information provided at the Create Mailbox screen, and click **Next**.

14. At the Completing the Exchange Task Wizard screen, ensure that the Results section lists Successes: 1, and click **Finish**.

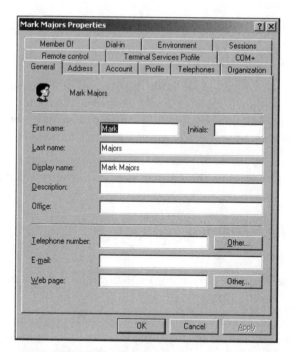

Figure 3-8   Properties of a user object prior to being mailbox-enabled

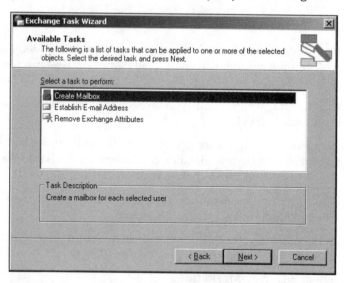

Figure 3-9   Using the Exchange Task Wizard to mailbox-enable a user

15. Right-click the **Mark Majors** user object, and then click **Properties**. The
     Properties window now includes the Exchange-related E-mail Addresses, Exchange
     Features, Exchange General, and Exchange Advanced tabs. Click **OK**.

16. Leave Active Directory Users and Computers open.

Creating New Mail-Enabled Groups

Exchange Server 2003 allows you to mail-enable both distribution and security group objects in Active Directory. Because these groups can only be mail-enabled (not mailbox-enabled), there is no Exchange mailbox defined for them. Instead, a message sent to the group's configured e-mail address is sent to all of the group's individual members.

When a new security or distribution group is created in an environment that includes Exchange Server, the wizard that walks you through the process includes an option to mail-enable the group.

ACTIVITY

Activity 3-3: Creating Mail-Enabled Groups

Time Required: 15 minutes

Objective: Raise a domain to the Windows Server 2003 functional level and then create a new mail-enabled universal distribution group.

Description: To simplify the process of sending e-mail messages to large groups of users, mail-enabled distribution groups are commonly used. In this activity, you create a new mail-enabled distribution group and add objects as members of the group.

1. In Active Directory Users and Computers, right-click the **Users** container, point to **New**, and click **Group**.

2. Notice that the only options available in the Group scope section are Domain local and Global. Universal groups cannot be created because your Active Directory domain's functional level is still set to Windows 2000 mixed mode. Click **Cancel**.

3. Right-click **secureXX.local** (where XX is your assigned student number), and click **Raise Domain Functional Level**.

4. At the Raise Domain Functional Level screen, note that the current domain functional level is set to Windows 2000 mixed. Click the **Select an available domain functional level** drop-down menu, and click **Windows Server 2003**. Click **Raise**.

5. When the Raise Domain Functional Level dialog box appears, read the message, and click **OK**. When the process completes, click **OK** again.

6. Right-click the **Users** container, point to **New**, and click **Group**. Notice that the Group scope section now allows you to select the Universal option.

7. In the Group name text box, type **Marketing**.

8. In the Group scope section, click **Universal**, as shown in Figure 3-10.

9. In the Group type section, click **Distribution**. Click **Next**.

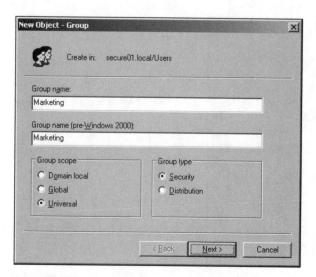

Figure 3-10   Creating a universal group

10. Ensure that the **Create an Exchange e-mail address** check box is checked, as shown in Figure 3-11, and click **Next**. Click **Finish** to create the mail-enabled Marketing group.

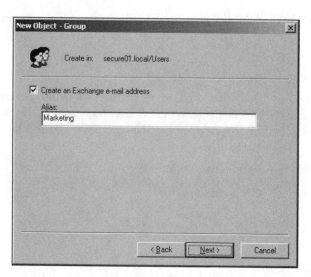

Figure 3-11   Mail-enabling a new group

11. Right-click the **Marketing** group and click **Properties**. Notice that the Properties screen includes three Exchange-related tabs—Exchange General, E-mail Addresses, and Exchange Advanced, as shown in Figure 3-12.

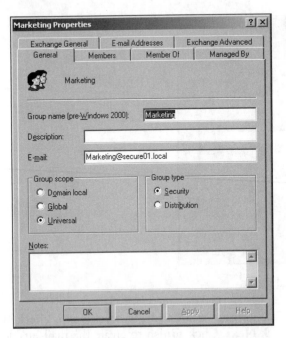

Figure 3-12   Properties of a mail-enabled group

12. Click the **E-mail Addresses** tab. Notice that the SMTP e-mail address to reach all members of the Marketing group is Marketing@secureXX.local, where XX is your assigned student number.

13. Click the **Members** tab, and then click the **Add** button.

14. At the Select Users, Contacts, Computers, or Groups screen, type **Mike Jones; Mark Majors** in the Enter the object names to select text box. Click **OK**. Both the Mike Jones and Mark Majors user accounts are listed as members of the Marketing group, as shown in Figure 3-13.

15. Click **OK** to close the Marketing Properties window.

16. Leave Active Directory Users and Computers open.

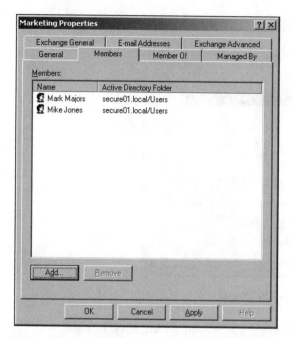

Figure 3-13   Marketing group members

Mail-Enabling Existing Groups

In much the same way that you can mailbox-enable an existing user after Exchange is installed, you can also mail-enable existing security and distribution groups. Again, this task is handled using the Exchange Task Wizard in Active Directory Users and Computers.

Activity 3-4: Mail-Enabling an Existing Group

Time Required: 10 minutes

Objective: Mail-enable an existing security group.

Description: Existing group objects might have been created prior to Exchange being installed, whereas others might have originally been added without creating an associated mailbox. In this activity, you mail-enable an existing security group object using the Exchange Task Wizard.

1. In the Active Directory Users and Computers Users container, right-click the **Domain Admins** group, and click **Exchange Tasks**.

2. At the Available Tasks screen, ensure that **Establish E-mail Address on Groups** is selected, as shown in Figure 3-14. Click **Next**.

3. At the Establish E-mail Address on Groups screen, accept the default Alias of DomainAdmins by clicking **Next**.

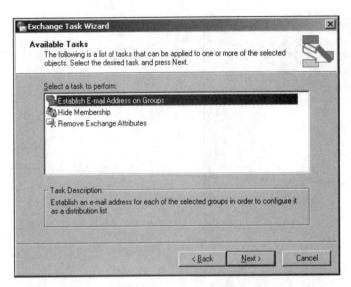

Figure 3-14   Mail-enabling a security group

4. At the Completing the Exchange Task Wizard screen, click **Finish**.

5. Right-click the **Domain Admins** group, and click **Properties**.

6. Click the **E-mail Addresses** tab. Notice that the SMTP address for this group is set to DomainAdmins@secureXX.local (as shown in Figure 3-15), where XX is your assigned student number (note that it might take up to 30 seconds for the address to appear). Sending a message to this address is the equivalent to sending a message to all members of the Domain Admins group. Click **OK**.

7. Leave Active Directory Users and Computers open.

Expanding Mail-Enabled Groups

When e-mail messages are sent to mail-enabled groups, a copy of the message is sent to each individual member of that group. For this process to occur, the membership of the group first must be expanded. Expanding a group is simply determining its individual members. If the group contains many members, the process can be very resource intensive for the Exchange server tasked with expanding the group.

By default, the first Exchange server that handles a message addressed to a group will expand its membership. However, it is also possible to designate a particular Exchange server as an expansion server to dedicate it to this task. Ultimately, this helps to reduce the load on other servers.

An expansion server is configured from the properties of a group on the Exchange Advanced tab. The default setting is Any server in the organization, as shown in Figure 3-16. However, you can also specify a specific server to act as the expansion server for that group by selecting it from the Expansion server drop-down menu instead.

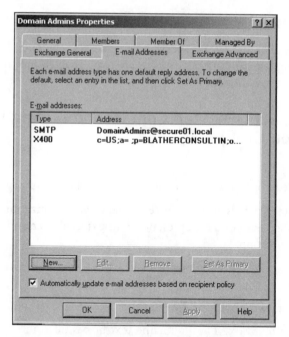

Figure 3-15   Viewing the e-mail address associated with a group

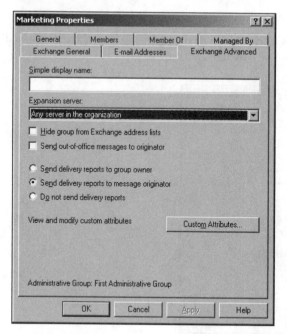

Figure 3-16   An expansion server can be configured from the Exchange Advanced tab in the properties of a group

Creating Mail-Enabled Contacts

As outlined earlier in the chapter, a contact is another valid Exchange recipient, typically a person from outside of an Exchange organization. Contacts are mail-enabled (not mailbox-enabled) and, as such, can only receive messages.

ACTIVITY

Activity 3-5: Creating a Mail-Enabled Contact and Adding It to a Distribution Group

Time Required: 10 minutes

Objective: Create a mail-enabled contact and then add it to a distribution group.

Description: Contact objects store details about users external to an organization. In this activity, you create a new mail-enabled contact representing an external user and add the contact to an existing distribution group.

1. In the Active Directory Users and Computers, right-click the **Users** container, point to **New**, and click **Contact**.

2. In the New Object – Contact window, type **Jon** in the First name text box.

3. Type **Frost** in the Last name text box. The Full name text box is filled in automatically.

4. Type **Jon Frost** in the Display name text box, and click **Next**.

5. Ensure that the **Create an Exchange e-mail address** check box is selected, as shown in Figure 3-17. Click the **Modify** button.

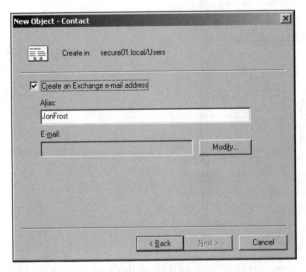

Figure 3-17   Mail-enabling a new contact

6. In the New E-mail Address window, click **SMTP Address**, and click **OK**.

7. In the Internet Address Properties window, type **jfrost@course.com**. Click **OK**.

8. Click **Next** and then click **Finish**. A contact with the name Jon Frost is added to the Users container.

9. Right-click the **Jon Frost** contact object, and click **Add to a group**.

10. At the Select Group window, type **Marketing** in the Enter the object name to select text box. Click **OK**. When the Active Directory dialog box appears, click **OK**.

11. Right-click the **Marketing** group and click **Properties**.

12. Click the **Members** tab. Notice that Jon Frost is now a member of the Marketing distribution group, as shown in Figure 3-18. When an e-mail message is sent to the Marketing group, Jon Frost also receives the message at his jfrost@course.com address. Click **OK**.

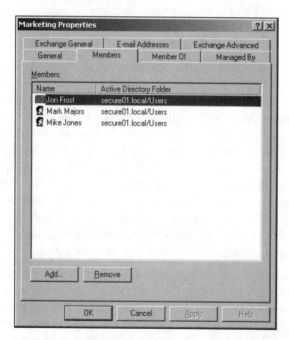

Figure 3-18   Viewing the members of the Marketing distribution group

13. Close **Active Directory Users and Computers**.

QUERY-BASED DISTRIBUTION GROUPS

Query-based distribution groups are a new feature to Exchange Server 2003 that allows the membership of a distribution group to be built dynamically according to the results of an LDAP query. These groups make it possible to send messages to multiple users based on specific criteria such as their location in Active Directory or a particular attribute. Ultimately, using query-based distribution groups makes it easier for an administrator to define group membership because group members are added to the group dynamically.

The benefit of using query-based distributions is best understood by using an example. Imagine an organization with tens of thousands of users. If an administrator is tasked with adding all of the users whose State/Province attribute is set to New York, the administrator first needs to determine which users' objects meet this criteria, and then add them to a static distribution group. Instead, the administrator can now use a query-based distribution group to create an LDAP query that effectively says "add all users with their State/province attribute set to New York to this query-based distribution group," and the task is completed automatically. An e-mail address is then added to the group, allowing all user objects listed as being in New York State to be sent an e-mail message using the group address.

Query-based distribution groups can also be combined as members of a single, normal distribution group to provide an even greater degree of flexibility. Consider an example in which a department manager requests that an e-mail address be created to contact all members of the Marketing Department as well as all users in New York State. If a single query-based distribution group is defined using both criteria (Marketing Department and New York State), only members of the Marketing Department located in New York State are added to the group. To solve this issue, the administrator could create two query-based distribution groups—one to find all members of the Marketing Department and another to find all users located in New York State. Then, these two query-based distribution groups could be added to a traditional distribution group (preferably a universal group in a multidomain environment). Sending a message to the new distribution group effectively sends the message to all members of both query-based distribution groups.

Although query-based distribution groups are a powerful option for sending e-mail messages to groups of users based on different criteria, they are computationally taxing for an Exchange server. When an Exchange server receives a message destined for a query-based distribution group, it must send an LDAP query to a **global catalog server**. The global catalog server must run the query and then return the results to the Exchange server. To ease this burden, you can specify an expansion server for the group from the Exchange Advanced tab in its properties.

 Query-based distribution groups can only be created in Exchange Server 2003 native mode organizations.

NOTE

Creating Query-Based Distribution Groups

To create a query-based distribution group, you need to define an LDAP query. Thankfully, no advanced knowledge of LDAP syntax is required because the Find Exchange Recipient window (in Active Directory Users and Computers) can be used to create the query in the same manner as searching for a recipient.

ACTIVITY

Activity 3-6: Creating a Query-Based Distribution Group

Time Required: 15 minutes

Objective: Create a query-based distribution group.

Description: Query-based distribution groups are built from the results of an LDAP query to dynamically add members to a group based on the specified search criteria. In this activity, you create a query-based distribution group that includes recipient objects with their State/province attribute set to New York.

1. Click **Start**, point to **All Programs**, point to **Microsoft Exchange**, and then click **Active Directory Users and Computers**.

2. Click the **plus sign (+)** next to secureXX.local to expand it, where XX is your assigned student number.

3. Click the **Users** container to view its contents.

4. Right-click the **Mark Majors** user object, and click **Properties**.

5. Click the **Address** tab.

6. In the State/Province text box, type **New York**, and click **OK**.

7. Right-click the **Jon Frost** contact object, and click **Properties**.

8. Click the **Address** tab.

9. In the State/Province text box, type **New York**, and click **OK**.

10. Right-click the **Users** container, point to **New**, and click **Query-based Distribution Group**.

11. At the New Object – Query-based Distribution Group window, type **New York** in the Query-based Distribution Group name text box. The Alias text box is populated with the same name automatically, as shown in Figure 3-19. Click **Next**.

12. Click **Customize filter**, as shown in Figure 3-20, and click the **Customize** button.

13. In the Find Exchange Recipients window, click the **Advanced** tab.

14. Click the **Field** button, select **User**, and then click **State/Province** (you need to scroll down to reach this item).

15. In the Value text box, type **New York**, and click **Add**.

16. Click the **Field** button, select **Contact**, and then click **State/Province**.

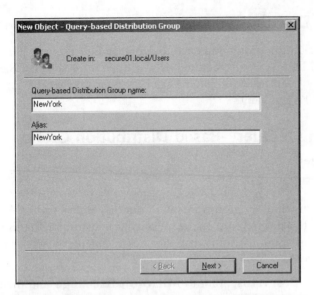

Figure 3-19   Creating a new query-based distribution group

Figure 3-20   Configuring a filter for a query-based distribution group

17. In the Value text box, type **New York**, and then click **Add**. Click **OK**, click **Next**, and then click **Finish**.

18. Right-click the **New York** Query-based Distribution Group, and click **Properties**.

3

19. Click the **Preview** tab. Notice that both the Mark Majors and Jon Frost objects are listed. The Preview tab displays the results of the query for user and contact objects in the Users container with their State/province attribute set to New York.

20. Click **OK** and leave Active Directory Users and Computers open.

CONFIGURING RECIPIENT SETTINGS

After objects are configured as mailbox-enabled or mail-enabled recipients, a number of tabs are added to their properties in Active Directory Users and Computers. The tabs added to the properties of a mailbox-enabled account include E-mail Addresses, Exchange General, Exchange Advanced, and Exchange Features (Exchange Features is added to mailbox-enabled recipients only). Ultimately, these settings allow you to configure a wide variety of Exchange-related settings for specific recipient objects. The following sections outline each tab added to the properties of a recipient object in more detail.

E-Mail Addresses

The E-mail Addresses tab in the properties of a mailbox-enabled or mail-enabled recipient lists all of the e-mail addresses assigned to that object. By default, objects have two e-mail addresses assigned—one SMTP address and one X.400 address. Other addresses for the object can be added, changed, or removed manually from this tab, or automatically through the use of recipient policy settings. Recipient policy settings are looked at in more detail later in this chapter.

For each e-mail address type listed on this tab, only one entry can be the default reply address. For example, if a user has two SMTP addresses listed, he receives messages sent to both addresses. However, all messages sent by the user list the address set as "primary" as the reply-to address. The primary address can be changed from the E-mail Addresses tab by selecting an address and clicking the Set As Primary option. The primary address for an object can be easily determined by looking for the capitalized entry in the Type column. For example, if the address type is listed as "SMTP," it is the primary SMTP address for that user. Nonprimary addresses for the same user are listed as type "smtp."

Exchange General

As its name suggests, the Exchange General tab allows you to configure a variety of general Exchange settings that apply to mailbox-enabled and mail-enabled recipients. Configurable settings found on or accessed via this tab include the following:

- *Mailbox store*—Found only in the properties of mailbox-enabled recipients, this setting lists the location of the user's associated mailbox, including server and mailbox store information.

- *Alias*—This setting lists the alias associated with the recipient as defined when the recipient was mailbox-enabled or mail-enabled. By default, a recipient object's alias will be the same as its Active Directory account name, but can be different if necessary.

- *Delivery Restrictions*—This setting allows you to configure sending and receiving message size limits, as well as control from whom the object can receive messages. For a mail-enabled recipient (such as a group), these settings are configured from the Message restrictions section of the Exchange General tab.

- *Delivery Options*—Found only in the properties of mailbox-enabled recipients, these settings allow you to configure other users who can send messages on this recipient's behalf, to specify a forwarding address to whom messages received by this recipient should be sent, and to configure the maximum number of recipients to whom this recipient can send a single message.

- *Message Size*—Found in the properties of a mail-enabled recipient, this setting allows you to configure the maximum message size that can be received by the recipient.

- *Storage Limits*—This item, found only in the properties of a mailbox-enabled recipient, allows you to configure mailbox storage limits for the recipient, and deleted item retention settings.

ACTIVITY

Activity 3-7: Configuring E-Mail Address and Exchange General Settings

Time Required: 15 minutes

Objective: Configure E-mail Address and Exchange General tab settings.

Description: In this activity, you configure settings on the E-mail Address and Exchange General tabs in the properties of a mailbox-enabled user object.

1. In the Active Directory Users and Computers Users container, right-click the **Mark Majors** user object, and click **Properties**.

2. Click the **E-mail Addresses** tab. Both the SMTP and X.400 addresses for Mark Majors are listed.

3. Click the **New** button. In the New E-mail Address window, click **SMTP Address**, and click **OK**.

4. In the E-mail address text box, type **markmajors@secureXX.local**, where XX is your assigned student number. Click **OK**.

5. In the E-mail addresses list, notice that the new address is listed, but the Type (smtp) is listed in lowercase, as shown in Figure 3-21. The E-mail addresses section always lists a user's primary address in caps, such as SMTP. With the new e-mail address added, Mark Majors will receive messages sent to both SMTP addresses, but all outgoing messages sent will use the mmajors@secureXX.local address as the return address by default.

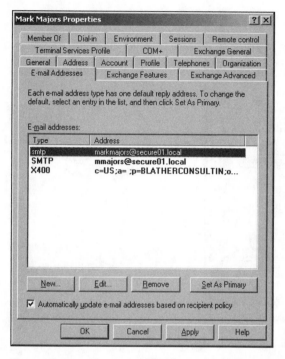

Figure 3-21   The E-mail Addresses tab for a user with multiple SMTP addresses defined

6. Click the **Exchange General** tab, as shown in Figure 3-22.

7. Click the **Delivery Restrictions** button.

8. In the Delivery Restrictions window, click **Maximum KB** in the Sending message size section, and type **1024** in the text box. This limits Mark Majors to sending messages up to 1 MB in size. Review the other options in this window, and then click **OK**.

9. Click the **Delivery Options** button. Click the **Add** button in the Send on behalf section. In the Select Recipient window, type **Mike Jones** in the Enter the object names to select text box, and click **OK**. This allows Mike Jones to send messages on behalf of Mark Majors.

10. In the Forwarding address section, click **Forward to**, and click **Modify**.

11. In the Select Recipient window, type **Mike Jones** in the Enter the object names to select text box, and click **OK**. This forwards all messages sent to Mark Majors to Mike Jones. Check the **Deliver messages to both forwarding address and mailbox** check box.

12. In the Recipient limits section, click **Maximum recipients**, and type **100**. This limits messages sent by Mark Majors to a maximum of 100 recipients, as shown in Figure 3-23. Click **OK**.

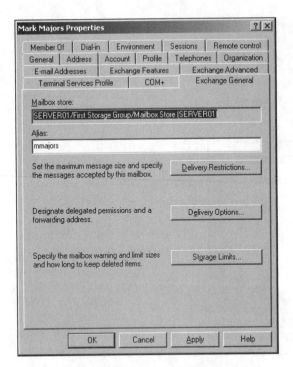

Figure 3-22   The Exchange General tab

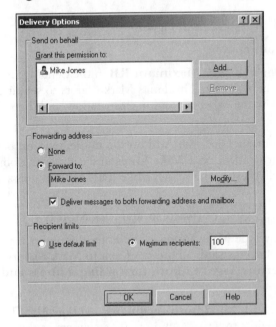

Figure 3-23   Setting a recipient limit for a user object

13. Click the **Storage Limits** button. Review the settings available in the window, but do not make any changes. Click **OK**.

14. Click **OK** to close the Mark Majors Properties window, and leave Active Directory Users and Computers open.

Exchange Features

The Exchange Features tab is only found in the properties of mailbox-enabled user and InetOrgPerson objects. The purpose of this tab is to control user access to certain Exchange features, such as certain mobile services or protocols. By selectively disabling certain features, you stop the mailbox-enabled recipient from accessing that feature.

For example, imagine that you want to stop a certain user from accessing any mobile services. You could access that user's Exchange Features tab, select each mobile service, and disable it. Similarly, you could stop a particular user from accessing certain protocols, such as POP3, IMAP4, or even Outlook Web Access, if desired.

Activity 3-8: Configuring Exchange Features Settings

Time Required: 10 minutes

Objective: Configure Exchange Features tab settings.

Description: The Exchange Features tab in the properties of a mailbox-enabled recipient allows you to enable or disable access to different mobile services and protocols. In this activity, you disable access to certain mobile services and protocols for a mailbox-enabled user.

1. Right-click the **Mark Majors** user object in the Users container in Active Directory Users and Computers, and click **Properties**.

2. Click the **Exchange Features** tab.

3. Click **Outlook Mobile Access** and click **Disable**.

4. Click **User Initiated Synchronization** and click **Disable**. This also automatically disables Up-to-date Notifications.

5. Click **POP3** and click **Disable**.

6. Click **IMAP4** and click **Disable**. Ultimately, the only Exchange feature that Mark Majors will have access to (outside of normal Microsoft Outlook connectivity) is Outlook Web Access, as shown in Figure 3-24.

7. Click **OK** to close the Mark Majors Properties window, but leave Active Directory Users and Computers open.

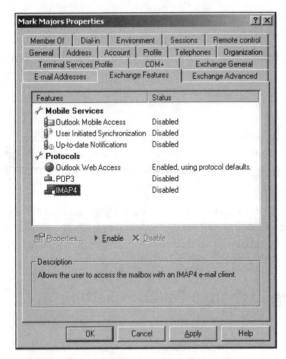

Figure 3-24   The Exchange Features tab

Exchange Advanced

The Exchange Advanced tab allows you to configure advanced Exchange-related settings for mailbox-enabled and mail-enabled recipients. The settings found on this tab for mailbox-enabled user and InetOrgPerson objects include the following:

- *Simple display name*—This text box can be used to assign a display name for mailbox-enabled recipients for systems that cannot interpret characters in different character sets, such as Kanji.

- *Hide from Exchange address lists*—Checking this box stops the recipient from being displayed in Exchange address lists.

- *Downgrade high priority mail bound for X.400*—Checking this box downgrades e-mail sent for high-priority delivery to X.400 e-mail addresses, making these messages compatible with the original X.400 e-mail standard.

- *Custom Attributes*—These settings allow you to specify up to 15 custom attributes to be associated with the object. Custom attributes are often used to track information not stored with Active Directory objects by default, such as employee ID numbers, cost center details, or other pertinent pieces of information about the object.

- *ILS Settings*—These settings are used to associate an Internet Locator Service server address and account with an object. ILS stores information about users that allows them to communicate with others online when visiting Web sites or using tools like NetMeeting.

- *Mailbox Rights*—These settings are used to grant or deny access to a mailbox. By default, only the SELF object has access to a user's mailbox. Other users or groups can be granted varying degrees of access to the mailbox by allowing (or denying) specific permissions to a mailbox.

Settings on the Exchange Advanced tab that are specific to mail-enabled group recipients include the following:

- *Expansion Server*—This setting allows you to specify the Exchange server on which the membership of a group will be expanded. By default, the first Exchange server that comes into contact with a message destined for a mail-enabled group expands the group's membership.

- *Out-of-office replies*—When checked, the sender receives out-of-office reply messages for all recipients of a message sent to this group who have out-of-office replies configured.

- *NDR settings*—These settings allow you to specify to whom (or whether) non-delivery reports will be sent in the event that a message destined for the mail-enabled group cannot be delivered.

Activity 3-9: Configuring Exchange Advanced Settings

Time Required: 10 minutes

Objective: Configure Exchange Advanced tab settings.

Description: Settings on the Exchange Advanced tab in the properties of a mailbox-enabled recipient allow you to configure everything from custom attributes to mailbox rights. In this activity, you configure a custom attribute and grant a user permission to read the contents of another user's mailbox.

1. Right-click the **Mark Majors** user object in the Users container in Active Directory Users and Computers, and click **Properties**.

2. Click the **Exchange Advanced** tab.

3. Click the **Custom Attributes** button. This opens the Exchange Custom Attributes window, as shown in Figure 3-25.

4. Click **extensionAttribute1** and click **Edit**.

5. In the Custom Attributes window, type **Cost Center NY**, and click **OK**. Click **OK** again to close the Exchange Custom Attributes window.

Figure 3-25   The Exchange Custom Attributes window

6. Click the **Mailbox Rights** button. This opens the Permissions for Mark Majors window, as shown in Figure 3-26. Notice that by default, only the SELF object is listed, with both the Allow Read and Allow Full mailbox access permissions.

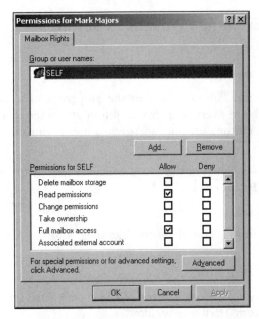

Figure 3-26   Viewing permissions associated with a user mailbox

7. Click the **Add** button.

8. In the Select Users, Computers, or Groups window, type **Mike Jones** in the Enter the object names to select text box, and click **OK**.

9. Uncheck the **Allow Delete mailbox storage** check box.

10. Check the **Allow Read permissions** check box. This allows Mike Jones to read the contents of Mark Major's mailbox.

11. Click **OK** to close the Permissions for Mark Majors window.

12. Click **OK** to exit the Mark Majors Properties window, and close **Active Directory Users and Computers**.

RECIPIENT POLICIES

To centralize the management and allocation of e-mail addresses, Exchange Server 2003 uses recipient policies. A **recipient policy** is a set of rules that applies to selected users and groups in an organization. Recipient policies can be used to apply additional e-mail addresses to users who meet the configured criteria, or manage user mailboxes.

When a new Exchange organization is created, so is a single recipient policy named Default. This policy is used to assign the generation rules for SMTP and X.400 addresses. For example, all new recipients created in the secureXX.local domain have a generation rule applied that automatically appends @secureXX.local to a new recipient's alias to create their e-mail address. Using recipient policies, you could change the rule used to generate all recipient e-mail addresses, or change the way e-mail addresses are assigned to certain recipients.

Understanding Recipient Policy Application

When no additional recipient policies exist, all recipients in an Exchange organization fall under the scope of the Default recipient policy. However, when other recipient policies are created, they are assigned a priority value that controls the order in which the policies are examined and replied. This is an important consideration—after a user falls under the scope of a particular recipient policy, settings in policies with a lower priority are ignored.

The application of recipient policies is best illustrated using an example. Consider a situation in which an administrator wants all members of a group called managers to have e-mail addresses in the format @mgmt.secureXX.local. The administrator would create a new recipient policy that applies to members of the managers group. Because the "Default" policy always has the lowest priority (and cannot be deleted), the new recipient policy would run first, and then apply the @mgmt.secureXX.local generation rule to all members of the management group (using an LDAP query to find the recipients to whom the policy should apply). The Default policy would be evaluated next, assigning all other users the @secureXX.local generation rule. Ultimately, all managers would have addresses ending in @mgmt.secureXX.local, whereas all other users would have @secureXX.local addresses.

When new recipient policies are created, you can specify priority by changing their order on the Recipient Policies list. It's critical to keep in mind that after a match is found (starting with the evaluation of the highest priority policy), additional recipient policies are not considered for a recipient. In the previous example, this means that all members of the managers groups are assigned @mgmt.secureXX.local addresses, and not @secureXX.local addresses. If you want managers to be assigned @secureXX.local addresses as well, both generation rules need to be specified in the recipient policy applied to the managers group.

Using recipient policies, you can also specify mailbox management setting such as the maximum message age and size limits. For these settings to actually be enforced, however, you must start the mailbox management process using the Mailbox Management tab in the properties of the Exchange server object in Exchange System Manager.

NOTE   You can stop e-mail addresses configured via recipient policies from being applied to a specific object from the object's properties in Active Directory Users and Computers. To do this, uncheck the Automatically update e-mail addresses based on recipient policy check box from the object's E-mail Addresses tab.

Creating and Applying Recipient Policies

When recipient policies are created, they are applied according to the schedule configured in the properties of the Recipient Update Service for the domain. By default, the Recipient Update Service for a domain is set to "Always run," but these settings can be changed. A recipient policy can be applied immediately by right-clicking on a recipient policy and selecting Apply this policy now.

ACTIVITY

Activity 3-10: Creating and Applying Recipient Policies

Time Required: 20 minutes

Objective: Create and apply a recipient policy.

Description: Recipient policies make it easy for an administrator to centralize the management of recipient e-mail addresses and mailbox management options. In this activity, you create a new recipient policy that adds an additional e-mail address generation rule to users who fall within the scope of an associated LDAP query.

1. Click **Start**, point to **All Programs**, point to **Microsoft Exchange**, and then click **System Manager**.

2. Click the **plus sign (+)** next to Recipients to expand it.

3. Click **Recipient Policies** to view its contents. The Default Policy is the only recipient policy listed, as shown in Figure 3-27.

4. Right-click **Default Policy** and click **Properties**.

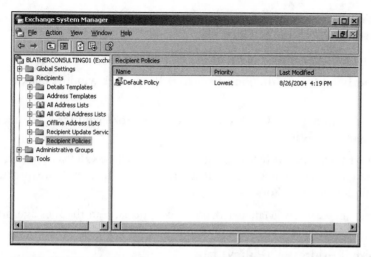

Figure 3-27 Viewing the contents of the Recipient Policies container

5. Click the **E-Mail Addresses (Policy)** tab. This tab lists the generation rules used to create SMTP and X.400 addresses, as shown in Figure 3-28. Click **OK** to close the Default Policy Properties window.

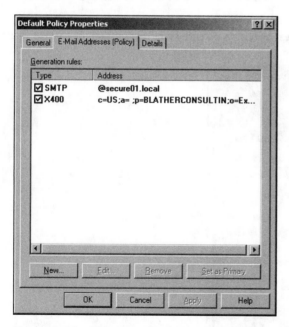

Figure 3-28 The E-Mail Addresses (Policy) tab for the Default recipient policy

6. Right-click **Recipient Policies**, point to **New**, and then click **Recipient Policy**.

7. In the New Policy window, check both the **E-Mail Addresses** and **Mailbox Manager Settings** check boxes. Click **OK**.

8. On the General tab, type **Test Policy** in the Name text box.

9. Click the **Modify** button. In the Find Exchange Recipients window, click the **Advanced** tab.

10. Click the **Field** button, select **User**, and then click **State/Province** (you need to scroll down to reach this item).

11. In the Value text box, type **New York**, and click **Add**. Click **OK** to complete the query. This new recipient policy applies to user objects with their State/province attribute configured as New York.

12. When the Exchange System Manager dialog box appears, read the message, and click **OK**.

13. Click the **E-Mail Addresses (Policy)** tab.

14. Click the **New** button. Click **SMTP Address**, and click **OK**.

15. In the Address text box, type **@ny.secureXX.local**, where XX is your assigned student number. Click **OK**.

16. In the Generation rules list, check the check box next to the **@ny.secureXX.local** address.

17. Click the **Mailbox Manager Settings (Policy)** tab, as shown in Figure 3-29.

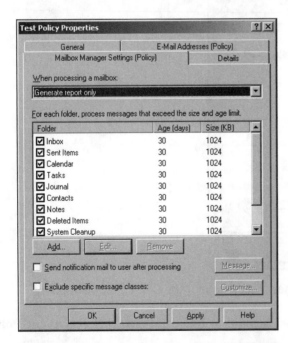

Figure 3-29   The Mailbox Manager Settings (Policy) tab

18. Click **Sent Items** and click **Edit**.

19. At the Folder Retention Settings window, type **512** in the Message Size (KB) text box. Click **OK**.

20. Check the **Send notification mail to user after processing** check box. Click the **Message** button to view the default message and settings, and click **OK**.

21. Click **OK** to close the Test Policy Properties window. When prompted to update all addresses, click **Yes**.

22. Right-click **Test Policy** and click **Apply this policy now**. When the Exchange System Manager dialog box appears, click **Yes**.

23. Close the **Exchange System Manager** window.

24. Click **Start**, point to **All Programs**, point to **Microsoft Exchange**, and then click **Active Directory Users and Computers**.

25. Click the **plus sign (+)** next to secureXX.local to expand it, where XX is your assigned student number.

26. Click the **Users** container to view its contents.

27. Right-click the **Mark Majors** user object, and click **Properties**.

28. Click the **E-mail Addresses** tab. Notice that the address mmajors@ny.secureXX. local has been added for the Mark Majors account as a result of the newly applied recipient policy, as shown in Figure 3-30.

29. Click **OK** to close the Mark Majors Properties window, and close **Active Directory Users and Computers**.

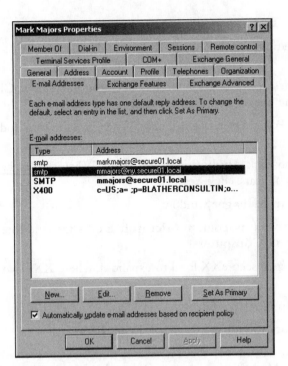

Figure 3-30   The E-mail Addresses tab, including a new address applied by the recipient policy

CHAPTER SUMMARY

- Recipients in an Exchange organization include user, InetOrgPerson, contact, security and distribution group, query-based distribution group, and public folder objects.

- Recipients that are mailbox-enabled can send and receive messages and have an associated storage mailbox. Recipients that are mail-enabled can receive messages only, and do not have a mailbox assigned.

- Examples of objects that can be mailbox-enabled include user and InetOrgPerson objects.

- Examples of objects that can be mail-enabled included user, InetOrgPerson, contact, security group, distribution group, query-based distribution group, and public folder objects.

- New objects can be mailbox-enabled or mail-enabled as part of their creation process after Exchange is installed. Existing objects can be mailbox-enabled or mail-enabled using the Exchange Task Wizard in Active Directory Users and Computers.

- Query-based distribution groups are a new feature in Exchange Server 2003 that allows an administrator to define the membership of the group dynamically through the use of an LDAP query.

❑ Exchange-specific settings found in the properties of recipient objects are configured from the E-mail Addresses, Exchange General, Exchange Advanced, and Exchange Features tabs.

❑ Recipient policies can be used to simplify and centralize the management of recipient settings, including e-mail addresses and mailbox management processes.

3

KEY TERMS

contacts — The objects that represent people external to a particular company or organization.

distribution group — An Active Directory group used for the purpose of distributing e-mail messages to all group members.

Global Address List (GAL) — A list of address and contact details for mail- and mailbox-enabled recipients in an Exchange organization.

global catalog server — A domain controller that holds a copy of all objects in an Active Directory forest and a subset of that object's attributes.

group — A collection of Active Directory objects that helps to simplify the management of objects with common requirements.

InetOrgPerson — A special user object with an extended set of attributes to support interactions with other directory services.

Lightweight Directory Access Protocol (LDAP) — The protocol used to query the Active Directory database.

mail-enabled recipient — A recipient object that can receive e-mail messages but cannot store messages on (nor send messages via) an Exchange server.

mailbox-enabled recipient — A recipient object that has a mailbox on an Exchange server, allowing it to send, receive, and store messages.

query-based distribution group — A special distribution group whose membership is defined dynamically according to the results of an LDAP query.

public folder — A storage area for e-mail messages and other files in an Exchange organization.

recipient — Any object that can receive e-mail messages in an Exchange organization.

recipient policy — A policy that allows the centralized configuration of e-mail address and mailbox management settings.

security group — An Active Directory group that is typically created for the purpose of assigning permissions or rights to group members.

REVIEW QUESTIONS

1. Which of the following objects can be mailbox-enabled? (Choose all that apply.)

   a. user

   b. InetOrgPerson

    c. security group

    d. public folder

2. Which of the following objects can be mail-enabled? (Choose all that apply.)

    a. user

    b. security group

    c. contact

    d. distribution group

3. Which of the following statements about mailbox-enabled recipients are true? (Choose all that apply.)

    a. they can store messages on an Exchange server

    b. they can receive messages via an Exchange server

    c. they can send messages via an Exchange server

    d. none of the above

4. Which of the following group types can be mail-enabled? (Choose all that apply.)

    a. security groups

    b. distribution groups

    c. query-based distribution groups

    d. universal security groups

5. Query-based distribution groups are only available in Exchange Server 2003 native mode organizations. True or False?

6. Which protocol is used to obtain the membership of a query-based distribution group?

    a. SMTP

    b. POP3

    c. IMAP

    d. LDAP

7. Which of the following tools is used to mail-enable an existing user object?

    a. Exchange System Manager

    b. Exchange Task Wizard

    c. Exchange Mail-enable Wizard

    d. Exchange User Manager

8. Which tool is used to create recipient policies?

    a. Exchange System Manager

    b. Active Directory Users and Computers

    c. Exchange Task Manager

    d. none of the above

9. Which of the following tabs are added to the properties of a contact after it is mail-enabled? (Choose all that apply.)

a. Exchange Advanced

b. E-mail Addresses

c. Exchange General

d. Exchange Features

10. From which Exchange-related tab in the properties of a mail-enabled recipient would an administrator make configuration changes to hide a recipient from Exchange address lists?

a. Exchange Advanced

b. Exchange Features

c. E-mail Addresses

d. Exchange General

11. Which of the following objects is not a valid Exchange recipient?

a. user

b. InetOrgPerson

c. organizational unit

d. distribution group

12. Which of the following are requirements to use query-based distribution groups?

a. Exchange Server 2003 running in native mode

b. Windows Server 2003 domain controllers

c. Windows Server 2003 global catalog server

d. Exchange Server 2003 running in mixed mode

13. How many expansion servers can be configured from the properties of a mail-enabled group?

a. 1

b. 2

c. 10

d. unlimited

14. Mail-enabled contacts are added to the Exchange GAL by default. True or False?

15. Which server in an Active Directory environment processes the LDAP query used to determine the membership of a query-based distribution group?

a. schema master

b. global catalog server

c. domain naming master

d. PDC emulator

16. Which of the following are requirements to mailbox-enabled InetOrgPerson objects?

    a. at least one Windows Server 2003 domain controller

    b. Exchange servers can be running Exchange Server 2003 only

    c. at least one Exchange Server 2003 system; other Exchange versions do not matter

    d. at least one Windows 2000 Server domain controller

17. A mail-enabled object has a mailbox stored on an Exchange server. True or False?

18. InetOrgPerson objects can be both mailbox-enabled and mail-enabled. True or False?

19. Query-based distribution groups can be added as members of a traditional distribution group. True or False?

20. Which of the following objects is assigned permission to access a user's mailbox by default?

    a. EVERYONE

    b. SELF

    c. Administrator

    d. Exchange Administrator

21. What is the maximum number of custom attributes that can be assigned to a mail- or mailbox-enabled recipient with Exchange Server 2003?

    a. 1

    b. 2

    c. 10

    d. 15

22. Mail-enabled contacts cannot be hidden from Exchange address lists. True or False?

23. Universal groups can only be created when a domain's functional level is raised from the Windows 2000 mixed level. True or False?

24. By default, the alias assigned to a mailbox-enabled user is the same as the user's Active Directory user name. True or False?

CASE PROJECTS

Case Project 3-1: Requirements to Mailbox-Enable an InetOrgPerson Object

The administrator at Magnetewan Industries plans to implement Exchange Server 2003 in their existing NetWare environment. They plan to use InetOrgPerson objects for user accounts rather than traditional user objects to help facilitate what might be a long transition period. What must be in place for InetOrgPerson objects to be mailbox-enabled after the Exchange server is installed?

Case Project 3-2: Query-Based Distribution Group Requirements

Super Siding Corporation is investigating some of the different recipient objects available with Exchange Server 2003. They are particularly interested in using query-based distribution groups as a way to send messages to different users and contacts. What must Super Siding Corporation do to be able to create query-based distribution groups?

Case Project 3-3: Defining Recipient Policies

Maple Sugar Systems is looking for a way to change the e-mail addresses of different recipient objects easily based on roles. Specifically, the company wants all users to be allocated an @maplesugarsystems.com address. They also want all managers to be assigned a second address, @mgmt.maplesugarsystems.com. Finally, all directors should have only one address, @directors.maplesugarsystems.com.

Based on these requirements, how many recipient policies would the administrator at Maple Sugar Systems need to define, which address should each policy list, and what should be the priority order in which policies should be applied?

4

CONFIGURING OUTLOOK AND OUTLOOK WEB ACCESS

After reading this chapter, you will be able to:

♦ Understand the different client access methods supported by Exchange servers

♦ Configure Microsoft Outlook 2003 to connect to an Exchange server

♦ Connect to an Exchange server using an Internet e-mail client such as Outlook Express

♦ Use Outlook Web Access to connect to an Exchange server from a Web browser

♦ Secure connections to Outlook Web Access

Exchange Server 2003 supports a wide variety of client access methods to meet the varying needs of users and organizations with different requirements. Although using the Outlook client remains the primary way for users to gain access to their mailbox and other Exchange features, alternatives include the use of Outlook Web Access, Outlook Mobile Access, and even Internet e-mail clients.

When used in conjunction with Outlook 2003, Exchange Server 2003 provides support for a number of new features and enhancements not previously available. These include integrated Kerberos authentication, the new Cached Exchange Mode, better compression and synchronization support, and even a new .pst file format. Many of the new client-related enhancements found in Exchange Server 2003 are only supported when Outlook 2003 is used as a client.

Companies also need to consider the security implications of allowing unsecured communications, especially for remote users. In this chapter, you learn more about configuring secure connections between Outlook 2003 and Exchange Server 2003 via RPC over HTTP, as well as how to implement Secure Sockets Layer (SSL) security for Outlook Web Access connections.

EXCHANGE CLIENT ACCESS

For users to interact with Exchange Server resources, such as their mailbox or public folders, client access software is required. Exchange Server 2003 allows client connections via a number of programs and methods, including the following:

- Microsoft Outlook
- Web browsers, using Outlook Web Access
- Outlook Mobile Access
- Internet e-mail clients, such as Outlook Express or Eudora

The ability to use different client access programs or methods depends upon the functionality supported by the client, as well as whether certain services on the Exchange server are installed and enabled. Although some methods provide access to all Exchange features, others provide access to a more limited subset of features. In the following sections, you learn more about the various client access programs and methods supported for connecting to a Microsoft Exchange Server 2003 system.

Microsoft Outlook

Microsoft Outlook is the primary client software package used to connect to and interact with an Exchange server. Outlook provides client access to the complete set of Exchange client messaging and collaboration features, including access to the user's mailbox, Public Folders, Tasks, Contacts, Journal, Calendar, Shortcuts, and more. In a nutshell, Outlook is designed to be a user's primary communication and information management tool.

The current version of Microsoft Outlook is **Outlook 2003**. When Outlook 2003 is used as a client in Exchange Server 2003 environments, a number of new features not available in previous configurations are supported. Examples include the following:

- Access from Outlook 2003 to Exchange Server 2003 over the Internet using the **RPC over HTTP** protocol. This allows an Outlook 2003 client to securely connect to an Exchange server over the Internet without the need for a dial-up or VPN connection into the server's network.
- Easier synchronization between Outlook 2003 and Exchange Server 2003 by way of data compression. Ultimately, these changes make the data transfer process between the client and server more efficient.
- A new .pst file format that includes support for a larger storage capacity and Unicode data. It should be noted that the new .pst format is incompatible with previous versions of Microsoft Outlook. However, Outlook 2003 can be configured to use the same .pst format as previous versions if required.
- Authentication from an Outlook 2003 client to an Exchange Server 2003 system using **Kerberos**. This changes the Exchange authentication model to work with

the Kerberos authentication methods used by Active Directory, and provides support for features like cross-forest authentication.

- Support for **Cached Exchange Mode**, in which a user works from a locally cached copy of the Exchange mailbox, rather than requiring a "live" connection at all times. Previously, users would be prompted with dialog boxes whenever the client needed to connect to the Exchange server. Now, many of these requests can be carried out on the local copy of the mailbox file. Cached Exchange Mode helps to significantly reduce network bandwidth consumption between Outlook 2003 and Exchange Server 2003.

Although using Outlook 2003 to connect to Exchange Server 2003 systems provides support for each of these new features, previous versions of Microsoft Outlook still can be used to connect to Exchange Server 2003 systems without issue.

Microsoft Outlook Web Access

As with previous versions of Exchange Server, Exchange Server 2003 supports connections to user mailboxes and related features from a Web browser using **Outlook Web Access**. Unlike previous versions, however, the version of Outlook Web Access provided with Exchange Server 2003 has been redesigned and now includes advanced features, such as spell check, support for rules, and a look and feel very similar to the full Outlook 2003 client.

Some of the new key features supported in Outlook Web Access with Exchange Server 2003 include the following:

- Compression support to reduce the size of data passed between the Exchange Server 2003 system and Outlook Web Access client
- **Forms-based authentication** that allows users to log on with their domain name, user name, and password, or their full user principal name (UPN)
- Support for **Secure MIME**, which allows the use of digital signatures and encryption with Outlook Web Access clients

Unlike previous releases, Outlook Web Access is now available in two different versions—the premium version and the basic version. The basic version is supported on almost all operating systems and Web browsers, and is very similar to previous versions of Outlook Web Access. The premium version of Outlook Web Access provides access to all of the new and advanced Web access features, but is not supported with all operating systems or browsers. As a general rule, any Microsoft operating system running Internet Explorer 6 SP1 has access to the premium version, although some operating systems can access the premium version at Internet Explorer 5.1 or higher. For a complete list of the Outlook Web Access versions supported by different operating system and browser combinations, visit *www.microsoft.com/exchange/techinfo/outlook/OWAandIE.asp*.

For comparative details on feature support in Outlook 2003 and the premium and basic versions of Outlook Web Access, visit *www.microsoft.com/ exchange/evaluation/OutlookVowa_1.asp*.

NOTE

Outlook Mobile Access

In a manner similar to Outlook Web Access, Exchange Server 2003 provides support for client connections from mobile devices, such as cell phones and Pocket PC devices. For a mobile user to connect to the Outlook Mobile Access feature, his device must include a browser that supports HTML, cHTML (Compact HTML), or xHTML (Extensible HTML).

Third-Party Software

For cases in which users simply need access to their Exchange mailbox for the purpose of sending or receiving messages via an Internet connection, Exchange Server 2003 also provides support for client connectivity using third-party e-mail client software. For example, an administrator could enable **Post Office Protocol 3 (POP3)** or **Internet Message Access Protocol 4 (IMAP4)** support on the Exchange Server 2003 system and allow Internet clients to gain access to their mailbox using these protocols. After being enabled, Internet e-mail clients like **Outlook Express** or Eudora can be used to allow users to send and receive messages via the Exchange server.

MICROSOFT OUTLOOK 2003

Of all the possible Exchange Server 2003 client access methods, Outlook 2003 is the only software option that provides complete interoperability with all Exchange messaging and collaboration features. Although previous versions of Microsoft Outlook will still function in Exchange Server 2003 environments, Outlook 2003 is required to take advantage of many new features like RPC over HTTP connections, support for Kerberos cross-forest authentication, the new .pst file format, Cached Exchange Mode, and more.

Installing Microsoft Outlook 2003

Microsoft Outlook 2003 is provided as a component of the Microsoft Office 2003 suite. In Activity 4-1, you connect to a shared folder on the instructor server and install Microsoft Outlook 2003 on your server.

Activity 4-1: Installing Microsoft Outlook 2003

Time Required: 15 minutes

ACTIVITY

Objective: Install Microsoft Outlook 2003.

Description: Outlook 2003 is installed as part of the Microsoft Office 2003 suite. In this activity, you install Outlook 2003 on your server.

1. Log on to your Windows Server 2003 system using the user name **Administrator** and the password **Password!**.

2. Click **Start**, click **Run**, type **\\serverinst\office\setup.exe** in the Open text box, and then click **OK**.

3. At the Product Key screen, enter the product key number provided by your instructor, and click **Next**.

4. At the User Information screen, type your full name in the User name text box, and click **Next**.

5. At the End-User License Agreement screen, check the **I accept the terms in the License Agreement** check box, and click **Next**.

6. At the Type of Installation screen, click **Custom Install**, and click **Next**.

7. At the Custom Setup screen, uncheck all check boxes with the exception of Microsoft Outlook, as shown in Figure 4-1. Click **Next**.

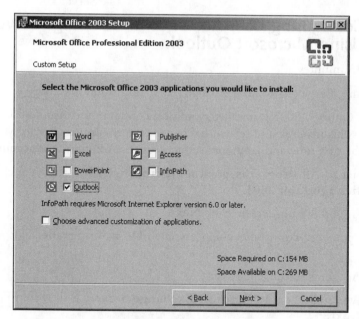

Figure 4-1   Installing Microsoft Outlook 2003

8. At the Summary screen, click **Install**.

9. At the Setup Completed screen, click **Finish**.

Configuring User Access

After being installed, Outlook 2003 can be configured to access a variety of different server types, including the following:

- Microsoft Exchange Server
- POP3 mail servers
- IMAP4 mail servers
- HTTP mail servers (such as Hotmail)
- Third-party mail servers (such as Novell GroupWise)

For Outlook 2003 users to connect to any of the servers just listed, appropriate user account settings first must be configured. When Outlook 2003 is opened for the first time, users are presented with the Outlook 2003 Startup screen, a wizard-based interface that supports upgrades from other mail systems, the configuration of new account settings, and so forth.

In Activity 4-2, you open Outlook 2003 for the first time and configure account settings for the Administrator account to access your Exchange Server 2003 system.

ACTIVITY

Activity 4-2: Configuring User Access to an Exchange Server Using Microsoft Outlook

Time Required: 15 minutes

Objective: Configure user access to an Exchange server from Outlook 2003.

Description: After Outlook 2003 is installed, you must configure user account settings to allow a user to access his mailbox and related Exchange features. In this activity, you open Outlook 2003 for the first time and configure settings for the Administrator account.

1. Click **Start**, point to **All Programs**, point to **Microsoft Office**, and then click **Microsoft Office Outlook 2003**.

2. At the Outlook 2003 Startup screen, click **Next**.

3. If the E-mail Upgrade Options screen appears, click **Do not upgrade**, and click **Next**.

4. At the E-mail Accounts screen, click **Next**.

5. At the Server Type screen, click **Microsoft Exchange Server**, as shown in Figure 4-2, and click **Next**.

6. At the Exchange Server Settings screen, type **SERVERXX** in the Microsoft Exchange Server text box, where XX is your assigned student number.

7. In the User Name text box, type **Administrator**, as shown in Figure 4-3. Click **Next**.

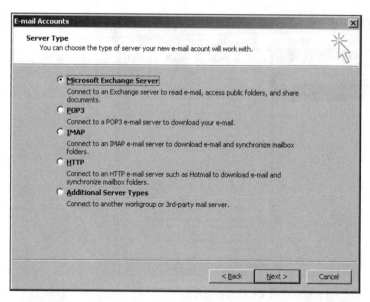

Figure 4-2   Selecting the option to connect Microsoft Outlook to an Exchange server

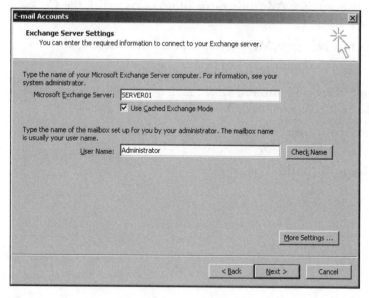

Figure 4-3   Configuring Exchange server and user name information

8. At the Congratulations! screen, click **Finish**. Microsoft Outlook opens to the Administrator's Inbox, as shown in Figure 4-4.

9. Click the list arrow to the right of New, and click **Mail Message**.

10. Click the **To** button, click **Mark Majors**, and then click **OK**.

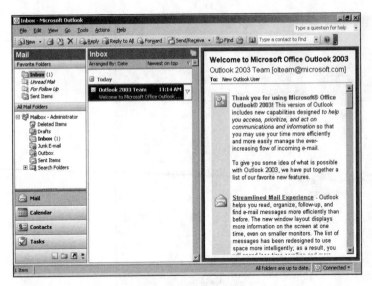

Figure 4-4   Welcome to Microsoft Outlook 2003

11. Click the **Cc** button, click **Administrator** (if necessary), click the **Cc – >** button, and then click **OK**.

12. In the Subject text box, type **Message to test account settings**.

13. In the message text box, type **test**, and click the **Send** button.

14. Click the **Send/Receive** button to view the new message. If you receive an error message in the Send/Receive dialog box, simply cancel the dialog box.

15. Click the **Message to test account settings** message in the Inbox window to view it, as shown in Figure 4-5.

16. Close the **Microsoft Outlook** window.

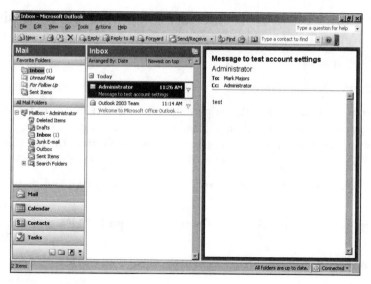

4

Figure 4-5   Viewing the received test message

USING INTERNET E-MAIL CLIENTS

In some cases, mailbox-enabled users might not have access to Microsoft Outlook and might need to connect to the Exchange server using a traditional Internet e-mail client such as Outlook Express. In these cases, the user typically connects to the Exchange server over the Internet (although a local network is also possible) using a mailbox-access protocol, such as POP3 or IMAP4.

Although protocols such as POP3 and IMAP4 don't provide the same degree of functionality and interoperability as found with client software like Outlook 2003, they do provide users with access to the mailboxes for the purpose of sending and receiving e-mail messages. Before users can connect using these methods, however, the appropriate Exchange virtual server associated with the protocol must be enabled. In addition, the user's account object must be enabled to allow access via the selected protocol on its Exchange Features tab. Access to the POP3 and IMAP4 protocols (as well as Outlook Web Access) are enabled for all new mailbox-enabled recipients by default, so in most cases, an administrator simply needs to enable the protocol's virtual server in Exchange System Manager.

In Activity 4-3, you enable the Default IMAP4 Virtual Server on your Exchange server using Exchange System Manager, and then configure Outlook Express to connect to your Exchange server using the IMAP4 protocol.

Activity 4-3: Connecting to Microsoft Exchange Server Using IMAP4

Time Required: 15 minutes

Objective: Configure Outlook Express to connect to an Exchange server using IMAP4.

Description: Internet e-mail client software packages that support POP3 and IMAP4 mail access can be configured to connect to an Exchange Server 2003 system after the appropriate virtual server is enabled and the client is properly configured. In this activity, you configure Outlook Express to access the Administrator's mailbox using the IMAP4 protocol.

1. Click **Start**, click **Run**, type **services.msc** in the Open text box, and then click **OK**.

2. In the Services window, right-click **Microsoft Exchange IMAP4**, and then click **Properties**.

3. In the Startup type drop-down box, select **Automatic**. Click **OK**.

4. Close the **Services** window.

5. Click **Start**, point to **All Programs**, point to **Microsoft Exchange**, and then click **System Manager**.

6. Click the **plus signs (+)** next to Administrative Groups, First Administrative Group, and Servers to expand them.

7. Click the **plus sign (+)** next to SERVERXX, where XX is your assigned student number.

8. Click the **plus sign (+)** next to Protocols to expand it.

9. Click the **IMAP4** node to view its contents, as shown in Figure 4-6.

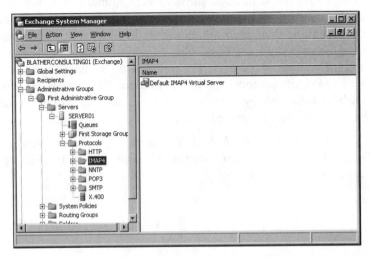

Figure 4-6   The Default IMAP4 Virtual Server is not started by default

10. Right-click **Default IMAP4 Virtual Server**, and click **Start**.

11. Close the Exchange System Manager window.

12. Click **Start**, point to **All Programs**, and then click **Outlook Express**.

13. When the Outlook Express dialog box appears, uncheck the **Always perform this check when starting Outlook Express** check box, and click **No**.

14. Click **Tools**, and click **Accounts**. (If the Your Name screen appeared after Step 13, move on to Step 16.)

15. Click the **Add** button, and click **Mail**. (If the Your Name screen appeared after Step 13, move on to Step 16.)

16. At the Your Name screen, type **Administrator** in the Display name text box, and click **Next**.

17. At the Internet E-mail Address screen, type **administrator@secureXX.local** in the E-mail address text box, where XX is your assigned student number. Click **Next**.

18. At the E-mail Server Names screen, click the drop-down menu to select My incoming mail server is a **IMAP** server, as shown in Figure 4-7.

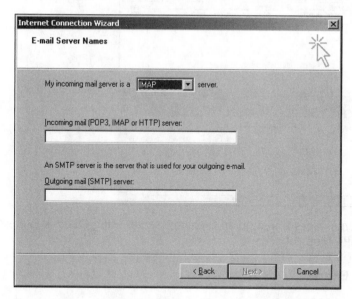

Figure 4-7   Configuring Outlook Express to connect to an IMAP4 server

19. In the Incoming mail (POP3, IMAP, or HTTP) server text box, type **serverXX.secureXX.local**, where XX is your assigned student number.

20. In the Outgoing mail (SMTP) server text box, type **serverXX.secureXX.local**, where XX is your assigned student number. Click **Next**.

21. At the Internet Mail Logon screen, type **Password!** in the Password text box. Click **Next**.

22. At the Congratulations screen, click **Finish**.

23. Click the **Close** button to close the Internet Accounts window. Close any windows related to importing messages if they appear on your screen, and do not import messages.

24. When the Outlook Express dialog box appears, click **Yes**. If another dialog box appears asking whether you want to go offline, click **Try Again**.

25. At the Show/Hide IMAP Folders window, click **OK**.

26. Click the **Inbox** icon under serverXX.secureXX.local, where XX is your assigned student number. Notice that both e-mail messages from Activity 4-2 are visible in your Inbox, as shown in Figure 4-8.

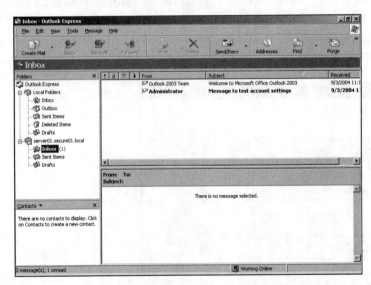

Figure 4-8   Viewing messages stored on an Exchange server using Outlook Express and the IMAP4 protocol

27. Close **Outlook Express**.

NOTE

After the associated POP3 or IMAP4 virtual server is enabled on an Exchange server system, any e-mail client that supports the POP3 or IMAP4 protocols can connect to the server—not just Outlook Express. Examples of popular third-party Internet e-mail clients include Qualcomm Eudora, Mozilla Thunderbird, and Netscape Mail.

Exploring Outlook Web Access

In most cases, users have one PC configured with Microsoft Outlook to access their e-mail, calendar, and other Exchange features. To facilitate user access to Exchange mailbox and collaboration features in cases in which users don't have access to the full Outlook client, Exchange Server 2003 allows connections via a Web browser using Outlook Web Access.

Although the version of Outlook Web Access provided with Exchange Server 2003 provides a higher degree of functionality than any previous version, it does not provide access to all of the features available to users who connect with the Outlook 2003 client. However, the premium version of Outlook Web Access does provide users with much of the same core functionality as the full Outlook client, and even goes as far as to supply a Web-based interface that is very consistent with the look and feel of Outlook 2003. The basic edition interface provides greater compatibility with a range of different Web browsers, but provides access to a much more limited set of tools.

Using Outlook Web Access provides users working from remote locations (or simply away from their primary PC) with a simple and effective way to access Exchange Server. In Activity 4-4, you connect to Outlook Web Access for the first time and explore its features and layout.

Activity 4-4: Exploring Outlook Web Access

Time Required: 15 minutes

Objective: Explore the premium version of Outlook Web Access.

Description: To allow remote users to access their mailbox and related Exchange features, Outlook Web Access provides access from a Web browser. In this activity, you access Outlook Web Access for the first time and explore its interface and features.

1. Click **Start**, point to **All Programs**, and then click **Internet Explorer**.

2. In the Address Bar, type **http://serverXX.secureXX.local/exchange** (where XX is your assigned student number), and click the **Go** button.

3. When the Connect to serverXX.secureXX.local dialog box appears, type **Administrator** in the User name text box and **Password!** in the Password text box.

4. Check the **Remember my password** check box, and then click **OK**. The Microsoft Outlook Web Access screen appears, as shown in Figure 4-9.

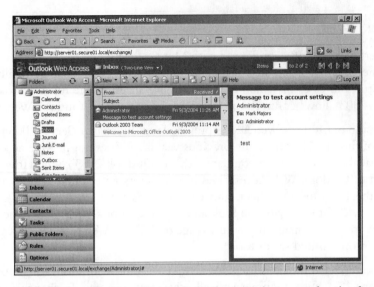

Figure 4-9   Opening Microsoft Outlook Web Access for the first time

5. Click the arrow next to the **New** button, and click **Message**. This opens a new message window, as shown in Figure 4-10. Notice that the message layout is similar to what you might expect from the full Microsoft Outlook 2003 client. Close the new message window.

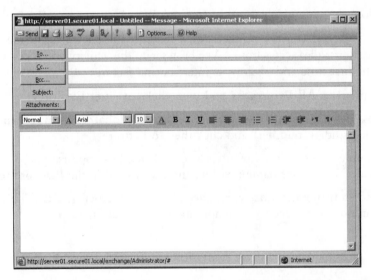

Figure 4-10   Creating a new message with Outlook Web Access

6. In the left navigation pane, click the **Options** button. This provides access to configuring a variety of Outlook options, as shown in Figure 4-11.

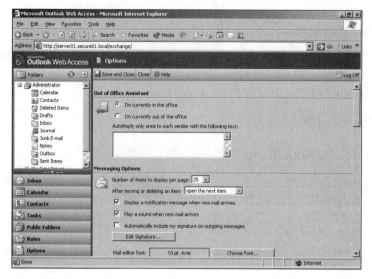

4

Figure 4-11   Viewing the Options screen in Outlook Web Access

7. As time permits, browse through the Microsoft Outlook Web Access interface to explore its general environment, options, and settings. When you are finished, close the **Internet Explorer** window.

Redirecting Client Requests

To make it easier for users to connect to the Exchange server running Outlook Web Access, it often helps to simplify the uniform resource locator (URL) used to connect to the server. Under normal circumstances, this URL is the fully qualified domain name of the server, followed by /exchange. However, you can use the redirection capabilities in the properties of an IIS-hosted Web site to make the URL easier for users to remember.

In Activity 4-5, you change the properties of the Default Web Site such that user requests to *http://serverXX.secureXX.local* are automatically redirected to the /exchange directory used to connect to Outlook Web Access.

ACTIVITY

Activity 4-5: Configuring Simplified User Access to Outlook Web Access

Time Required: 15 minutes

Objective: Configure a simplified URL for Outlook Web Access.

Description: To simplify access to Outlook Web Access, you can configure IIS redirection settings such that users do not need to input an entire URL. In this activity, you configure IIS to redirect requests to the fully qualified domain name of your server to the /exchange directory.

1. Click **Start**, point to **Administrative Tools**, and then click **Internet Information Services (IIS) Manager**.

2. Click the **plus sign (+)** next to SERVERXX to expand it, where XX is your assigned student number.

3. Click the **plus sign (+)** next to Web Sites to expand it.

4. Click **Default Web Site** to view its contents, as shown in Figure 4-12.

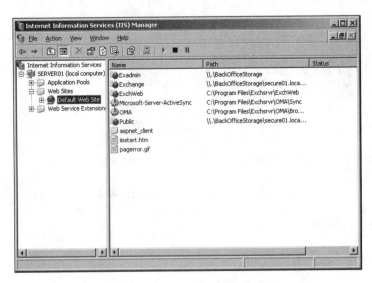

Figure 4-12   Contents of the Default Web Site

5. Right-click **Default Web Site** and click **Properties**.

6. Click the **Home Directory** tab.

7. Under The content for this resources should come from, click **A redirection to a URL**.

8. In the Redirect to text box, type **/exchange**.

9. Check the **A directory below URL entered** check box, as shown in Figure 4-13. Click **OK**.

10. At the Inheritance Overrides window, click **Cancel**.

11. Close the **Internet Information Services (IIS) Manager** window.

12. Click **Start**, point to **All Programs**, and then click **Internet Explorer**.

13. In the Address Bar, type **serverXX.secureXX.local** (where XX is your assigned student number), and click **Go**.

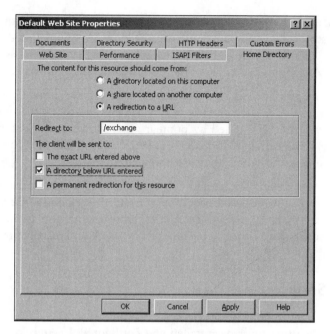

Figure 4-13   Redirecting client requests to a different URL

14. At the Connect to serverXX.secureXX.local window, type **Password!** in the Password text box, and click **OK**. The Microsoft Outlook Web Access screen appears, the request having been redirected to the /exchange folder automatically.

15. Close **Internet Explorer**.

SECURING OUTLOOK AND OUTLOOK WEB ACCESS

When Exchange Server 2003 is initially installed, user connections to Outlook Web Access are authenticated, but all communications between the user's Web browser and the Exchange server are unsecured. In cases in which you plan to allow users to connect to Outlook Web Access over the Internet, you should secure the session between the user's browser and the Exchange server using **Secure Sockets Layer (SSL)** communication.

To implement SSL to take advantage of its encryption capabilities, the Default Web Site on which Outlook Web Access is running must be configured with a Web server certificate. This certificate is used to identify the server, whereas the associated public and private key pair is used to securely exchange the session key that is used to encrypt all communications between clients and the server.

By default, Web sites running on IIS do not have any certificates installed, and are, thus, incapable of using SSL to secure communications. To implement SSL, you first must obtain the required Web server certificate from a **certificate authority (CA)**.

A CA is an organization entrusted with validating or "vouching for" the identity of an organization. CAs issue certificates to companies and organizations, certifying the identity of that organization. After the identity of the organization has been verified and any associated fees have been paid, the CA signs and then issues the certificate to the requesting entity.

In cases in which the general public accesses a Web server, most organizations obtain their server certificates from a trusted CA, such as Thawte or VeriSign. Almost all Web browsers include the public keys for certificates signed by popular CAs, allowing the Web browser (and by extension, the user) to be certain that the server's certificate is valid, thus confirming the identity of the server and site to which they are connecting.

Although using a certificate provided by a trusted CA is generally preferable, organizations running Windows 2000 Server or Windows Server 2003 can alternatively install **Certificate Services** and issue their own certificates for everything from identifying users to Web servers. In this case, the organization effectively becomes its own CA, and manages the entire certificate granting process.

Installing Certificate Services

For an organization running Windows 2000 Server or Windows Server 2003 to issue certificates, Certificate Service first must be installed and configured. In Activity 4-6, you install Certificate Services on your Windows Server 2003 system.

ACTIVITY

Activity 4-6: Installing Certificate Services

Time Required: 15 minutes

Objective: Install Windows Server 2003 Certificate Services.

Description: To issue your own Web server certificate, Certificate Services first must be installed. In this activity, you install Certificate Services on your Windows Server 2003 system.

1. Click **Start**, click **Control Panel**, and then click **Add or Remove Programs**.

2. In the Add or Remove Programs window, click **Add/Remove Windows Components**.

3. At the Windows Components screen, check the check box next to **Certificate Services**. When the Microsoft Certificate Services dialog box appears, read the message, and then click **Yes**. The Windows Components screen with Certificate Services selected is shown in Figure 4-14. Click **Next**.

4. At the CA Type screen, click **Next**.

5. At the CA Identifying Information screen, type **BLATHERCONSULTING** in the Common name for this CA text box, and click **Next**.

6. At the Certificate Database Settings screen, click **Next**.

7. When the Microsoft Certificate Services dialog box appears, click **Yes**. When prompted, insert your Windows Server 2003 CD, and click **OK**.

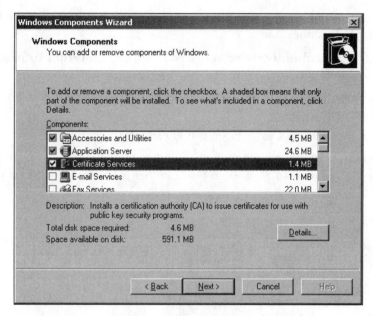

4

Figure 4-14   Installing Certificate Services

8. At the Completing the Windows Components Wizard screen, click **Finish**.

9. Close the **Add or Remove Programs** window.

Obtaining and Installing a Server Certificate

After Certificate Services is installed, an organization can create certificate requests and implement its own policies to control how certificates are issued. In cases in which a Web server certificate is required for the purpose of implementing SSL encryption, IIS simplifies the certificate request and installation process using a tool known as the Web Server Certificate Wizard. This tool can be used to request certificates from a third-party trusted CA, or to submit requests to an organization's internal certificate server.

In Activity 4-7, you request and install a new certificate for your Web server, and configure the Default Web Site to require SSL communications for all client connections.

ACTIVITY

Activity 4-7: Installing a Server Certificate to Require SSL Communications

Time Required: 15 minutes

Objective: Install a Web server certificate and configure Outlook Web Access to require SSL communications.

Description: To allow secure SSL-based connections to Outlook Web Access, a Web server certificate must be installed, and the Default Web Site must be appropriately configured. In this activity, you request and install a Web server certificate and then configure the Default Web Site to require SSL connections.

1. Click **Start**, point to **Administrative Tools**, and then click **Internet Information Services (IIS) Manager**.

2. Click the **plus sign (+)** next to SERVERXX to expand it, where XX is your assigned student number.

3. Click the **plus sign (+)** next to Web Sites to expand it.

4. Right-click **Default Web Site** and click **Properties**. Notice that, by default, the TCP port for the site is set to 80, and no port number is assigned for SSL, as shown in Figure 4-15.

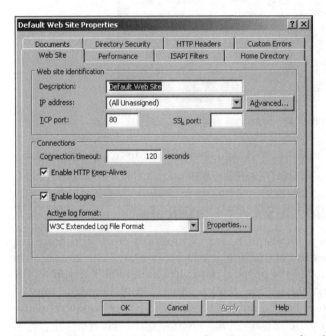

Figure 4-15   Reviewing port number assignments for the Default Web Site

5. Click the **Directory Security** tab.

6. In the Secure communications section, click the **Server Certificate** button.

7. At the Welcome to the Web Server Certificate Wizard screen, click **Next**.

8. At the Server Certificate screen, ensure that **Create a new certificate** is selected, as shown in Figure 4-16. Click **Next**.

9. At the Delayed or Immediate Request screen, click **Send the request immediately to an online certification authority**, and click **Next**.

10. At the Name and Security Settings screen, click **Next**.

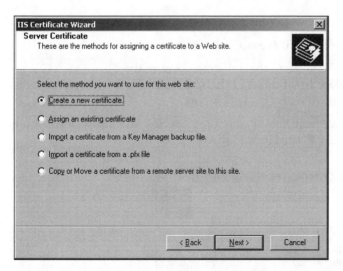

Figure 4-16   Using the Web Server Certificate Wizard to create a new certificate

11. At the Organization Information screen, type **Blather Consulting** in the Organization text box, and **North America** in the Organizational unit text box, as shown in Figure 4-17. Click **Next**.

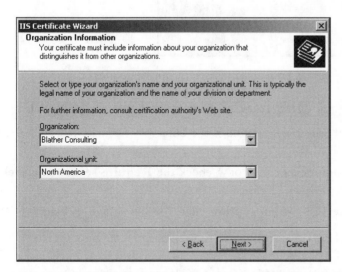

Figure 4-17   Supplying organization information during the certificate request process

12. At the Your Site's Common Name screen, click **Next**.

13. At the Geographical Information screen, ensure that **US (United States)** is selected in the Country/Region drop-down menu.

14. In the State/Province text box, type **New York**.

15. In the City/locality text box, type **New York**. Click **Next**.

16. At the SSL Port screen, click **Next**.

17. At the Choose a Certificate Authority screen, ensure that **serverXX.secureXX.local\BLATHERCONSULTING** is selected (where XX is your assigned student number), and click **Next**.

18. At the Certificate Request Submission screen, review the information you entered, as shown in Figure 4-18. Click **Next**.

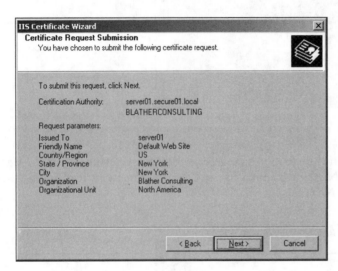

Figure 4-18   Reviewing details prior to sending a certificate request

19. At the Completing the Web Server Certificate Wizard screen, click **Finish**.

20. In the Secure communications section of the Directory Security tab, click the **Edit** button.

21. In the Secure Communications window, check the **Require secure channel (SSL)** check box.

22. Check the **Require 128–bit encryption** check box, as shown in Figure 4-19. Click **OK**.

23. Click the **Web Site** tab.

24. In the SSL port text box, type **443**. Click **OK**. If the Inheritance Overrides window appears, click **Cancel**.

25. Close the **Internet Information Services (IIS) Manager** window.

Figure 4-19   Configuring the Default Web Site to require 128-bit encryption

Testing a Secure Connection

After installing your Web server certificate, requiring SSL communications, and specifying the SSL port, it's important to be certain that secure connections to Outlook Web Access are functioning correctly.

When SSL is enabled and required for user connections, the Secure HTTP protocol identifier, HTTPS://, must precede the address specified to connect to Outlook Web Access. In Activity 4-8, you first attempt to connect to Outlook Web Access using an unsecured connection, and then connect over an SSL connection.

ACTIVITY

Activity 4-8: Testing an SSL-Secured Outlook Web Access Connection

Time Required: 15 minutes

Objective: Test an SSL connection.

Description: After a Web server certificate is installed and SSL settings are configured, it's important to test that the server will allow SSL-based connections only. In this activity, you attempt to connect to Outlook Web Access using both unsecured and SSL-secured connections.

1. Click **Start**, point to **All Programs**, and then click **Internet Explorer**.

2. In the Address Bar, type **http://serverXX.secureXX.local/exchange** (where XX is your assigned student number), and click the **Go** button. The screen shown in Figure 4-20 appears. You cannot connect to the server because you selected the option to require a secure connection in Activity 4-7.

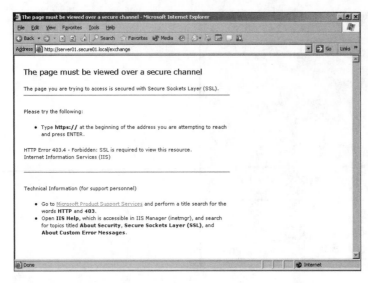

Figure 4-20 Message encountered when attempting to connect to the server without SSL

3. In the Address Bar, type **https://serverXX.secureXX.local/exchange** (where XX is your assigned student number), and click the **Go** button. At the Security Alert box, click **OK**.

4. When the Security Alert window shown in Figure 4-21 appears, click **Yes**.

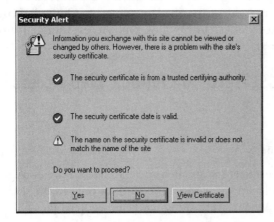

Figure 4-21 Reviewing the alert associated with the Web server's certificate

5. When the Connect to serverXX.secureXX.local window appears, type **Password!** in the Password text box, and click **OK**.

6. The Microsoft Outlook Web Access screen appears over the secure connection, as shown in Figure 4-22. Close the **Internet Explorer** window.

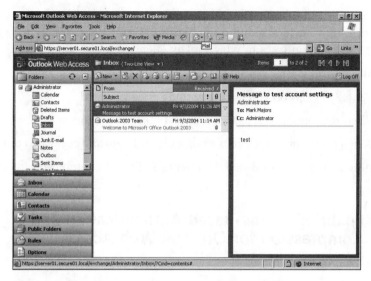

Figure 4-22   Connected to Outlook Web Access over an SSL connection

Forms-Based Authentication and Outlook Web Access Compression

The version of Outlook Web Access included with Exchange Server 2003 supports a new feature known as forms-based authentication. When enabled, users are prompted with a logon screen in which they need to supply their domain, user name, and password credentials. The information supplied by the user is stored in a cookie that is automatically deleted when the user closes her Web browser. In addition, this cookie is deleted automatically after a certain period of inactivity. When the Public or shared computer option is selected, the cookie is deleted automatically after 15 minutes of inactivity. When the Private computer option is selected, the cookie remains valid for inactivity periods of up to 24 hours by default.

NOTE The default inactivity timeout values associated with the public and private computer options can be changed by editing the registry. To change these settings, create PublicClientTimeout and TrustedClientTimeout DWORD values in HKEY_LOCAL_MACHINE\SYSTEM\CurrentControlSet\Services\ MSExchangeWEB\OWA and specify timeout values in minutes. Values between 1 and 432,000 are supported.

To enable forms-based authentication, the server running Outlook Web Access must be configured to require SSL client connections. A reminder message is presented when you enable forms-based authentication in Exchange System Manager.

After forms-based authentication is enabled, you can also enable Outlook Web Access data compression. Data compression helps to reduce the amount of data transferred from the

Outlook Web Access server to user Web browsers, thus significantly improving access speeds. However, enabling compression can result in significant resource utilization on the Outlook Web Access server, especially in cases in which many clients connect simultaneously.

Three levels of compression are supported for Outlook Web Access:

- *None*—When this option is selected, nothing is compressed.
- *Low*—When this option is selected, only static pages are compressed.
- *High*—When this option is selected, both static and dynamic pages are compressed.

In Activity 4-9, you enable both forms-based authentication and compression for Outlook Web Access.

ACTIVITY

Activity 4-9: Enabling Forms-Based Authentication and Compression for Outlook Web Access

Time Required: 15 minutes

Objective: Enable forms-based authentication and compression for Outlook Web Access.

Description: After SSL is enabled for the Default Web Site, it is possible to enable both forms-based authentication and compressions settings for Outlook Web Access. In this activity, you enable and test both features.

1. Click **Start**, point to **All Programs**, point to **Microsoft Exchange**, and then click **System Manager**.

2. Click the **plus signs (+)** next to Administrative Groups, First Administrative Group, and Servers to expand them.

3. Click the **plus sign (+)** next to SERVERXX, where XX is your assigned student number.

4. Click the **plus sign (+)** next to Protocols to expand it.

5. Click the **HTTP** folder to view its contents. The Exchange Virtual Server should be visible, as shown in Figure 4-23.

6. Right-click **Exchange Virtual Server** and click **Properties**.

7. Click the **Settings** tab.

8. Check the **Enable Forms Based Authentication** check box, as shown in Figure 4-24.

9. In the Compression drop-down list, click **High**. Click **OK**.

10. When the Exchange System Manager dialog box appears, read the message shown in Figure 4-25, and click **OK**.

11. Close the **Exchange System Manager** window.

12. Click **Start**, point to **All Programs**, and then click **Internet Explorer**.

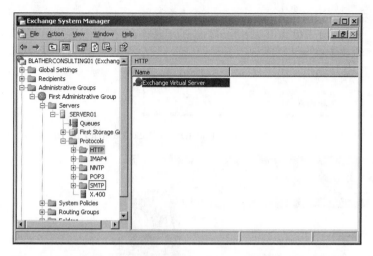

Figure 4-23   The Exchange Virtual Server used to configure HTTP settings

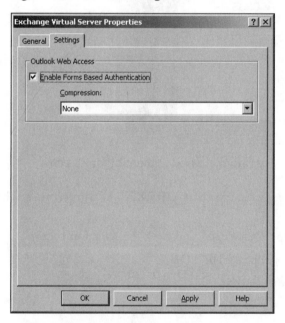

Figure 4-24   Enabling forms-based authentication

13. In the Address Bar, type **https://serverXX.secureXX.local/exchange** (where XX is your assigned student number), and click **Go**. At the Security alert dialog box, click **OK**.

14. When the Security Alert dialog box appears, click **Yes**.

15. The Outlook Web Access forms-based authentication screen now appears, as shown in Figure 4-26.

Figure 4-25   Reviewing the requirements to use forms-based authentication

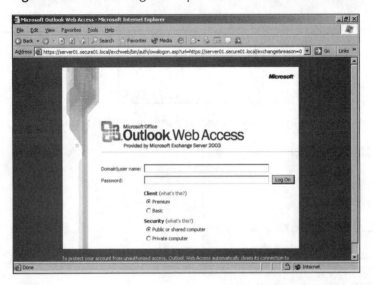

Figure 4-26   The Outlook Web Access forms-based authentication screen

16. In the Domain\user name text box, type **SECUREXX\Administrator**, where XX is your assigned student number.

17. In the Password text box, type **Password!**, and click the **Log On** button.

18. When the Privacy dialog box appears, click **OK**.

19. Close the **Internet Explorer** window.

RPC over HTTP

In the past, companies that wanted to allow remote Outlook users to gain access to Exchange servers located on the company's private network have relied on VPN connections for security. In this scenario, the remote user would be connected using dial-up or broadband Internet, and then initiate a VPN tunnel to provide a secure connection between the PC and the corporate network.

Although this setup is still absolutely valid, remote users running Outlook 2003 can now securely connect to an Exchange Server 2003 system using a secure RPC over HTTP connection. In this configuration, the Outlook 2003 clients sends remote procedure call (RPC) requests within HTTP or HTTPS (HTTP, Secure) requests, which are ultimately processed by an RPC over HTTP Proxy system on the corporate network. SSL is used to secure the HTTP connection such that data passed between the client and server remains encrypted and confidential.

The primary reason why RPC over HTTP connections are now supported with Outlook 2003 is to ensure that any user with access to the HTTP or HTTPS protocols can connect to an Exchange Server 2003 system over the Internet. In many cases, a firewall on the client side of the connection might restrict access to all protocols with the exception of HTTP and HTTPS (thus making VPN connections impossible). In these cases, users behind the restrictive firewall can still access their Exchange mailbox without issue.

Front-End and Back-End Exchange Servers

In environments that include multiple Exchange servers, companies might opt to deploy what is known as a front-end/back-end Exchange architecture. In this configuration, an Exchange Server 2003 system is usually deployed at the perimeter of the corporate network, or in a demilitarized zone (DMZ) network created between the Internet and the private corporate network. Known as a **front-end server**, this system acts as the intermediary between client connections from the Internet and the back-end Exchange servers located on the private network.

In effect, when Internet clients make requests to access their mailbox using techniques like RPC over HTTP, Outlook Web Access, POP3, or IMAP4, these requests are sent to the front-end Exchange server. The front-end Exchange server is then responsible for connecting to and communicating with the **back-end server** that holds the user's mailbox. Ultimately, this setup ensures that Internet-based clients don't have direct access to Exchange servers on the private network, which helps to provide additional security.

Any Exchange Server 2003 system can be designated as a front-end server from the General tab in the properties of the server's object in Exchange System Manager. To configure an Exchange server as a front-end server, simply check the This is a front-end server check box, as shown in Figure 4-27.

For an Exchange Server 2003 system to be designated as a front-end server to process RPC over HTTP requests, the following requirements must be met:

- The Windows Server 2003 system on which Exchange Server 2003 is installed must have the RPC over HTTP Proxy networking component installed.
- The Exchange server cannot host any user mailboxes.
- The Exchange server cannot host any public folders.
- The Exchange server must be part of the same Exchange organization as the back-end servers to which it will connect.
- SSL must be enabled for the RPC virtual directory in IIS.

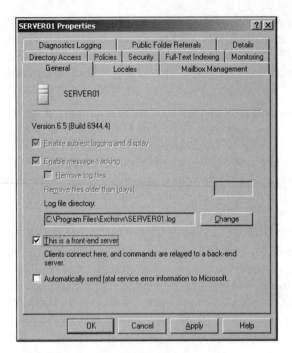

Figure 4-27   Configuring Exchange Server 2003 as a front-end server

In addition, systems running Outlook 2003 on Windows XP must have Windows XP Service Pack 1 or higher installed.

When RPC over HTTP Proxy connections are enabled on a network with Exchange Server deployed in a front-end/back-end configuration, the RPC over HTTP Proxy connections are established between the Outlook 2003 client and the front-end server running Exchange Server 2003. To further secure the environment, many companies opt to use techniques such as Internet Protocol Security (IPSec) to encrypt all traffic passed between the front-end and back-end servers.

NOTE   Exchange Server 2003 can be deployed in a number of different front-end/back-end configurations to meet the security needs of different organizations. The Planning an Exchange Server 2003 Messaging System document at *http://go.microsoft.com/fwlink/?linkid=21766* provides comprehensive details of different configurations along with information about required firewall settings.

Implementing RPC over HTTP Connectivity

To implement RPC over HTTP connections between an Outlook 2003 client and Exchange Server 2003 server, both the client and server must be properly configured. In Activity 4-10, you install the RPC over HTTP Proxy protocol, and then configure both Outlook 2003 and Exchange Server 2003 to support RPC over HTTP connections.

ACTIVITY

Activity 4-10: Implementing RPC over HTTP Connections for Outlook 2003

4

Time Required: 15 minutes

Objective: Implement RPC over HTTP connections for Outlook 2003.

Description: Outlook 2003 can be configured to connect to an Exchange Server 2003 system using the RPC over HTTP protocol. In this activity, you configure both your Exchange server and Outlook 2003 to support RPC over HTTP connections.

1. Click **Start**, click **Control Panel**, and then click **Add or Remove Programs**.

2. In the Add or Remove Programs window, click **Add/Remove Windows Components**.

3. At the Windows Components screen, click **Networking Services**, and click the **Details** button.

4. In the Networking Services window, check the check box next to **RPC over HTTP Proxy**, as shown in Figure 4-28. Click **OK**.

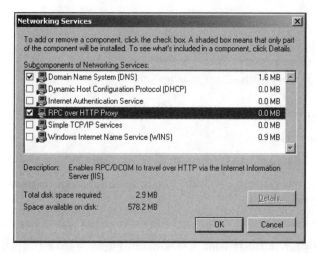

Figure 4-28   Installing the RPC over HTTP Proxy networking service

5. Click **Next** at the Windows Components Wizard screen. When prompted, insert your Windows Server 2003 CD, and click **OK**.

6. At the Completing the Windows Components Wizard screen, click **Finish**.

7. Close the Add or Remove Programs window.

8. Click **Start**, point to **Administrative Tools**, and then click **Internet Information Services (IIS) Manager**.

9. Click the **plus sign (+)** next to SERVERXX to expand it, where XX is your assigned student number.

10. Click the **plus sign (+)** next to Web Sites to expand it.

11. Click **Default Web Site** to view its contents, as shown in Figure 4-29.

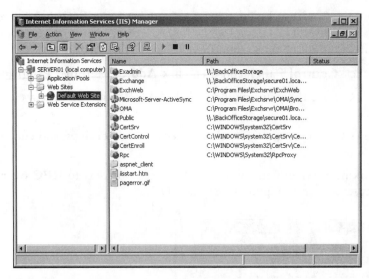

Figure 4-29 Viewing the contents of the Default Web Site

12. Right-click the **RPC** virtual directory, and click **Properties**.

13. Click the **Directory Security** tab.

14. In the Authentication and access control section, click the **Edit** button.

15. In the Authentication access section, check the **Basic authentication (password is sent in clear text)** check box.

16. When the IIS Manager dialog box appears, read the message, and click **Yes**.

17. Close the **Authentication Methods** window shown in Figure 4-30 by clicking **OK**.

18. Click **OK** to close the **RPC Properties** window.

19. Close the Internet Information Services (IIS) Manager window.

20. Click **Start**, click **Control Panel**, and then click **Mail**. The Mail Setup – Outlook window appears, as shown in Figure 4-31.

21. Click the **Show Profiles** button.

22. On the Mail window, click the **Add** button.

23. In the New Profile window, type **RPC over HTTP mail**, and click **OK**.

24. When the E-mail Accounts window opens, click **Next**.

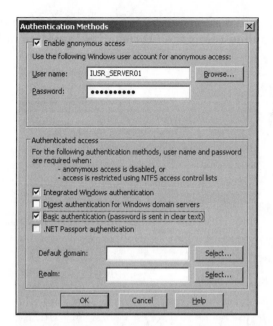

4

Figure 4-30   Configuring authentication methods for the Default Web Site

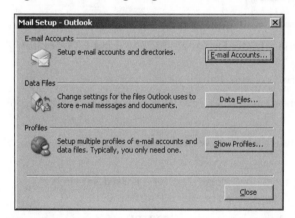

Figure 4-31   The Mail Setup – Outlook window

25. At the Server Type screen, click **Microsoft Exchange Server**, and click **Next**.

26. At the Exchange Server Settings screen, type **serverXX.secureXX.local** in the Microsoft Exchange Server text box, where XX is your assigned student number.

27. In the User Name text box, type **Administrator**.

28. Click the **More Settings** button.

29. Click the **Connection** tab. In the Exchange over the Internet section, check the **Connect to my Exchange mailbox using HTTP** check box, as shown in Figure 4-32.

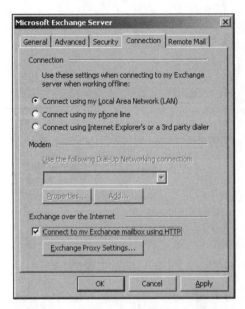

Figure 4-32   Selecting the Connect to my Exchange mailbox using HTTP option

30. Click the **Exchange Proxy Settings** button.

31. In the https:// text box, type **serverXX.secureXX.local**, where XX is your assigned student number.

32. Check the **Mutually authenticate the session when connecting with SSL** check box.

33. In the Principal name for proxy server text box, type **msstd:serverXX.secureXX.local**, where XX is your assigned student number.

34. Check the **On fast networks, connect using HTTP first, and then connect using TCP/IP** check box.

35. In the Proxy authentication settings section, select **Basic Authentication** from the drop-down list, as shown in Figure 4-33.

36. Click **OK** twice, and click **Next**.

37. At the Congratulations! screen, click **Finish**.

38. At the Mail screen, select **RPC over HTTP mail** in the Always use this profile drop-down list, and click **OK**.

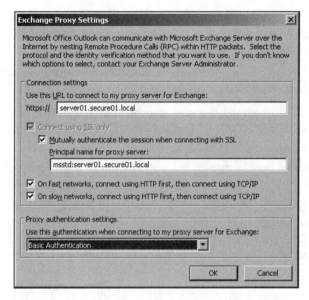

Figure 4-33   Configuring Proxy authentication settings

39. Click **Start**, point to **All Programs**, point to **Microsoft Office**, and then click **Microsoft Office Outlook 2003**.

40. When the Connect to serverXX.secureXX.local window appears, enter **SECUREXX\Administrator** in the User name box, and **Password!** in the Password text box. In all cases, XX represents your assigned student number. Click **OK**. Microsoft Outlook is now connected to the Exchange server via an RPC over HTTP connection. If you are prompted about importing a new account, click No.

41. Click **Start**, click **Control Panel**, and then click **Mail**.

42. Click the **Show Profiles** button.

43. At the Mail screen, select **Outlook** in the Always use this profile drop-down list, and click **OK**. Close the **Control Panel** window. Close **Microsoft Outlook**.

CHAPTER SUMMARY

❏ Exchange Server 2003 supports a variety of client connectivity options, including those from Microsoft Outlook, Web browsers using Outlook Web Access, mobile Web browsers using Outlook Mobile Access, and traditional e-mail clients such as Outlook Express.

❏ Outlook 2003 is the most fully featured client software package for connecting to Exchange Server 2003 systems.

❑ Outlook Web Access allows users to connect to their Exchange mailbox and related collaboration features using a Web browser such as Internet Explorer. Outlook Web Access comes in two different editions, basic and premium.

❑ To secure Outlook Web Access communications, a Web server certificate should be installed and the server should require SSL connections.

❑ The server certificates required to implement SSL can be acquired from a trusted CA, such as Thawte or VeriSign, or created using Windows 2000 Server or Windows Server 2003 Certificate Services.

❑ Outlook Web Access supports both forms-based authentication and compression on systems configured for SSL communication.

❑ To facilitate connections between Outlook 2003 clients and Exchange Server 2003 systems over TCP/IP networks, such as the Internet, RPC over HTTP connections can be used. Using RPC over HTTP connections in conjunction with SSL encryption helps to eliminate the need for clients to first connect to the network hosting Exchange Server using a VPN connection.

❑ In environments with multiple Exchange servers, users typically create a secure connection with a front-end Exchange server located on a DMZ network. The front-end Exchange server then acts as a Proxy for all communications between the client and the back-end server on which the user's mailbox resides.

KEY TERMS

back-end server — An Exchange server in a multiserver environment that stores user mailboxes and public folders.

Cached Exchange Mode — A new feature available when using Exchange Server 2003 with Outlook 2003 that caches a copy of the user mailbox on the client system, allowing many tasks to be carried out on the cached version rather than requiring access to the "live" Exchange server.

certificate authority (CA) — A trusted organization responsible for issuing digital certificates.

Certificate Services — The Windows 2000 Server or Windows Server 2003 service that allows an organization to issue its own certificates.

forms-based authentication — An Outlook Web Access feature that allows users to log on with their domain name, user name, and password, or their full user principal name (UPN).

front-end server — An Exchange Server 2003 system that does not store user mailboxes or public folders and is configured to act as an intermediary for connections to back-end servers.

Internet Message Access Protocol 4 (IMAP4) — A protocol used to access the contents of a user mailbox where messages are stored on the server.

Kerberos — The primary authentication protocol used in Active Directory environments.

Outlook 2003 — The primary messaging and collaboration software package used to interact with an Exchange server.

Outlook Express — The free Internet e-mail client provided with Microsoft operating systems.

Outlook Web Access — The Exchange Server 2003 feature that allows users to access an Outlook-like environment from a Web browser.

Post Office Protocol 3 (POP3) — A protocol used to access the contents of a user mailbox where messages are typically downloaded to the client computer and removed from the server.

RPC over HTTP — A method that allows an Outlook client to connect to an Exchange server over the Internet by encapsulating RPC requests within HTTP packets.

Secure MIME — A technique used to secure e-mail messages through the use of encryption and digital signatures.

Secure Sockets Layer (SSL) — A protocol developed to securely transmit data over the Internet in an encrypted format.

REVIEW QUESTIONS

1. Which of the following represent versions of Outlook Web Access supported with Exchange Server 2003? (Choose all that apply.)

   a. basic

   b. advanced

   c. premium

   d. deluxe

2. Which of the following protocols can be used to connect to an Exchange Server 2003 system? (Choose all that apply.)

   a. POP3

   b. IMAP4

   c. RPC over HTTP

   d. HTTP

3. Which of the following client software packages support RPC over HTTP connections? (Choose all that apply.)

   a. Outlook 2002

   b. Outlook Express

   c. Outlook 2003

   d. Outlook 97

4. Which of the following protocols supported by Outlook 2003 allows for cross-forest authentication?

   a. NTLM

   b. Kerberos

   c. IPSec

   d. HTTP

5. Outlook 2002 cannot connect to an Exchange Server 2003 system. True or False?

6. Which of the following elements must be configured in order to use forms-based authentication with Outlook Web Access?

   a. IPSec

   b. SSL

   c. SSH

   d. PPTP

7. Which of the following elements should not be present on an Exchange Server 2003 system configured as a front-end server?

   a. user mailboxes

   b. public folders

   c. Exchange System Manager

   d. Active Directory Users and Computers

8. Which port is used for secure HTTP connections by default?

   a. TCP 80

   b. TCP 443

   c. TCP 433

   d. TCP 411

9. Which feature supported by Outlook 2003 allows a copy of a user's Exchange mailbox to be stored on her local system?

   a. Cached Exchange Mode

   b. Cache Mode

   c. Synchronization Mode

   d. mixed mode

10. Which of the following statements about the new .pst file format used by Outlook 2003 are true? (Choose all that apply.)

   a. The new .pst format supports Unicode.

   b. The new .pst format is compatible with previous versions.

   c. The new .pst format is not compatible with previous versions.

   d. The new .pst format provides greater storage capacity than previous versions.

11. If a person using Outlook Web Access chooses the Public computer option when logging on via forms-based authentication, after what period of inactivity is his cookie deleted?

    a. 5 minutes

    b. 10 minutes

    c. 30 minutes

    d. 15 minutes

12. If a person using Outlook Web Access chooses the Private computer option when logging on via forms-based authentication, after what period of inactivity is her cookie deleted?

    a. 6 hours

    b. 12 hours

    c. 24 hours

    d. never

13. Which of the following services must be installed for an organization to issue its own Web server certificate?

    a. Web Services

    b. Certificate Services

    c. WINS

    d. RPC over HTTP

14. Which of the following are compression choices available when configuring Outlook Web Access via the properties of the (HTTP) Exchange Virtual Server? (Choose all that apply.)

    a. Low

    b. High

    c. None

    d. Default

15. Which IIS-based tool can be used to generate a Web server certificate request?

    a. Web Server Certificate Wizard

    b. Certificate Services Wizard

    c. Certificate Wizard

    d. none of the above

16. Which of the following protocol identifiers precedes the address of a Web site where SSL-based connections are required?

    a. HTTP://

    b. SSL://

    c. HTTPS://

    d. GOPHER://

17. Outlook Express supports connections to both POP3 and IMAP4 servers. True or False?

18. The Default POP3 Virtual Server is enabled on an Exchange Server 2003 system by default. True or False?

19. Mailbox-enabled recipients have access to Outlook Web Access by default. True or False?

20. The Exchange Server 2003 version of Outlook Web Access does not provide the ability to sign or encrypt messages digitally using Secure MIME. True or False?

CASE PROJECTS

CASE PROJECTS

Case Project 4-1: Choosing a Client Solution

Maple Sugar Systems is looking for an effective way to grant its salespeople access to the newly implemented Exchange Server 2003 system. These users will connect to the system using their own PC, and the administrators cannot be certain what software they have installed. Assuming that all users have at least dial-up Internet access, what solution will work best for the company's salespeople? What potential limitations apply?

CASE PROJECTS

Case Project 4-2: Evaluating Client Access Methods

Many of the users at Magnetewan Industries are deployed to client locations for periods ranging from a week to many months. All of these users are provided with laptop computers that include the Office 2003 suite. What options should the administrators at Magnetewan consider implementing to allow deployed staff to access the new Exchange Server 2003 system? What are the pros and cons of each method?

CASE PROJECTS

Case Project 4-3: Granting Selective Access to POP3

Super Siding Corporation creates mailbox-enabled user accounts for all of its staff and contractors. Recently, a number of contractors have asked to be granted POP3 access to the Exchange server to allow them to download their mail at home, from their preferred e-mail client. The administrator at Super Siding Corporation is willing to allow this, but would prefer that regular staff not have any access to the server via POP3. What does the administrator need to do to allow POP3 access for the contractors only?

CHAPTER 5

MANAGING ADDRESSES

After reading this chapter, you will be able to:

♦ Understand and create the different types of address lists that are used within Exchange Server 2003

♦ Understand how recipient policies work

♦ Describe how the Recipient Update Service works

Sending and receiving information is the foundation of Exchange Server 2003. Exchange Server 2003 facilitates this by providing a multitude of messaging components that allow receivers or recipients to receive information transferred by a messaging system. A recipient represents an object or resource within Active Directory. A recipient might be a mailbox where a user receives mail, a public folder where information is shared among many users, or even a newsgroup on the Internet.

No matter where a resource resides, however, a recipient object for that resource is always created within Active Directory. One of your main tasks of administering your Exchange Server 2003 infrastructure is to create and maintain these recipient objects.

Microsoft Outlook users generally search for other recipients within their company in the Global Address List (GAL), which is an aggregation or list of all messaging recipients. A feature of Exchange Server 2003 is its ability to create custom address lists, which allow you to group recipients in the GAL according to attributes. Essentially, an address list allows you to add a hierarchical structure to an otherwise flat view provided by the GAL.

Another type of address list that is provided with Exchange Server 2003 is called the offline address list. An offline address list provides a user with a downloadable copy of an address list, or lists. This enables users to compose messages without having to be connected to the server. It provides the user with the ability to search the content of the offline address list and address the messages offline. Next time the user is online, these messages are automatically sent to the recipient. The Default Global Address List is usually selected as the source for generating an offline address list, as it is the most comprehensive of all address lists.

The Recipient Update Service (RUS) is a feature of Exchange Server 2003 that builds and maintains address lists. The RUS runs as a thread of the System Attendant service and polls Active Directory for updated recipient information on a predetermined schedule, which is once a minute by default. If there are new recipients, new address lists, or changes to existing address lists, the address lists are updated by the RUS.

This chapter focuses on address lists, the RUS, and recipient policies. It provides detail on the inner workings of the RUS, how it maintains address lists and how recipient policies are configured.

Address Lists

When using Outlook to send messages, you need a way to address the message to the other user. Knowing the unique address of a destination recipient is not something that users remember for every individual that might have a mailbox. In large organizations, there can typically be thousands of users. To address this, Outlook makes use of a GAL, which is an aggregation of all messaging recipients within the Exchange Server 2003 organization. Indeed, along with custom connectors, it is possible to have **Global Address Lists (GALs)** that contain not only the aggregation of all messaging recipients within the Exchange Server 2003 organization, but also the aggregation of all users within a foreign e-mail system connected by a dedicated connector, such as the Lotus Notes Connector or the GroupWise Connector. In this chapter, the focus is on Exchange Server 2003, however, and foreign connectors are not considered further.

The GAL is, in fact, composed of several address lists. Each address list contains a subset of all users in the Exchange organization and can be used to address e-mail messages, choose meeting attendees, and look up locations and phone numbers of other users within the organization. Address lists can be broken down into three different types:

- *Default address lists* — These consist of address lists that are created by default when Exchange Server 2003 is installed.

- *Custom address lists* — These consist of address lists that you create based on fields of recipient objects.

- *Offline address lists* — These consist of local copies of address lists that users download to their computers.

The following sections look at each of these in turn.

Default Address Lists

Default address lists are address lists that have been installed by default during an Exchange Server 2003 installation. These address lists help organize the presentation of Exchange recipient information to end users. They can be used as is, or modified to suit the needs of the organization. Table 5-1 lists the default address lists that are installed as part of an Exchange Server 2003 installation along with a description of these address lists, and the build rules that are used to construct these address lists.

Table 5-1   Default address lists

Address Lists	Description	Build Rule
All Contacts	This list consists of all mail-enabled contacts in the organization. Mail-enabled contacts appear in address lists but do not have an Exchange mailbox in the associated Exchange organization.	(&(mailnickname=*) (l(&(objectCategory=person) (objectClass=contact))))
All Groups	This list consists of all mail-enabled groups in the organization. Mail-enabled groups appear in address lists and can be either distribution groups or security groups.	(&(mailnickname=*) (l(objectCategory=group)))
All Users	This list consists of all mailbox-enabled and mail-enabled users in the organization. Mailbox-enabled users have Exchange mailboxes. Mail-enabled users appear in address lists but do not have Exchange mailboxes.	(&(mailnickname=*) (l(&(objectCategory=person) (objectClass=user)(!(homeMDB=*)) (!(msExchHomeServerName=*))) (&(objectCategory=person) (objectClass=user)(l(homeMDB=*) (msExchHomeServerName=*)))))
Public Folders	This list consists of all mail-enabled public folders in the organization that are not hidden from address lists. Mail-enabled public folders appear in address lists and can receive messages.	(&(mailnickname=*) (l(objectCategory=publicFolder)))
Default Global Address List	This list consists of all recipients in the organization: mailbox-enabled users, mail-enabled users, groups, contacts, and public folders.	(& (mailnickname=*) (l (&(objectCategory=person) (objectClass=user)(!(homeMDB=*)) (!(msExchHomeServerName=*))) (&(objectCategory=person) (objectClass=user)(l(homeMDB=*) (msExchHomeServerName=*))) (&(objectCategory=person) (objectClass=contact))(objectCategory=group) (objectCategory=publicFolder) (objectCategory=msExchDynamicDistributionList)))

5

NOTE Exchange Server 2003 has reduced the number of default address lists from Exchange 2000 Server. In Exchange 2000 Server, an additional default address list called "All Conference resources" was available. This address list was used primarily by the Exchange Conferencing server, which was included with Exchange 2000 Server. This service has been removed from Exchange Server 2003, and, as such, the associated default address list that was associated with this service has also been removed.

Custom Address Lists

Default address lists do a good job of aggregating recipients for the end user, but you might have requirements to build customized address lists to meet your users' needs. These **custom address lists** can be created according to location, department, teams, or any other Active Directory attribute that is available for query.

To create an address list, you need to define to whom the policy will be applied. Exchange Server 2003 makes use of a dialog box–based Find command that presents you with a set of menus that allows you to select and filter the desired set of recipients that will make up an address list. This interface is based on an LDAP (Lightweight Directory Access Protocol) query, which allows you to filter by any Active Directory attribute. You can restrict membership within the address list to specific recipient types, limit the address list to a specific server or mailbox store, or you can create a custom LDAP filter that will give you more granular control over what is included in your address list.

When restricting the membership within an address list, you have the following options available:

- *Users with an Exchange Mailbox*—Used to add all mailbox-enabled users to the custom address list
- *Users with external e-mail addresses*—Used for all mail-enabled users
- *Groups*—Used to add all mail-enabled groups to the custom address list
- *Contacts*—Used to add all mail-enabled contacts to the custom address list
- *Public folders*—Used to add all mail-enabled public folders that are not hidden from address lists to the custom address list

When limiting the address list membership based on storage location, you have the following options available:

- *Mailboxes on any server*—Used to add recipients on all servers to the custom address list
- *Mailboxes on this server*—Used to add recipients who have mailboxes on the specified server to the custom address list
- *Mailboxes in this mailbox store*—Used to add recipients who have mailboxes on the specified store to the custom address list

Finally, if you want to have more granular control, you can create a custom query filter rule that specifies which recipients should be allowed membership to your custom address list. Creating a filter rule helps you fine-tune membership to a list. Multiple filter rules for an address list can be created to define complex membership requirements.

You create custom filter rules by defining the Active Directory field, condition, and value on which you want to search. By default, all filter rules use a logical AND to form an LDAP query. This means that all the conditions of the rule must be met for the recipient to be a member of the address list.

The value you specify in the Find Exchange Recipients dialog box is compared with the value in Active Directory for the recipients to identify which recipients are eligible to be added to the address list.

Table 5-2 lists the conditions that are available for building custom filter rules.

Table 5-2 Custom filter rule conditions

Condition	Description
Starts with	The value for the selected field must start with the characters specified in the Value box.
Ends with	The value for the selected field must end with the characters specified in the Value box.
Is (exactly)	The value for the selected field must exactly match the contents of the Value box. However, case sensitivity is not checked.
Is not	The value for the selected field must not match the contents of the Value box.
Present	The selected field must contain a value.
Not present	The selected field must not contain a value.

ACTIVITY

Activity 5-1: Creating a New Address List

Time Required: 10 to 20 minutes

Objective: Create a new address list for an Exchange Server 2003 organization.

Description: In this activity, you create a new address list to identify the users within the city associated with each particular server. To accomplish this activity, you must ensure that the Country attribute for each user has been set appropriately. For this activity, ensure that you have mailbox-enabled users for each of the classroom servers. For ServerXX, create a temporary user called TempUserXX, where XX is the student number assigned. Each user will have its Country field set to a unique country name. TempUser01 would have its Country field set to Canada, whereas TempUser02 should have its Country field set to the United States, TempUser03 should have its Country field set to Brazil, and so on.

1. If necessary, log on to your server as **Administrator**.

2. From the Windows desktop, click **Start**, point to **All Programs**, point to **Microsoft Exchange**, and then click **System Manager**.

3. Click the **plus sign (+)** next to the Recipients container, and right-click the **All Address Lists** container. On the shortcut menu, point to **New**, and then click **Address List**. The Create Exchange Address List dialog box opens, as shown in Figure 5-1.

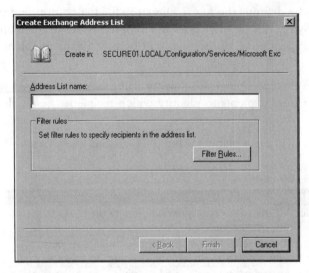

Figure 5-1   Create Exchange Address List dialog box

4. In the Address List name text box, type **Country Recipients List**, where Country is the country assigned to your server.

5. Click the **Filter Rules** button. The Find Exchange Recipients dialog box opens, as shown in Figure 5-2. This dialog box is used to specify the criteria that will be used to include recipients within the address list.

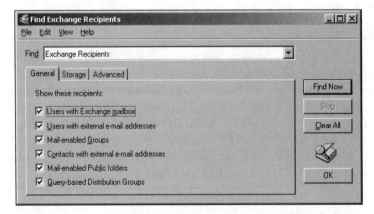

Figure 5-2   Find Exchange Recipients dialog box

6. On the General tab, uncheck all check boxes with the exception of the **Users with Exchange mailbox** option.

7. To specify the criteria to use to select your users, click the **Advanced** tab.

8. Click the **Field** button, point to **User**, and then click **Country**.

9. In the Value field, type the name of the country that is associated with the temporary user located on your server. After you have done this, click the **Add** button to add it to the Condition List.

10. Click **OK** when finished to return to the Create Exchange Address List dialog box.

11. Click **Finish** to return to Exchange System Manager.

12. Close **Exchange System Manager**.

After you have created a custom address list, you can perform various administrative tasks with it. You have the ability to rename address lists, delete address lists, and edit existing address lists. With the exception of editing default address lists, you have the ability to perform rename and delete tasks on default address lists. However, it is recommended that you avoid doing so and confine these administrative tasks to custom address lists.

As in previous versions of Exchange, Exchange Server 2003 gives you the ability to create address lists that group recipients in any way you like, to make it easier for you to find the recipient you are looking for in your organization. You can create a new top-level address list right in the All Address Lists folder, or you can create an address list inside an existing address list.

NOTE

When you create subordinate address lists, you must specify the conditions that you used to create the parent list and add any extra conditions to distinguish the child list from the parent list or specify distinct criteria that will distinguish the recipients within the child list from the recipients in the parent list. Nested lists do not inherit their rules from the parent address list. This differs from address book views in Exchange Server 5.5, in which subordinate address views inherited the criteria from parent address views.

ACTIVITY

Activity 5-2: Nesting Address Lists

Time Required: 10 to 20 minutes

Objective: Nest address lists within an existing address list.

Description: In this activity, you create a nested address list under the country address list that was created in the previous activity. To complete this activity, you need to ensure that the City attribute for each temporary user has been set appropriately. Each temporary user will have its City attribute set to a unique city name associated with the country. TempUser01 would have its City field set to Toronto, whereas TempUser02 would have its City field set to San Francisco, TempUser03 would have its City field set to Sao Paolo, and so on.

1. From the Windows desktop, click **Start**, point to **All Programs**, point to **Microsoft Exchange**, and then click **System Manager**.

2. Click the **plus sign (+)** next to the Recipients container. Click the **plus sign (+)** next to the All Address Lists container. Right-click the **Country Recipients List**, where Country is associated with the country assigned to your server. On the short-cut menu, click **Properties**. The Country Recipients List Properties dialog box opens for this address list, as shown in Figure 5-3.

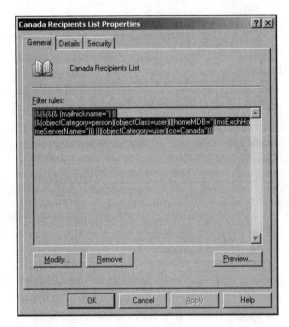

Figure 5-3   Country Recipients List Properties dialog box

3. Click the **Remove** button to remove the current conditions for the filter rule. This essentially creates a shell container that can be used for nesting. Click **OK** to return to the Exchange System menu.

4. Right-click the **Country Recipients List**, where Country is the country assigned to your server. On the shortcut menu, point to **New**, and then click **Address List**. The Create Exchange Address List dialog box opens.

5. In the Address List name text box, type **City Recipients List**, where City is the city assigned to your server.

6. Click **Filter Rules**. The Find Exchange Recipients dialog box opens, which allows you to specify the criteria that will be used to include recipients within the address list.

7. On the General tab, uncheck all the check boxes with the exception of the **Users with Exchange mailbox** option.

8. To specify the criteria to use to select your users, click the **Advanced** tab.

9. Click the **Field** button, point to **User**, and then click **City**.

10. In the Condition field, click **Starts with** from the drop-down list, if necessary.

11. In the Value field, type **City**, where City is the city assigned to your server. Click the **Add** button to add it to the Condition List.

12. Click **OK** when finished to return to the Create Exchange Address List dialog box.

13. Click **Finish** to return to Exchange System Manager.

14. Close **Exchange System Manager**.

In large organizations, multiple companies might be hosted within the same Exchange Server 2003 organization. An example is an umbrella company that owns a number of subsidiary companies. In this particular scenario, you might have a requirement to define address lists that contain recipients from each of the subsidiary companies. Further, you might have a requirement to restrict individual users to see the recipients within their own respective address lists and not have the ability to access other address lists that are not related to the company to which the user belongs.

By default, Exchange Server 2003 grants users the ability to access all address lists. If you want to deny users access to particular address lists, you need to configure directory security on Active Directory objects. Directory security restricts what users can see in the directory, and, if done properly, restricts one company from viewing the information of other companies or divisions.

Although you can prevent users and groups from viewing the contents of an address list by using the Open Address List permission, it does not prevent users from viewing the address list itself. To hide an address list, create an empty address list that acts as a container for other address lists that, in turn, contain recipients. Then deny the user the Open Address List permission on a container address list, so the user will not be able to view its contents. You must also either remove or deny the List Contents permission to hide an address book.

ACTIVITY

Activity 5-3: Assigning Permissions to Address Lists

Time Required: 30 to 40 minutes

Objective: Set the permissions on an address list so that recipients can see their own respective address list and the address lists of other users.

Description: In this activity, you assign permissions so that only a select set of individuals can see it. In this activity, you set permissions on the city recipient lists that were created in the previous activity.

For this activity to succeed, you need to create a global group that will be used to permission the address list. The name of this global security group will be called "city" Address List Access, where city is the name of the city hosted by your server. You also need to ensure there is more than one recipient in the organization, one of which will not be a member of the group and one of which will be a member. For this activity, ensure that two mailbox-enabled test users called Test1 and Test2 are created. Test1 will be a member of the group you are creating, whereas Test2 will not. This allows you to log on to the Exchange 2003 server with each account to determine if the permissions took effect.

You must also ensure that you have configured Exchange System Manager to view the Security Permissions tab for objects.

1. From the Windows desktop, click **Start** and click **Run**. The Run dialog box opens. Type **REGEDT32** in the Open text box, and click **OK**. This starts the Registry Editor, as shown in Figure 5-4.

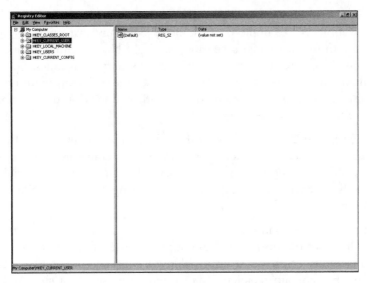

Figure 5-4   Registry Editor interface

2. Click the **plus sign (+)** next to HKEY_CURRENT_USER, click the **plus sign (+)** next to Software, click the **plus sign (+)** next to Microsoft, and, finally, click the **plus sign (+)** next to Exchange.

3. Right-click the **EXAdmin key**, point to **New**, and then click **DWORD Value** from the shortcut menu.

4. Type **ShowSecurityPage** for the name of the new entry.

5. Right-click the **ShowSecurityPage** entry, and click **Modify** from the shortcut menu. The Edit DWORD Value dialog box opens.

6. Within the Value data text box, type the value **1** and click **OK**.

7. Click the **File** menu and click **Exit** to quit the Registry Editor. The changes should take effect immediately and only affects the currently logged-on user.

8. From the Windows desktop, click **Start**, point to **All Programs**, point to **Microsoft Exchange**, and then click **System Manager**.

9. Click the **plus sign (+)** next to the Recipients container, and click the **plus sign (+)** next to the All Address Lists container. Finally, click the **Country Recipients List** container, where Country is the country assigned to your server.

10. In the details pane, right-click the **City Recipients List**, where City is the city assigned to your server. On the shortcut menu, click **Properties**. The City Recipients List Properties dialog box opens for this address list, where City is the city assigned to your server, as shown in Figure 5-5.

5

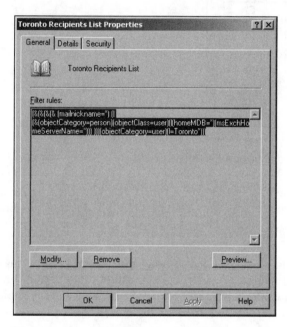

Figure 5-5   City Recipients List dialog box

11. Click the **Security** tab, as shown in Figure 5-6, and then click the **Advanced** button. The Advanced Security Settings for City Recipients List dialog box opens for this address list, where City is the city assigned to your server. Click the **Allow inheritable permissions from the parent to propagate to this object** check box to clear it.

12. You are prompted with a dialog box asking if you want to copy or remove the existing permissions. Click **Copy** to copy the current permissions from the parent object. Do not click Remove. If you do, system permissions will be affected.

13. Click **Add** to grant the group that was created for this activity access to this address list. The Select User, Computer, or Group dialog box opens.

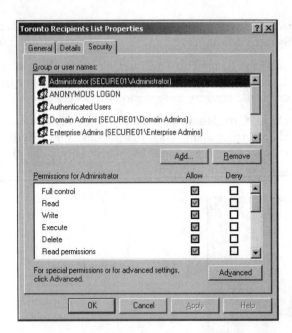

Figure 5-6   City Recipients List dialog box Security tab

14. In the Enter the object name to select text box, type **City Address List Access**, where City is the city assigned to your server. Click **OK**. The Permissions Entry for City Recipients List dialog box opens, where City is the city assigned to your server, as shown in Figure 5-7.

15. Click the **Allow** check box for the Read permission, Open Address List permission, and List object permission. Checking these settings also causes other permissions to be allowed. Click **OK** to return to the Advanced Security Settings for City Recipients List dialog box, where City is the city assigned to your server.

16. In the Permissions entries scroll box, click **Authenticated Users** and click the **Remove** button. This removes access for all other users except those specifically identified within the group defined for this activity. Repeat this for any other reference to Authenticated Users.

17. Click **OK** to return to the City Recipients List Properties dialog box. You are prompted with a Security Warning dialog box indicating that you are setting a deny permissions entry. Click **Yes** to continue.

18. You are then prompted with a Permissions Warning dialog box, indicating that you are about to change permissions. Click **Yes** to continue.

19. Click **OK** to close the City Recipients List Properties dialog box, where City is the city assigned to your server.

20. Close **Exchange System Manager**.

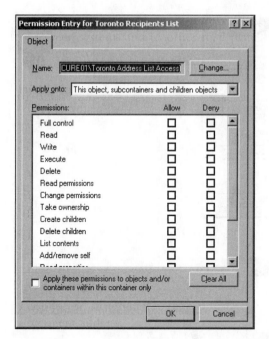

Figure 5-7   Permissions Entry for City Recipients List dialog box

NOTE   The remaining steps in this activity require the use of a client machine, as specified in the beginning of this book. If you do not have an available client machine, simply skip the rest of this activity; the rest of the chapter will not be affected.

21. To test this, you need to create separate profiles for each user that you will be testing in addition to the default profile that is set up. This should be done on a separate client machine. To do this, log on to your client machine. From the desktop, click **Start**, and then click **Control Panel**. The Control Panel opens. Click **Switch to Classic View**, if necessary, and in the details pane, double-click **Mail**. This opens the Mail Setup window, similar to the one shown in Figure 5-8.

22. Click **Show Profiles**. The Mail dialog box opens, similar to the one shown in Figure 5-9.

23. Click **Prompt for a profile to be used**, if necessary.

24. Click **Add**. The New Profile dialog box opens. Type **TEST User X**, where X is one of the test users that exists on your server and with which you are working. Click **OK** to continue. The E-Mail Accounts Wizard starts.

25. Click **Next** on the initial screen.

26. On the Server Type screen, click **Microsoft Exchange Server**, and click **Next** to continue.

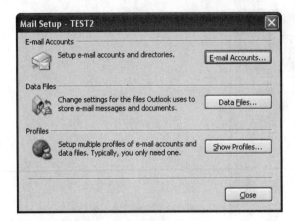

Figure 5-8   Mail Setup window

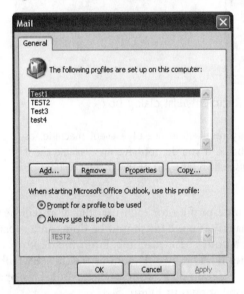

Figure 5-9   Mail dialog box

27. On the Exchange Server Settings screen, type **SERVERXX** in the Microsoft Exchange Server field, where XX is the student number assigned.

28. Uncheck the **Use Cached Exchange Mode** check box.

29. Type **TestX** in the User Name field, where X is the number associated with the user you are setting up. Click **Next** to continue.

30. On the Congratulations! screen, click **Finish**.

31. Repeat Steps 24 through 30 for the second account. When finished, click **OK** to close the Mail dialog box.

5

32. Using Outlook, log on using each profile that was created, one that is a member of the group and one that is not. One profile should be able to see the address list, whereas the other should not be able to see the contents of the address list.

33. Close **Outlook**.

34. Log off your client machine and return to your server.

By default, Microsoft configures the Display Name field in Active Directory in "Firstname Lastname" format. When users browse through the GAL, they see the order of entries sorted in "Firstname Lastname" order. This differs from earlier versions of Exchange, which displayed and ordered based on "Lastname, Firstname". Therefore, when your users open the address list in their mail client, the recipients are sorted by First Name. This is not something that is desirable for most organizations that typically search for users based on "Lastname, Firstname" format.

ACTIVITY

Activity 5-4: Change the Display Order of Names Within the Global Address List

Time Required: 10 to 20 minutes

Objective: Change the display format for names within the GAL from "Firstname Lastname" format to "Lastname, Firstname" format.

Description: In this activity, you configure Active Directory to change the display format of the display name within the GAL from "Firstname Lastname" to "Lastname, Firstname" format. For this activity to succeed, it is necessary to have ADSI Edit installed. ADSI Edit can be installed as part of the Windows 2000/2003 support tools, which are available on the Windows 2000/2003 installation CD.

1. From the Windows desktop, click **Start** and click **Run**. The Run dialog box opens.

2. In the Open text box, type **adsiedit.msc** and click **OK**. This starts ADSI Edit, as shown in Figure 5-10.

3. Click the **plus sign (+)** next to Configuration [serverxx.securexx.local], where XX is the student number assigned to your server, and click the **plus sign (+)** next to CN=Configuration, DC=secureXX, DC=local, where XX represents the student number assigned to your domain. Click the **plus sign (+)** next to CN=DisplaySpecifiers. Click **CN=409**, as shown in Figure 5-11.

4. In the right pane, scroll down until you see "CN=user-Display." Right-click **CN=user-Display** and click **Properties** from the shortcut menu. The CN=user-Display Properties dialog box opens.

5. Within the Attributes field, scroll down and click **createDialog**. Click the **Edit** button. The String Attribute Editor dialog box opens.

6. In the Value field, enter "**%<sn>, %<givenName>**". Ensure you type the string as shown without the quotes. Click **OK** after you have finished. This returns you to the CN=user-Display Properties dialog box.

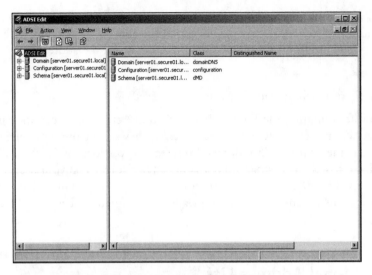

Figure 5-10   ADSI Edit main interface

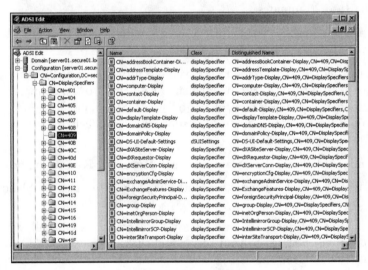

Figure 5-11   Expanding to the 409 display specifier

7. Click **OK** to return to the ADSI Edit window.

8. Close **ADSI Edit**.

9. Create a new mailbox-enabled user within Active Directory Users and Computers using your first and last names. After you have created it, open up Outlook and start the address book. Scroll through to look at the entry to determine if the display name is in "Lastname, Firstname" format. Note that setting the display specifier does not change existing entries, but only changes entries that are newly created. To change

existing entries, you need to make use of a utility, a script, or set them manually. When finished, close **Outlook**.

After you have configured address lists on the back end, you can then configure how address lists are used on the client. Note that, when checking names, you'll usually want the GAL to be listed before the users' own contacts or other types of address lists. This is important because users often put internal mailboxes in their personal address lists. The danger of doing this without first resolving names against the GAL, however, is that although the display name might be identical, the properties of a mailbox might change. When changes occur, the entry in the user's address book is no longer valid and any mail sent bounces back to the sender with a nondelivery receipt. To correct this, the user should either remove that mailbox from his personal address list and add it based on the current entry in the GAL, or change the check names resolution order to use the GAL before any personal lists.

ACTIVITY

Activity 5-5: Configure Clients to Make Use of Address Lists

Time Required: 10 to 20 minutes

Objective: Configure Outlook to make use of a custom address list.

Description: In this activity, you configure Outlook to make use of the custom City Recipients List address list that was created in a previous activity. To complete this activity, complete the following:

1. Start **Microsoft Outlook 2003**. Outlook opens the Administrator account. In order to see the City Recipients List address list, the Administrator account needs to be set to not use cached mode. To do this, click **Tools**, and then click **E-mail Accounts**. Click **Next** on the initial screen. On the E-mail Accounts screen, click the **Change** button. On the Exchange Server Settings screen, uncheck the **Use Cached Exchange Mode** check box, and then click **Next**. Click **OK** in the Microsoft Office Outlook dialog box, and then click **Finish**. Exit **Outlook,** and then reopen it.

2. Within Outlook 2003, click the **Tools** menu, and click **Address Book**. The Address Book opens.

3. Click the **Tools** menu and then click **Options**.

4. Within the Show this address list first drop-down list, click **City Recipients List**, where City represents the city assigned to your server.

5. Within the Keep personal addresses in drop-down box, click **Contacts**, if necessary. This is where all new addresses will be stored. Within the When sending mail, check names using these address lists in the following order field, click the **Global Address List** and use the up arrow to ensure it is at the top of the list, if necessary. Click **OK** when finished to return to the Address Book.

6. Click the **File** menu and click **Close** to return to Outlook.

7. Close **Outlook**.

Offline Address Lists

An **offline address list** is a set of address lists in files that are created and stored on an offline address lists server. Users who work offline can connect to an Exchange 2003 server and download offline address lists remotely to obtain information about other users in the organization.

When you install the first Exchange 2003 server into an organization, the Default Offline Address List is created. The Default Offline Address List is based on the Default Global Address List.

Exchange Server 2003 allows you to create multiple offline address lists, which are composed of any combination of existing address lists. Each mailbox store is associated with an offline address list. When users whose mailboxes are on that store connect to the Exchange server remotely, they can download offline address lists. They can choose to download only updates that were made since the last download. When the offline address list is created, the specified address lists are converted to a single data file and stored in a public folder. When users download the offline address list, this data file is used as the source of the information.

ACTIVITY

Activity 5-6: Configuring an Offline Address List

Time Required: 10 to 20 minutes

Objective: Configure an offline address list on your server.

Description: In this activity, you configure an offline address list that will be composed of the Default Global Address List and the custom address lists that were created as part of previous activities.

1. From the Windows desktop, click **Start**, point to **All Programs**, point to **Microsoft Exchange**, and then click **System Manager**.

2. Click the **plus sign (+)** next to the Recipients container. Right-click the **Offline Address Lists** container. On the shortcut menu, point to **New**, and then click **Offline Address List**. The New Object – Offline Address List dialog box opens.

3. In the Offline address list name field, type **SERVERXX Offline Address List**, where XX is the student number assigned to your server.

4. Click the **Browse** button. The Select Exchange Server dialog box opens. In the Enter the object name to select text box, type **SERVERXX**, where XX is the student number assigned to your server. Click **OK** to return to the New Object – Offline Address List dialog box. Click the **Next** button to continue.

5. Specify the address lists to include in your offline address list. By default, the Default Global Address List is included. Click the **Add** button to add additional address lists. The Select Address Lists dialog box opens.

6. In the Enter object names to select text box, enter the name of the additional address lists you want to configure on your machine. In this activity, specify the **City**

Recipients List that was created in a previous activity, where City is the city assigned to your server. Click **OK** when finished to return to the New Object - Offline Address List dialog box. Click **Next** to continue.

7. You are prompted that the public folder where the offline address list will be located needs to be created and that the offline address list will not be available until that time. Click **Next** to continue.

8. You are prompted where the offline address list will be created. Click **Finish** to complete the task and return to Exchange System Manager.

9. Close **Exchange System Manager**.

After you have configured your offline address list, you can then modify it later by configuring its properties. You have the ability to add or remove additional address lists to the set of offline address lists, as well as configure the server from which the offline address list is managed and propagated. Finally, if you have multiple offline address lists, you can designate which one should be downloaded by default. This address list is known as the default address list.

To use an offline address list, the client must be configured to have a local copy of the server mailbox, or use personal folders. Offline address lists are available only when users are working offline.

ACTIVITY

Activity 5-7: Configuring Clients to Make Use of Offline Address Lists

Time Required: 5 to 10 minutes

Objective: Configure an Outlook client to make use of an offline address list.

Description: In this activity, you configure your Outlook client to make use of offline address lists.

1. Start **Microsoft Outlook 2003**.

2. Within Outlook 2003, click **Tools**, point to **Send/Receive**, and then click **Download Address Book**. The Offline Address Book dialog box opens.

3. If necessary, click **Download Changes since last Send/Receive** to download only items that have changed since the last time you synchronized the address list.

4. Click **No Details**. Clicking No Details causes the address book to be downloaded without address information details. This reduces the download time for the address book. Clicking Full Details causes the entire address book with all address information details to be downloaded. Full details are necessary if the user needs to encrypt messages when using remote mail.

5. Click **OK** when you are finished. If you receive an error message in the Send/Receive dialog box, simply cancel the dialog box.

6. Close **Outlook**.

RECIPIENT POLICIES

You can simplify administration of Exchange objects by using a **recipient policy**. A recipient policy is a collection of configuration settings that can be applied to one or more Exchange objects. Two types of recipient policies are available in Exchange Server 2003: Mailbox Manager recipient policies and e-mail address recipient policies. Both types of policies are applied to recipient objects using LDAP queries.

When you install Exchange Server 2003, a default recipient policy is generated. This default policy automatically creates SMTP and X.400 addresses for all mail-enabled objects in the organization. If other components, such as the cc:Mail connector, are installed, the e-mail address for cc:Mail is also configured but not automatically generated for recipients. By modifying the default policy, you can update the default e-mail addressing throughout the organization. Your updates can either override the existing e-mail addresses or be added as primary addresses (with the current defaults set as secondary addresses).

E-Mail Address Recipient Policies

E-mail address recipient policies control e-mail address generation in the organization, and you also use them to establish new default e-mail addresses on a global basis. You can create multiple e-mail address recipient policies, each with their own e-mail addresses configured. Through filters, you can then apply the policy to specific recipients matching specific filter parameters that you specify. When you create e-mail address recipient policies, you need to specify the information outlined in Table 5-3.

Table 5-3 E-mail address recipient policy configuration information

Item	Description
Define search criteria	When you create a recipient policy, you must define the search criteria that determines the recipients to which the policy is applied. You define the search criteria by configuring filter rules, or by creating a custom search and entering LDAP query code manually to define the search criteria.
Define primary and secondary e-mail addresses	If you create multiple e-mail addresses of the same type in a recipient policy, the first one created is the primary e-mail address for that address type. Each subsequent e-mail address is a secondary address for that address type. A secondary e-mail address can replace the primary address by highlighting the secondary address, and selecting the Set as Primary button in the E-mail Addresses tab of the recipient policy.

Table 5-3 E-mail address recipient policy configuration information (continued)

Item	Description
Define e-mail address values by using variables	You can use the following variables to define e-mail address values: %g - Given Name (First Name) %i - Middle Initial %s - Surname (Lastname) By default, the SMTP address uses the alias value of the recipient to define the left side of the SMTP address. You can override this default using wildcards. For example, the default SMTP address for users is *alias@domainname*. To generate the SMTP address *firstname.lastname@domainname*, you can create a new recipient policy that specifies the SMTP address value as *%g.%s@domainname*.

ACTIVITY

Activity 5-8: Creating an E-Mail Address Recipient Policy

Time Required: 10 to 20 minutes

Objective: Create an e-mail address recipient policy to configure a primary address to represent your organization.

Description: In this activity, you create an e-mail address recipient policy that will be used to stamp your users with the organization name. The addresses will have the form *firstname.lastname@blatherconsultingXX.com*, where XX is the student number assigned to you. Complete the following steps to implement the recipient policies for users within your organization:

1. From the Windows desktop, click **Start**, point to **All Programs**, point to **Microsoft Exchange**, and then click **System Manager**.

2. Click the **plus sign (+)** next to the Recipients container. Right-click the **Recipient Policies** container. On the shortcut menu, point to **New**, and then click **Recipient Policy**. The New Policy dialog box opens and you are presented with the option to create an e-mail address recipient policy or a Mailbox Manager recipient policy. In this activity, you create an e-mail address recipient policy; therefore, check the **E-Mail Addresses** check box and click **OK**. The E-mail Address Recipient Policy Properties dialog box opens.

3. In the Name field, type **BlatherConsultingXX E-Mail Addresses Recipient Policy** for the name of your recipient policy, where XX is the student number assigned to you.

4. Click the **Modify** button. The Find Exchange Recipients dialog box opens. On the General tab, uncheck all entries with the exception of the **Users with Exchange mailbox** option.

5. Click the **Advanced** tab. Click the **Field** button, point to **User**, and then click **Alias**. In the Value field, type "*****". Click the **Add** button. When finished, click **OK** to return to the E-mail Address Recipient Policy Properties dialog box.

6. You are prompted with a warning indicating that you should enable the Apply this policy now option to apply this policy immediately. Click **OK** to continue.

7. Click the **E-Mail Addresses (Policy)** tab. Click the **New** button; the New E-mail Address dialog box opens.

8. Click **SMTP Address** and click **OK**. The SMTP Address Properties dialog box opens.

9. In the Address field, type **@blatherconsultingXX.com**, where XX is the student number assigned. Click **OK** to return to the Properties dialog box.

10. Click the **blatherconsultingXX.com** check box that you have just created, where XX is the student number assigned. This enables the address for all mailboxes within your organization; however, it only enables it as a secondary address. To enable it as the primary address for your users, ensure that your address is selected and click the **Set as Primary** button. Notice that the new address becomes bold and the previous SMTP address becomes nonbold. This indicates that the primary address is now the new address you have created. Click **OK** when you are finished to return to Exchange System Manager.

11. You are prompted with a warning indicating that the e-mail addresses of type SMTP have been modified, and whether you want to update the corresponding e-mail addresses on recipients to match the new addresses. Click **Yes** to continue. If necessary, click **Yes** again. This returns you to Exchange System Manager.

12. Close **Exchange System Manager**.

In some cases, you might have a need to exclude individual users from a particular e-mail address recipient policy. This is typically the case for organizations running in a mixed mode environment in which you still have legacy Exchange 5.5 servers as well as Exchange 2003 servers and you host multiple domain names. In this case, you might need to exclude or create exceptions to any policies that might be in effect. The following activity outlines the steps for accomplishing this.

ACTIVITY

Activity 5-9: Creating Exceptions to E-Mail Address Recipient Policies

Time Required: 5 to 10 minutes

Objective: Exclude individuals from having e-mail address recipient policies applied to them.

Description: In this activity, you modify a test user created on your server to exclude her from having e-mail address recipient policies applied to her. To do this, complete the following steps.

1. From the Windows desktop, click **Start**, point to **All Programs**, point to **Microsoft Exchange**, and then click **Active Directory Users and Computers**.

2. If necessary, click the **plus sign (+)** next to secureXX.local to expand it, where XX is your assigned student number. Click the **Users** container.

3. In the details pane, right-click **Test1**. On the shortcut menu, click **Properties**. The Test1 Properties dialog box opens.

4. Click the **E-mail Addresses** tab.

5. Click the **Automatically update e-mail addresses based on recipient policy** check box to clear it. This ensures that the user does not have recipient policies applied against her. After you are finished, click **OK** to return to Active Directory Users and Computers.

6. Close **Active Directory Users and Computers**.

In an organization that has many e-mail address recipient policies in effect, only one policy is applied to a particular object. To determine which of the policies is applied to an object, Exchange Server 2003 checks the policies priority. Policies with a higher priority are applied before policies with a lower priority. The default policy is set to the lowest priority. This means that the default policy is applied only when no other policy is available for a particular object. You do not have the ability to change the priority of this policy; however, you can change the priority of any other custom policy that you create. To do so, right-click the policy within the Recipient Policies node, point to All Tasks, and then select Move Up or Move Down, as appropriate.

Mailbox Manager Recipient Policies

Mailbox Manager recipient policies are designed to help manage user mailboxes so that users experience fewer problems. Mailbox Manager does this by helping you to keep track of mailbox usage. You can also notify users when their mailboxes have messages that should be cleaned up, or you can take action to clean up mailboxes by moving or deleting messages explicitly.

When activated, Mailbox Manager processes messages according to which folder the messages are stored in, and you can configure different settings for each type of folder. By default, items in folders older than 30 days and larger than 1 MB are processed by Mailbox Manager and the following message processing options are available to you:

- *Generate Report Only*—This option generates a report that is delivered to designated administrators. You can send either a summary report or a detailed report.

- *Move to Deleted Items Folder*—This option moves items that exceed the age and size limits to the Deleted Items folder. The items are purged from this folder based on the deletion settings for the mailbox store in which the mailbox is located or the individual settings for the user's mailbox.

■ *Move to System Cleanup Folders*—This option moves items that exceed the age and size limits to the System Cleanup folders. Items in the folder are marked for cleanup at the next cleanup interval, which can happen automatically or when the user chooses.

■ *Delete Immediately*—This option deletes the items permanently. The items are not copied to the Deleted Items folder.

You can apply Mailbox Manager recipient policies to all mailbox-enabled objects. Unlike e-mail address recipient policies, Exchange doesn't create a default Mailbox Manager recipient policy and mailbox management isn't activated. Activating Mailbox Manager is a two-part process. You must first create and configure a Mailbox Manager recipient policy, and then you must specify when and how mailbox management occurs.

As with an e-mail address recipient policy, you can create multiple Mailbox Manager policies and you can use filters to custom-tailor the list of mailboxes that are affected by the various policies. For example, you could create different Mailbox Manager policies for executives, managers, and users. Or, you could create policies for each business unit in your organization, such as Marketing, Administration, Finance, and Human Resources. Keep in mind that regardless of whether a mailbox matches multiple filter criteria, only one Mailbox Manager policy is applied to a particular object, as determined by the priority of the policy.

Activity 5-10: Creating a Mailbox Manager Policy

Time Required: 10 to 20 minutes

Objective: Create a Mailbox Manager policy that will notify users when they should clean up their mailboxes.

Description: Creating a Mailbox Manager policy helps users to be aware that they need to clean up their mailboxes on occasion. By reducing the size of the mailbox, you save disk space either on the server or on the user's computer. By reducing mailbox clutter, you make it easier for users to find current information and reduce distraction. Less size and clutter also means that the mailbox is easier to manage and that it is less likely for the mailbox to get corrupted.

1. From the Windows desktop, click **Start**, point to **All Programs**, point to **Microsoft Exchange**, and then click **System Manager**.

2. Click the **plus sign (+)** next to the Recipients container. Right-click the **Recipient Policies** container. On the shortcut menu, point to **New**, and then click **Recipient Policy**. The New Policy dialog box opens and you are presented with the option to create an e-mail address recipient policy or a Mailbox Manager recipient policy. In this activity, you create a Mailbox Manager recipient policy; therefore, click the **Mailbox Manager Settings** check box and then click **OK**. The Properties dialog box for your Mailbox Manager recipient policy opens.

3. In the Name field, type **BlatherConsultingXX Mailbox Managers Recipient Policy** for the name of your recipient policy, where XX is the student number assigned.

4. Click the **Modify** button. The Find Exchange Recipients dialog box opens. On the General tab, uncheck all entries with the exception of the **Users with Exchange mailbox** option.

5. Click the **Advanced** tab. Click the **Field** button, point to **User**, and then click **Alias**. In the Value field, type "*****". Click the **Add** button. When finished, click **OK** to return to the Properties dialog box for the Mailbox Manager recipient policy.

6. You are prompted with a warning indicating that you should enable the Apply this policy now option to apply this policy immediately. Click **OK** to continue.

7. Click the **Mailbox Manager Settings (Policy)** tab. This presents the options shown in Figure 5-12.

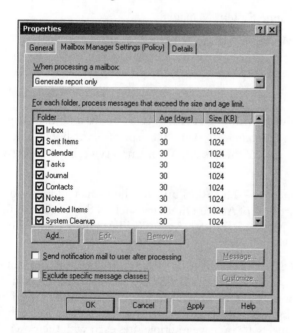

Figure 5-12   Mailbox Manager policy settings

8. Click **Generate report only** within the When processing a mailbox drop-down list, if necessary.

9. Within the list of folders that is presented, uncheck the **Calendar**, **Contacts**, and **Tasks** check boxes. Typically, calendar items do not contain large attachments and users typically like to keep a record of the events of their past for time-control purposes. Contacts are permanent records of individuals you maintain information about and as such should not be deleted. Tasks is another such item.

10. Change the size and age limit on the Inbox folder. To do this, click the **Inbox** folder and click the **Edit** button. The Folder Retention Settings dialog box opens.

11. Type **10** in the Age Limit field. Type **512** in the Message Size field. Click **OK** to return to the Properties dialog box.

12. Check the **Send notification mail to user after processing** check box, and click the **Message** button. The Notification Message dialog box opens.

13. Check the **Insert the number of messages processed** check box, and click **OK** to return to the Properties dialog box.

14. Click **OK** to return to Exchange System Manager.

15. Close **Exchange System Manager**.

RECIPIENT UPDATE SERVICE

As mentioned earlier, the **Recipient Update Service (RUS)** builds and maintains address lists by creating and maintaining Exchange Server 2003 specific attribute values within Active Directory. RUS runs as a thread of the System Attendant service. By default, two RUS objects are created:

- *RUS (Enterprise Configuration)*—This RUS updates the e-mail addresses of objects in the configuration partition of Active Directory, such as the Exchange Information Store object, the Message Transfer Agent (MTA) object, and the System Attendant.

- *RUS (installation Active Directory domain)*—For each Active Directory domain that has an installation of Exchange Server 2003, a RUS object is created and updates e-mail addresses for recipient objects in the respective domain partition of Active Directory with which this RUS object is associated. At least one RUS object for each domain contains mail-enabled objects. If you have multiple sites each with their own domain controller, you need to have multiple instances of the RUS. In this scenario, an instance of the RUS is run against a domain controller within each site.

When a domain without an Exchange 2003 server has recipients, you must create an additional RUS on an existing Exchange 2003 server and configure the RUS to point to a domain controller within the domain without an Exchange 2003 server. Before adding the RUS for a domain without Exchange Server 2003, you must first run Exchange 2003 Setup with the /domainprep switch in the domain without Exchange Server 2003.

The RUS is responsible for the automatic generation of SMTP addresses and any other proxy addresses that you have defined for recipients, and stamps the proxyAddresses attribute on recipient objects within Active Directory. The RUS does this by polling Active Directory for objects to update. The Recipient Update Service searches the directory for objects to update in three ways:

- Update only new and modified objects through regularly scheduled updates or by initiating an Update Now event through Exchange System Manager.

- Update all objects by initiating a Rebuild event through Exchange System Manager.

- Update objects that correspond to a specific recipient policy when a policy is modified or applied.

If the update is administrator initiated, then it depends on the type of action that was initiated by the administrator within Exchange System Manager. The following sections look at each of these options in turn.

Updating New and Modified Objects

The default behavior for the RUS is to update new and modified objects each time it runs to search for objects to update. By default, this is once a minute. The RUS keeps track of the latest change that has occurred on the domain controller against which the RUS is configured. Based on the schedule that is set for the RUS, the RUS periodically checks for objects that have been created or updated since it last checked. If there are new recipients, new address lists, or changes to existing address lists, the recipient objects are updated by the RUS. Activity 5–11 looks at an example of how to configure the scheduling of e-mail address recipient policy updates.

ACTIVITY

Activity 5-11: Scheduling E-Mail Address Recipient Policy Updates

Time Required: 5 to 10 minutes

Objective: Modify the schedule with which the RUS applies recipient policies.

Description: In this activity, you configure the RUS to make modifications to e-mail addresses based on recipient policy changes. These updates are made at a specific interval that is defined for the service. You can view the update interval and modify it as necessary by completing the following steps.

1. From the Windows desktop, click **Start**, point to **All Programs**, point to **Microsoft Exchange**, and then click **System Manager**.

2. Click the **plus sign (+)** next to the Recipients container. Click the **Recipient Update Services** node. You can now see the available Recipient Update Services in the details pane. You will have the enterprise configuration service and an additional service for the domain of which the server is a member.

3. Right-click **Recipient Update Service (Enterprise Configuration)**. On the shortcut menu, click **Properties**. The Recipient Update Service (Enterprise Configuration) Properties dialog box for the Recipient Update Service opens.

4. Use the Update interval list box to choose a new update interval. The following options are available. In this activity, click **Run every hour**.

   - Always run

   - Run every hour

   - Run every 2 hours

   - Run every 4 hours

   - Never run

   - Use custom schedule

5. Click **OK** to apply the changes and return to Exchange System Manager.

6. Close **Exchange System Manager**.

This is also the action that the RUS performs to search for objects to update when the Administrator selects an Update Now action within Exchange System Manager. When the Administrator clicks Update Now, Exchange System Manager sets the msExchReplicateNow attribute within Active Directory to true and causes the RUS to temporarily ignore its schedule and immediately query for any new changes and take any appropriate actions on those objects based on the recipient policies that apply to them. When the Update Now process is finished, msExchReplicateNow is set back to false.

Updating All Objects

To update all objects instead of just new and modified objects, the Exchange Administrator can use the Rebuild option within Exchange System Manager. When this option is selected, the msExchDoFullReplication attribute on the RUS service within Active Directory is set to true. The next time that the RUS is started by the schedule or by the Update Now command, the RUS starts at the beginning and looks at every object within Active Directory instead of querying only for new or modified objects. When the Rebuild process is finished, msExchDoFullReplication is set back to false.

Updating Objects Corresponding to a Specific Policy

Finally, you can modify the filter on a policy to make the RUS take action outside of its default behavior. When you modify the filter on a policy, the policy can apply to a completely different set of users than it did before. Because of this, if the filter on a policy has been modified, the RUS queries for every user who matches both the new filter and the old filter the next time the RUS is started by the schedule or by the Update Now command. This causes each object to have their msExchPoliciesIncluded attribute set to reflect the policy that is associated with them. This does not cause their addresses to be updated, however. To have e-mail addresses updated automatically for those users who match the new filter, the Administrator must use the Apply Now option to apply the policy.

NOTE   If you only modify the e-mail addresses on a policy, you do not change the default behavior of the RUS. If you have not changed the filter on the policy, the RUS does not automatically query for all users who match that policy to update them.

When the RUS is started by its schedule or by the initiation of an Update Now within Exchange System Manager, the RUS decides what to do in the following way:

1. First, the RUS determines which recipient policy to apply to the object. To do so, the RUS sorts the list of policies and selects the policy with the highest priority that has a filter which applies to this object and that is not present in the msExchPoliciesExcluded attribute on the user. In other words, the RUS selects the highest priority nonexcluded policy that applies to the user. When the choice is made, the RUS stamps the objectGUID attribute of that policy into the msExchPoliciesIncluded attribute on the recipient.

2. Second, the RUS determines whether the recipient is new. If the recipient has no proxy addresses, it is considered to be new and the RUS stamps the recipient with all the checked addresses on the policy. If the recipient is not new, the RUS performs the following:

    - If any of the primary addresses for this policy are populated in the gatewayProxy attribute of the RUS and the addresses that are currently on the object do not match the policy, the RUS regenerates those primary addresses. The previous primary address becomes a secondary address.

    - If any secondary addresses that are listed in gatewayProxy do not already exist on the recipient, the RUS adds those secondary addresses to the recipient.

    - If any address type is set for removal (by being unchecked on the policy), the RUS removes all addresses of that type from the recipient.

3. If the recipient has no addresses of an address type that is selected on the policy, the RUS adds the selected primary address of that type. The RUS does not add any secondary addresses in this step and does not evaluate whether the address of a type matches the format of the address specified on the policy. The RUS checks only to see if an address of that type exists.

The RUS regenerates primary addresses on a recipient to match their policy only if the policy has been applied and the gatewayProxy attribute is populated. Otherwise, the RUS never verifies that the addresses on a recipient match the policy on that recipient. Secondary addresses are only added when the recipient is new or when the policy has already been applied. If an Administrator adds a new secondary proxy to an existing policy, the new address is not added to existing users until the policy is applied.

5

Finally, if you clear the check box for a primary address on a policy, all addresses of that type are removed when you apply the policy. When you click to clear the address on the policy, the RUS does not prompt you to apply the policy, and the addresses are not removed. However, if you apply the policy at a later date, the addresses are removed. This also applies if you remove the address type from the policy. If you remove the address type and do not apply the policy, the addresses of that type are not removed from the recipients. If you apply the policy at a later date, the address type is not removed because the gatewayProxy attribute is not populated with the instruction to delete the address type. If you want to remove the addresses, you must add an address of that type back to the policy, click to clear the check box for that address, and then apply the policy.

CHAPTER SUMMARY

- GALs are composed of several address lists. Each address list contains a subset of all users in the Exchange organization and can be used to address e-mail messages, choose meeting attendees, and look up locations and phone numbers of other users within the organization.

- Default address lists are address lists that have been installed by default during an Exchange Server 2003 installation. These address lists help organize the presentation of Exchange recipient information to end users.

- Customized address lists allow you to build customized address lists to meet the needs of the users. Custom address lists can be created according to location, department, teams, or any other Active Directory attribute that is available for query.

- To create an address list, you need to define to whom the policy will be applied. Exchange Server 2003 makes use of a dialog box–based Find command that presents you with a set of menus that allows you to select and filter the desired set of recipients that will make up an address list. This interface is based on an LDAP query, which allows you to filter by any Active Directory attribute.

- As in previous versions of Exchange, Exchange Server 2003 gives you the ability to create address lists that group recipients in any way you like, to make it easier for users to find the recipient they are looking for in your organization. You can create a new top-level address list right in the All Address Lists folder, or you can create an address list inside an existing address list.

- When checking names, you'll usually want the GAL to be listed before the users' own contacts or other types of address lists. This is important because users often put internal mailboxes in their personal address lists. The danger of doing this without first resolving names against the GAL, however, is that although the display name might be identical, the properties of a mailbox might change. When changes occur, the entry in the user's address book is no longer valid and any mail sent bounces back to the sender with a nondelivery receipt.

❑ An offline address list is a set of address lists in files that are created and stored on an offline address lists server. Users who work offline can connect to an Exchange 2003 server and download offline address lists remotely to obtain information about other users in the organization.

❑ A policy is a collection of configuration settings that can be applied to one or more Exchange objects. Two types of policies are available in Exchange Server 2003, mailbox policies and e-mail address recipient policies.

❑ Mailbox Manager is designed to help manage user mailboxes so that users experience fewer problems. Mailbox Manager does this by helping you to keep track of mailbox usage. You can also notify users when their mailboxes have messages that should be cleaned up or you can take action to clean up mailboxes by moving or deleting messages explicitly.

❑ RUS builds and maintains address lists by creating and maintaining Exchange Server 2003 specific attribute values within Active Directory.

5

KEY TERMS

custom address list — An address list that has been created and customized.

default address lists — The address lists that have been installed by default during an Exchange Server 2003 installation.

e-mail address recipient policies — The policies that control e-mail address generation in the organization, and you can also use them to establish new default e-mail addresses on a global basis.

Global Address List (GAL) — The address list that contains an aggregation of all messaging recipients within the Exchange Server 2003 organization as well as all users within a foreign e-mail system connected by a dedicated connector, such as the Lotus Notes Connector or the GroupWise Connector.

Mailbox Manager recipient policies — The policies that help manage user mailboxes so that users experience fewer problems. Mailbox Manager does this by helping you to keep track of mailbox usage. You can also notify users when their mailboxes have messages that should be cleaned up, or you can take action to clean up mailboxes by moving or deleting messages explicitly.

offline address list — A set of address lists in files that are created and stored on an offline address lists server. Users who work offline can connect to an Exchange 2003 server and download offline address lists remotely to obtain information about other users in the organization.

recipient policy — A collection of configuration settings that are applied to users and groups.

Recipient Update Service (RUS) — The service that builds and maintains address lists by creating and maintaining Exchange Server 2003–specific attribute values within Active Directory.

REVIEW QUESTIONS

1. You want to create an address list that contains all users from the Marketing or Finance Departments. How can this be accomplished?

   a. You create a custom LDAP query with the AND operator to accomplish this.

   b. You create a custom LDAP query with the OR operator to accomplish this.

   c. You create a custom filter with the OR operator to accomplish this.

   d. You create a custom filter with the AND operator to accomplish this.

2. Where in ADSI Edit will you find the attribute to modify a user's full name display? Assume you are working in the secure01.local domain.

   a. CN=Configuration, DC=secure01, DC=local, CN=DisplaySpecifiers, CN=409, CN=user-Display

   b. CN=Configuration, DC=local, CN=DisplaySpecifiers, CN=409, CN=user-Display

   c. CN=Configuration, DC=secure01, DC=local, CN=DisplaySpecifiers, CN=Exchange, CN=409, CN=user-Display

   d. CN=Configuration, DC=secure01, DC=local, CN=DisplaySpecifiers, CN=Exchange, CN=user-Display

3. Which of the following attributes is a valid setting to change the default full name display to LastName, FirstName?

   a. %<Surname>, %<GivenName>

   b. $<sn>, $<GivenName>

   c. %<sn>, %<gn>

   d. $<sn>, $<gn>

4. Which attribute does the Recipient Update Service make use of to populate the proxyAddresses attribute when policies are being applied?

   a. addressGateway

   b. gatewayAddress

   c. msExchAddressProxy

   d. msExchProxyGateway

5. Changes to recipient policies take effect immediately. True or False?

6. Which of the following are not part of the default address lists installed with Exchange Server 2003?

   a. All Contacts

   b. All Groups

   c. All Conferencing Resources

   d. Public Folders

7. Which of the following options are available when specifying an LDAP query to populate an address list? (Choose all that apply.)

    a. Users with an Exchange mailbox. Add all mailbox-enabled users to the custom address list.

    b. Users with external e-mail addresses. This includes all mail-enabled users.

    c. Groups. Add all mail-enabled groups to the custom address list.

    d. Objects considered as shared mailboxes. Add all mailbox-enabled shared mailboxes to the custom address list.

8. When limiting address list membership to a particular store, which of the following options are available?

    a. Mailboxes on any server. Add recipients on all servers to the custom address list.

    b. Mailboxes on this server. Add recipients who have mailboxes on the specified server to the custom address list.

    c. Mailboxes in this mailbox store. Add recipients who have mailboxes on the specified store to the custom address list.

    d. All of the above.

9. When configuring a Mailbox Manager policy, which of the following options are available? (Choose all that apply.)

    a. Generate Report Only

    b. Move to Deleted Items folder

    c. Move to System Cleanup Folder

    d. Delete Immediately

10. How do you create exceptions to an e-mail address recipient policy?

    a. Make the user a member of the NoPolicy group.

    b. Add the user to the list of users the policy should not be applied to within the properties of the recipient policy.

    c. Hide the user from the GAL.

    d. Use Active Directory Users and Computers to uncheck the option to have addresses updated via recipient policies.

11. How do you hide an address list so that it can't be viewed by users?

    a. Create an empty address list that acts as a container for other address lists. Deny the user the Open Address List permission on the container.

    b. Hide the address from the GAL through Active Directory Users and Computers.

    c. Configure the address lists the user is allowed to see through ADSI Edit.

    d. None of the above.

5

12. Which of the following Recipient Update Services modifies the e-mail addresses for the System Attendant and the MTA?

    a. The Enterprise Configuration Recipient Update Service.

    b. The domain Recipient Update Service.

    c. None; the System Attendant and MTA do not have e-mail addresses.

    d. Both the Enterprise Configuration RUS and Domain RUS update the e-mail addresses.

13. Which methods does the RUS use to locate objects within Active Directory for updating?

    a. update only new and modified objects through regularly scheduled updates or by initiating an Update Now event through Exchange System Manager

    b. update all objects by initiating a Rebuild event through Exchange System Manager

    c. update objects that correspond to a specific recipient policy when a policy is modified or applied

    d. all of the above

14. What is the default behavior of the RUS?

    a. update only new and modified objects

    b. update all objects

    c. update objects that correspond to a specific recipient policy

    d. A and C

    e. B and C

15. Which of the following permissions apply to address lists? (Choose all that apply.)

    a. Open Address List

    b. List Contents

    c. Read Address List

    d. Write Address List

16. What is the default threshold for when Mailbox Manager processes items? (Choose all that apply.)

    a. 30 days

    b. 1 MB

    c. 15 days

    d. 10 MB

17. Nested address lists inherit conditions from their parent address list? True or False?

18. The priority on the default recipient policy is configurable. True or False?

5

19. When are offline address lists available to the end user?

    a. They are always available.

    b. They are available only when you are working offline.

    c. They are available when the user requests to use an offline address list.

    d. None of the above.

20. What is the default display name within the Global Address List when Exchange Server 2003 is installed?

    a. Firstname Lastname

    b. Lastname Firstname

    c. Firstname, Lastname

    d. Lastname, Firstname

21. Which address list provides a listing of all recipients who are external to your organization?

    a. All Users list

    b. All Contacts list

    c. All Groups list

    d. All Resources list

CASE PROJECTS

CASE
PROJECTS

Case Project 5-1: Configuring Address Lists

As the e-mail administrator for a large university, you have been asked by the faculties to define individual address lists for each individual faculty. Further, they require that each faculty list be hidden from users who are not members of the faculty. What are the steps you would go through to configure these address lists?

CASE
PROJECTS

Case Project 5-2: Implementing Mailbox Manager Policies

You are the e-mail architect for a large financial services company. You have noticed that the storage for your e-mail servers has grown significantly over the last year. What are the possible approaches to curbing the growth of storage?

CASE
PROJECTS

Case Project 5-3: Implementing a Custom SMTP Address

As the person in charge of implementing e-mail services for a startup company called Arctic Services, you are just in the process of installing your first e-mail infrastructure. You want to configure your recipients to have the articservices.com domain name associated with them as their primary address. What do you need to do to configure this for them?

Case Project 5-4: Configuring Offline Address Lists

As the Administrator of your e-mail environment, you have been receiving numerous calls about users getting nondelivery receipt when they send messages. These complaints seem to have arisen after you modified the SMTP address for your users. Upon further investigation, you notice the problem occurs with some users, yet not with others. What might be the problem?

6

PUBLIC FOLDERS

After reading this chapter, you will be able to:

♦ Describe public folders, the advantages of multiple public folder trees, and create and configure public folders and public stores

♦ Configure public folder permissions and how they are propagated to subfolders

♦ Describe how public folders are replicated

♦ Manage public folder replication

♦ Understand public folder referrals

♦ Troubleshoot public folders

Public folders are the foundation for collaboration within Exchange Server 2003. Public folders are contained in public folder stores managed by the Information Store service. It is important to understand the use of public folders so you can manage your information storage and retrieval effectively. Public folders enable public access to, and collaboration on, centralized messaging information. When members of a team are located in geographically different locations, the ability to share information is even more important. Exchange Server 2003 offers collaborative capabilities through its implementation of public folders.

Public folders are used to share files and messages within an organization. They are used as a repository for many different types of information that can be shared among users in an Exchange organization. When a public folder is used in combination with customized forms, it becomes the basis for collaboration applications, such as bulletin boards, discussion groups, customer tracking systems, and so on. Understanding the features and architectural elements of public folders in Exchange Server 2003, in addition to allowing you to create and manage public folders, enables you to develop an environment in which users can access and use data efficiently and productively.

This chapter introduces you to the concepts of public folders. It provides you with insight into the features and concepts surrounding the implementation of public folders. The chapter presents information on how to create and configure public folder stores and public folder trees, as well as presents the advantages of implementing multiple public folder trees. The chapter presents how public folder permissions can be configured and how they can be propagated to subfolders. In addition, the chapter discusses how to create and monitor a public folder replica, and how public folder referral can be implemented within an Exchange Server 2003 organization. Finally, the chapter finishes up with a discussion on troubleshooting.

INTRODUCTION TO PUBLIC FOLDERS

Public folders provide a shared repository for Exchange Server 2003. They provide a number of features that provide a number of benefits to an organization considering a collaborative architecture for their organization. Public folders in Exchange Server 2003 provide the following capabilities that contribute to a collaborative environment:

- *Multiple public folder trees*—Multiple public folder trees, also known as hierarchies or **public folder trees**, enable you to store public folders in more than one tree.

- *Secure items in public folders*—You have the ability to secure items in public folders through Exchange Installable File System (EXIFS).

- *Accessibility from the Web*—This feature enables you to use a Web browser to gain access to public folders by specifying a URL (uniform resource locator) to the folder.

- *Accessibility from the file system*—This feature enables you to use EXIFS to share public folders.

- *All-text indexing capabilities for public folders provided through MSSearch*—Microsoft Outlook clients automatically use this index when using the Advanced Find function.

- *Referrals enabled by default*—Public folder referrals enable clients to gain access to any folder in the organization. Exchange Server 2003 enables referrals by default between routing groups.

- *Public folders*—are used to share messages and files in an organization.

These features and benefits are realized using **public folder stores**. When you create a public folder, that folder is placed in the public folder store of a particular Exchange server. Each Exchange organization has a default public folder store, which is referred to as the **public root store**. Any Exchange server that has a public folder store can host a public folder and have that public folder replicated to the public folder stores of multiple additional servers.

Public Folder Trees

An Exchange organization can host multiple public folder trees, as shown in Figure 6-1.

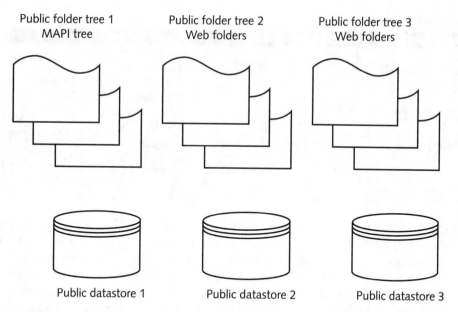

Figure 6-1 Public folder tree hierarchies

Each tree consists of a separate hierarchy of public folders and must be unique. Each public folder tree can be assigned to a single public folder store only. It is not possible to have two stores on a single server sharing the same tree. Within a public folder tree, the folders at the first level are referred to as **top-level public folders**. When a user creates a top-level public folder, it is placed in the public folder store on that user's home server. When a user creates a lower-level public folder, it is placed in the public folder store containing the parent folder in which the new folder is created. In addition, each public folder can be replicated to other servers in the organization. As you can see, this situation can get complicated. Public folders exist on different servers, and some public folders have instances on multiple servers.

Additional trees and hierarchies can be created and used as file repositories for departments, groups, or projects. You can also use general-purpose public folder trees for collaboration with browsers and applications, such as Office 2003, which can use HTTP to access the Information Store. Table 6-1 describes the hierarchies.

Table 6-1 Folder types

Hierarchy Type	Folder Tree Use Appears As	Access Methods
Default (All Public Folders)	MAPI clients	MAPI clients (such as Outlook) Applications (such as Microsoft Word and Microsoft Excel) Web browsers IFS shares
Alternate	General purpose	Applications (such as Word and Excel) Web browsers IFS shares

As can be seen, two different types of public folder trees can be created within Exchange Server 2003. As with previous versions of Exchange, an organization can have only one default root-level public folder tree, named All Public Folders. This is the only public folder tree that is accessible to MAPI (Messaging Application Programming Interface) mail clients such as Outlook. Exchange Server 2003, however, allows you to create multiple root-level public folders, which appear alongside of the All Public Folders tree. These other trees, however, can only be viewed from Outlook Web Access, Internet Explorer, Windows Explorer, or another application that makes use of the **Installable File System**.

Each public folder tree uses a separate database on an Exchange server, with the default root-level public folder tree, or All Public Folders tree, being maintained on the public root store. When configuring mailbox stores, you should ensure that you point them to the public root store. If the mailbox stores don't point to it, the default public folder tree is inaccessible to a user's mail client. To ensure that information about public folders is distributed throughout the Exchange system, Active Directory maintains a public folder hierarchy for each public folder tree. This is a single hierarchical structure that contains information about all of the public folders in that tree. The public folder hierarchies are automatically made available to every Exchange user in the organization.

When planning support for public folder trees, you need to consider the following issues:

- *Replication*—Because the default public folder tree is created on every public folder server, and its list of folders is always replicated, additional public folder trees only affect the servers on which they are configured. This means that you can create a set of departmental or local folders on only one server or on a subset of servers. You do not have to replicate these additional public folder trees to every public folder server.

- *Size minimization*—You can use additional public folder trees to minimize the overall size of the default public folder tree (simplifying navigation) and to reduce the cost of replicating the hierarchy of the default tree.

- *Permissions*—MAPI top-level hierarchy client permissions are the traditional MAPI permission (Editor, Owner, and so on). General-purpose, top-level hierarchy client permissions are based on Microsoft Windows Server 2003.

- *Top-level hierarchies*—There can only be one MAPI top-level hierarchy per organization. However, you can have multiple general-purpose, top-level hierarchies per organization.

- *Deep traversal searches*—MAPI top-level hierarchy does not support deep traversal searches (the ability to search the entire tree), whereas general-purpose trees do support deep traversal searches.

- *Mixed/native mode settings*—In mixed mode, MAPI top-level hierarchy folders are mail-enabled by default, whereas general–purpose, top-level hierarchy folders are not. In native mode, both types of folders are mail-disabled by default.

Creating a new public folder tree involves three steps. First, you must create a new top-level root folder that will house the new tree structure. Second, you must create a new public folder store on the server to hold the contents of that new tree structure. Finally, you must connect the new top-level folder to the new public folder store.

Creating a New Top-Level Root Folder

The only type of tree that you can create, change, or delete is a general-purpose tree. You can't create, change, or delete the default public folder tree. The default tree is created automatically when Exchange Server 2003 is installed; and it is managed by Exchange Server 2003. When you create a new public folder tree, Exchange Server creates an object in Active Directory that represents the tree. The directory object holds the properties and attributes of the tree and must be stored in a specific container. A default container is automatically created in the Exchange organization. If you want to use a different container, you must create the container before you create the public folder tree. You need to create additional containers for public folder trees only when you use administrative groups. With administrative groups, each group that you create after the first group can have a public folders container.

Activity 6-1: Creating a Top-Level Public Folder Tree

Time Required: 5 to 10 minutes

Objective: Create a general-purpose, top-level public folder tree.

Description: In this activity, you create a general-purpose, top-level public folder tree. Because you have not configured separate administrative groups, you cannot create a separate container. As such, this activity looks at how a public folders container can be created, not at actually creating one.

1. Log on to your Windows Server 2003 system using the user name **Administrator** and the password **Password**.

2. From the Windows desktop, click **Start**, point to **All Programs**, point to **Microsoft Exchange**, and then click **System Manager**.

3. Click the **plus sign (+)** next to Administrative Groups, and click the **plus sign (+)** next to the First Administrative Group. If the group already has a folders node, a public folder tree has already been created and you will not be able to create

another. If the group doesn't have a folders node, right-click the administrative group, point to **New**, and then click **Public Folders Container**. Note that if the administrative group does not contain a server, or already has a folders container, this option will not be available.

4. After a public folders container has been created, right-click the **Folders** container, point to **New**, and then click **Public Folder Tree**. The Properties dialog box for a new public folder tree opens, as shown in Figure 6-2.

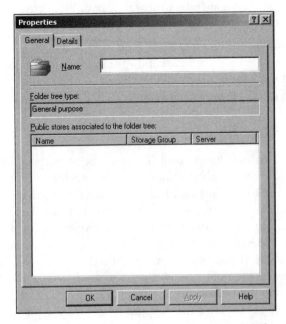

Figure 6-2   Public Folder Tree Properties dialog box

5. In the Name field, type **"First Public Folder Tree"** as the descriptive name for your public folder tree. Click **OK** when you are finished to return to Exchange System Manager.

6. Close **Exchange System Manager**.

Creating a Public Folder Store

Now that the public folder container and the public folder tree have been created, you need to associate the public folder tree with a public folder store. You do this by creating the public folder store.

One thing you should consider when configuring the public store is the Limits tab. Public folders help users share messages, documents, and ideas; they are an important part of any Exchange organization. Over time, however, public folders can become cluttered, with dated information consuming storage with information that is no longer relevant. To reduce the clutter and help alleviate these issues, you should consider modifying the age limit and deleted item retention settings.

The age limit and deleted item retention are two separate values. Deleted item retention is designed to ensure that postings and documents that could be needed in the future aren't permanently deleted. When retention is turned on, deleted items are retained for a specified period of time before they are permanently deleted and made nonrecoverable.

The age limit applies to deleted items as well. If a deleted item reaches the age limit, it is permanently deleted along with other items that have reached their age limit.

ACTIVITY

Activity 6-2: Creating a Public Folder Store

Time Required: 10 to 20 minutes

Objective: Create a public folder store for the public folder tree that was created in the previous activity.

Description: In this activity, you create a public store that will be associated with the public folder tree that was created in the previous activity and then walk through the different options that can be set for the public folder store. To create a public folder store, complete the following steps.

1. From the Windows desktop, click **Start**, point to **All Programs**, point to **Microsoft Exchange**, and then click **System Manager**.

2. Click the **plus sign (+)** next to Administrative Groups, and click the **plus sign (+)** next to First Administrative Group. Click the **plus sign (+)** next to the Servers container, and click the **plus sign (+)** next to SERVERXX, where XX is the student number assigned. Right-click the **First Storage Group**, point to **New**, and then click **Public Store**. The Properties dialog box for the public store you are defining opens, as shown in Figure 6-3.

3. Type **"First Public Store"** in the Name field for your public store.

4. Click the **Browse** button to the right of the Associated public folder tree field. The Select a Public Folder Tree dialog box opens. If necessary, click **First Public Folder Tree**, the public folder tree that you created in the previous activity, and then click **OK**. This returns you to the Public Store Properties dialog box.

5. Click the **Database** tab; the options outlined in Figure 6-4 appear. Here, you have the option to change the locations of where your database files will be located. For this activity, leave these in the default location.

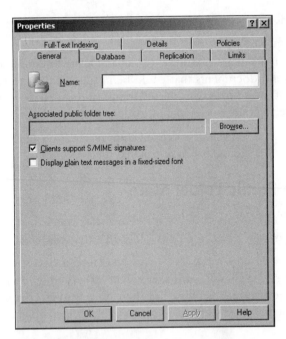

Figure 6-3   Public Store Properties dialog box

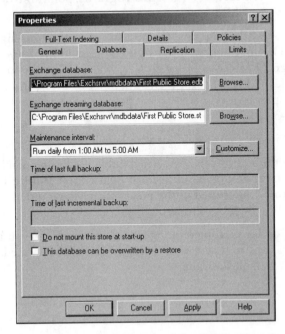

Figure 6-4   Database tab of the Public Store Properties dialog box

6. Click the **Replication** tab. The options shown in Figure 6-5 appear. This tab can be used to configure the replication intervals and limits for all folders in the public folder store. The options include the following:

- *Replication interval*—Determines when changes to public folders are replicated. Click **Run every hour** from the drop-down list provided.

- *Replication interval for always (minutes)*—Sets the interval (in minutes) that's used when you select Always Run as the Replication interval. Because we have set the Replication interval to be every hour, this option will not be changed.

- *Replication message size limit (KB)*—Sets the size limit (in kilobytes) for messages that are replicated. Messages over the size limit aren't replicated. Change the size to **500 KB** instead of the default size limit of 300 KB.

6

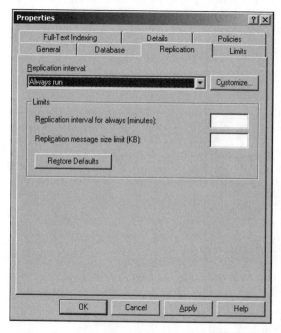

Figure 6-5 Replication tab of the Public Store Properties dialog box

7. Click the **Limits** tab. The options outlined in Figure 6-6 appear.

- *Issue warning at (KB)*—Sets the size, in kilobytes, of the data that a user can post to the public store before a warning is issued to the user. The warning tells the user to clean out the public store. Type **2048** for this activity.

- *Prohibit post at (KB)*—Sets the maximum size, in kilobytes, of the data that a user can post to the public store. The restriction ends when the total size of the user's data is under the limit. Type **4096** for this activity.

- *Maximum item size (KB)*—Sets the maximum size, in kilobytes, for postings to the data store. Type **1024** for this activity.

- *Warning message interval*—Sets the interval for sending warning messages to users whose total data size exceeds the designated limits. The default interval is daily at midnight. Change this by clicking **Run daily at 1:00 AM** from the drop-down list.

- *Keep deleted items for (days)*—Sets the number of days to retain deleted items. Type **14** for this activity. Note that if you set the retention period to 0, deleted postings aren't retained, and you cannot recover them.

- *Do not permanently delete items until the store has been backed up*—Ensures that deleted items are archived into at least one backup set before they are removed. Click this check box to ensure this item is enabled.

- *Age limit for all folders in this store (days)*—Sets the number of days to retain postings in the store. Postings older than the limit are automatically deleted. Type **356** in the age limit value field. This automatically checks the associated check box for you.

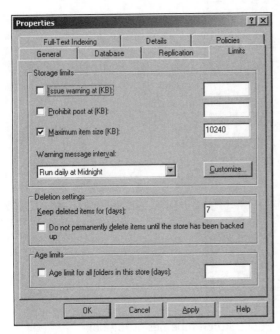

Figure 6-6   Limits tab of the Public Store Properties dialog box

8. Click **OK** to finish defining the public store and return to Exchange System Manager.

9. When prompted, click **Yes** to mount the store. By mounting the store, you make it available for use.

10. When prompted that the store was successfully mounted, click **OK** to return to Exchange System Manager.

11. Close **Exchange System Manager**.

Creating Public Folders

After the public folder tree has been created, you can then create public folders within the tree. Public folders provide a storage point for common information that can be either centralized or distributed. Creating public folders can be done by the administrator using Exchange System Manager or, if the client has sufficient permissions, by the clients themselves using Outlook. Both the client and the administrator have the ability to set up a hierarchy of folders and associated permissions that allow them to organize information specific to their requirements.

6

Activity 6-3: Creating Public Folders

Time Required: 10 to 20 minutes

Objective: Create public folders under the default public folder tree.

Description: In this activity, you create two public folders. The public folders will be created under the default public folder tree, which is the only public folder tree accessible to MAPI (Outlook) clients. This activity illustrates the creation of public folders through Exchange System Manager and prepares for future activities. Prior to creating a public folder, you will need to remove SSL from the Exadmin virtual directory, as shown in the first few steps of this activity.

1. From the Windows desktop, click **Start**, point to **Administrative Tool**, and then click **Internet Information Services (IIS) Manager**.

2. Click the **plus sign (+)** next to SERVERXX to expand it, where XX is your assigned student number. Click the **plus sign (+)** next to Web Sites, and then click the **plus sign (+)** next to Default Web Site.

3. Right-click the **Exadmin** virtual directory, and then click **Properties**. In the Exadmin Properties dialog box, click the **Directory Security** tab, and then, under Secure communications, click **Edit**.

4. In the Secure Communications dialog box, click to clear the **Require secure channel (SSL)** check box, and then click **OK** to return to the Exadmin Properties dialog box. Click the **OK** to return to Internet Information Services (IIS) Manager.

5. Close **Internet Information Services (IIS) Manager**.

6. From the Windows desktop, click **Start**, point to **All Programs**, point to **Microsoft Exchange**, and then click **System Manager**.

7. Click the **plus sign (+)** next to Administrative Groups, and click the **plus sign (+)** next to the First Administrative Group. Click the **plus sign (+)** next to the Folders container. Right-click **Public Folders**, point to **New**, and then click **Public Folder**. The Properties dialog box for a new public folder opens, as shown in Figure 6-7.

8. In the Name field, enter a descriptive name for the public folder. For this activity, use the name **"First Public Folder."**

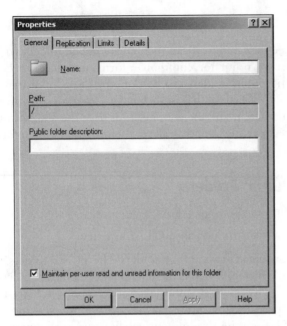

Figure 6-7   New Public Folder Properties dialog box

9. Click the **Limits** tab and, under Storage limits, click the **Use public store defaults** option. This configures the public folder to use the global limits set on the public folder store. Click **OK** to return to Exchange System Manager.

10. Click the **plus sign (+)** next to Public Folders. Right-click **First Public Folder,** point to **New**, and click **Public Folder**. The Properties dialog box for a new public folder opens.

11. In the Name field, type **"First Sub Folder"** as the descriptive name for the public folder.

12. Click the **Limits** tab and, under Storage limits, click the **Use public store defaults** option. This configures the public folder to use the global limits set on the public folder store. Click **OK** to return to Exchange System Manager.

13. Close **Exchange System Manager**.

After the public folders have been created and deleted item retentions have been configured, you might be required to recover items after they have been deleted. Clients have the ability to do this themselves through Outlook, freeing the administrator from this task. This is significant because recovering deleted items can be a laborious task for the administrator.

Activity 6-4: Recovering Deleted Items

Time Required: 5 to 10 minutes

Objective: Outline the steps that are required to recover deleted items.

Description: You can recover deleted items from public folder stores as long as you've set a deleted item period for the public folder store from which the items were deleted and the retention period for this data store hasn't expired. If both of these conditions are met, you can recover deleted items by completing the following steps.

1. Start Outlook by clicking **Start**, pointing to **All Programs**, pointing to **Microsoft Office**, and then clicking **Microsoft Office Outlook 2003**.

2. If necessary, log on to the Administrator account. In the Folders List, click the **plus sign (+)** next to Public Folders. Click the **plus sign (+)** next to All Public Folders. Click **First Public Folder**.

3. Click the **New** button. In the Subject field, enter "This is a test," and enter "This is text in the post" in the Text field. Click the **File** menu and click **Post**. The message will be posted to the public folder.

4. Right-click the previously created message, and click **Delete** from the shortcut menu provided. You are prompted to confirm whether you want to delete the message. Click **Yes**.

5. Click the **Tools** menu and click **Recover Deleted Items**. The Recover Deleted Items From dialog box opens.

6. If necessary, click the **This is a test** item, and click the **Recover Selected Items** button.

7. Close **Microsoft Outlook**.

CONFIGURING PUBLIC FOLDER PERMISSIONS

When you create a public folder, Exchange Server 2003 assigns a set of permissions that specify the individuals with the right to perform designated activities in that folder. You can assign permissions to folders, items, and properties. Permissions can be inherited from higher-level objects, such as the public folder tree and the administrative group.

If you configure public folder permissions by using Outlook, which displays the legacy roles such as Publishing Author, Editor, and Owner to control access to folders, Exchange Server 2003 automatically configures the corresponding Windows Server 2000/2003 permissions.

Exchange Server 2003 relies on Active Directory in Windows Server 2000/2003 to enforce security on Exchange Server 2003 objects. The operating system manages and enforces permissions that are specific to Exchange Server 2003, such as the ability to create a top-level public folder. The following principles are used to implement security within Exchange Server 2003:

- You can apply access control to any resource, not just the folder. Specifically, you can apply security separately to folders, items in the folders, and the properties of an item.

- You apply the same type of permissions for a folder, or items within it, and assign them to a user account or security group in Windows Server 2000/2003.

- The access control list (ACL) uses security identifiers (SIDs) of Windows Server 2000/2003 users and groups. Exchange Server 2003 assigns the Anonymous access permissions to the special ANONYMOUS LOGON account and the Default access permission to the Everyone group. When evaluating access to a resource in Windows Server 2000/2003, all of the entries in the ACL are processed until:

  - An entry denies permission.

  - All of the requested permissions are granted.

  - The end of the list is reached without all permissions granted.

- Permissions can be denied. This feature can be used to exclude a user or group from permissions granted to a larger group. Denied permissions are processed first and take precedence over granted permissions.

Configuring Client Permissions

To specify client settings for a public folder, you can use either Exchange System Manager or Outlook itself. By default, all users including those accessing the folder anonymously over the Web have permission to access the folder and read its contents. Users who log on to the network or to Outlook Web Access have additional permissions. These permissions allow them to create subfolders, to create items in the folder, to read items in the folder, and to edit and delete items they have created.

To change permissions for anonymous and authenticated users, you need to set a new role for the special users Anonymous and Default, respectively. Initially, anonymous users have the role of Contributor and authenticated users have the role of Publishing Author. Table 6-2 describes the permissions granted to each role.

Table 6-2   Role permissions

Role	Permission
Owner	All rights in the folder: Create, Read, Modify, Delete all items and files, and Create Subfolders. The owner can also change permission levels that other users are assigned for the folder.
Publishing Editor	Create, Read, Modify, Delete all items and files, and Create Subfolders.
Editor	Create, Read, Modify, and Delete all items and files.
Publishing Author	Create and Read items and files, Modify and Delete items and files you create, and Create subfolders.
Author	Create and Read items and files, and Modify and Delete items and files you create.
Nonediting Author	Create and Read items and files, and Delete items and files you create.
Reviewer	Read items and files only.
Contributor	Create items and files only. The contents of the folder do not appear.

Table 6-2 Role permissions (continued)

Role	Permission
None	Grants no permission in the folder. Use this as the default permission when you want to limit the folder audience to only users you specifically add to the Name/Role box.

ACTIVITY

Activity 6-5: Setting Client Permissions

Time Required: 5 to 10 minutes

Objective: Configure client permissions for a public folder using Exchange System Manager.

Description: In this activity, you use Exchange System Manager to configure the client permissions for a public folder to allow users to manipulate folder contents. Prior to completing this, you need to configure the First Public Folder to be mail-enabled. This is addressed within the activity. To configure client permissions, complete the following steps.

1. From the Windows desktop, click **Start**, point to **All Programs**, point to **Microsoft Exchange**, and then click **System Manager**.

2. Click the **plus sign (+)** next to Administrative Groups, and click the **plus sign (+)** next to First Administrative Group. Click the **plus sign (+)** next to the Folders container, and click the **plus sign (+)** next to Public Folders. Right-click **First Public Folder**, point to **All Tasks**, and then click **Mail Enable**.

3. Right-click **First Public Folder** and click **Properties**. The First Public Folder Properties dialog box opens.

4. Click the **Permissions** tab and click the **Client permissions** button. The Client Permissions dialog box opens, as shown in Figure 6-8.

5. The Name and Role lists display account names and their permissions on the folder. To grant users permissions that are different from the default permission, click **Add**; the Add Users dialog box opens. Click **Test1** and click the **Add** button; this moves the user to the Add Users scroll box. Click **OK** to return to the Client Permissions dialog box.

6. In the Name and Role lists, click **Test1** and in the Roles drop-down list, click **Owner**.

7. When you're finished granting permissions, click **OK**. This returns you to the First Public Folder Properties dialog box. Click **OK** to return to Exchange System Manager.

8. Close **Exchange System Manager**.

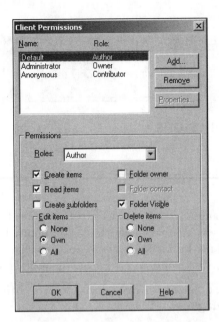

Figure 6-8   Client Permissions dialog box

Client permissions allow users to manipulate folder contents, but they do not let users manage the permissions on the folder itself. Only administrators can set folder permissions and modify public folder properties. If you want other users to be able to set permissions, you need to grant the users directory rights to the folder. If you want users to be able to administer a public folder as well, you need to grant them administrative rights to the folder.

ACTIVITY

Activity 6-6: Setting Directory Rights and Designating Administrators

Time Required: 5 to 10 minutes

Objective: Configure directory and administrative rights to a public folder.

Description: In this activity, you use Exchange System Manager to configure directory and administrative rights on a public folder. To configure directory and administrative rights on a public folder, complete the following steps.

1. From the Windows desktop, click **Start**, point to **All Programs**, point to **Microsoft Exchange**, and then click **System Manager**.

2. Click the **plus sign (+)** next to Administrative Groups. Click the **plus sign (+)** next to First Administrative Group. Click the **plus sign (+)** next to the Folders container, and click the **plus sign (+)** next to Public Folders. Right-click **First Public Folder** and click **Properties** from the shortcut menu.

3. Click the **Permissions** tab and click the **Directory rights** button. The Permissions for First Public Folder dialog box opens, as shown in Figure 6-9. Click the **Add** button. The Select Users, Computers, or Groups dialog box opens.

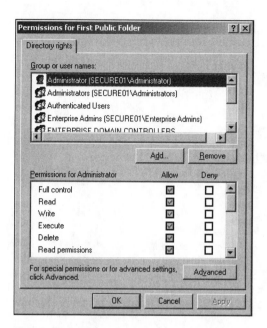

Figure 6-9 Directory Rights tab of the Permissions for First Public Folder dialog box

4. In the Enter the object names to select field, type **Test1** and click the **Check Names** button. Click **OK** to grant permissions to change the e-mail related attributes of the mail-enabled folder and return to the Permissions for First Public Folder dialog box. Click **OK** to return to the First Public Folder Properties dialog box.

5. Click the **Administrative rights** button. The Permissions for First Public Folder dialog box opens, as shown in Figure 6-10. Click the **Add** button. The Select Users, Computers, or Groups dialog box opens.

6. In the Enter the object names to select field, enter **Test1** and click the **Check Names** button. Click **OK** to grant permissions to administer and modify the permissions on the public folder and return to the Permissions for First Public Folder dialog box. Click **OK** to return to the First Public Folder Properties dialog box. Click **OK** to return to Exchange System Manager.

7. Close **Exchange System Manager**.

Propagating Permissions

You can assign permissions to higher-level objects and then have them propagated to lower-level objects. The top-level folder in a public folder tree is referred to as a parent folder. Assigning permissions to a parent folder causes them to propagate to all the folders within the tree. A parent folder inherits permissions from folders above it in the administrative hierarchy, including the administrative group permissions and organization permissions. Table 6-3 describes the permissions that are available in Exchange Server 2003 and their inheritance hierarchy.

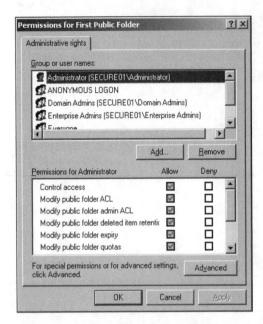

Figure 6-10   Administrative Rights tab of the Permissions for First Public Folder
dialog box

Table 6-3   Inheritance hierarchy

Permission	Inheritance Hierarchy	Description
Create public folder	Organization Administrative group Public folder tree	Gives administrative permission to create a public folder. Overrides other permissions, such as create container.
Create top-level public folder	Organization Administrative group Public folder tree	Specifies who can define top-level folders, which, in turn, define the tree structure.
Modify public folder Deleted item retention Modify public folder expiry Modify public folder quotas	Administrative group Public folder tree	Specifies who can change these configuration properties.
Modify public folder replica list	Organization Administrative group Public folder tree	Specifies who can configure where a public folder is replicated.
Modify public folder ACL	Public folder tree	Specifies who can configure permissions.
Modify public folder admin ACL	Organization Administrative group Public folder tree	Specifies who can configure administrator rights.

Table 6-3 Inheritance hierarchy (continued)

Permission	Inheritance Hierarchy	Description
Administer Information Store	Organization Administrative group Public folder tree	Specifies who can manage the public Information Store.
Create named properties in the Information Store	Organization Administrative group Public folder tree	Specifies who can create named properties. Use this to prevent unauthorized properties from being created (possibly from a denial of service attempt).
View Information Store	Organization Administrative group Public folder tree	Specifies who can view status on the public Information Store.

6

The permissions for public folders in Exchange Server 2003 are divided into three different categories. Using the facilities of Exchange System Manager, Exchange Server 2003 enables you to control the details of public folder access and administration using these rights.

- *Client rights*—Client rights enable you to control the permissions of users accessing the folder and messages contained within. For example, you can control who has Read/Write permission on a public folder.

- *Directory rights*—Mail-enabling a public folder creates an object in Active Directory. Directory rights enable you to control which users can manipulate this object.

- *Administrative rights*—Administrative rights enable you to assign specific rights to specific administrators.

Properties that you set for a parent folder can be applied to all subfolders using Exchange System Manager. After the parent's settings are applied, you can still change the subfolders' settings. Changing the settings on the subfolders does not affect the settings on the parent or other subfolders.

ACTIVITY

Activity 6-7: Propagating Folder Settings

Time Required: 5 to 10 minutes

Objective: Propagate public folder settings to subfolders.

Description: In this activity, you propagate public folder settings to lower-level subfolders within the public folder tree. Any property changes you make to public folders aren't automatically applied to subfolders, only to newly created subfolders. In addition, any changes you make specifically to the child folder are lost if you choose to propagate settings from the parent folder. You can, however, manually propagate setting changes if you need to. To do this, complete the following steps.

1. From the Windows desktop, click **Start**, point to **All Programs**, point to **Microsoft Exchange**, and then click **System Manager**.

2. Click the **plus sign (+)** next to Administrative Groups. Click the **plus sign (+)** next to First Administrative Group. Click the **plus sign (+)** next to the Folders container, and click the **plus sign (+)** next to Public Folders. Right-click **First Public Folder**, point to **All Tasks**, and then click **Propagate Settings**. Note that if the public folder does not have any subfolders, this option will not be available. The Propagate Folder Settings dialog box opens, as shown in Figure 6-11.

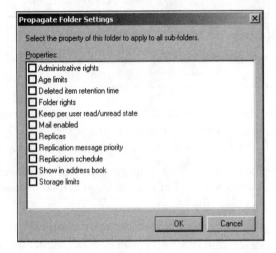

Figure 6-11   Propagate Folder Settings dialog box

3. Check the following check boxes and click **OK**. This propagates the settings to the subfolders:

   - **Age limits**

   - **Replicas**

   - **Storage limits**

4. Close **Exchange System Manager**.

REPLICATING PUBLIC FOLDERS

Public folder replication is a mail-based process that makes use of SMTP to transport messages between servers that contain replicas of the information.

Client Access to Public Folders

When a client attempts to access public folder data on a server, the client must be able to connect to a server that contains a replica of the data. The client attempts to connect to any replica to present the requested data to the user.

To maximize efficiency, the client attempts a connection to servers in the following order:

1. A call is made to the Information Store. The Information Store then returns a list of all Exchange servers in the organization that currently have a copy of the requested public folder.

2. The Information Store then makes a call to the routing service. This routing service returns the cost associated with the route to that public folder. Note that the store caches the cost for each server that has the requested public folder for one hour. This is done to prevent repeated calls into the routing service. You can purge this cache by restarting MSExchangeIS.

6

3. The Information Store then uses the following criteria to determine how to route the client to the closest copy of the public folder.

   - If the original public folder store is local (for example, when the mailbox of the client/user is on the same server as the public folder), the client is directed to this server for the public folder contents.

   - If the public folder server that contains the public folder is in the same routing group as the client's mailbox, the client is sent to the public folder server within that routing group.

   - If there is not a copy of the public folder contents in the local routing group, the Information Store initiates the process of calculating the lowest cost route to a server in the organization that has a copy of the public folder. Note that the Information Store discards any servers that are down or have an infinite cost associated with them.

   - If none of the previous criteria are true, the client will not be able to view the contents of this public folder.

Server Replication

When servers need to replicate public folder information among themselves, the **Public Folder Replication Agent (PFRA)**, which is part of the Information Store service, monitors changes, additions, and deletions to the public folder. The PFRA also makes use of change numbers, time stamps, and predecessor change lists to keep track of replication progress and to identify whether a public folder is synchronized.

Any time a user posts information to a public folder, or modifies existing information within a public folder, Exchange Server 2003 makes use of a change number to keep track of the public folder item. The change number that is used by the PFRA is made up of a globally unique Information Store identifier and a server-specific change counter. This ensures that change numbers are Information Store specific, but also reflect sequential changes as indicated by the change counter. The change counter is not sequential for a single message or folder, but is sequential across all the messages and folders on that Information Store. The change counter is incremented as any user in the organization makes additions, modifications, or deletions to any message within a public folder on that server. When public folder contents are modified, the PFRA for that Information Store assigns a new change number to the message.

The PFRA on the Information Store also assigns a time stamp to messages when they arrive in a public folder. When a message instance on an Information Store is modified, the PFRA for that Information Store assigns a new time stamp, using the greater of either the current system time or the old time stamp.

The predecessor change list for a message is a list of the Information Stores that have made changes to the message and the last change number made by each Information Store. For example, a predecessor change list on an individual message might look like the following:

- Information Store 1–4
- Information Store 2–9
- Information Store 3–6

This example indicates that the last change that Information Store 1 made to the message was change number 4, the last change that Information Store 2 made to the message was change number 9, and so on. When a message is modified, the PFRA on the Information Store where the modification occurs adds the current change number to its entry in the predecessor change list. The predecessor change list is used to identify public folder conflicts.

During message creation, Information Stores receiving the replication message simply create the message in their instance of the public folder, using the change number assigned by the Information Store on which the message was originally created. When a message is deleted, the originating Information Store sends a replication message to all other Information Stores maintaining instances of the public folder, indicating that the message has been deleted. Each receiving Information Store deletes its own instance of the message. Message expirations occur slightly differently than message deletions. Each Information Store uses message expiration information to verify when a message should be deleted. Although the end result is the same in that the message is deleted, the difference is that no expiration message is replicated. Each Information Store is responsible for managing its own message expirations.

When a change is made to an instance of a message in a replicated public folder, the original message on a particular Information Store (the originating Information Store) is modified by the PFRA for that Information Store to update the state information for that message. The PFRA then sends a replication message, containing the modified message and all of its attachments, to all of the other Information Stores that have been configured to maintain a replica of the public folder in which the message resides. The list of Information Stores maintaining replicas is stored in the Information Store and they can be viewed on the Replication tab for each public folder.

When an Information Store receives a replication message, the new message contained in the replication message (the update message) is used to replace the existing message that already exists in the public folder, if the modification that caused the replication was made against the same message or a later version of the message. That is, if the change number of the local message is included in the predecessor change list of the update message, the change is made.

If the change number of the local message is not included in the predecessor change list of the update message, it indicates that the original message was not the same as the local message. This indicates that the original message was in fact older than the local message. The change was made to a version of the message that had not incorporated some previous change on some other Information Store, resulting in a conflict. That is, a conflict occurs when a user edits an item located in a public folder on one server, and then, before the changes can be replicated to all instances of the public folder, another user on a different server edits the same item. Figure 6-12 provides an example of a conflict.

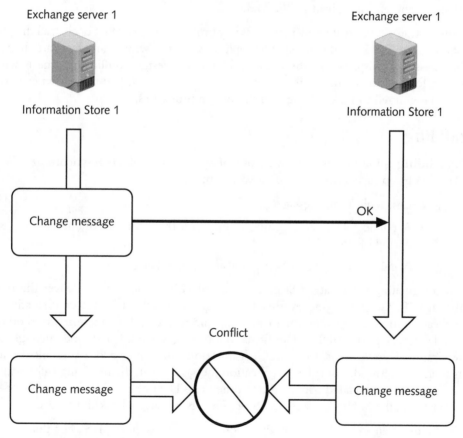

Figure 6-12   Message conflict

Two types of public folder conflicts exist: **message edit conflicts** and **folder edit conflicts**.

A message edit conflict occurs when the content and/or properties associated with a message are modified on any server. When you replicate these changes, conflicts can occur. A replication server determines which set of message properties to use, the local copy or the copy from the remote server. The goal of conflict resolution is to ensure that public folder content is the same at all replicas. When a message edit conflict occurs, the following process occurs:

- A conflict resolution message is generated and sent to the folder contact.
- The messages in conflict are attached to the conflict message.
- The contact can choose to keep one or all the messages in conflict.

A folder edit conflict occurs when two or more public folder contacts change a public folder design at the same time. In this case, the last design change is saved, overwriting previous changes. The exception to this is a change to the replica list, which is a list of all servers that replicate content of a given public folder.

Administrators can create new replicas at any time. When a conflict occurs, all the properties of the losing folder are discarded. The replica lists of the winner and loser are then merged. No message is displayed in the public folder, but a design conflict message is sent to the public folder contact, or public folder owner if there are no contacts. Owner permissions must be granted to make changes to the design properties.

Backfilling

Backfilling is the process by which out-of-sync public folders resynchronize themselves. Backfilling can recover from the following situations:

- Lost replication message(s)
- A public folder server going offline, and then coming online after an extended period of time
- A public folder server being restored from a backup

The originating Information Store relies on SMTP to successfully deliver the replication message. To save messaging overhead, there are no mechanisms for confirmation of each replication message between the originating and receiving Information Stores other than a nondelivery report (NDR). Confirmation messages would add one message to every replication message sent. In a large organization, this could add a substantial amount of messaging overhead. Instead, if a replication message is lost, the receiving Information Store no longer has an updated copy of the lost message. The public folder is now out-of-sync. To correct this, the public Information Store process initiates a backfill process.

Let's look at an example of how this backfilling process takes place. For this example, the scenario is outlined in Figure 6-13.

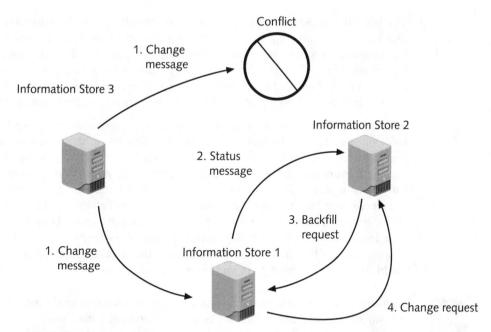

Figure 6-13   Backfilling example

Here, Information Store 2 chooses Information Store 1. Next, Information Store 1 receives the backfill request, and then sends the missing changes to Information Store 2, which implements the changes. Information Store 1, Information Store 2, and Information Store 3 are now synchronized. The end result of the backfill process is that after it is complete, all the public folders are once again synchronized. Let's consider how this occurs.

1. Replication to Information Store 2 fails. Information Store 3 sends the replication message to Information Store 1 and Information Store 2, but for some reason the replication message does not reach Information Store 2. Information Store 1 and Information Store 3 are synchronized, but Information Store 2 has an old version of the replicated message. Information Store 1 and Information Store 3 have a change number that has not been implemented by Information Store 2.

2. Status messages are sent and analyzed. When Information Store 1 sends its status message to Information Store 2 and Information Store 3, Information Store 2 determines whether the change numbers are the same for all the public folders that are being replicated. If the change numbers are the same (for those public folders being replicated between Information Store 1 and Information Store 2), Information Store 1 and Information Store 2 are synchronized. If not, Information Store 2 determines whether there are any higher change numbers in the list of changes for Information Store 1 that are not in the list of changes for Information Store 2.

3. The backfill request is sent. In this case, there are changes to Information Store 1 that have not been implemented by Information Store 2, as indicated by the higher change number received in the status message from Information Store 1. Information Store 2 then creates a backfill request for those changes that have not been received. This backfill request is placed in an e-mail message, and is sent by Information Store 2 to a public folder server (in this case, Information Store 1).

4. Changes are sent. If Information Store 1 does not respond to the backfill request, Information Store 2 chooses another Information Store based on e-mail transit time and routing group connector costs. Each Information Store maintains an average transmission time for the other servers with which it is replicating. The Information Store uses this value to establish an order within a routing group of the servers to which it sends the backfill request. The Information Store first tries all the servers within its own routing group in order of average transmission time. The Information Store then uses routing group connector costs to pick the next routing group, the Information Store uses the average transmission time to establish an order within that routing group, and so on.

NOTE   The process as outlined in this section for a lost replication message works the same way to recover a server that has been offline and has missed multiple replication messages, and to recover a server that has been restored from an old backup. The way that public folder contents are sent does not differ between backfill and normal replication (multiple public folder messages are bundled into a larger single message according to the maximum message size).

MANAGING PUBLIC FOLDER REPLICATION

Public folder replicas provide multiple, redundant information points and load balancing for accessing data. It is important that you understand the concepts and processes of replication so that users can access data without taxing your server or using unnecessary bandwidth over your network. Different components of public folder replication are controlled in different ways, as follows:

- Active Directory controls the replication of public folder directory objects.

- The Exchange Server 2003 Information Store controls the replication of public folder hierarchies.

- An Exchange Server 2003 administrator controls the replication of the content of public folders. Content is considered to be the message headers, message body, and any attachments. By default, when you create a public folder, only one copy of the public folder exists within the organization. A public folder can exist in an organization either as a single copy or as multiple copies. Multiple copies are known as replicas.

Configuring Replicas

You can configure a public folder to have replicas on multiple public folder servers. Replicas are useful for distributing the user load on servers, distributing public folders geographically, and backing up public folder data. A replica copied from one server to another is a separate instance of a public folder and its contents. All replicas of a public folder are equal. There is no master replica. This means that you can directly modify replicas of public folders, and the folder changes are then replicated automatically to other servers. This type of replication is known as a **multimaster replication**.

During public folder replication, the Information Store replicates the public folder hierarchy to every server using system messages. The contents, however, are replicated only to servers on which an administrator has set up replicas. When a user creates a public folder, its location in the hierarchy is replicated to every server. If the new public folder is a top-level folder, the contents of the new folder are on the user's public folder server. If the new public folder is not a top-level folder, the contents are located on every server on which the parent folder's contents reside. During replication, the Information Store sends changes made to items in a replica to all other replicas of the public folder throughout the organization. The Information Store replicates changes made to the folder, the folder's properties, or the public folder hierarchy to all servers. When you no longer want a public folder replica, you can delete it from its database. The following activity outlines the steps needed to create a public folder replica.

ACTIVITY

Activity 6-8: Configuring Public Folder Replication

Time Required: 5 to 10 minutes

Objective: Walk through the steps to replicate a folder to another server within the Exchange Server 2003 organization.

Description: In this activity, you use Exchange System Manager to configure public folder replication for a folder on your system. By default, the content of a public folder is replicated only to the default public store for the tree. You can replicate the folder to additional public stores by completing the following steps.

It is not possible to replicate public folders to additional servers within the organization at this point because each of the servers within the class have been configured as single servers within their own organization. This activity walks through the steps necessary to create replicate folders. After servers have been reconfigured to participate in groups, replication to additional servers can be accomplished.

1. From the Windows desktop, click **Start**, point to **All Programs**, point to **Microsoft Exchange**, and then click **System Manager**.

2. Click the **plus sign (+)** next to Administrative Groups, and click the **plus sign (+)** next to the First Administrative Group. Click the **plus sign (+)** next to the Folders container, and click the **plus sign (+)** next to Public Folders. Right-click **First Public Folder** and click **Properties** from the shortcut menu. The First Public Folder Properties dialog box opens, as shown in Figure 6-14.

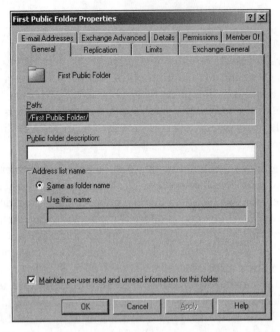

Figure 6-14   First Public Folder Properties dialog box

3. Click the **Replication** tab. The Replicate content to these public stores field shows where replicas of the folders are currently being created.

4. To replicate the folder to other servers in the Exchange organization, click **Add**. Because there are no other servers within the organization at this point, it is not possible to replicate folders to another server. In the warning that appears, click **OK**.

5. The Public folder replication interval determines when changes to public folders are replicated. To customize the schedule, you can click the Customize button, or you can select a preconfigured replication interval from the drop-down list. Leave the selection to Use public store schedule to use the settings configured for the public store.

6. The Replication message priority determines how items placed in folders are replicated. The available priorities are Urgent, Normal, and Not Urgent. Messages in folders with a higher priority are replicated before messages in other folders. Leave this selection set to Normal.

7. Click **OK** to return to Exchange System Manager.

8. Close **Exchange System Manager**.

When designing your Exchange Server 2003 environment, you might need to create additional replicas of system folders to control your network traffic. Table 6-4 describes common system folders that are automatically created on a server when it is installed as the first server in an administrative group.

Table 6-4 Exchange 2003 system folders

Folder Name	Description
EFORMS REGISTRY	Contains all rights in the folder: Create, Read, Modify, Delete all items and files, and Create Subfolders. The owner can also change permission levels that other users are assigned for the folder.
Events Root	Contains scripts for an Exchange Server 5.5 compatible Event Service.
OFFLINE ADDRESS BOOK	Stores offline address books for clients to download.
SCHEDULE+FREE BUSY	Stores schedule information for users. Outlook uses this to determine meeting availability.
Schema-root	Defines properties for objects kept in the public folder store.
StoreEvents	Contains Exchange 2003 event sink code for a specific server.
SYSTEM CONFIGURATION	Contains public folder expiry information.
OWAScratchPad	Is used as a staging area for attachments submitted with posts to public folders by OWA clients. When you click the Attachment button, the post is staged to the OWAScratchPadMDB_GUID folder (where MDB_GUID is the Messaging Database globally unique identifier), where the post remains during composition.

Configuring Replication Priority

You can set the priority for replication messages sent by a public folder. The priority determines the order in which Exchange Server 2003 sends messages. The following list outlines the priorities that can be assigned to a public folder. Messages within that public folder take on the priorities of the public folder. For instance, messages with an urgent priority are delivered first.

- *Not Urgent*—Messages with this priority are delivered last.
- *Normal*—Messages with this priority are sent before nonurgent messages; however, all urgent messages are delivered first.
- *Urgent*—Messages with this priority are sent before messages with a priority of normal or not urgent.

Checking Replication Status

The replication status is the best way to keep track of public folder replication, and you need to periodically check the status of replication on each public folder store. To do this, access the public folder store in Exchange System Manager, and then click the replication status container. In the Details pane, you see the following columns:

- *Name*—The name of the affected public folder store
- *Last Received Time*—The time the last replica was received

- *Number of Replicas*—The number of replicas received
- *Replication Status*—The status of the replication, either completed or failed

You can also check the replication status of public folders by examining the replication for the individual public folder itself. Through this process, you can confirm that an individual folder was replicated and check the average amount of time it took to complete the replication. The following activity outlines the steps for checking the individual replication status of a public folder.

NOTE

In most cases, you need to use the normal priority, which is the default. However, if a folder contains items that need to be replicated quickly throughout the organization, you might want to use the urgent priority setting. Watch out, though; too many folders with urgent priority can degrade performance in the Exchange organization.

ACTIVITY

Activity 6-9: Checking the Replication Status of a Public Folder

Time Required: 5 to 10 minutes

Objective: Walk through the steps to check on the status of replication for public folders that have been configured for replication.

Description: In this activity, you go through the steps of checking the replication status for a public folder. You need to periodically check the status of replication on each public folder store. Note that because servers have not been configured in groups at this point, replication cannot be configured. This activity walks through the steps for checking on the status only. To check on status, complete the following steps.

1. From the Windows desktop, click **Start**, point to **All Programs**, point to **Microsoft Exchange**, and then click **System Manager**.

2. Click the **plus sign (+)** next to Administrative Groups. Click the **plus sign (+)** next to First Administrative Group. Click the **plus sign (+)** next to the Servers container. Click the **plus sign (+)** next to SERVERXX, where XX is the student number assigned. Click the **plus sign (+)** next to First Storage Group, and click the **plus sign (+)** next to Public Folder Store (SERVERXX), where XX is the student number assigned. Click the **Replication Status** container. The status of the public folder replication appears, as shown in Figure 6-15.

3. In the Details pane, you can check on the status of the particular folder you have replicated.

4. After you have reviewed the status of public folders, close **Exchange System Manager**.

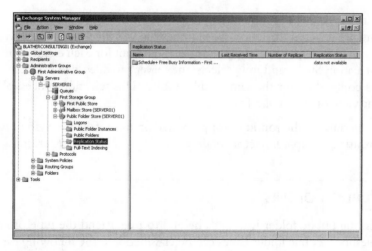

Figure 6-15   Replication status

PUBLIC FOLDER REFERRALS

Public folder referrals enable you to route information requests to specific servers. Public folder referrals to servers within another routing group are configured on routing group connectors between two routing groups. The routing group connector is unidirectional and requires two instances to be configured for bidirectional traffic. You can configure public folder referrals for the routing group going in each direction. Public folder referrals between routing groups are transitive and allow all referrals over the connection when enabled. For example, if Routing Group A allows public folder referrals to Routing Group B, and Routing Group B allows public folder referrals to Routing Group C, this means that Routing Group A allows public folder referrals to Routing Group C, and vice versa.

Each Exchange Server 2003 connector (SMTP, X.400, or routing group connector) has a cost associated with it. You can configure the cost value with a number from 1 to 100. The cost associated with each connector is used to optimize message flow. Exchange Server 2003 routes messages according to lowest cost. If two or more routes are available with the same cost, Exchange Server 2003 distributes the load as equally as possible between them. This cost is also used in calculating the most appropriate route the client will use to access public folders on remote servers (via public folder referrals).

The Information Store discards any route with an infinite cost. An infinite cost indicates that, for an available route to the public folder, one or more connectors have the Do not allow public folder referrals check box selected. In this case, this route is discarded, and is not used to access the public folder. In other words, the Information Store and the routing service do not use routes with an infinite cost. These routes are discarded from the list of available routes during the public folder server selection process.

If multiple servers in the same routing group have a copy of the requested public folder contents, the Information Store returns a list of these servers from which the client can choose. The client then randomly selects one server, and assigns a corresponding number associated with that server. For all future attempts to access this public folder, the client first tries the server initially selected (based on the number that it assigned to this server). Each client selects its own random number, so the number is different for each client. The process in which the Information Store randomly selects one server provides load balancing among the various clients contending for the same public folder. This selection process also gives clients a consistent view of the public folder.

To configure the referrals on the routing group connector, use Exchange System Manager to configure the routing group connector to allow or deny public folder referrals.

TROUBLESHOOTING PUBLIC FOLDERS

When troubleshooting public folder issues, it's helpful to understand the type of issue you are tying to troubleshoot. Public folder issues can be classified into the following categories:

- *Accessibility issues*—These issues relate to accessing the content of public folders. Typically, they relate to configuration issues with IIS or Internet Explorer.

- *Permissions issues*—These issues relate to accessing the content of public folders because of problems with permissions. These can be especially prevalent after a migration.

- *Deleted site and system folder issues*—These issues relate to problems with site and system folders. Typically, folders have been inadvertently deleted.

- *Replication issues*—These issues relate to problems with replicating content to different Exchange servers within the organization.

The following sections delve into each of these categories in more detail.

Accessibility Issues

When managing access to public folders through Exchange System Manager or through the client, you might receive error messages indicating that the operation failed, with an ID number of 80004005. This type of error message is a result of problems with the infrastructure that is used to provide access to public folders. Exchange Server 2003 makes use of HTTP DAV to manage access to public folders. It does this by communicating with the EXAdmin virtual root in IIS, which then performs the commands on the client's behalf.

To help resolve these issues, you need to investigate things such as whether the World Wide Web (WWW) service is running. If the WWW service is not running, you cannot obtain HTTP access to the public folders and, as such, you receive this error. You also need to investigate potential configuration changes to Internet Explorer or the IIS service on the server. If you have made configuration changes, especially security configuration changes, you might need to undo those changes. It is always best to bring the server up in its default state and then ensure that everything is working before making these changes. Before making changes, ensure you document each change you make so that you have clear direction on how to back out, if necessary.

Permissions Issues

Permissions are a problematic area for Exchange Server 2003 if not dealt with carefully. In addition, Exchange Server 2003 modifies the way with which permissions are handled for public folders. In Exchange Server 5.5, permissions were always handled by Exchange itself. In Exchange 2000/2003, security is now handled by Active Directory. The Exchange Web storage system can not only handle requests to modify permissions from Exchange through Exchange System Manager, but it can also handle modifications to permissions through file system calls. This is because Exchange Server 2003 can present the information within a public folder database as a file system to the end user. Herein lies the potential for issues with permissions. The problem is that the permission formats between Windows 2000/2003 and Exchange/Outlook are different.

Because Exchange Server 2003 can present its information as a file system to the end user, it allows permissions to be set using Windows Explorer, in addition to the utilities provided by the application, such as Exchange System Manager or through the Outlook mail client. The reason this causes a problem is that Windows Explorer uses the Windows 2000/2003 access control list (ACL) format, whereas Outlook and Exchange System Manager make use of MAPI ACL formats. When modifying public folder permissions, you should ensure that you are always consistent in how you modify them. Preferably, you should modify all permissions through Exchange System Manager or the Outlook client as opposed to using file system permissioning provided by Windows Explorer. By using Exchange System Manager or Outlook, you then allow the synchronization to Active Directory permissions to occur through IIS. To help resolve issues with folder rights, refer to Knowledge Base Articles Q270905 and Q251606.

Deleted Site and System Folder Issues

Other potential public folder issues might have nothing to do with user-created public folders, but with system folders. For instance, clients might experience issues accessing free/busy information or exhibit problems with downloading the offline address book. If these types of problems arise, you should investigate if there are issues with the system folders. The information in these folders might have become corrupted, or the folder might have been inadvertently deleted. If the public folder store where these folders originate has been lost, or an administrator has deleted one of the folders, you need to take measures to replace these folders.

Replacing system folders means running a utility from Microsoft called Guidgen.exe. This tool creates new globally unique identifiers (GUID) that are then used to rebuild the site folders. For more information, refer to Knowledge Base Article Q822444. Note that when you reset the GUID for the site folders within an administrative group, all previous information within site folders is lost.

Replication Issues

Replication issues typically manifest themselves during the backfilling process. As was discussed earlier in the chapter, backfilling is the process by which out-of-sync public folders resynchronize themselves. This typically occurs when a public folder's server goes offline, and then comes back online after an extended period of time. In this type of situation, you might find that newly created public folders, or old public folders, might not be correctly replicated to servers in different routing groups.

In some cases, these problems might be related to how long the backfill process takes. Under certain circumstances, the backfill process can take hours and, in some cases, days. For these types of scenarios, you can really do nothing more than wait until the backfill process completes. In other cases, the problems can be more directly related to configuration issues in the environment. For instance, because public folder replication is mail-based, you might see issues arise when public folders do not have e-mail addresses associated with them. To help troubleshoot these issues, make use of message tracking to help find out what might be causing these issues. For further information on using message tracking to troubleshoot public folder replication issues, refer to Knowledge Base Article Q260330.

CHAPTER SUMMARY

- You can mail-enable public folders so that you can send messages to the folder using the entries from the GAL instead of having to post them directly.

- Public folders enable you to use a Web browser to gain access to public folders by specifying a URL to the folder.

- Exchange Server 2003 supports multiple public folder trees, also known as hierarchies. Public folder trees enable you to store public folders in more than one hierarchy.

- Public folder referrals enable clients to gain access to any folder in the organization. Exchange Server 2003 enables referrals by default between routing groups.

- Exchange Server 2003 supports both MAPI-based public folder trees and general-purpose public folder trees. There can only be one MAPI public folder, and it is known as the All Public Folders tree. General-purpose public folder trees are SMTP-enabled.

- If you configure multiple public folder trees, you need to configure additional public stores on each server that hosts content from that tree, because each public store contains the contents of one public folder tree. You cannot split a public folder tree across multiple stores.

- Exchange Server 2003 relies on Active Directory in Windows Server 2003 to enforce security on Exchange Server 2003 resources. The operating system manages and enforces permissions that are specific to Exchange Server 2003, such as the ability to create a top-level public folder.

- Child folders inherit parent folder settings at time of creation only. Any changes you make to the parent folder are not automatically inherited by existing child folders. In addition, any changes you make specifically to the child folder are lost if you choose to propagate settings from the parent folder.

❑ All replicas of a public folder are equal. There is no master replica. This is known as a multimaster replication model.

❑ The public Information Store uses change numbers, time stamps, and predecessor change lists to keep track of replication progress and determine whether a public folder is synchronized.

❑ A public folder conflict occurs when a user edits an item located in a public folder on one server, and then, before the changes can be replicated to all instances of the public folder, another user on a different server edits the same item.

6

KEY TERMS

backfilling — The process by which out-of-sync public folders resynchronize. Backfill can recover from the following situations: lost replication message(s), a public folder server going offline, and then coming online after an extended period of time. A public folder server being restored from a backup.

folder edit conflict — A folder edit conflict occurs when two or more public folder contacts change a public folder design at the same time.

Installable File System — An API that allows you to access files stored on disk in formats other than FAT and HPFS, and access files that are stored on a network file server.

message edit conflict — A conflict that occurs when the content and/or properties associated with a message are modified on any server.

multimaster replication — A replication mechanism that does not involve a centralized master copy of the information. When data is modified at each source, the changes are then automatically replicated from that source to all other replicas within the infrastructure.

public folder — A folder that facilitates the exchange of all types of information between groups of people in an organization.

public folder referral — A referral that enables you to route information requests to specific folders. Public folder referrals between routing groups are transitive and allow all referrals over the connection when enabled.

public folder replica — A replica that provides multiple, redundant information points and load balancing for accessing data.

Public Folder Replication Agent (PFRA) — The agent that monitors changes, additions, and deletions. This agent also sends change messages to other Information Stores on which replicated instances are located.

public folder store — A database for storing public folders in Exchange Server 2003.

public folder tree — An object in Active Directory that defines the folder hierarchy.

public root store — The default public folder store for an Exchange Server 2003 organization.

top-level public folder — Referred to as the parent folder. The top-level folder represents the top of a public folder tree. If the new public folder is a top-level folder, the contents of the new folder are on the user's public folder server.

REVIEW QUESTIONS

1. What do administrators and users use to create public folders?

   a. Administrators use Exchange System Manager, whereas users can use a MAPI client such as Outlook.

   b. Administrators use a MAPI client such as Outlook, whereas users can use Exchange System Manager.

   c. Administrators and users use Exchange System Manager.

   d. Administrators and users use a MAPI client such as Outlook.

2. Which of the following are types of rights permissions for public folders in Exchange Server 2003? (Choose all that apply.)

   a. user rights

   b. client rights

   c. directory rights

   d. administrative rights

3. Where is the master replica found in Exchange Server 2003?

   a. The master replica is found on the first Exchange server installed in a domain.

   b. The master replica is stored in the Information Store.

   c. The master replica is stored in the StoreEvents system folder.

   d. There is no master replica. All replicas are equal.

4. What is the process by which out-of-sync public folders resynchronize?

   a. backfill

   b. synchronize

   c. resynchronize

   d. harmonize

5. Exchange Server 2003 controls the replication of public folder directory objects. True or False?

6. Which of the following are valid replication message priorities? (Choose all that apply.)

   a. normal

   b. urgent

   c. not urgent

   d. not normal

7. Which of the following are valid system folders? (Choose all that apply.)

   a. Schedule+Free Busy

   b. EForms Registry

   c. Calendar Forms

   d. StoreEvents

8. Which of the following is not a valid role within Exchange Server 2003? (Choose all that apply.)

  a. Publishing Author

  b. Publishing Editor

  c. Contributing Author

  d. Contributing Editor

9. What is the primary reason for replicating system folders?

  a. so that end users have access to the contents

  b. so that public folder referrals do not need to be turned on

  c. to minimize network traffic

  d. all of the above

10. What is the purpose of public folder referrals?

  a. to provide access to the Global Address List

  b. to provide access to the offline address book

  c. to provide access to permissions for public folders

  d. to provide access to public folders that are not local to the site

11. Where are public folder referrals configured?

  a. on the public folder itself

  b. on the public folder store

  c. on the server

  d. on the routing group connector

12. Which of the following rights enable a user to gain access to messages sent to a public folder?

  a. directory rights

  b. client rights

  c. message rights

  d. none of the above

13. What is the primary purpose of public folders?

  a. to provide centralized access to common content

  b. to provide distributed access to common content

  c. to minimize the use of storage on your system

  d. all of the above

6

14. What type of conflicts can occur during public folder replication? (Choose all that apply.)
    a. folder conflicts
    b. message conflicts
    c. item conflicts
    d. all of the above

15. Why should age limits and deleted item retention be configured on public folders? (Choose all that apply.)
    a. to reduce clutter
    b. to manage storage
    c. to minimize replication traffic
    d. to maximize availability

16. Which of the following ensures that items are recoverable from public folders after they are deleted?
    a. age limits
    b. recovery storage groups
    c. deleted item retention
    d. all of the above

17. Existing child folders receive permissions settings when the permissions are changed on a parent folder? True or False?

18. Exchange Server 2003 controls the replication of directory rights. True or False?

19. Which of the following are replicated to every server? (Choose all that apply.)
    a. public folder content
    b. public folder hierarchy
    c. public folder permissions
    d. all of the above

20. When are confirmation messages used during public folder replication?
    a. when the folder structure has been replicated
    b. when messages have been replicated
    c. when permissions have been replicated
    d. none of the above

21. Which of the following is used to keep track of replication? (Choose all that apply.)
    a. change numbers
    b. index counters
    c. time stamps
    d. predecessor change lists

CASE PROJECTS

Case Project 1-1: Planning Public Folder Replication

Bob Jones, an Arts professor, has written an e-mail message to the head of Network Operations complaining about how slow it is to access public folders. After investigation, you identify that the Arts Department is separated by a slow WAN connection. Write an e-mail response to Bob explaining the likely cause of the problem and what you can do to correct it.

6

Case Project 1-2: Monitoring Public Folder Replication

As the e-mail administrator for your network, you want to proactively monitor your server environment. What can you do to check that your public folder infrastructure is not encountering any issues?

Case Project 1-3: Managing Permissions on Public Folders

As the e-mail architect for your organization, you have been asked by security to clean up permissions on the public folder infrastructure. You have conducted your analysis and identified a consistent set of permissions that you can apply to all your public folders. What can you do to implement this?

Case Project 1-4: Implementing Multiple Public Folder Trees

As the e-mail architect for your organization, you have been asked by the business to implement a public folder solution that will allow them to access content from the server using a Web browser. What is the best approach for meeting their requirements?

7

CONFIGURING AND MANAGING EXCHANGE SERVER

After reading this chapter, you will be able to:

♦ Understand how and why additional administrative groups should be created

♦ Understand how and why additional routing groups should be created

♦ Describe front-end and back-end server configurations

♦ Describe how to manage virtual servers and virtual directories

I n medium-sized to large companies, Exchange Server 2003 is rarely installed on a single server. Rather, more than one server is installed into the organization to support the volume of users that can be hosted by your organization, or they can be configured to act as dedicated servers for processing specific tasks, thereby load-balancing the processing across servers. This chapter examines scenarios in which additional servers will be installed into an Exchange Server 2003 organization.

Prior to installing additional servers into an organization, it is necessary to define how the servers will be organized both from a connectivity perspective and from an administrative perspective. This chapter examines how servers can be organized into groups that enjoy permanent, high-bandwidth connectivity and how these groups can be defined administratively. Not only can Exchange 2003 servers be configured into groups to take advantage of high-bandwidth connectivity, but they can also be configured administratively into separate groups to reflect the different administrative topologies that different organizations might support. This chapter looks at the different administrative models that can be defined and how they can be implemented.

Typically, servers are installed to host additional mailboxes, or public folders. However, they can also be installed to serve more specific tasks, such as providing a dedicated routing server between different groups of servers or acting in a front-end/back-end configuration that will offload specific tasks between servers and, thereby, balance the load across multiple servers providing increased scalability.

No discussion of front-end/back-end server configurations can occur without having an understanding of HTTP (Hypertext Transfer Protocol) virtual servers. HTTP virtual servers hosted by Exchange Server 2003 work behind the scenes to grant access and transfer files to client workstations. As your organization grows, you might find that you need additional HTTP virtual servers to handle the needs of remote users or that you want to offload HTTP services to separate Exchange servers. You can handle both of these tasks by installing Exchange Server 2003 on new servers and then creating additional HTTP virtual servers as necessary. This chapter explores how to do this.

Finally, administering HTTP virtual servers is a bit different from other administrative tasks you perform within Exchange Server 2003, primarily because administering HTTP virtual servers involves using a different tool called the Internet Services Manager. This chapter explores how HTTP virtual servers can be administered.

ADMINISTRATIVE GROUPS

Administrative groups are used to define the administrative topology for your Exchange organization. They are logically defined, meaning that on a conceptual level they can be based on geography, department, division, or function. For example, if your company has five offices in five different states, it is likely that you will have one or more Exchange servers in each location, with an Exchange administrator in each location as well. Depending on how your organization is administered, it might be best, in this scenario, to create an administrative group for each of the five locations so that the local Exchange administrator can administer the local Exchange servers. Another possible arrangement is for one group to manage all of the routing group functions, another to manage all of the public folder functions, and still another to manage all of the recipient policy functions. With administrative groups, members of the larger Exchange 2003 administration team can specialize in one area of administration, even if your Exchange Server 2003 organization is countrywide.

An administrative group makes it easier to assign administrative permissions. After you have set the permissions for the administrative group object, any objects that are created or moved into the object inherit its permission. Hence, it is easier to set permission for an administrative group first and then to create objects inside the group and have them inherit the group's permissions. As always, it's best to set permissions at the highest object level and then have those permissions flow down the object hierarchy.

Objects that can be created in an administrative group include the following:

- Policies
- Routing groups
- Public folder trees
- Servers

Administrative Models

You can use three administrative models to organize your administrative groups:

- Centralized
- Decentralized
- Mixed

In a **centralized administrative model**, one group maintains complete control over all of the Exchange servers. You might have only one group or a few tightly controlled groups for administrative purposes. Your routing group topology does not need to be the same as the administrative topology, which means that you can have multiple routing groups that reflect your physical topology while maintaining centralized administrative control in one administrative group. Figure 7-1 shows a centralized administrative model.

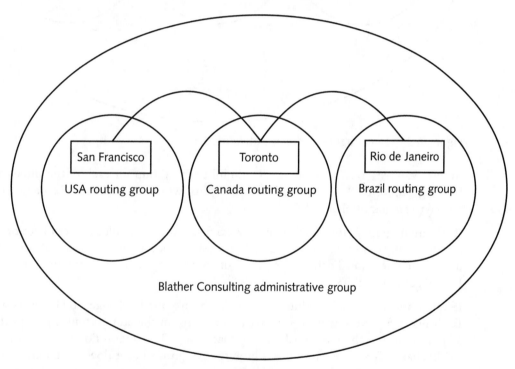

Figure 7-1   Centralized administrative model

In the **decentralized administrative model**, each location has its own team of Exchange administrators and allows them administrative control over any objects placed inside their administrative group. These groups are often based on geographical locations or on the departmental needs of the company. Each of these groups can contain policies, servers, public folder trees, and other objects specific to the group. Figure 7-2 shows a decentralized administrative model.

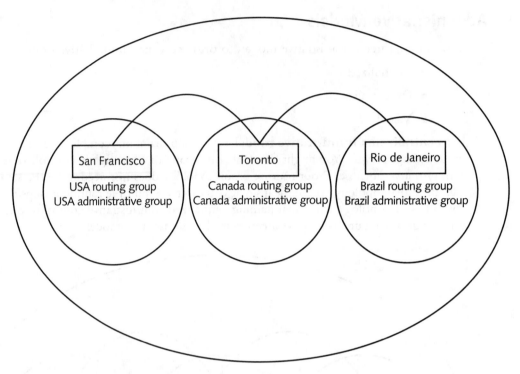

Figure 7-2 Decentralized administrative model

In this example, you would set up an administrative group for each of the three cities and have a group of Exchange administrators, each of whom manages the Exchange servers in her own geographical area.

If you are migrating from Exchange Server 5.5 and you had multiple sites in your Exchange Server 5.5 organization, you are forced into using a decentralized model of administration during the migration. Each Exchange 5.5 site is created as a separate administrative group in Exchange Server 2003.

If you want to centralize administration for both your Exchange 2003 servers and your Exchange 5.5 servers, you need to set permissions on the administrative groups that limit administration to the individuals within that group. This action doesn't really incorporate the Exchange 5.5 servers into one administrative group, but it does limit administration to one group of administrators.

The **mixed administrative model** is best for restricting certain administrative functions to certain people while not creating specializations for every administrative function. In this model, you create administrative groups by function rather than by departmental boundaries. For instance, you might create an administrative group whose only child object is policies. In this scenario, you can restrict to a handful of people the ability to create new policies or alter existing policies for your Exchange Server 2003 organization. However, all other administrative functions remain under the default First Administrative Group and are not placed in their own administrative group.

You can also use this model to combine specialized administrative functions and geographical considerations into one administrative model. For instance, you might create an administrative group to manage the routing groups, a second group to manage policies, a third group for the New York division, a fourth group for the California division, and a fifth group to manage all of the public folder trees. Figure 7-3 provides an example of a mixed administrative model.

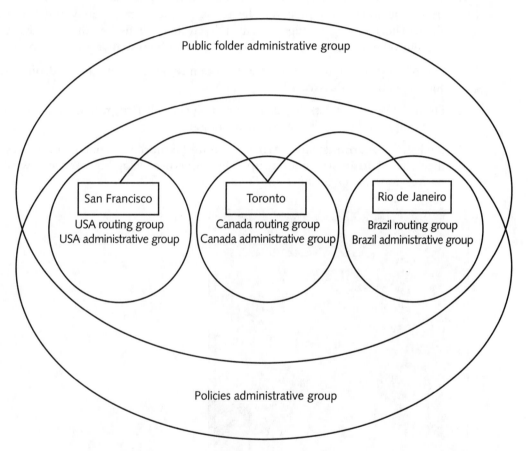

Figure 7-3   Mixed administrative model

In this model, day–to–day administration is decentralized to the geographic regions. However, public folder trees, policies, and routing group administration are centrally managed.

ACTIVITY

Activity 7-1: Creating an Administrative Group

Time Required: 10 to 20 minutes

Objective: Create an additional administrative group.

Description: In this activity, you create an additional administrative group for your organization. By default when you install your first Exchange 2003 server, a default administrative group called First Administrative Group is created.

When the first server is installed into an administrative group, the servers container is created as part of the installation process. The server is then subsequently installed into the container. The Routing Groups container is created when the administrative group is created. The other containers can be created after the administrative group has been created.

1. Log on to your Windows Server 2003 system using the user name **Administrator** and the password **Password!**.

2. From the Windows desktop, click **Start**, point to **All Programs**, point to **Microsoft Exchange**, and then click **System Manager**.

3. Right-click **Administrative Groups**. From the shortcut menu, point to **New**, and then click **Administrative Group**. The Properties dialog box for the new administrative group opens, as shown in Figure 7-4.

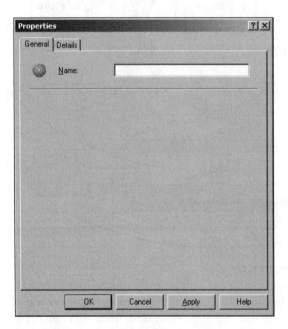

Figure 7-4   New Administrative Group Properties dialog box

4. In the Name text box, type the name of your administrative group. For this activity, use **Second Administrative Group**. Click **OK** to return to Exchange System Manager.

5. Close **Exchange System Manager**.

Prior to installing additional servers into an organization, you should have your administrative topology defined because you need to define your administrative groups before installing an Exchange Server 2003 server. Moving servers between administrative groups after the server has been installed is not possible. Only during installation do you get the opportunity to define into which administrative group you want to install the server.

Managing Administrative Groups

How you manage administrative groups depends on the operations mode in use. Exchange Server 2003 has the following two modes of operation:

- *Mixed mode*—When operating in mixed mode, Exchange Server 2003 can support pre-Exchange 2000 Server installations.

- *Native mode*—When operating in native mode, Exchange Server 2003 supports only Exchange 2000 Server and Exchange Server 2003 installations.

Mixed Mode

By default, when you install Exchange Server 2003, the operations mode is set to mixed. The mixed mode configuration provides for interoperability with Microsoft Exchange Server 5.5, but limits the capabilities of Exchange Server 2003. These limitations directly affect the way administrative groups are used and effectively force Exchange Server 2003 to handle administrative groups in the same way that Exchange Server 5.5 handles sites.

When running in mixed mode operations, Exchange Server 2003 has the following limitations:

- When Exchange Server 2003 coexists with Exchange Server 5.5, Exchange Server 2003 uses the site concept to define both administrative groups and routing groups. This limitation means that each administrative group has only one functional routing group even if you create additional routing groups.

- You can't move mailboxes from a server in one administrative group to a server in another administrative group. This limitation reduces your flexibility in managing mailboxes.

Additional limitations apply if Exchange Server 2003 is installed in an Exchange Server 5.5 site. These additional limitations are as follows:

- Some System Manager commands don't apply to Exchange Server 5.5. Because of this, you can't use these commands to manipulate an Exchange Server 5.5 server.

- Exchange Server 5.5 directory service objects are replicated into Active Directory with read-only properties. This means you can't edit these properties through Active Directory. You need to use the Microsoft Exchange Server 5.5 Administrator tool for this, which can be installed as part of Exchange Server 2003.

- InetOrgPerson and query-based distribution groups are available only in Microsoft Windows Server 2003 domains and when Exchange is running in native mode. Further, to use query-based distribution groups, all servers must be using at least Exchange 2000 Server with Service Pack 3.

Native Mode

When operating in native mode, Exchange Server 2003 isn't subject to these limitations. You can enable routing group support and create additional routing groups as necessary. It also means that Exchange Server 2003 cannot work with versions of Exchange Server 5.5 or earlier.

ROUTING GROUPS

As you have seen, an administrative group is a collection of server objects that are grouped together to allow administrative activities to be performed on those objects as a unit. By contrast, a **routing group** is a collection of servers that enjoy permanent, high-bandwidth connectivity. The links between routing groups are assumed to be either slow or unreliable. Connectors are used to connect routing groups over these slow WAN links. Although administrative groups are logical in nature, routing groups are determined by the physical topology of your network.

Routing groups allow you to specify the routes that messages will take to get from the sender to the recipient within your Exchange Server 2003 organization. By implementing costs on the connectors, you can channel the physical path you want messaging to take within your organization.

NOTE   After a server is connected to a particular routing group, you can't move it to another routing group without reinstalling Exchange Server. Because of this, you should plan the messaging topology for your organization very carefully.

Message transfer and communication within routing groups is handled directly with a target server, greatly reducing administration on your part. Message transfer, and communication among routing groups, is handled by a bridgehead server.

A **bridgehead server** is the point of entry and exit for all message traffic among routing groups. Bridgehead servers also handle the link state information, which is used to determine optimal routing paths. You must designate a bridgehead server in each routing group. To communicate, bridgehead servers use a **routing group connector**, which provides the direct connection among routing groups. You use one routing group connector to connect two routing groups.

A general rule of thumb is that you want to keep the number of routing groups within your organization to a minimum. If you can get away with having just one routing group, you should do so. However, there are also many good reasons to use multiple routing groups. If your company is spread over two or more geographic regions, you might want to implement a routing group for each region. The primary reason for doing so is to help manage network bandwidth consumption. A single routing group is easy to set up because much of the communication between the servers in a routing group occurs automatically. Unfortunately, this automatic communication consumes a considerable amount of bandwidth, which grows with the size of the routing group. If your network contains WAN links, which typically have a smaller amount of bandwidth available, it is best to divide the organization so that an Exchange routing group does not span a WAN link.

When determining whether to set up a routing group, you should take the following into consideration:

- *Persistent connectivity*—Because of the constant and automatic communication between Exchange servers within a routing group, these servers must be able to communicate using SMTP over permanent connections or connections that are always online and available. In addition, all servers within a routing group must be able to contact the routing group master at all times. If you have network segments that are connected by a switched virtual circuit or a dial-up connection, you must implement separate routing groups for those segments.

- *Common Active Directory forest*—All servers within a routing group must belong to the same Active Directory forest.

- *Relatively high bandwidth*—Servers in a routing group require enough bandwidth on the connections between them to support whatever traffic they generate. Microsoft recommends that the connection between servers support at least 128 Kbps. Keep in mind that if a network link is heavily used, 128 Kbps will not be sufficient for Exchange Server traffic. The network link should have a fair amount of bandwidth available for new traffic generated by Exchange Server, if an Exchange routing group will span that link.

Routing groups in Exchange Server 2003, like sites in Exchange Server 5.5, are based on available bandwidth. However, Exchange Server 2003 uses SMTP, which is more tolerant of lower bandwidths and higher latency. This capability means that you can group servers into routing groups that you could not have grouped into sites in Exchange Server 5.5. Because of this, you might want to divide Exchange servers into multiple routing groups for a number of reasons:

- The minimum requirements outlined previously are not met.

- The messaging path between servers must be altered from a single hop to multiple hops.

- The messages must be queued and sent according to a schedule.

- Bandwidth between servers is less than 16 Kbps, which means that the X.400 connector is a better choice.

- You want to route client connections to specific public folder replicas because public folder connections are based on routing groups.

The most important factor to consider when planning your routing group boundaries is the stability of the network connection, not the overall bandwidth of the connection. If a connection is prone to failure or is often so saturated that the pragmatic effect is a loss of connectivity, you should place the servers that the connection serves in separate routing groups.

Be certain to have a global catalog server in each routing group and preferably in each Windows 2000/2003 site. This arrangement decreases look-up traffic across your slower WAN links and makes the directory information for client lookups more available to your clients.

After you have identified whether you need to create a separate routing group within your organization, you can then make use of Exchange System Manager to create a separate routing group.

ACTIVITY

Activity 7-2: Creating a Routing Group

Time Required: 10 to 20 minutes

Objective: Create an additional routing group using Exchange System Manager.

Description: In this activity, you create an additional routing group within your organization. Routing groups help you to control mail flow and public folder referrals. Within a routing group, all servers communicate and transfer messages directly to one another.

1. From the Windows desktop, click **Start**, point to **All Programs**, point to **Microsoft Exchange**, and then click **System Manager**.

2. Click the **plus sign (+)** next to Administrative Groups to expand it.

3. Right-click the **Second Administrative Group**, point to **New**, and then click **Routing Groups Container**. This creates a new routing groups container.

4. Click the **plus sign (+)** next to Second Administrative Group, and then right-click the **Routing Groups** container. From the shortcut menu, point to **New**, and then click **Routing Group**. The Properties dialog box for a New Routing Group opens, as shown in Figure 7-5.

5. In the Name text box, type **Second Routing Group** for the name of your new routing group. Click **OK** to return to Exchange System Manager.

6. Close **Exchange System Manager**.

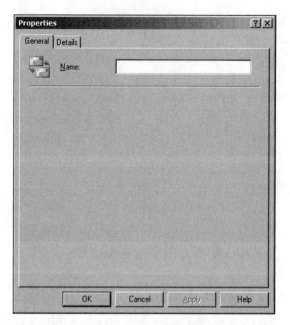

Figure 7-5   Routing Group Properties dialog box

After you have configured your administrative groups and routing groups, the installation process for new servers into the organization changes. The following activity outlines the steps for installing a server into a separate administrative and routing group.

ACTIVITY

Activity 7-3: Installing a Server into a New Administrative Group and Routing Group

Time Required: 90 to 120 minutes

Objective: Install an Exchange Server 2003 server into a second administrative and second routing group.

Description: With administrative groups already preconfigured, you are prompted during the installation of any new servers as to which administrative group and routing group you want to install the server into. This activity walks you through the steps of installing a new Exchange server into the administrative and routing groups you configured in previous activities.

This activity is rather involved and requires that you work with another student in your class as partners. Your group will consist of two servers: your machine and your partner's machine. Your partner's machine will act as the second server in your BLATHERCON-SULTINGXX organization, where XX is the student number assigned to the first server. You will keep this setup for the remainder of the book. To complete this activity, perform the following seven steps on the second server, unless otherwise noted.

NOTE

Some steps need to be performed on the first server, so be certain to pay close attention to which of the two servers is referenced for any steps that you perform.

1. Uninstall Exchange Server 2003

2. Remove Certificate Services

3. Uninstall Active Directory

4. Undo IIS changes

5. Reinstall Active Directory

6. Configure DNS

7. Reinstall Exchange Server 2003

The following sections provide the details of each step to reconfigure the second server.

ACTIVITY

Step 1: Uninstall Exchange Server 2003

1. Before uninstalling Exchange Server 2003 on the second server, you have to delete all mailboxes on the server. This is done first. If necessary, log on to the second Windows Server 2003 system using the user name **Administrator** and the password **Password!**.

2. Click **Start**, point to **All Programs**, point to **Microsoft Exchange**, and then click **Active Directory Users and Computers**. The Active Directory Users and Computers window opens.

3. Click the **plus sign (+)** next to secureYY.local to expand it, where YY is the assigned student number. Click the **Users** container to view its contents.

4. In the right pane, right-click **Administrator**, and then click **Exchange Tasks**. The Exchange Task Wizard opens.

5. At the Available Tasks screen, click **Delete Mailbox** in the Select a task to perform list box, and then click **Next**. Click **Next** again to confirm deletion, and then click **Finish** when the mailbox is successfully deleted.

6. Repeat Steps 4 and 5 for each mail-enabled user. Close **Active Directory Users and Computers** when finished.

7. Click **Start**, point to **Control Panel**, and then click **Add or Remove Programs**. The Add or Remove Programs window opens.

8. To remove Microsoft Exchange Server 2003, click **Microsoft Exchange** in the Currently installed programs list box. Click the **Change/Remove** button. This starts the Microsoft Exchange Installation Wizard.

9. On the Welcome to the Microsoft Exchange Installation Wizard screen, click the **Next** button. When prompted for the action to take, select **Remove** in the Action column, as shown in Figure 7-6. Note the installation path in the Install Path text box, and then click **Next** to continue.

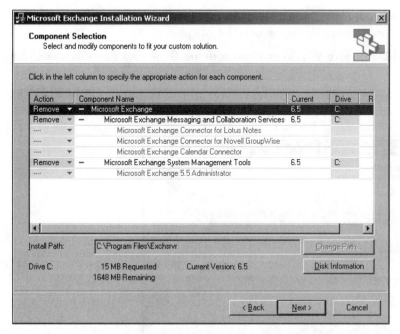

Figure 7-6   Component Selection screen when uninstalling Exchange Server 2003

10. Click **Next** on the Installation Summary screen to start the removal process. If you receive a warning about Web Store Platform–based applications becoming inoperable, click **OK** to continue.

11. During the uninstall, you are prompted with a warning dialog box indicating that the organization will be removed from Windows Active Directory. Click **OK** to continue.

12. If prompted, insert your Microsoft Exchange Server 2003 CD, and click **OK**.

13. When you are finished, click **Finish** on the Completing the Microsoft Exchange Wizard screen. If prompted to restart the computer, click **Yes**, and then after the computer restarts, log back on to the second server using the user name **Administrator** and the password **Password!**.

14. Use Windows Explorer to delete the folder, C:\Program Files\Exchsrvr, which is the installation location noted in Step 9. If prompted to delete shared files, click **Yes**.

15. Close all open windows.

Step 2: Remove Certificate Services

After Exchange Server 2003 has been uninstalled, you then need to remove Certificate Services on the second server. In preparation for future activities and chapters, you also need to remove Certificate Services from the first server as follows:

1. Click **Start**, point to **Control Panel**, and then click **Add or Remove Programs**. The Add or Remove Programs window opens.

2. Click **Add/Remove Windows Components**. This starts the Windows Components Wizard.

3. Uncheck the **Certificate Services** check box, as shown in Figure 7-7. Click **Next**. The wizard then proceeds with removing Certificate Services.

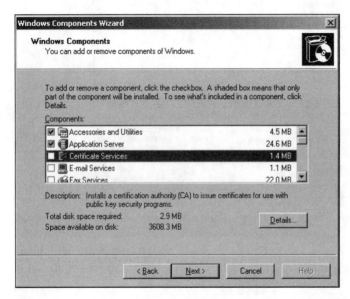

Figure 7-7   Windows Components screen when uninstalling Certificate Services

4. On the Completing the Windows Components Wizard screen, click **Finish**.

5. Close **Add or Remove Programs**.

6. Repeat Steps 1 to 5 on the second server.

Step 3: Uninstall Active Directory

To uninstall Active Directory from the machine that will act as the second server in your organization, run the DCPROMO command.

1. Click **Start** and then click **Run**. The Run dialog box opens. Type **DCPROMO** in the Open text box, and then click **OK**. This starts the Active Directory Installation Wizard.

2. Click **Next** at the Welcome to the Active Directory Installation Wizard screen to continue.

3. You are prompted with an informational message indicating that this domain controller is a global catalog server. Click **OK** to continue.

4. At the Remove Active Directory screen, check the **This server is the last domain controller in the domain** check box, and then click **Next**.

5. At the Application Directory Partitions screen, you are presented with the list of application directory partitions that this server maintains. Click **Next** to continue.

6. At the Confirm Deletion screen, click the **Delete all application directory partitions on this domain controller** check box, and then click **Next**.

7. At the Administrator Password screen, type **Password!** in the New Administrator Password and Confirm password text boxes, and then click **Next** to continue.

8. At the Summary screen, click **Next** to continue. This starts the process to remove Active Directory from your server.

9. When Active Directory is removed, click **Finish** on the Completing the Active Directory Installation Wizard screen.

10. You are prompted to restart the server. Click **Restart Now** to restart the computer.

11. After the computer has restarted, log back on to the second server using the user name **Administrator** and the password **Password!**.

12. If the Manage Your Server window opens, check the **Don't display this page at logon** check box, and then close the window.

ACTIVITY

Step 4: Undo IIS Changes

After you have completed removing Active Directory, the second server will be configured as a stand-alone server. In preparation for the activities in this chapter, you need to undo the IIS changes on both of the servers within your group.

1. Click **Start**, point to **Administrative Tools**, and then click **Internet Information Services (IIS) Manager**.

2. Click the **plus sign (+)** next to SERVERXX, where XX is the student number assigned. Click the **plus sign (+)** next to Web Sites.

3. Right-click the **Default Web Site**, and then click **Properties** on the shortcut menu. The Default Web Site Properties dialog box opens.

4. Click the **Directory Security** tab.

5. In the Secure communications section, click the **Edit** button. The Secure Communications dialog box opens. Uncheck the **Require secure channel (SSL)** check box. Click **OK** to return to the Default Web Site Properties dialog box.

6. Click **OK** to return to Exchange System Manager. If the Inheritance Overrides window opens, click **Cancel** until you return to the Exchange System Manager.

7. Close **Exchange System Manager**.

8. Repeat Steps 1 to 7 on the second server.

ACTIVITY

Step 5: Reinstall Active Directory

At this point, you are ready to add the second server as another domain in your forest. The name of the new domain will be the same as the name that was used for the stand-alone domain on the second server. You should not install it as a child domain, but instead as a separate domain.

To reinstall Active Directory on the second server, complete the following steps (on the second server):

1. Click **Start** and then click **Run**. The Run dialog box opens. Type **DCPROMO** in the Open text box, and then click **OK**. This starts the Active Directory Installation Wizard.

2. At the Welcome to the Active Directory Installation Wizard screen, click **Next** to continue.

3. At the Operating System Compatibility screen, click **Next** to continue.

4. For the Domain Controller Type, click the **Domain controller for a new domain** option button, if necessary, and then click **Next**.

5. When prompted for the type of domain to create, click **Domain tree in an existing forest**, as shown in Figure 7-8. Click **Next** to continue.

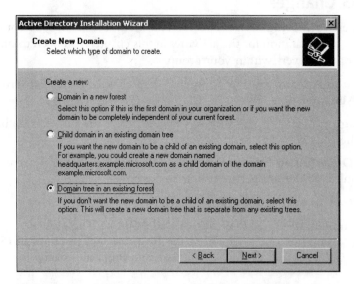

Figure 7-8 Active Directory Installation Wizard

6. At the **Network Credentials** screen, type **Administrator** in the User name text box, **Password!** in the Password text box, and **SECUREXX**, where XX is the student number assigned to the first server, in the Domain text box, and then click **Next** to continue.

NOTE   If you receive an error stating that the domain controller could not be contacted, click **OK** to close the error message, click **Cancel** in the Active Directory Installation Wizard, and then click **Yes** to confirm. Click **Start**, point to **Control Panel**, point to **Network Connections**, right-click **Classroom**, and then click **Properties**. In the list box, click **Internet Protocol (TCP/IP)**, and then click the **Properties** button. In the Preferred DNS Server field, type **192.168.0.XX**, where XX is the student number assigned to the first server, click **OK**, and then click **Close**. Repeat Steps 1 to 6.

7. At the New Domain Tree screen, in the Full DNS name for new domain text box, type **SECUREYY.LOCAL**, where YY is the student number assigned to the second server, and then click **Next**.

8. When prompted for the NetBIOS name, use the name that is provided (SECUREYY, where YY is the student number assigned to the second server), and click **Next** to continue.

9. At the Database and Log Folders screen, accept the defaults, and then click **Next** to continue.

10. At the Shared System Volume screen, accept the default, and then click **Next** to continue.

11. When prompted to install DNS, click **Install and configure the DNS server on this computer, and set this computer to use this DNS server as its preferred DNS server**, if necessary, and then click **Next** to continue.

12. At the Permissions screen, click **Permissions compatible only with Windows 2000 or Windows Server 2003 operating systems**, if necessary, and then click **Next** to continue.

13. Type **Password!** in the Restore Mode Password text box and the Confirm password text box, and then click **Next**.

14. Click **Next** on the Summary screen to continue. This installs Active Directory on the second server, installing the server as a domain controller for a new domain within your group's forest.

15. When the Active Directory installation is complete, click **Finish** on the Completing the Active Directory Installation Wizard screen.

16. You are prompted to restart the server. Click **Restart Now** to restart the computer.

17. After the computer has restarted, log back on to the second server using the user name **Administrator** and the password **Password!**.

7

Step 6: Configure DNS

Before you reinstall Exchange Server 2003 on the second server, you need to configure DNS on each of the servers within the forest for Exchange Server 2003 to resolve names properly. Because you configured each server as a domain controller within its own domain and the domains were not child domains of each other, you need to configure each to replicate their zone information to the other. This allows each domain to resolve the names contained in the other domain correctly. You do this by configuring a secondary zone on each server.

Before you configure a secondary zone to replicate information, you must configure the current zone on each server to allow zone transfers to other servers. To do this, complete the following steps on the second server:

1. Start the DNS Management console by clicking **Start**, pointing to **Administrative Tools**, and then clicking **DNS**.

2. If necessary, click the **plus sign (+)** next to SERVERYY, where YY is the student number assigned.

3. Click the **plus sign (+)** next to Forward Lookup Zones, and click the zone for the current domain, **secureYY.local**, where YY is the student number assigned. Right-click the zone. Click **Properties** on the shortcut menu.

4. Click the **Zone Transfers** tab, and ensure that the **Allow zone transfers** check box is checked. Click to select the **Only to servers listed on the Name Servers tab** option button, if necessary.

5. Click the **Name Servers** tab, and then click the **Add** button. The New Resource Record dialog box opens.

6. Type **SERVERXX.SECUREXX.LOCAL** in the Server fully qualified domain name (FQDN) field, where XX is the student number assigned to the other server. Click **Resolve** and then click **OK**.

If the FQDN will not resolve, enter the IP address of the other server in the IP address field, and then click **Add**.

7. After you are finished, click **OK** to return to the DNS Management console. Leave the DNS Management console open.

8. Repeat Steps 1 to 7 on the first server. To replicate the zone information of the other domain to the current domain, configure secondary zones on each server to replicate zone information from the other domain. To do this, complete the following steps on the second server:

9. Within the DNS Administration console, right-click **Forward Lookup Zones**, and click **New Zone** on the shortcut menu. This starts the New Zone Wizard.

10. At the Welcome to the New Zone Wizard screen, click **Next** to continue.

11. On the Zone Type screen, click **Secondary zone**, as shown in Figure 7-9. Click **Next** to continue.

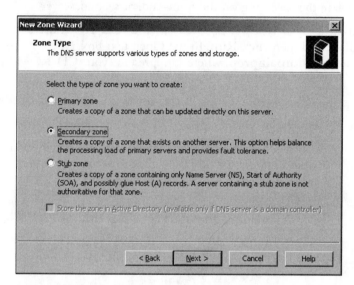

Figure 7-9 New Zone Wizard

12. When prompted for the name of the zone, in the Zone name text box, type **SECUREXX.LOCAL**, where XX is the student number assigned to the other server. Click **Next** to continue.

13. You are then prompted for the IP address of the Master DNS Server for the zone information you want to replicate. Enter the IP address of the other server in the IP address field, click **Add**, and then click **Next**.

14. At the Completing the New Zone Wizard screen, click **Finish**.

15. Close the **DNS Management** console.

16. Repeat Steps 9 to 15 on the first server.

ACTIVITY

Step 7: Reinstall Exchange Server 2003

Finally, it's time to reinstall Exchange Server 2003 as a new server within your group's existing Exchange Server 2003 organization. This new server, the second server in your group, will be installed into the administrative and routing groups that were created in previous activities and will act as the front-end server for the remainder of the activities in this book. The server that already exists within your organization, the first server, will act as the back-end server for the remainder of the book.

Before reinstalling Exchange Server 2003, it is necessary to first run DomainPrep on the newly created domain. (Note that it is not necessary to run ForestPrep again because the new server is being installed into an existing forest.) You then need to delegate Exchange

Full Administrator permissions to the administrator of the newly created domain to allow that account to install Exchange Server 2003 into the existing organization. To do these preliminary tasks, complete the following on the front-end, or second, server.

1. Insert your Microsoft Exchange Server 2003 CD in your CD-ROM drive if necessary. Click **Start** and then click **Run**. In the Open text box, type **D:\setup\i386\setup /domainprep**, where D represents your CD-ROM drive letter. Click **OK**.

2. At the Welcome to the Microsoft Exchange Installation Wizard screen, click **Next**.

3. At the License Agreement screen, click **I agree**, and then click **Next**.

4. At the Component Selection screen, ensure that **DomainPrep** is specified in the Action column, as shown in Figure 7-10, and then click **Next** to continue.

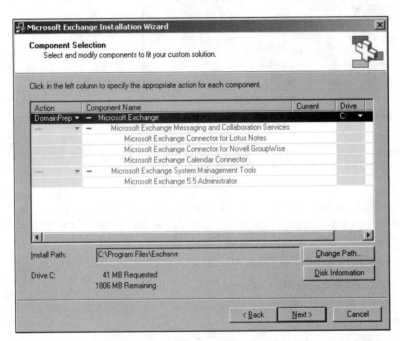

Figure 7-10   Microsoft Exchange Installation Wizard Component Selection screen

5. You are prompted with a warning dialog box indicating that the domain has been identified as an insecure domain for mail-enabled groups with hidden DL membership. Click **OK** to continue.

6. When complete, click **Finish**.

7. Switch to the back-end, or first, server, and start Exchange System Manager by clicking **Start**, pointing to **All Programs**, pointing to **Microsoft Exchange**, and then clicking **System Manager**.

8. Right-click **BLATHERCONSULTINGXX (Exchange)**, where XX is the student number assigned to the back-end, or first, server. On the shortcut menu, click **Delegate control**. This starts the Exchange Administration Delegation Wizard.

9. At the Welcome to the Exchange Administration Delegation Wizard screen, click **Next** to continue.

10. At the Users or Groups page, click the **Add** button to open the Delegate Control dialog box.

11. Click the **Browse** button to open the Select Users, Computers, or Groups dialog box. In the Enter the object name to select text box, type **administrator**, and ensure that the From this location text field is set to **Entire Directory**. Click the **Check Names** button to resolve the name.

12. The Multiple Names Found dialog box opens, displaying all matches for "administrator." From the list that is presented, select the **Administrator** for the domain that currently does not have Exchange Server 2003 installed, which is the front-end, or second, server, as shown in Figure 7-11. Click **OK**.

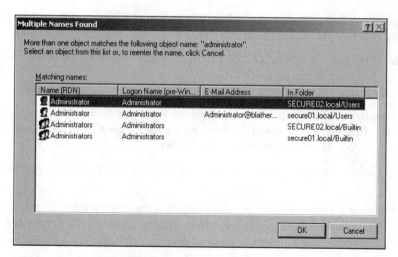

Figure 7-11   Administrator user for back-end server selected

13. Click **OK** on the Select Users, Computers, or Groups dialog box to return to the Delegate Control dialog box.

14. Within the Role drop-down list, click **Exchange Full Administrator** and click **OK** to return to the Exchange Administration Delegation Wizard. The Administrator on the new domain now has Exchange Full Administrator permissions on the Exchange organization. Click **Next** to continue.

15. At the Exchange Administration Delegation Wizard summary screen, click **Finish** to complete the delegation.

16. You are prompted with a warning dialog box indicating that, to administer an Exchange server, the delegated user or group must be a member of the local machine administrator group. Click **OK** to continue.

17. Close **Exchange System Manager**. After the domain has been prepped and permissions have been modified to allow the Administrator of the new domain to install the server, Exchange Server 2003 can be installed on the new domain controller. To do this, complete the following steps on the front-end, or second, server:

18. Click **Start** and then click **Run**. In the Open text box, type **D:\setup\i386\setup**, where D represents your CD-ROM drive letter. Click **OK**.

19. At the Welcome to the Microsoft Exchange Installation Wizard screen, click **Next**.

20. At the License Agreement screen, click **I agree**, and then click **Next**.

21. At the Component Selection screen, ensure that the Action column next to both **Microsoft Exchange Messaging and Collaboration Services** and **Microsoft Exchange System Management Tools** is set to **Install**, and then click **Next** to continue.

22. At the Licensing Agreement screen, click **I agree that I have read and will be bound by the license agreements for this product**, and then click **Next**.

23. When prompted for the administrative group in which you want to create the server, click **Second Administrative Group** from the Admin Group Name drop-down list, and then click **Next**.

24. When prompted to specify the routing group in which to create the server, click **Second Administrative Group/Second Routing Group** from the Routing Group Name drop-down list, and then click **Next**.

25. At the Installation Summary screen, review the selected components, and then click **Next**.

26. The Component Progress Screen provides details about the progress of the Exchange Server 2003 installation process. During the installation, you might be prompted with dialog boxes indicating that you will be replacing files that already exist. Click **Yes** to continue.

27. After you are finished, click **Finish** on the Completing the Microsoft Exchange Wizard screen. If prompted to restart the computer, click **Yes**, and then after the computer restarts, log back on to the front-end, or second, server using the user name **Administrator** and the password **Password!**.

FRONT-END/BACK-END CONFIGURATIONS

Microsoft Exchange Server 2003 supports the deployment of Exchange in a manner that distributes server tasks among front-end and back-end servers. A front-end server accepts requests from clients and proxies them to the appropriate back-end server for processing.

A front-end/back-end server topology is recommended for multiple server organizations that use Microsoft Outlook Web Access, POP, IMAP, or Outlook 2003 clients that will make use of RPC over HTTP. A **front-end server** is a specially configured server running Exchange Server 2003. A **back-end server** is a server with a standard configuration running Exchange Server 2003. There is no configuration option to designate a server as a back-end server. After a front-end server has been configured, it makes use of LDAP to query Active Directory to determine which back-end server holds the requested resource.

Advantages of Front-End/Back-End Configuration

Using a front-end/back-end server deployment has the following advantages:

- *Single namespace*—The primary advantage of a front-end/back-end server configuration is the ability to expose a single, consistent namespace for all the servers within your organization. Without a front-end server, the user must know the name of the server that hosts their mailbox when accessing it using a Web, POP, or IMAP interface.

- *Ability to load-balance across servers*—Using Web, POP, IMAP, or RPC over HTTP to access mailboxes introduces security concerns because the traffic is communicated in clear text. To resolve this issue, SSL encryption can be used to encrypt the traffic between the client and server. However, encrypting and decrypting message traffic uses processor time. When SSL encryption is in use, front-end and back-end server architecture provides an advantage because the front-end servers can handle all encryption and decryption processing, offloading it from the back-end server infrastructure.

- *Ability to use firewalls to protect the back-end infrastructure*—You can position the front-end server as a single point of access to your Exchange Server 2003 organization. By placing the front-end server behind a firewall and configuring it as the single point of access, it provides an additional layer of security for the organization. This prevents hackers from gaining insight into the configuration of your back-end infrastructure. By configuring front-end servers, you can also have them authenticate requests for access to mailbox or public folder information before the request is passed on to the back-end server. This protects the back-end servers from denial of service attacks.

Front-End/Back-End Functionality

The general functionality of a front-end/back-end configuration is for the front-end server to proxy requests to the back-end server on behalf of client computers. Typically, most scenarios that involve a front-end/back-end server configuration fall into one of two categories, those that involve the use of a firewall and those that do not involve the use of a firewall.

Scenarios that involve a firewall require complex configuration because of the way with which Exchange Server 2003 communicates with Active Directory. Exchange Server 2003 makes use of a component called DSAccess that accesses and stores directory information in a local cache to improve performance. DSAccess is used to detect the directory servers it should contact, based on criteria such as site information and availability of servers. The directory server, in turn, is used to query for information regarding the particular server that contains a user's mailbox, the SMTP addresses that exist for a user object, the servers that contain public folder stores, and so on.

To communicate with the directory, DSAccess makes use of LDAP and RPCs. The use of RPCs for communication with a directory server can cause issues for people who maintain the security of your network. This is because RPC communication typically requires a large number of ports to be opened on your firewall, which can introduce security issues. As such, special consideration must be taken to configure your front-end/back-end server topology when firewalls are introduced. This chapter does not consider how to configure Exchange Server 2003 front-end/back-end server topologies that include firewalls. For further information, it is recommended that you refer to the white paper "Exchange Server 2003 and Exchange 2000 Server Front-end and Back-end Topology" at *www.microsoft.com/technet/prodtechnol/exchange/2003/library/febetop.mspx*.

Scenarios that do not involve a firewall are typically considered when an organization wants to maintain a single namespace for all their e-mail servers or to provide a highly scalable Outlook Web Access, POP, or IMAP infrastructure. This type of deployment results in a standard front-end/back-end server deployment and is much easier to implement than scenarios that involve a firewall. How this works depends on how the front-end/back-end server topology is being accessed.

When accessing the front-end/back-end server topology using IMAP or POP access, the client sends the front-end server a log-on request that contains the name of the mailbox to be accessed. The front-end server then determines which back-end server contains the user's mailbox. The front-end server then proxies the log-on request to the appropriate back-end server where they are authenticated. The back-end server then sends the results of the log-on operation back to the front-end server, which in turn presents the results of the authentication back to the user. This type of proxy communication then continues for the remainder of the time that the client has a session established with the front-end/back-end topology.

Activity 7-4: Setting Up a Front-End Server Configuration for POP and OWA Access

ACTIVITY

Time Required: 20 to 30 minutes

Objective: Configure a front-end server to act as a POP server for the Exchange Server 2003 organization.

Description: In this activity, you configure the newly installed server that was created in the previous activity as a front-end server for POP access to the organization. This server will accept POP connections and proxy the requests to the back-end server on behalf of the client to retrieve information from the mailbox. When you configure a front-end/back-end configuration like this, mailboxes are hidden from the users. Client computers connect to one host name shared by the front-end servers. As a result, moving users between servers is transparent to the users and requires no reconfiguration of client computers. Before you configure the server as a front-end server, you need to rehome the Recipient Update Service for this server, as Exchange Server 2003 does not allow you to configure a server as a front-end server if it is used as a Recipient Update Service server.

NOTE You will only be able to retrieve messages as part of this activity. Because the new server was installed in a separate administrative group and routing group from the back-end server, Exchange Server 2003 does not know how to route messages that are received through SMTP to the back-end server mailbox. After a routing group connector is in place, messages route properly. You will configure a routing group connector in Chapter 8, "Managing Routing and Internet Connectivity."

1. From the Windows desktop of the front-end, or second, server, click **Start**, point to **All Programs**, point to **Microsoft Exchange**, and then click **System Manager**.

2. Click the **plus sign (+)** next to the Recipients container, and click the **Recipient Update Services** folder. In the right pane, right-click the **Recipient Update Service (SECUREYY)**, where YY is the student number assigned to the server that will be configured as the front-end server. On the shortcut menu, click **Properties**. This opens the Recipient Update Service (SECUREYY) Properties dialog box for the Recipient Update Service for that domain.

3. On the General tab, click the **Browse** button next to the Exchange server field. The **Select Exchange Server** dialog box opens. Within the Enter the object name to select text box, type **SERVERXX**, where XX is the student number assigned to the server that will act as the back-end server. Click **OK** to return to the Recipient Update Service (SECUREYY) Properties dialog box. Click **OK** to return to Exchange System Manager.

4. Click the **plus sign (+)** next to Administrative Groups, and then click the **plus sign (+)** next to the Second Administrative Group. Click the **plus sign (+)** next to the Servers container, and right-click **SERVERYY**, where YY is the student number assigned to the server that will be configured as the front-end server. On the shortcut menu, click **Properties**. This opens the SERVERYY Properties dialog box, where YY is the student number assigned to your front-end server, as shown in Figure 7-12.

5. On the General tab, click the **This is a front-end server** check box, and then click **OK**. You are prompted with a warning indicating that you are about to change the role of this server and that it will not become effective until the server is rebooted or until POP, IMAP, HTTP, and all Exchange services are stopped and restarted. Click **OK** to continue.

6. Close **Exchange System Manager**.

7. Manually restart the server. After the computer restarts, log back on to the front-end server using the user name **Administrator** and the password **Password!**.

7

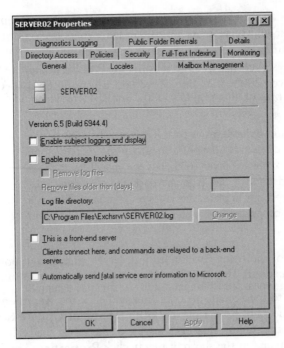

Figure 7-12   Front-end Server Properties dialog box

8. To ensure that POP access will work, you need to ensure that the POP service is started on both servers. To do this on the front-end server, click **Start**, point to **Administrative Tools**, and then click **Services**. The Services console opens.

9. Scroll down within the detail pane, and right-click **Microsoft Exchange POP3**. Click **Properties** on the shortcut menu. Click **Automatic** on the Startup type drop-down list. Click **OK** to return to the Services console.

10. Right-click **Microsoft Exchange POP3**, and then click **Start** on the short-cut menu.

11. Close the **Services** console.

12. Repeat Steps 8 to 11 on the back-end server.

    To test the front-end/back-end configuration, use two test accounts on the back-end server, Administrator and Mike Jones.

13. Using Microsoft Outlook on the back-end server, connect to the Administrator account. Send a message to Mike Jones. After the message has been sent, close **Outlook**.

14. Start Outlook Express on the front-end server by clicking **Start**, pointing to **All Programs**, and then clicking **Outlook Express**.

15. If the Outlook Express dialog box opens, uncheck the **Always perform this check when starting Outlook Express** check box, and then click **No**.

16. Click **Tools** and then click **Accounts**. (If the Your Name screen appeared after Step 15, move on to Step 18.)

17. Click the **Add** button and then click **Mail**. (Again, if the Your Name screen appeared after Step 15, move on to Step 18.)

18. At the Your Name screen, type **Mike Jones** in the Display name text box, and then click **Next**.

19. At the Internet E-mail Address screen, type **mjones@blatherconsultingXX.com** in the E-mail address text box, where XX is the student number assigned to your back-end server. Click **Next**.

20. At the E-mail Server Names screen, ensure **POP3** is selected in the drop-down list, type **serverXX.secureXX.local** in the Incoming mail (POP3, IMAP, or HTTP) server and Outgoing mail (SMTP) server text boxes, and then click **Next**.

21. At the Internet Mail Logon screen, type **Password!** in the Password text box. Click **Next**.

22. At the Congratulations screen, click **Finish**.

23. If necessary, click the **Close** button to close the Internet Accounts window. Close any windows related to importing messages if they appear on your screen, and do not import messages.

24. If the Outlook Express dialog box opens, click **Yes**. If another dialog box opens asking whether you want to go offline, click **Try Again**.

25. If the Show/Hide IMAP Folders window opens, click **OK**.

26. If necessary, expand the **Local Folders** node, and then click **Inbox**.

27. If no messages appear in your Inbox, click the **Send/Recv** button on the toolbar. You should receive the message sent from the Administrator account in Step 1.

 You may also receive a test message sent to Mark Majors in Chapter 4, "Configuring Outlook and Outlook Web Access." Remember that the account was configured such that all mail sent to Mark Majors is also delivered to
NOTE Mike Jones.

28. Close **Outlook Express**.

29. The final test is to test the functionality of Outlook Web Access. To do this on the front-end server, click **Start**, point to **All Programs**, and then click **Internet Explorer**.

30. If the Internet Explorer Security Configuration message appears, click the **In the future, do not show this message** check box, and then click **OK**.

31. You might need to reset the security level. Click **Tools** and then click **Internet Options**. In the Internet Options dialog box, click the **Security** tab. Ensure that the

Internet Security level is set to **Medium-low**. Reset the level as necessary, clicking **Yes** if asked to confirm changes. Click **OK**.

32. In the Address field, type **http://serverXX.secureXX.local/Exchange**, where XX is the student number assigned to the back-end server, and then click the **Go** button.

33. Type **SECUREXX\Administrator**, where XX is the student number assigned to the back-end server, in the User name text box, type **Password!** in the Password text box, and then click **OK**. The Microsoft Outlook Web Access screen should open.

34. Close **Internet Explorer**.

To allow IMAP or POP clients to send information through the front-end/back-end infrastructure, it is necessary to configure SMTP on the front-end server as SMTP is the protocol that is used by IMAP and POP clients for outgoing communication. To run SMTP on the front-end server and have it accept inbound mail (mail for your domains), you must have a mailbox store mounted on the front-end server. The reason for this is that NDRs (nondelivery reports) may be generated on the front-end server, and the NDRs must be routed through the store for formatting. By default, Exchange Server 2003 allows relaying only from authenticated clients. As such, you need to ensure that you configure your servers to require authentication before allowing the clients to send e-mail through the server.

When accessing a front-end/back-end server topology using Outlook Web Access, HTTP requests from the client computer are sent to the front-end server. The front-end server then uses Active Directory to determine to which back-end server to proxy the request. After determining the appropriate back-end server, the front-end server then forwards the request to the back-end server. The request is identical to the original request sent from the client. In particular, the HTTP host header, which matches the name of the front-end server to which the request was sent, remains unchanged. The front-end server contacts the back-end server using the host name of the back-end server, but in the HTTP headers of the request, the front-end server sends the host header used by the client. This ensures that the appropriate back-end Exchange Server 2003 virtual server handles the request. The back-end server processes the HTTP request from the front-end normally, and the response is sent unchanged through the front-end server back to the client. In most cases, the back-end server handles the front-end server as if it were another HTTP client. The client, therefore, never needs to know that the request was not handled on the front-end server.

Microsoft Exchange 2000 Server was the first version of Microsoft Exchange to introduce the concepts of a front-end/back-end server configuration. With Exchange 2000 Server, you could only configure the Enterprise Edition as a front-end server. With Exchange Server 2003, you can configure both the Enterprise and Standard Editions as front-end servers. Exchange Server 2003 has introduced other improvements for front-end/back-end server configurations. Some of these additional improvements include the following:

- *Kerberos authentication*—Exchange Server 2003 introduced the ability for Exchange front-end servers to use Kerberos authentication for HTTP sessions between front-end and back-end servers. This does not imply that the session between the front-end and back-end servers is encrypted, only that the authentication is encrypted. If you require the entire session to be encrypted, it is necessary to make use of IPSec (Internet Protocol Security) or VPN connectivity to secure all communication between the front-end and back-end servers.

- *RPC over HTTP*—This feature enables users with Outlook 2003 the ability to access their information from the Internet by encapsulating the RPC within HTTP for communication with the back-end server.

- *Forms-based authentication*—Exchange Server 2003 includes a new authentication feature for Outlook Web Access clients. Forms-based authentication uses a cookie to identify the user when the user has done the initial logon. Tracking the use of this cookie allows Exchange to time out inactive sessions. However, the initial user's name and password is still transmitted in clear text, similar to basic authentication. As such, you should make use of SSL encryption when using forms-based authentication.

7

MANAGING HTTP VIRTUAL SERVERS

When you install Exchange Server 2003, it integrates with Windows 2000/2003 IIS (Internet Information Services). Not only does Exchange store configuration in Active Directory, it also stores configuration within the IIS metabase. The Directory Service/ Metabase Synchronization (DS2MB) process that is part of the Exchange System Attendant service then replicates relevant configuration changes made in Active Directory through Exchange System Manager to the metabase at regular intervals. The DS2MB process always overrides changes made directly to the IIS metabase. As such, you should always make use of Exchange System Manager when making changes to virtual servers on computers running Exchange Server 2003.

Exchange uses IIS virtual servers to provide the transport services you need to access public folders and mailboxes using an Internet protocol such as HTTP, POP, or IMAP. When your Exchange Server 2003 organization supports more than one domain namespace or hosts additional public folder trees, you need to configure these domains as additional HTTP virtual servers or as additional HTTP virtual directories. Each HTTP virtual server is represented as a Web site, as shown in Figure 7-13.

The Default Web Site represents the default HTTP virtual server. If you examine the directory structure for HTTP virtual servers, you find several important directories, including the following:

- *Exadmin*—Exadmin is used for Web-based administration of the HTTP virtual server. By default, this directory is configured for integrated authentication only.

- *Exchange*—Exchange is the directory to which users connect to access their mailboxes. By default, this directory is configured for both basic and integrated Windows authentication with the default domain set to the pre-Windows 2000 domain name.

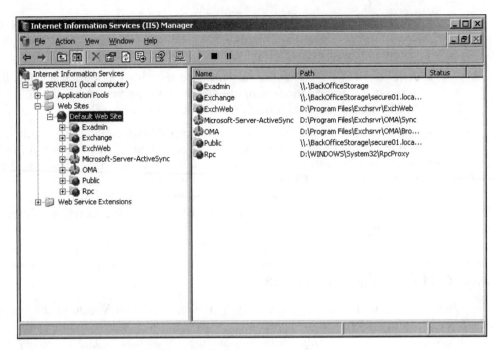

Figure 7-13   Default HTTP virtual server

- *ExchWeb*—ExchWeb is used with Outlook Web Access and provides calendaring, address book, and other important control functions. By default, this directory is configured for anonymous access, but the bin directory that provides the controls is restricted and uses both basic and integrated Windows authentication.

- *OMA*—OMA is the directory to which Outlook Mobile Access users connect to access their Exchange data. By default, this directory is configured for basic authentication with the default domain set to \.

- *Public*—Public is the directory to which users connect to access the default public folders tree. By default, this directory is configured for both basic and integrated Windows authentication with the default domain set to the pre-Windows 2000 domain name.

If your organization is large and complex, you likely host more than one domain name. For example, companies that are the target of acquisition might be required to preserve their domain name because of branding purposes. To address this within a front-end/back-end topology, you need to create additional virtual servers or virtual directories.

Additional virtual servers give you more flexibility and allow you to connect to your server using your domain address as the main identifier. The disadvantages of using this approach is that if you are going to make use of virtual servers and want to encrypt traffic with the front-end server, you need to install and configure a certificate for each virtual server. This is because certificates are installed at the virtual server level. Creating additional virtual servers implies additional certificates.

Activity 7-5: Configuring an Additional Virtual Server

Time Required: 20 to 40 minutes

Objective: Create an additional HTTP virtual server to host an additional domain.

Description: In this activity, you create an additional HTTP virtual server that will be configured to host an additional SMTP domain in three stages. A fourth stage will test the new virtual server.

For this activity, it is necessary to assign numbers to each group of front-end/back-end server groups.

Start by modifying an existing recipient policy to include the domain address for your new domain.

1. Open Exchange System Manager on the back-end server by clicking **Start**, pointing to **All Programs**, pointing to **Microsoft Exchange**, and then clicking **System Manager**.

2. Click the **plus sign (+)** next to the Recipients container. Click the **Recipient Policies** container, and in the right pane, right-click the **BlatherConsultingXX E-Mail Addresses Recipient Policy**, where XX is the student number assigned to the back-end server, that was configured in a previous chapter. On the shortcut menu, click **Properties**. The BlatherConsultingXX E-Mail Addresses Recipient Policy Properties dialog box opens.

3. Click the **E-Mail Addresses (Policy)** tab, and then click the **New** button. The New E-mail Address dialog box opens.

4. Click **SMTP Address** and then click **OK**. The SMTP Address Properties dialog box opens. Type **@blatherconsultingsrvZZ.com** in the Address text box, where ZZ is the number assigned to your group. Click **OK** to return to the BlatherConsultingXX E-Mail Addresses Recipient Policy Properties dialog box.

5. Click the check box next to the new SMTP address you just created, and then click **OK**.

6. You are prompted with a warning that the e-mail addresses have been modified. Click **Yes** to update all corresponding recipient e-mail addresses to match the new address and return to System Manager. Next, you create the new HTTP virtual server on the front-end server.

7. On the front-end server, open System Manager by clicking **Start**, pointing to **All Programs**, pointing to **Microsoft Exchange**, and then clicking **System Manager**.

8. Click the **plus sign (+)** next to Administrative Groups, and then click the **plus sign (+)** next to Second Administrative Group.

9. Click the **plus sign (+)** next to Servers, and then click the **plus sign (+)** next to SERVERYY, where YY is the student number assigned to the front-end server. Click the **plus sign (+)** next to the Protocols container, and then click the **HTTP** container.

10. Right-click the HTTP container, point to **New**, and then click **HTTP Virtual Server** on the submenu. The Properties dialog box for a new HTTP virtual server opens, as shown in Figure 7-14.

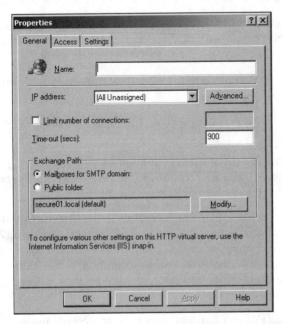

Figure 7-14   New HTTP Virtual Server Properties dialog box

11. In the Name text box, type **blatherconsultinggroupZZ.com**, where ZZ is the number assigned to the group consisting of you and your partner.

12. Click the **Mailboxes for SMTP domain** option button, if necessary. Ensure that **secureXX.local** is specified in the Exchange Path text field, where XX is the student number assigned to the back-end server.

13. Click the **Advanced** button. The Advanced dialog box opens. Highlight the existing entry and then click **Modify**. The Identification dialog box opens.

14. Type **www.blatherconsultingsrvZZ.com** in the Host name text box, where ZZ is the number assigned to your group, and then click **OK** until you return to Exchange System Manager.

15. Right-click the newly created HTTP virtual server, and then click **Start** on the shortcut menu.

If you are not able to start the virtual server, move on to the next step.

NOTE

16. Close **Exchange System Manager**. Next, you need to configure a matching HTTP virtual server on the back-end server to match the virtual server created on your front-end server.

17. Return to the open Exchange System Manager on your back-end server, and then click the **plus sign (+)** next to Administrative Groups.

18. Click the **plus sign (+)** next to the First Administrative Group, click the **plus sign (+)** next to the Servers container, click the **plus sign (+)** next to SERVERXX, where XX is the number assigned to the back-end server, click the **plus sign (+)** next to the Protocols container, and, finally, click the **HTTP** container. Right-click the **HTTP** container, point to **New**, and then click **HTTP Virtual Server**. The Properties dialog box for the new HTTP virtual server opens.

19. In the Name text box, type **blatherconsultinggroupZZ.com (Back-end)**, where ZZ is the number assigned to the group consisting of you and your partner.

20. Click the **Modify** button. This brings up the list of domains that have been configured for your organization, as shown in Figure 7-15. Click the **blatherconsultingsrvZZ.com** domain for which you are configuring the HTTP virtual server, where ZZ is the number assigned to your group. Click **OK**.

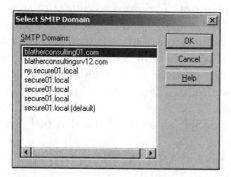

Figure 7-15   Select SMTP Domain dialog box

21. Click the **Advanced** button. The Advanced dialog box opens. Click on the existing entry, and then click the **Modify** button. The Identification dialog box opens.

22. Type **www.blatherconsultingsrvZZ.com** for the host name, where ZZ is the number assigned to your group, and then click **OK** until you return to Exchange System Manager.

23. Right-click the newly created HTTP virtual server, and then click **Start** on the shortcut menu.

NOTE

If you are not able to start the virtual server, move on to the next step.

24. Close **Exchange System Manager**. Finally, you test this new virtual server using your back-end server as a client machine. You need to add a record to the hosts file on both the front-end and back-end servers to ensure that the mail clients can resolve the new domain name to the correct address. To do this, complete the following steps:

25. Using Notepad on the back-end server, open the c:\Windows\System32\Drivers\ Etc\hosts file and associate the entry **www.blatherconsultingsrvZZ.com**, where ZZ is the number assigned to your group, with the IP address of your front-end server. Save and close the file. Repeat this step on the front-end server to add this same front-end server entry into the hosts file on that machine.

26. On the back-end server, open Internet Explorer, enter **www.blatherconsultingsrvZZ.com** in the Address Bar, where ZZ is the number assigned to your group, and then click **Go**. When prompted for credentials, type **administrator@secureXX.local** in the User name text box, where XX is the student number assigned to the back-end server; type **Password!** in the Password text box; and then click **OK**. The Microsoft Outlook Web Access screen should appear. When you are finished, close **Internet Explorer**.

Instead of making use of separate HTTP virtual servers to address the multiple domain issue, you can make use of additional virtual directories. The main advantage to using virtual directories pertains to SSL. SSL certificates are issued for a specific host or domain name. When you have multiple virtual servers with different domain names, you need one SSL certificate for each domain name. This introduces additional management and potentially additional cost depending on which certificate provider you use. Using virtual directories, clients access a single domain, the default domain, and then access a brand name domain as a virtual directory off of the main domain. This saves the potential cost of additional certificates and the additional configuration of SSL on each individual virtual server.

ACTIVITY

Activity 7-6: Configuring Additional Virtual Directories

Time Required: 20 to 40 minutes

Objective: Create an additional HTTP virtual directory to host an additional domain.

Description: In this activity, you create an additional HTTP virtual directory that will be configured to host an additional SMTP domain in two stages.

First, you need to modify an existing recipient policy to include the domain address for your new domain.

1. On the back-end server, open Exchange System Manager by clicking **Start**, pointing to **All Programs**, pointing to **Microsoft Exchange**, and then clicking **System Manager**.

2. Click the **plus sign (+)** next to the Recipients container. Click the **Recipient Policies** container, and in the right pane, right-click the **BlatherConsultingXX E-Mail Addresses Recipient Policy**, where XX is the student number assigned to the back-end server, that was configured in a previous chapter. On the shortcut menu, click **Properties**.

3. Click the **E-Mail Addresses (Policy)** tab, and then click the **New** button. The New E-mail Address dialog box opens.

4. Click **SMTP Address** and then click **OK**. The SMTP Address Properties dialog box opens. Enter **@blatherconsultingdirZZ.com** in the Address text box, where ZZ is the number assigned to your group. Click **OK** to return to the BlatherConsultingXX E-Mail Addresses Recipient Policy Properties dialog box.

5. Click the check box next to the new SMTP address you just created, and then click **OK**. You are prompted with a warning that the e-mail addresses have been modified. Click **Yes** to update all corresponding recipient e-mail addresses to match the new address and return to Exchange System Manager.

6. After you have completed setting up the environment, you can then proceed with defining additional virtual directories on the front-end and back-end servers. On the front-end server, start Exchange System Manager by clicking **Start**, pointing to **All Programs**, pointing to **Microsoft Exchange**, and then clicking **System Manager**.

7. Click the **plus sign (+)** next to Administrative Groups, click the **plus sign (+)** next to the Second Administrative Group, and then click the **plus sign (+)** next to the Servers container. Click the **plus sign (+)** next to SERVERYY, where YY is the student number assigned to your front-end server, click the **plus sign (+)** next to the Protocols container, click the **plus sign (+)** next to the HTTP container, and, finally, click the **Exchange Virtual Server**.

8. Right-click the **Exchange Virtual Server**. On the shortcut menu, point to **New**, and then click **Virtual Directory**. The Properties dialog box for a new virtual directory opens.

9. In the Name text box, enter the name of your virtual directory. This name is important because this is what the client must enter in his browser. For this activity, type **blatherconsultingdirZZ**, where ZZ is the number assigned to your group.

10. Click the **Mailboxes for SMTP domain** option button, if necessary. Click the **Modify** button. The Select SMTP Domain dialog box opens. Click the **blatherconsultingdirZZ.com** domain, where ZZ is the number assigned to your group. Click **OK** until you return to Exchange System Manager.

11. Close **Exchange System Manager**.

12. Return to the open Exchange System Manager on your back-end server, and then click the **plus sign (+)** next to Administrative Groups.

13. Click the **plus sign (+)** next to First Administrative Group, click the **plus sign (+)** next to the Servers container, click the **plus sign (+)** next to the back-end server, and, finally, click the **plus sign (+)** next to the Protocols container. Click the **plus sign (+)** next to the HTTP container, and then click **Exchange Virtual Server**. Right-click the **Exchange Virtual Server**, point to **New**, and then click **Virtual Directory**. The Properties dialog box for the new virtual directory opens.

14. In the Name text box, type **blatherconsultingdirZZ**, where ZZ is the number assigned to your group. This name is important as this is what the client must enter in his browser.

15. Click the **Mailboxes for SMTP domain** option button, if necessary. Click the **Modify** button. The Select SMTP Domain dialog box opens. Click the **blatherconsultingdirZZ.com** domain, where ZZ is the number assigned to your group. Click **OK** until you return to Exchange System Manager.

16. Close **Exchange System Manager**.

17. To test this new virtual directory, your back-end server will act as a client machine. From the back-end server, open Internet Explorer, type **http://serverYY.secureYY.local/blatherconsultingdirZZ** in the Address Bar, where YY is the student number assigned to your front-end server and ZZ is the number assigned to your group, and then click **Go**. When prompted for credentials, type **administrator@secureXX.local** in the User name text box, where XX is the student number assigned to the back-end server; type **Password!** in the Password text box; and then click **OK**. The Microsoft Outlook Web Access screen should appear. When you are finished, close **Internet Explorer**.

After you have configured HTTP virtual servers, part of the ongoing job is to administer them. One of the administration tasks is to control connections to your HTTP virtual server. Normally, virtual servers accept an unlimited number of connections. However, at times your virtual server might become overloaded. As such, you might want to limit the number of simultaneous connections. After the limit is reached, no other clients are permitted to access the server. The clients must wait until the connection load on the server decreases.

The connection timeout value determines when idle user sessions are disconnected. With the default HTTP virtual server, sessions time out after they have been idle for 15 minutes. You might want to lower this value to force users to log back on to the server.

If you don't disconnect idle sessions within a reasonable amount of time, unauthorized persons could gain access to your messaging system.

CAUTION

ACTIVITY

Activity 7-7: Configuring Connection Values

Time Required: 10 to 15 minutes

Objective: Walk through the steps outlining how to configure connection settings for your HTTP virtual server.

Description: In this activity, you walk through the steps for how you could configure the connection limits and connection timeout values for your SMTP virtual server.

1. From the Windows desktop of your front-end server, click **Start**, point to **Administrative Tools**, and then click **Internet Information Services (IIS) Manager**.

2. In IIS Manager, click the **plus sign (+)** next to SERVERYY, where YY represents the student number assigned to the front-end server. Click the **plus sign (+)** next to Web Sites. Each HTTP virtual server is represented by a Web site. The Default Web Site represents the default HTTP virtual server.

3. Right-click the **Default Web Site**, and then click **Properties** on the shortcut menu. The Default Web Site Properties dialog box opens. Click the **Performance** tab.

4. To set a connection limit, in the Web site connections area click the **Connections limited to** option button. Leave the limit set at 1000.

5. Click the **Web Site** tab. The Connection timeout field controls how long idle user sessions remain connected to the server. Type **60** in the text box to change the current timeout value to 60 seconds.

6. Click **OK** when finished to return to IIS Manager.

7. If necessary, click **Cancel** in all Inheritance Overrides windows that open.

8. Close **Internet Information Services (IIS) Manager**.

HTTP virtual servers run under a server process that you can start, stop, and pause much like other server processes. If you're changing the configuration of a virtual server or performing other maintenance tasks, you might need to stop the virtual server, make the changes, and then restart it. When a virtual server is stopped, it doesn't accept connections from users and can't be used to deliver or retrieve mail.

An alternative to stopping a virtual server is to pause it. Pausing a virtual server prevents new client connections, but it doesn't disconnect current connections. When you pause an HTTP virtual server, clients who are already connected can still continue to retrieve documents, messages, and public folder data. No new connections, however, are accepted.

The World Wide Web publishing service is the service that controls all HTTP virtual servers. Stopping this service stops all virtual servers using the process and all connections are disconnected immediately. Starting this service restarts all virtual servers that were running when you stopped the World Wide Web publishing service.

7

Activity 7-8: Starting and Stopping Virtual Servers and the World Wide Web Service

Time Required: 10 to 20 minutes

Objective: Walk through the steps outlining how to start and stop an HTTP virtual server and the World Wide Web publishing service.

Description: In this activity, you walk through the steps that you can take to stop and start HTTP virtual servers within your Exchange Server 2003 organization as well as the World Wide Web publishing service.

1. From the Windows desktop of your front-end server, click **Start**, point to **All Programs**, point to **Microsoft Exchange**, and then click **System Manager**.

2. Click the **plus sign (+)** next to Administrative Groups. Click the **plus sign (+)** next to Second Administrative Group. Click the **plus sign (+)** next to the Servers container, click the **plus sign (+)** next to the front-end server, click the **plus sign (+)** next to the Protocols container, click the **plus sign (+)** next to the HTTP container, and, finally, click the **Exchange Virtual Server**.

3. Right-click **Exchange Virtual Server**. The shortcut menu presents you with the following options. For this activity, click **Stop** to stop the server.

   - *Start*—To start the virtual server; is only available if the virtual server is currently stopped or paused

   - *Stop*—To stop the virtual server; is only available if the virtual server is started

   - *Pause*—To pause the virtual server; is only available if the virtual server is started

4. Right-click **Exchange Virtual Server**, and then click **Start** to restart the virtual server.

5. Close **Exchange System Manager**.

6. To start and stop the World Wide Web publishing service on the front-end server, open the Computer Management Console by clicking **Start**, pointing to **Administrative Tools**, and then clicking **Computer Management**.

7. Click the **plus sign (+)** next to the Services and Applications node, and then click **Services**.

8. In the right pane, right-click the **World Wide Web Publishing Service**. You are provided with options to Start, Stop, Pause, Resume, or Restart the service. Click **Stop** to stop the service.

9. Right-click the **World Wide Web Publishing Service**, and click **Start** to restart the service.

10. Close the **Computer Management** console.

CHAPTER SUMMARY

- ☐ Administrative groups are used to define the administrative topology for your Exchange organization. They are logically defined, meaning that at a conceptual level, they can be based on geography, department, division, or function.

- ☐ Different approaches can be taken to administrative group design. These approaches include centralization, decentralization, and a mixed administrative model.

- ☐ How you operate administrative groups depends on the mode for which your Exchange Server 2003 organization is configured. In mixed mode, Exchange Server 2003 can support the administration of pre-Exchange 2000 Server infrastructures. In native mode, Exchange Server 2003 can only support Exchange 2000 and Exchange 2003 installations.

- ☐ A routing group is a collection of servers that enjoy permanent, high-bandwidth connectivity. The links between routing groups are assumed to be either slow or unreliable. Connectors are used to connect routing groups over these slow WAN links. Although administrative groups are logical in nature, routing groups are determined by the physical topology of your network.

- ☐ By default, Exchange Server 2003 functions as though all servers in an organization belong to a single, large routing group.

- ☐ A front-end/back-end configuration supports the deployment of Exchange Server 2003 in a manner that distributes server tasks among front-end and back-end servers. A front-end server accepts requests from clients and proxies them to the appropriate back-end server for processing.

- ☐ Typically, most scenarios that involve a front-end/back-end server configuration fall into one of two categories, those that involve the use of a firewall and those that do not involve the use of a firewall.

- ☐ Exchange uses IIS virtual servers to provide the transport services you need to access public folders and mailboxes using an Internet protocol such as HTTP, POP, or IMAP.

- ☐ If your organization is large and complex, you likely host more than one domain name. To address this within a front-end/back-end topology, you need to create additional virtual servers or virtual directories.

- ☐ The main advantage to using virtual directories pertains to SSL. SSL certificates are issued for a specific host or domain name. When you have multiple virtual servers with different domain names, you need one SSL certificate for each domain name.

- ☐ Additional virtual servers give you more flexibility and allow you to connect to your server using your domain address as the main identifier.

- ☐ HTTP virtual servers run under a server process called the World Wide Web Publishing Service that you can start, stop, and pause much like other server processes.

7

KEY TERMS

administrative group — A group used to define the administrative topology for your Exchange organization. It is logically defined, meaning that at a conceptual level, it can be based on geography, department, division, or function.

back-end server — A server that hosts the mailboxes and public folders and accepts requests from clients through the front-end server. All interaction is with the front-end server, not with the clients directly.

bridgehead server — The server running Exchange 2000 Server that hosts routing group connectors. Exchange 2000 Server passes messages that are delivered between routing groups through bridgehead servers.

centralized administrative model — A model in which one group maintains complete control over all of the Exchange servers.

decentralized administrative model — A model in which a separate administrative group is created for each group of Exchange administrators who will manage the Exchange servers and users within their own administrative jurisdiction.

front-end server — A server that accepts requests from clients and proxies them to the appropriate back-end server for processing. Front-end servers do not host mailboxes or public folders directly.

mixed administrative model — A model in which day-to-day administration is decentralized, however, functional administration, such as public folder trees management, policy management, and so on, is centralized into another administrative group.

routing group — A group that is a collection of servers that enjoy permanent, high-bandwidth connectivity. By default, Exchange Server 2003 functions as though all servers in an organization belong to a single, large routing group.

routing group connector — A connector specifically designed to allow servers to communicate with servers in other routing groups. This is the preferred method of connecting routing groups.

REVIEW QUESTIONS

1. Your company has three regional offices, each connected with Integrated Services Digital Network (ISDN) lines to the home office. Administration personnel are located in the home office. How many administrative groups should you define?

   a. one

   b. two

   c. three

   d. There is not enough information to determine the need for administrative groups.

2. Why would you implement front-end/back-end servers? (Choose all that apply.)

   a. to provide a single name to Internet clients for client access

   b. to offload SSL processing from the back-end server

   c. to improve performance for MAPI clients

   d. to increase Information Store capacity

3. What objects can be created within an administrative group? (Choose all that apply.)

   a. policies

   b. routing groups

   c. recipients

   d. servers

4. What are the limitations of leaving an organization in mixed mode? (Choose all that apply.)

   a. Some Exchange System Manager commands do not apply to the Exchange Server 5.5 environment.

   b. Exchange Server 5.5 directory service objects are replicated into Active Directory with read-only properties.

   c. Recipient policies do not take effect for Exchange Server 5.5 users.

   d. Query distribution lists do not function.

5. Front-end/back-end server configurations can only be defined on the Enterprise Edition of Exchange Server 2003. True or False?

6. What are the advantages of a front-end/back-end server configuration?

   a. can provide a single namespace for the organization

   b. provides the ability to load-balance across servers

   c. provides the ability to use firewalls to protect the data stored within public folders and mailbox stores

   d. all of the above

7. When creating a front-end/back-end server design to host an additional SMTP domain based on additional HTTP virtual servers, what requirements must you meet? (Choose all that apply.)

   a. A separate front-end HTTP virtual server must be created to host the SMTP domain.

   b. A separate back-end HTTP virtual server must be created to host the SMTP domain.

   c. The mailboxes to be associated with the SMTP domain must be configured to point to the proper HTTP virtual server.

   d. all of the above

7

8. Which of the following processes is used to synchronize Active Directory with the IIS metabase?

   a. MBSync

   b. DS2MB

   c. IISSync

   d. DS2IIS

9. Which of the following are virtual directories defined on the Default Virtual Server?

   a. Exadmin

   b. Exchange

   c. OMA

   d. OAB

10. When configuring multiple HTTP virtual servers, what must you take into consideration with regard to securing communication?

    a. Each HTTP virtual server must be configured behind a firewall.

    b. Each HTTP virtual server must be configured on a distinct port.

    c. Each HTTP virtual server must have its own certificate.

    d. all of the above

11. When configuring OWA on a front-end/back-end server configuration, which of the following is the TCP port that can be used to communicate between the front end and back end?

    a. 8080

    b. 443

    c. 80

    d. all of the above

12. What is the default connection timeout value on HTTP virtual servers?

    a. 10 minutes

    b. 15 minutes

    c. 20 minutes

    d. 5 minutes

13. What is the default connection limit on HTTP virtual servers?

    a. 100 connections

    b. 150 connections

    c. 200 connections

    d. unlimited connections

14. Which of the following tools can be used to start and stop HTTP virtual servers?
    a. Exchange System Manager
    b. IIS Manager
    c. Services Management Console
    d. all of the above

15. When operating in mixed mode, which of the following can't you accomplish?
    a. create recipient policies
    b. move mailboxes between servers in different administrative groups
    c. create routing groups
    d. create additional message stores

16. Which of the following are not containers within an administrative group?
    a. system policies
    b. routing groups
    c. servers
    d. recipient policies

17. By default, when you first install Exchange Server 2003, the organization is configured as mixed mode. True or False?

18. A front-end/back-end server configuration can be defined to communicate using one port and one protocol. True or False?

19. Which of the following protocols are supported in a front-end/back-end server configuration?
    a. POP
    b. RPC
    c. HTTP
    d. all of the above

20. Which component is responsible for interacting with Active Directory in a front-end/back-end server configuration?
    a. DRAccess
    b. DSAccess
    c. DSConfig
    d. DSSync

7

21. What improvements were introduced as part of Exchange Server 2003 to better support front-end/back-end server configurations? (Choose all that apply.)

   a. Kerberos authentication

   b. forms-based authentication

   c. pass-through authentication

   d. RPC over HTTP

CASE PROJECTS

Case Project 7-1: Choosing an Administrative Groups Model

As the e-mail architect for your company, you are in the process of designing your Exchange Server 2003 migration from Exchange Server 5.5. You are at the point at which you are considering how the new organization can be administered. Explain the different options available to you in your transition from Exchange Server 5.5

Case Project 7-2: Designing Routing Groups

As the e-mail architect for your organization, you are looking at transitioning from another e-mail platform to Exchange Server 2003. You are in the process of trying to determine a routing group model for your new organization. What are some of the factors you should take into consideration when designing a routing group model for the new organization?

Case Project 7-3: Designing Front-End/Back-End Server Implementations

As the chief technical officer for a large application service provider, you are using Exchange Server 2003 to provide Web e-mail services to organizations that sign up to be hosted. What is the best approach for implementing each organization within the Exchange Server 2003 infrastructure used to provide service for your customers?

Case Project 7-4: Managing HTTP Virtual Servers

As the administrator of your e-mail environment, you have been monitoring your e-mail infrastructure and notice that the SMTP service that relays your e-mail to external organizations is becoming heavily loaded. What are the courses of action you can take to help alleviate this situation?

8

MANAGING ROUTING AND INTERNET CONNECTIVITY

After reading this chapter, you will be able to:

♦ Understand SMTP and how it works

♦ Understand how Exchange Server 2003 makes use of SMTP

♦ Understand how message routing works within an Exchange Server 2003 infrastructure

♦ Describe the link state algorithm and how Exchange Server 2003 makes use of it

♦ Describe how external messaging is handled within Exchange Server 2003

A well-designed Microsoft Exchange system within a reasonably large organization will reflect skillful interweaving of various messaging technologies. Message routing is the process through which a message eventually reaches its intended recipient. Because of the many connector options available in Exchange, setting up efficient message routing can be an intricate process throughout your enterprise. This chapter covers basic routing concepts to give you a feel for how Exchange handles messages.

One of the most significant differences between Microsoft Exchange Server 2003 and Exchange Server 5.5 lies in the basic architecture of an Exchange system. The message routing topology in Exchange Server 5.5 is based on sites. A site is a logical grouping of servers that enjoys permanent, high-bandwidth connectivity. Architecturally, each site defines three distinct boundaries: the boundary for single-hop routing, the administrative unit, and a namespace hierarchy in the directory structure.

In Exchange Server 2003, these three boundaries have been separated into individual elements. Single-hop routing is defined by a routing group; the unit of administration is defined by the administrative group; and the namespace hierarchy exists in Active Directory in the form of a domain. This architecture gives administrators much more flexibility in determining how an Exchange

Server 2003 server is administered because administrative assignments can be divided along functions and activities rather than geography.

Fortunately for the end user, the complex message routes are abstracted into the single Inbox metaphor. As a system administrator, however, it is essential for you to understand all the possible instances of message routing to be able to create the most efficient routes in your Exchange organization.

This chapter focuses on the routing architecture used in Exchange Server 2003 and the facilities for administering that routing architecture. It describes what routing groups are, how they connect, and how link state information works to provide better message routing than Exchange Server 5.5. It also presents the steps necessary to configure and administer routing within your organization.

THE SIMPLE MAIL TRANSFER PROTOCOL

Simple Mail Transfer Protocol (SMTP) is the primary messaging protocol that is used by Exchange Server 2003 to send and receive e-mail. SMTP has its origins in the Internet, and, like many other protocols, it is designed to work on top of TCP/IP (the de facto standard for network communications).

SMTP requires that when one server connects to another server to send e-mail, it uses only certain commands in a certain way and expects specific replies. In fact, this is the very definition of a protocol; a set of rules for how two computers will interact with each other. SMTP does not stop there, however. SMTP is made up of several different protocols that define its functionality. The group of commands that make up the communication and interaction between two servers is only one of the protocols that make up SMTP (RFC 2821, to be specific). Table 8-1 provides an example of the interaction between two servers, as defined by the RFC 2821 protocol.

Table 8-1   SMTP dialogue

SMTP Command	Description
HELO host.company.com	The sending host sends a Hello greeting that includes its name. In this case, the sending host responds "Hello, my name is host.company.com."
250 receiver.hostedcompany.com	The receiving host responds with a "250" response along with the name of the server doing the responding indicating that all is well.
MAIL FROM: <user1@mycompany.com>	The sending host says it has mail from an individual named user1@mycompany.com.
250 sender OK	The receiving host responds with a "250" indicating that all is well.

Table 8-1 SMTP dialogue (continued)

SMTP Command	Description
RCPT TO: <user2@hostedcompany.com>	The sending host says the mail is for user2@hostedcompany.com.
250 recipient OK	The receiving host says the format of the recipient's address is fine.
DATA	The sending host lets the receiving host know that what follows is the actual message itself.
354 Start data input end with <crlf>.<crlf>	The receiving system says it is ready, and to end the data with a period (.) on a line by itself so that the receiving system knows when the message is completed.
The data of the message .	The sending host sends the message, followed by a period on a separate line.
250 OK	The receiving host sends back a "250" response saying all is well.
QUIT	The sending host sends a quit message to end the connection.

Table 8-1 outlines what occurs when two servers interact with each other, but what about the data part of the interactions? All that was mentioned within the example was that the "data of the message" would be transferred. What is the data? How is it formatted? This is defined by the specifications of RFC 2822, which covers the basic header or envelope elements of a message. An example based on the dialogue from Table 8-1 is shown here.

```
FROM: Larry Chambers <user1@mycompany.com>
TO: myfriend <user2@hostedcompany.com>
SUBJECT: The results you were looking for
```

Table 8-2 lists some of the other headers that make up the RFC 2822 specification.

Table 8-2 SMTP headers

SMTP Header	Description
RETURN-PATH	This field is added by the final transport system that delivers the message to its recipient. This field is intended to contain definitive information about the address and route back to the message's originator.
RECEIVED	A copy of this field is added by each transport service that relays the message. The information in the field can be quite useful for tracing transport problems.
FROM/RESENT-FROM	This field contains the identity of the person(s) who wanted this message to be sent.
SENDER/RESENT-SENDER	This field contains the authenticated identity of the person/system that sends the message.

Table 8-2   SMTP headers (continued)

SMTP Header	Description
REPLY-TO/RESENT-REPLY-TO	This field provides a method for indicating any mailboxes to which responses are to be sent.
TO	This field contains the identity of the primary recipients of the message.
CC/RESENT-CC	This field contains the identity of the secondary recipients of the message.
BCC/RESENT-BCC	This field contains the identity of additional recipients of the message. The contents of this field are not included in copies of the message sent to the primary and secondary recipients.
MESSAGE-ID/RESENT-MESSAGE-ID	This field contains a unique identifier for the message.
IN-REPLY-TO	The contents of this field identify previous correspondence that this message answers.
REFERENCES	The contents of this field identify other correspondence that this message references.
SUBJECT	This is intended to provide a summary, or indicate the nature, of the message.
COMMENTS	This permits adding text comments onto the message without disturbing the contents of the message's body.
ENCRYPTED	Sometimes, data encryption is used to increase the privacy of message contents. If the body of a message has been encrypted, to keep its contents private, this field can be used to note that and to indicate the nature of the encryption.

Now that you know how messages are communicated back and forth and the format of those messages, you still have one more thing to worry about: attachments. A mail message is limited in the information it can convey in its body without attachments. To handle this, **Multipurpose Internet Mail Extension (MIME)** was introduced. MIME provides a way to describe a message as consisting of many parts, each of which could be formatted differently. One part of a message could be audio, another video, and yet another text. But how are binary files to be included as attachments? SMTP can only handle sending textual information, not binary information. The original answer to this was to convert the binary information to a format that resembled text. This was accomplished by using a process known as uuencode (the name comes from Unix-to-Unix Encoding, for which uuencode was originally designed).

MIME added six headers to a standard RFC 2822 envelope. Three are mandatory, whereas the other three are optional. Table 8-3 lists the headers that were added.

Table 8-3   MIME headers

MIME Header	Description
Mime-Version:	Specifies the version of the MIME standard that is in use. Currently, v1.0 is the only standard available.
Content-Type:	Defines the type of data within the message. The content is defined in terms of MIME types, which are strings that identify the format of the content. MIME types have the format major type/minor type (subtype), where major type represents the content category and minor type represents the specific content type within that category. For instance, video/mpeg is the MIME type for MPEG videos. In this case, the major type is video, and the subtype is MPEG, which identifies the specific format of the content.
Content-Transfer-Encoding:	Specifies the encoding that is used for the attachment within the message. Two types of encoding can be used, base64 and quoted-printable. Typically, base64 is used for attaching binary data and quoted-printable is used for text data.
Content-Disposition:	Describes how parts of the message should be handled. If the Content-Disposition value is inline, it should be displayed as part of the larger message. If the Content-Disposition value is an attachment, the part is treated as a separate file that can be saved or opened.
Content-ID:	Assigns each message part a name that is unique among all message parts in all messages. No two messages will ever have parts with the same Content-ID.
Content-Description:	Describes a message part. No particular standards exist for the information placed in here.

MIME works by concatenating all of the attachments, and placing message headers between them that define what sort of content is in the attachment (plain text, HTML, graphics, and so forth) and how it's encoded for transfer through the mail system. Each content type consists of both a top-level media type and a corresponding subtype. It is possible to define additional types other than those specified in the RFCs to accommodate proprietary formats. Table 8-4 lists some of the more common top-level types and corresponding subtypes.

Some of the content types are "multipart," meaning that they define a complex message structure with more than one part, each of which has headers of its own.

8

Table 8-4   Top-level media types

Media Type	Subtype
Text	Plain, richtext, enriched
Image	jpeg, gif
Audio	Basic
Video	mpeg
Application	Octet-stream, postscript
Multipart	Mixed
Message	rfc822

SMTP AND EXCHANGE SERVER 2003

Exchange Server 2003 makes use of the SMTP service that comes standard with Windows 2000 and Windows 2003. The Windows SMTP service is a component of IIS (Internet Information Services) and runs as part of Inetinfo.exe. Exchange Server 2003 uses SMTP as its native transport protocol. Exchange Server 2003 enhances the functionality of the SMTP service in the following ways:

- SMTP management is removed from the IIS Manager and is added to Exchange System Manager.

- Exchange Server 2003 added support for link state information and the SMTP commands that support it. Link state information is used to determine the best path for messages to travel through an Exchange network. Link state routing determines the best path based on the cost assigned to different segments in the path.

- Advanced queuing capabilities are added to improve message delivery times and provide additional information for tracking messages through the system.

- The message categorizer communicates with a global catalog to obtain information such as recipient policies. This information is used for tasks such as ensuring that message sizes are not above the specified maximum limits. It is also used to obtain configuration information for Exchange virtual servers.

- An Installable File System (IFS) store driver provides access to the Exchange store through file management utilities such as Windows Explorer.

- The location of the mail queue is moved from the \inetpub\mailroot\queue folder to \exchsrvr\mailroot\vsi 1\queue. An additional folder is created in \exchsrvr\mailroot for each additional SMTP virtual server.

Exchange Server 2003 does not work in isolation. It is highly dependent on other services offered by the infrastructure, particularly Active Directory and the IIS metabase. Making changes to the configuration of Exchange Server 2003 changes the configuration information stored in Active Directory and the IIS metabase. This allows the SMTP service, which is a part of IIS, to read the configuration changes. This also allows other sites within the infrastructure to read the configuration that is replicated by Active Directory. When modifications are made to Exchange Server 2003, these modifications are stored directly in Active Directory. The DS2MB process, which is part of the System Attendant service, then replicates this information to the IIS metabase for use by the SMTP service.

Although there is only one SMTP service, you can configure multiple virtual SMTP servers on each Exchange Server 2003 server. Each virtual server can be started, stopped, or paused independently of other virtual servers.

Activity 8-1: Creating SMTP Virtual Servers

Time Required: 10 to 20 minutes

Objective: Create an SMTP virtual server within Exchange Server 2003 to allow the delivery of messages via SMTP to external SMTP servers.

8

Description: In this activity, you create an additional SMTP virtual server on the back-end server. Reasons for creating an additional SMTP virtual server include adding additional fault tolerance to your environment and allowing your organization to host multiple default domains. When you have multiple SMTP virtual servers, one of the servers can go offline without stopping message delivery in the Exchange organization. If you are hosting multiple domains and you want to have more than one default domain, you might want to create an additional SMTP virtual server.

1. Log on to the back-end server using the user name **Administrator** and the password **Password!**.

2. From the Windows desktop, click **Start**, point to **All Programs**, point to **Microsoft Exchange**, and then click **System Manager**.

3. Click the **plus sign (+)** next to Administrative Groups, click the **plus sign (+)** next to First Administrative Group, and then click the **plus sign (+)** next to the Servers node.

4. Click the **plus sign (+)** next to SERVERXX, where XX is the number assigned to your back-end server, and then click the **plus sign (+)** next to the Protocols node.

5. Right-click the **SMTP** node, point to **New**, and then click **SMTP Virtual Server**. This starts the New SMTP Virtual Server Wizard, as shown in Figure 8-1.

6. Type **BLATHER SMTP Virtual Server** in the Name text box, and then click **Next**.

7. Use the IP Address drop-down list to select an available IP address. The IP address/ TCP port combination must be unique on every virtual server. Because an SMTP virtual server is already installed, you cannot choose (All Unassigned). In this case, click **192.168.0.XX**, where XX is the number assigned to your back-end server, and then click **Finish**.

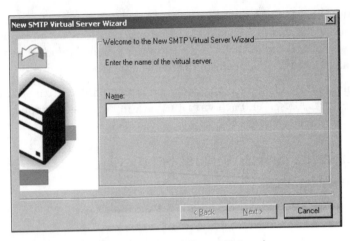

Figure 8-1   New SMTP Virtual Server Wizard

8. Because the default SMTP virtual server is making use of port 25, you need to change the port assigned to your new SMTP virtual server. To do this, click the **plus sign (+)** next to the SMTP node, right-click the newly created **BLATHER SMTP Virtual Server**, and then click **Properties** on the shortcut menu. The BLATHER SMTP Virtual Server Properties dialog box opens, as shown in Figure 8-2.

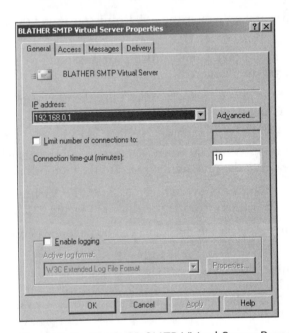

Figure 8-2   BLATHER SMTP Virtual Server Properties dialog box

9. On the General tab, click the **Advanced** button. The Advanced dialog box opens.

10. Click the **IP address** within the address list, if necessary, and then click the **Edit** button.

11. In the TCP port text box, type **5025** instead of the default port 25. Click **OK** when finished.

12. Click **OK** to return to the BLATHER SMTP Virtual Server Properties dialog box.

13. Click **OK** to return to Exchange System Manager.

14. If necessary, right-click - **BLATHER SMTP Virtual Server**, and then click **Start** on the shortcut menu.

15. Close **Exchange System Manager**.

As implied by the activity, you have the option to create multiple SMTP virtual servers on the same physical server to provide separate configurations for different messaging services. Each virtual server has its own distinct configuration, including IP address, port number, and authentication settings. Each Exchange Server 2003 server has, by default, at least one virtual server that listens on port 25 on all IP addresses. Every virtual server on any one single physical server must belong to the same routing group.

In most cases, additional virtual servers are not needed. However, if you are hosting multiple domains or want to have more than one default domain name, you can create multiple virtual servers to meet your needs. Multiple virtual servers do not increase your throughput, but they are very handy if you need to configure different options for different sets of users.

Activity 8-2: Configuring SMTP Virtual Server Options

Time Required: 10 to 20 minutes

Objective: Configure your SMTP virtual server to restrict access to it.

Description: By default, virtual servers are accessible to all IP addresses, which can present a security risk that could allow your server to be misused. For instance, if a virus with an SMTP daemon takes control of a workstation that is on the same domain as your Exchange Server 2003 server, it can relay messages off of your SMTP virtual server because of the unrestricted connections. To control use of a virtual server, you can grant or deny access by IP address, subnet, or domain.

1. From the Windows desktop of the back-end server, click **Start**, point to **All Programs**, point to **Microsoft Exchange**, and then click **System Manager**.

2. Click the **plus sign (+)** next to Administrative Groups, click the **plus sign (+)** next to the First Administrative Group, and then click the **plus sign (+)** next to Servers.

3. Click the **plus sign (+)** next to SERVERXX, where XX is the number assigned to your back-end server, click the **plus sign (+)** next to the Protocols node, and then click the **plus sign (+)** next to the SMTP node.

4. Right-click **BLATHER SMTP Virtual Server**, and then click **Properties** on the shortcut menu.

5. Click the **Access** tab and then click the **Connection** button. The Connection dialog box opens with the list of computers that currently are allowed to connect to your SMTP virtual server. Initially, this is blank, as shown in Figure 8-3.

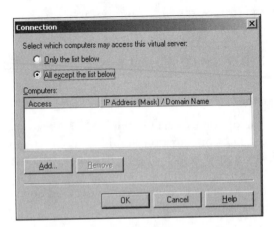

Figure 8-3   Connection dialog box

6. To grant access to specific computers and deny access to all others, click the **Only the list below** option button.

7. Create the grant or deny list by clicking the **Add** button, and then adding the computer, group of computers, or domain to which you want to grant access. If you are adding a single computer, click the **Single computer** option button and specify the IP address. If you are adding a group of computers, click the **Group of computers** option button and specify the subnet address, such as 192.168.5.0, and the subnet mask, such as 255.255.255.0. If you are configuring a domain, click the **Domain** option button, and specify the fully qualified domain name.

NOTE

If you grant or deny based on domain name, your server might experience performance degradation. This is because the Exchange Server 2003 server must perform a reverse DNS lookup on each connection to determine whether the connection comes from the domain.

8. For this activity, click the **Single computer** option button, if necessary, and then type **192.168.0.XX**, where XX is the number of your back-end server, in the IP address text box.

9. Click **OK** to return to the Connection dialog box.

10. Click **OK** to return to the BLATHER SMTP Virtual Server Properties dialog box.

11. Click **OK** to return to Exchange System Manager.

12. Close **Exchange System Manager**.

UNDERSTANDING MESSAGE ROUTING

To have an understanding of message routing, it is helpful to have an understanding of how the underlying message routing subsystem functions. This will help you to understand how messages are processed internally and how they flow between servers both inside and outside of your Exchange organization. This will also help to complete the explanation of the overall concepts that make up the routing picture.

Exchange Server 2003 delivers messages through the least expensive available route. This is determined based on the costs that are configured in the routing connectors that connect routing groups. If the least expensive route has a link that is down, the next least expensive route is used.

Routing Groups and Connectors

8

A routing group in an Exchange organization consists of a collection of well-connected Exchange servers for which full-time, full mesh connectivity is guaranteed. Within a routing group, any Exchange server can send mail to and receive mail from any other Exchange server without configuring any special connectivity.

By default, all Exchange servers are configured in a single routing group named after the administrator group. You must manually add additional routing groups and move servers into them.

In addition to being routed within a routing group, messages can be routed outside the routing group to external e-mail systems or to other routing groups that make up the Exchange organization. Alternate routing groups can be configured within an Exchange organization for a variety of reasons, including limited capacity/availability of network connections, policy limits or restrictions on the size of mail messages, and a need for scheduling the flow of e-mail. To connect to outside e-mail systems or connect routing groups together within the same organization, Exchange makes use of connectors. There are four types of connectors that are available with Exchange Server 2003:

- *Routing group connector*—The **routing group connector** is used to route messages between routing groups. Each connector is one-way. To provide bidirectional communication, two routing group connectors must be configured. This provides maximum flexibility in designing routing paths. Routing group connectors use SMTP as a messaging protocol. However, this type of connector offers different options than an SMTP connector.

- *SMTP connector*—The **SMTP connector** is designed to route mail to external e-mail systems such as Internet mail hosts or another Exchange organization. They can also be used to route mail between routing groups within an Exchange organization but Microsoft recommends against it.

- *X.400 connector*—The **X.400 connector** is designed to connect Exchange servers with legacy X.400 systems or between Exchange servers in low-bandwidth scenarios. The X.400 connector can also be used to connect Exchange Server 2003 routing groups or Exchange Server 5.5 systems that are not connected by other means. X.400 connectors are only available to Exchange Server 2003, Enterprise Edition administrators.

- *Specialty connectors*—These types of connectors include the Lotus Notes connector and the GroupWise connector. These connectors provide e-mail connectivity, format conversion, and calendaring between Exchange Server 2003 and the respective e-mail systems.

These connectors provide e-mail connectivity outside of the routing group. Other than the X.400 connector and the specialty connectors, connectivity between servers in a routing group and between routing groups is based entirely on SMTP. Using SMTP instead of RPC (remote procedure call), as was used in Exchange Server 5.5, is more advantageous in that it provides a more flexible routing and administrative scheme because SMTP is more tolerant of low-bandwidth and high-latency topologies than its RPC-based communications predecessor. It also provides the advantage of dividing the routing architecture and the grouping of servers for administrative purposes. In Exchange Server 5.5, both of these elements were dictated by the site, forcing many companies to map their administrative boundaries to their site boundaries. Finally, SMTP requires less overhead and bandwidth than RPC-based communication.

Activity 8-3: Installing a Routing Group Connector

Time Required: 10 to 20 minutes

Objective: Install a routing group connector to provide connectivity between two routing groups.

Description: In this activity, you install a routing group connector between two routing groups. The routing group connector will be installed on each bridgehead server within their respective routing group, and configured appropriately to allow connectivity. By default, all servers in the originating routing group act as local bridgehead servers. In this activity, you specify that only the bridgehead server is allowed to send mail over the connector instead of allowing every server within the routing group to have this ability. Because routing group connectors are always one-way connections, after you have created one end of the connector, you are prompted to have Exchange Server 2003 automatically create a routing group connector in the remote routing group. If you choose to do so, the connector that is created in the remote routing group will inherit the settings you have chosen for the local connector.

1. From the Windows desktop of the back-end server, click **Start**, point to **All Programs**, point to **Microsoft Exchange**, and then click **System Manager**.

2. Click the **plus sign (+)** next to Administrative Groups, and then click the **plus sign (+)** next to First Administrative Group.

3. Click the **plus sign (+)** next to Routing Groups, and, finally, click the **plus sign (+)** next to First Routing Group.

4. Within the First Routing Group, right-click **Connectors**. On the shortcut menu, point to **New**, and then click **Routing Group Connector**. The Properties dialog box for the routing group connector opens, as shown in Figure 8-4.

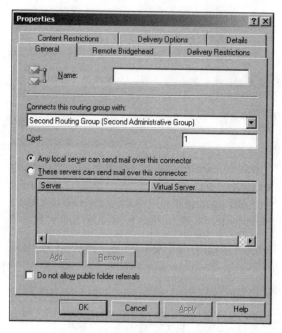

8

Figure 8-4   Routing Group Connector Properties dialog box

5. On the General tab, type **RGXX to RGYY Connector** in the Name text box, where XX is the number assigned to your back-end server and YY is the number assigned to your front-end server.

6. Click **Second Routing Group (Second Administrative Group)** from the Connects this routing group with drop-down list, if necessary.

7. Click the **These servers can send mail over this connector** option button, and then click the **Add** button. The Add Bridgehead dialog box opens. Click the **Default SMTP Virtual Server** on SERVERXX, where XX is the number assigned to your back-end server, as shown in Figure 8-5. Click **OK** to return to the Properties dialog box.

8. Click the **Remote Bridgehead** tab, and then click the **Add** button. You are presented with a list of available routing groups and servers within those routing groups to connect to. In this activity, click **SERVERYY**, where YY is the number assigned to your front-end server. Click **OK** to continue.

9. Click **OK** to install the connector.

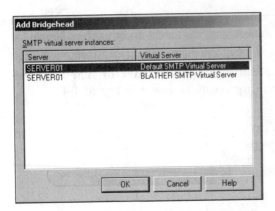

Figure 8-5   Add Bridgehead dialog box

10. You are prompted with a warning dialog box asking if you want to create the routing group connector in the remote routing group. Click **Yes** to continue.

11. Close **Exchange System Manager**.

Other Transport Methods

A routing group connector provides one method for your messages to flow into an Exchange Server 2003 server. Other methods of message flow into a server are depicted in Figure 8-6.

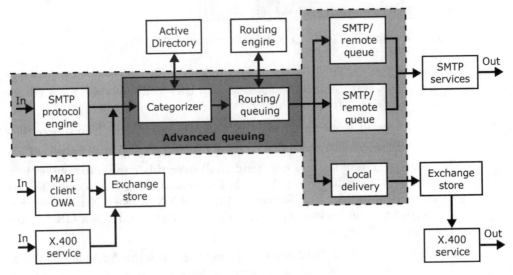

Figure 8-6   Exchange Server 2003 transport architecture

The first is through the SMTP service, such as Internet e-mail or a routing group connector, as just mentioned. The second is through a store submission, such as a message created by a Microsoft Outlook MAPI client or an OWA (Outlook Web Access) client. The third way is for the message to come in via the MTA (Message Transfer Agent) using X.400 connectivity.

SMTP messages are first sent to an NTFS queue because not all messages coming in from SMTP are destined for the local Exchange store. SMTP messages are then delivered from the NTFS queue to the precategorization queue where the message awaits being processed by the categorizer.

Messages submitted via either a store submission or the MTA are handled differently. These messages are dropped into the Exchange store driver. The Exchange store driver picks up these messages and passes them to the precategorization queue where they are processed in a manner similar to the way SMTP messages are processed.

After the message makes its way to the precategorization queue, the message is processed by the message categorizer, which is essentially a collection of event sinks. An event sink is a script that is run against a message to perform certain functions.

It is at this point that distribution list expansion is conducted as well. In addition, the message categorizer retrieves attributes from Active Directory that apply to the message, such as the originators or recipient size limits for outgoing and incoming messages, delivery restrictions, forwarding specifications, and other settings that might restrict the message in some way. Any restrictions that do exist are applied to the message. These restrictions are generally configured on the connector itself, as you will see in the following activity. After these tasks have been accomplished, the message is placed into a postcategorization queue.

ACTIVITY

Activity 8-4: Configuring Routing Group Connector Delivery Options

Time Required: 10 to 20 minutes

Objective: Configure delivery options to deliver large messages during nonpeak hours.

Description: In this activity, you configure the delivery options for the new routing group connector. Delivery options control when messages are sent through the connector. One of the key features is the ability to set connection schedules for all messages or messages of different size. This activity assumes that you have a relatively slow link between your routing groups and you will set a separate schedule for large messages and small messages to ensure that oversized messages don't use all the available bandwidth during peak usage hours.

1. From the Windows desktop of the back-end server, click **Start**, point to **All Programs**, point to **Microsoft Exchange**, and then click **System Manager**.

2. Click the **plus sign (+)** next to Administrative Groups. Click the **plus sign (+)** next to First Administrative Group, click the **plus sign (+)** next to the Routing Groups node, and then click the **plus sign (+)** next to First Routing Group.

3. Click the **plus sign (+)** next to the Connectors node, and right-click the **RGXX to RGYY Connector**, where XX is the number assigned to your back-end server and YY is the number assigned to your front-end server. On the shortcut menu, click **Properties**. The RGXX to RGYY Connector Properties dialog box opens, as shown in Figure 8-7.

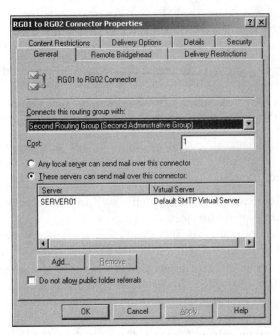

Figure 8-7   RGXX to RGYY Connector Properties dialog box

4. Click the **Delivery Options** tab. In the Connection time drop-down list, click **Run daily at 2:00 AM** to specify the time when messages are sent through the connector.

5. To set separate delivery options for standard and large messages, click the **Use different delivery times for oversize messages** check box. In the Oversize messages are greater than (KB) text box, type **1512**.

6. Click **OK**.

7. If you are prompted to configure a similar connector on the remote bridgehead server, click **Yes** to continue and return to Exchange System Manager.

8. Close **Exchange System Manager**.

After the message is processed in the postcategorization queue, it is given to the routing engine, which parses the destination address against its domain mapping and domain configuration table. The routing engine then decides whether the message is destined for the local store, or if a temporary outbound queue called a destination message queue should be created to pass the message to another SMTP server.

Destination message queues are created based on the destination domain name. The advanced queuing engine is able to create as many destination message queues as needed, each having a name based on the destination domain name. From these queues, the SMTP service reads the message out of the destination message queue and then passes the message to the next SMTP server. If the message is destined for the local store, it is placed in the local delivery queue. The store.exe process then reads the message out of the local delivery queue and writes it to the local database. At this point, the recipient is notified that new mail has arrived.

LINK STATE ALGORITHM

Before a message is delivered to its final destination, the routing engine is consulted for the best possible route to the destination. If the message is destined for another Exchange Server 2003 server within the same routing group, a DNS query is made to determine the address of the destination server at which point the SMTP service contacts the destination server directly to deliver the message. When the message is delivered outside of the routing group, the routing engine typically routes the message differently. It determines the best route based on different criteria, such as link availability, cost, and so on. To do this, the routing engine makes use of something called a **link state algorithm**.

The link state algorithm is based on a routing algorithm that has been in existence for many years and is used extensively in network routing as the Open Shortest Path First (OSPF) protocol. The link state algorithm propagates the state of the messaging system almost in real time to all servers in the organization. This has several advantages, including the following:

- Each Exchange server can make the best routing decision before sending a message downstream where a link might be down.

- Message delivery becomes deterministic in that messages will no longer bounce back and forth between servers because each Exchange Server 2003 server has the latest information about all the paths within the organization.

- Message looping is eliminated because alternate route information is propagated to each Exchange Server 2003 server.

Routing Group Master

The link state algorithm operates over TCP port 691 within the routing group. In each routing group, one server is configured as the **routing group master**. The routing group master receives link state information and propagates this information to the other servers in the routing group. It also propagates this information to other routing groups through a server known as the **bridgehead server**. When one bridgehead server connects to another bridgehead server in a different routing group, the exchange of link state information occurs over TCP port 25, using SMTP. The routing group master keeps track of which servers are up and which are down and propagates that information to the routing group master in every other routing group.

Link state information is rather important when an organization has multiple routing groups with multiple paths between the groups, or if the Exchange organization connects to external e-mail systems. The routing group master maintains the link state information, sending it to and receiving it from the routing group masters in other routing groups. The routing group master is not necessarily the same server as the bridgehead server, which is the server that you designate to send and receive messages across a given connector to another bridgehead server. You can, however, manually configure one server to perform both roles.

The routing group master ensures that all the servers in its routing group have correct link state information about the availability of the messaging connectors and servers in other groups. In addition, it ensures that other groups have correct information about its servers.

Only two states are available for any given link: up or down. The link state information does not include any connection information, such as whether a link is in a retry state. This information is known only to the server involved in the message transfer. When a bridgehead server determines that a link is unavailable, it marks the link as down. It then sends this information to all the servers in its own routing group (over TCP port 691) and to the bridgehead servers in the other routing groups (over TCP port 25).

Link State Information

Link state information is held in memory, not on disk. If the routing group master goes down or needs to be rebooted, it needs to have link state information replicated from other routing group masters in the organization. Because the routing group information is held in the naming partition of Active Directory, the definitions of connectors and costs are also held in Active Directory. The link state algorithm references each connector by its GUID (globally unique identifier).

In Exchange Server 2003, link state propagation has been improved in two different ways. The first improvement involves scenarios in which no alternate path exists within the routing topology; the second is for situations in which the connection is intermittent. For these scenarios, Exchange Server 2003 attempts to determine if the connector state is intermittent or if no alternate path exists and suppresses the propagation of link state information if either of these conditions exist. If no alternate path exists for a link, the link state is always marked as up. Exchange does not change the link state to unavailable if no alternate path exists. Exchange simply lets mail queue for delivery and sends it when the route becomes available. This change enhances performance because it reduces the propagation of link state information.

For intermittent or oscillating connections, Exchange Server 2003 reviews the link state queue and determines if there are multiple conflicting state changes in a given interval for a connector. If so, the connector is considered an oscillating connection and its link state remains up. This is preferred as it is better to leave the connector up than continually change the link state and propagate this information throughout the organization. This reduces the amount of link state traffic that is replicated between servers.

How Exchange Makes Use of Link State Information

To understand how Exchange Server 2003 makes use of link state information and connector costs, the concepts are illustrated through an example. Figure 8-8 provides a routing topology for a fictitious company, Importers of the Americas, which has operations in five cities in both North and South America.

8

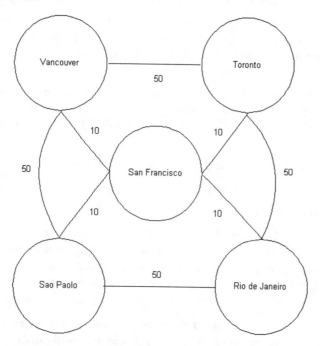

Figure 8-8   Link state routing topology example

Each of the sites is represented as a distinct routing group within the Exchange Server 2003 organization as illustrated in the diagram. Connectors are established between each routing group and their associated costs are depicted.

Routing cost plays a key role in optimizing message routing. When two or more connectors link the same servers or routing groups, the connector with the lowest routing cost has preference over the other connectors. If the connector with the lowest cost is unavailable for any reason, Exchange Server 2003 uses the connector with the next lowest routing cost. By having multiple connectors and setting routing costs, administrators can ensure that messages are delivered even when a primary connector fails.

Activity 8-5: Setting Routing Costs for a Connector

Time Required: 10 to 20 minutes

Objective: Configure routing costs for a connector.

Description: In this activity, you configure the routing cost for a connector. If you had two connectors, you could configure them both with the same cost to balance the messaging load over the two servers. Configuring multiple connectors with the same routing cost tells Exchange Server 2003 to distribute the load as evenly as possible among connectors.

1. From the Windows desktop of the back-end server, click **Start**, point to **All Programs**, point to **Microsoft Exchange**, and then click **System Manager**.

2. Click the **plus sign (+)** next to Administrative Groups, click the **plus sign (+)** next to First Administrative Group, click the **plus sign (+)** next to the Routing Groups node, click the **plus sign (+)** next to First Routing Group, and, finally, click the **plus sign (+)** next to the Connectors node.

3. Right-click on **RGXX to RGYY Connector**, where XX is the number assigned to your back-end server and YY is the number assigned to your front-end server. On the shortcut menu, click **Properties**. The RGXX to RGYY Connector Properties dialog box opens.

4. On the General tab, type **5** in the Cost text box to set the cost for the connector.

5. Click **OK** to return to Exchange System Manager.

6. Close **Exchange System Manager**.

If all the connections between the routing groups in Figure 8-8 are available, a server in Toronto sends a message to Rio de Janeiro via the San Francisco routing group. This is because the cost of sending the message through the San Francisco routing group is lower than sending it directly from Toronto to Rio de Janeiro. The costs between these two offices might be higher for any number of reasons, such as network speed, line utilization, and so forth.

Now assume that there is a link failure between San Francisco and Rio de Janeiro. Because the organization is based on Exchange Server 2003, the link state protocol causes the routing processes to propagate the status of this link throughout the organization so that mail flow can still be maintained. When the bridgehead server in Toronto sends a message to the bridgehead server in San Francisco, the message is delivered successfully. Now, the bridgehead server in San Francisco tries to connect to the server in Rio de Janeiro and finds that the connection is down. The San Francisco bridgehead server then goes into retry mode and waits 60 seconds before attempting the transfer again. After three unsuccessful attempts to connect to the destination bridgehead server, the San Francisco bridgehead server marks the connection as down and updates the link state information using TCP port 691 on the routing group master within the San Francisco routing group. The routing group master, upon receiving the notification that the link is down, immediately sends updates to all other Exchange Server 2003 servers within the San Francisco routing group.

At this point, the San Francisco bridgehead server is still waiting to deliver the message to its final destination. However, because the connection is down, it recalculates an alternate route to Rio de Janeiro through Toronto (because the message originated in Toronto) and notifies the Toronto bridgehead server about the downlink to Rio de Janeiro. The bridgehead server in Toronto immediately connects to the routing group master in the Toronto routing group over TCP port 691 and transfers the information about the down link. The routing group master within the Toronto routing group then sends updates to all the servers within the Toronto routing group. Using the new link state information, the bridgehead server in the Toronto routing group calculates the best route to Rio de Janeiro based on the known information for each connection. Given that the connection from San Francisco to Rio de Janeiro is down, it uses the direct connection from Toronto to Rio de Janeiro as the route for all subsequent messages.

Before routing the message to Rio de Janeiro, the bridgehead server in the Toronto routing group propagates the link state information to the bridgehead server in Rio de Janeiro. This process continues until all of the routing groups know of the downlink between San Francisco and Rio de Janeiro. Any subsequent messages that are generated within the Toronto routing group will then be routed directly to Rio de Janeiro via the connection with the higher cost. This occurs until the connection from San Francisco to Rio de Janeiro comes back up. To check if the connection is up, the bridgehead server in San Francisco continues to try to contact the bridgehead server in Rio de Janeiro every 60 seconds, or according to the specified schedule, even if no messages are awaiting transfer. When the link becomes active again, the new link status is replicated to all of the other Exchange Server 2003 servers in the organization, in much the same way the down status of the link was propagated throughout the organization.

Now what happens if more than one connection fails? The beauty of the link state algorithm is that it ensures that the message doesn't bounce back and forth between routing groups in a continual attempt to find an open message path.

For example, using the routing infrastructure outlined previously, if the link between Toronto and San Francisco is down, and the link between Toronto and Rio de Janeiro is down, what happens when a message is sent from Toronto to Rio de Janeiro? Based on the cost of the routes, the bridgehead server in Toronto sends a message to Rio de Janeiro via the San Francisco routing group. The bridgehead server opens a connection to the bridgehead in San Francisco, but before sending the message, it propagates the down status of the connection between Toronto and Rio de Janeiro. The bridgehead server in San Francisco then forwards the link status information to the routing group master, which, in turn, propagates the information to each of the other Exchange Server 2003 servers in the routing group. After the link status has been propagated, the bridgehead server in the Toronto routing group sends the message to the bridgehead server in San Francisco.

The bridgehead server in San Francisco then attempts to open a connection to the bridgehead server in Rio de Janeiro, at which time it discovers that the attempt will fail and will go into retry mode every 60 seconds or based on the schedule defined on the Delivery tab of the SMTP virtual server (configured in the next activity). If it cannot establish a connection, it marks the link as down and notifies the routing group master, which, in turn, propagates the status to each of the other Exchange Server 2003 servers in the San Francisco routing group. The bridgehead server then recalculates a new route for the message. However, because both of the routes to the Rio de Janeiro routing group are down, the cost that is calculated is infinite. After the cost has been calculated as infinite, the message is then routed via an alternative route. In this scenario, the message is then routed through Sao Paolo to Rio de Janeiro.

Activity 8-6: Configuring the Retry Intervals for SMTP Virtual Servers

Time Required: 10 to 20 minutes

Objective: Configure the retry interval for an SMTP virtual server.

Description: In this activity, you configure the retry interval on your SMTP virtual server. In Exchange Server 2003, if a message cannot be delivered on the first attempt, Exchange Server 2003 tries to send it again after a specified time. You can configure the interval between delivery attempts. After the time limit is reached, the message is returned to the sender with an NDR. Copies of the message and the NDR are sent to a location that you designate on the Messages tab. The NDR then goes through the same delivery process as messages.

1. From the Windows desktop on the back-end server, click **Start**, point to **All Programs**, point to **Microsoft Exchange**, and then click **System Manager**.

2. Click the **plus sign (+)** next to Administrative Groups. Click the **plus sign (+)** next to First Administrative Group, click the **plus sign (+)** next to the Servers node, and then click the **plus sign (+)** next to SERVERXX, where XX is the number assigned to your back-end server. Click the **plus sign (+)** next to the Protocols node, and, finally, click the **plus sign (+)** next to the SMTP node.

3. Right-click the **BLATHER SMTP Virtual Server**, and then click **Properties** on the shortcut menu. The BLATHER SMTP Virtual Server Properties dialog box opens.

4. Click the **Delivery** tab. Type **5** in the First retry interval (minutes) text box to specify how long to attempt delivery before posting the first notification. The default is 10 minutes.

5. Type **5** in the Second retry interval (minutes) text box to specify how long to attempt delivery after the first retry interval before posting the second notification. The default is 10 minutes.

6. Type **5** in the Third retry interval (minutes) text box to specify how long to attempt delivery after the second retry interval before posting the third notification. The default is 10 minutes.

7. Type **7** in the Subsequent retry intervals (minutes) text box to specify how long to attempt delivery after the third retry interval before posting a notification. The default is 15 minutes.

8. Type **20** in the Delay notification text box, and then click **Minutes** in the drop-down list to set a delay period before sending a delivery notification. The minimum value is 1 Minute, the default is 12 Hours, and the maximum value is 9999 Days.

9. The settings on the Delivery tab should appear as shown in Figure 8-9. Click **OK** to finish.

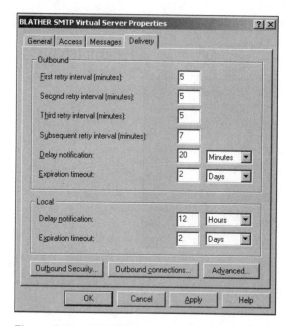

Figure 8-9   BLATHER SMTP Virtual Server Properties dialog box, Delivery tab

10. Close **Exchange System Manager**.

USING LINK STATE INFORMATION TO ROUTE EXTERNALLY

What happens when a message is destined for a foreign e-mail system, such as the Internet? How does Exchange Server 2003 use link state information for external mail delivery? The answer to this question is that Exchange Server 2003 routes messages based on the information contained in the link state routing table, similar to the way in which it routes internal messages. It first evaluates the connector with the address space that most closely matches the destination, and then evaluates the costs associated with using those connectors. Consider the routing architecture presented in Figure 8-10.

Figure 8-10 contains three Internet connectors, as follows:

- One connector that routes addresses based on *.br with a cost of 10
- A second connector that routes addresses based on *.net with a cost of 20
- A third connector that routes all other addresses with a cost of 10

When mail is sent to an external user with an e-mail address of ryan@importsofamerica.br, Exchange Server 2003 first looks for a connector with an address space that most closely

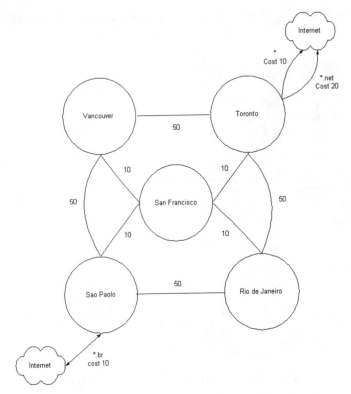

Figure 8-10   Link state routing topology with external connectors example

matches the destination recipient address, in this case, importsofamerica.br. Exchange Server 2003 then determines that the connector for *.br most closely matches the destination address and routes the message through the SMTP connector in Sao Paolo. The routing infrastructure then delivers the message using this connector regardless of cost. If the message is sent to an address of Sheryl@importsofamerica.com, Exchange Server 2003 makes use of the SMTP connector with the address space of * that routes through Toronto, because it is the closest match.

If there are two connectors that match a specific address space, the lower cost connector is always used. However, if one of the connectors is unavailable, routing does not fail over to a connector with a less specific address space. For instance, if the connector serving *.net were to fail, traffic would not be routed out the connector serving * in the Toronto routing group.

Activity 8-7: Installing an SMTP Connector

Time Required: 10 to 20 minutes

Objective: Provide some perspective on how Exchange Server 2003 routes external SMTP mail; install and configure an SMTP connector.

Description: In this activity, you install an SMTP connector for your Exchange Server 2003 organization. When you install an SMTP connector, you must define which local bridgehead servers the connector will use as well as the connector scope, message routing technique, and address space. SMTP virtual servers act as local bridgehead servers for SMTP connectors. As mentioned, SMTP connectors have a specific scope that controls how the connector routes messages. You can use an SMTP connector with a routing group scope to transfer messages within your organization. You can use an SMTP connector with an organizational scope to connect independent Exchange organizations or to connect Exchange servers with other SMTP-compatible servers on the Internet.

1. From the Windows desktop of the back-end server, click **Start**, point to **All Programs**, point to **Microsoft Exchange**, and then click **System Manager**.

2. Click the **plus sign (+)** next to Administrative Groups. Click the **plus sign (+)** next to First Administrative Group, click the **plus sign (+)** next to the Routing Groups node, and, finally, click the **plus sign (+)** next to First Routing Group.

3. Right-click **Connectors**, point to **New** on the shortcut menu, and then click **SMTP Connector**. The Properties dialog box for the SMTP connector opens, as shown in Figure 8-11.

8

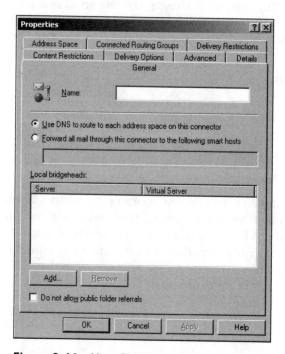

Figure 8-11 New SMTP connector Properties dialog box

4. On the General tab, type **External SMTP Connector** in the Name text box.

5. You have the option of using either DNS to route mail or to use a smart host for routing. To use a smart host, select Forward all mail through this connector to the following smart hosts, and then type the fully qualified domain name or IP address of the server through which you want to route messages. In this activity, you configure the SMTP connector to make use of DNS for routing. To do this, click **Use DNS to route to each address space on this connector**, if necessary.

6. You must specify at least one local bridgehead server. To do so, click the **Add** button. The Add Bridgehead dialog box opens. Click the **Default SMTP Virtual Server** on SERVERXX, where XX represents the number assigned to your back-end server. Click **OK** to return to the Properties dialog box for the new SMTP connector.

7. To specify an address space and the scope of the connector, click the **Address Space** tab. If you are connecting two Exchange organizations, set the connector scope as Entire organization. If you are connecting two routing groups, set the connector scope as Routing group. For this activity, click **Routing group**.

8. Click the **Add** button. The Add Address Space dialog box opens. If necessary, click **SMTP**, and then click **OK**. The Internet Address Space Properties dialog box opens. If necessary, type * in the E-mail domain text box, and then, if necessary, type **1** in the Cost text box. Click **OK** to return to the External SMTP Connector Properties dialog box.

9. To set this connector up as an open relay, click the **Allow messages to be relayed to these domains** check box.

10. Click **OK** to install the connector.

11. You are prompted that you are allowing the connector to relay and that it is overriding restrictions on the SMTP virtual server. Click **OK** to continue.

12. Close **Exchange System Manager**.

SMTP connectors are a bit more complex than the routing group connector you configured earlier. However, the additional settings SMTP connectors make available puts these connectors at an advantage. With SMTP connectors, you can encrypt message traffic sent over the link, and require stricter authentication than with routing group connectors. You can transmit messages to a designated server called a smart host, which then transfers the message, or you can use DNS records to route messages.

Activity 8-8: Configuring Delivery Options for SMTP

Time Required: 10 to 20 minutes

Objective: Configure the delivery options for an SMTP connector.

Description: In this activity, you configure the delivery options for an SMTP connector. SMTP connectors have delivery options that determine when messages are sent through the connector as well as whether messages are queued for remote delivery. To control when messages are sent, schedules can be configured based on the different message sizes. This allows you to better utilize limited bandwidth. To control message queuing, you can enable or disable it for remote delivery on an individual basis. When a user logs on to the system, Exchange Server 2003 then triggers delivery of all queued messages for that user. This allows you to more efficiently manage how messages are delivered to remote clients with temporary connections.

1. From the Windows desktop of the back-end server, click **Start**, point to **All Programs**, point to **Microsoft Exchange**, and then click **System Manager**.

2. Click the **plus sign (+)** next to Administrative Groups. Click the **plus sign (+)** next to First Administrative Group, click the **plus sign (+)** next to the Routing Groups node, click the **plus sign (+)** next to First Routing Group, and, finally, click the **plus sign (+)** next to the Connectors node.

3. Right-click the **External SMTP Connector**, and then click **Properties** on the shortcut menu. The External SMTP Connector Properties dialog box opens.

4. Click the **Delivery Options** tab. Click **Run daily at 11:00 PM** in the Connection time drop-down list. This specifies the times when messages are sent through the connector.

5. To set separate delivery options for standard and large messages, click the **Use different delivery times for oversize messages** check box. Type **1024** in the Oversize messages are greater than (KB) text box to designate the minimum size in kilobytes of messages that will be considered as oversized. The default is 2000 KB.

6. Click **Run every 2 hours** in the second Connection time drop-down list. This sets the delivery times for large messages. The external SMTP connector's delivery options are configured, as shown in Figure 8-12.

7. When you are finished, click **OK** to return to Exchange System Manager.

8. Close **Exchange System Manager**.

8

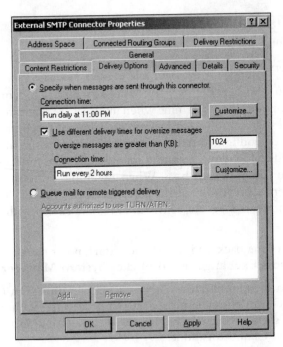

Figure 8-12   External SMTP Connector Properties dialog box, Delivery Options tab

CHAPTER SUMMARY

- ❑ SMTP provides a set of rules for communicating messages between servers and defines the format of those messages.

- ❑ MIME extends the headers of traditional SMTP messages to define how attachments are to be encapsulated within your message.

- ❑ Exchange Server 2003 uses virtual servers to implement SMTP messaging within an Exchange Server 2003 organization. The SMTP service that monitors these virtual servers originates with Windows 2000/2003 and is extended by an Exchange Server 2003 installation to provide additional functionality.

- ❑ You can have more than one SMTP virtual server per computer. This gives you the ability to host different default domains or to configure different delivery options for different groups of individuals.

- ❑ A routing group in Exchange Server 2003 consists of a collection of well-connected Exchange servers for which full-time, full mesh connectivity is guaranteed. By default, Exchange Server 2003 functions as though all servers in an organization belong to a single, large routing group.

- ❑ Alternate routing groups can be configured and are usually defined to address issues with limited capacity/availability of network connections.

◻ Four types of connectors are available with Exchange Server 2003 to provide connectivity between systems and to other mail platforms. These include the SMTP connector, the routing group connector, the X.400 connector, and specialty connectors, such as the Lotus Notes connector and the Groupwise connector.

◻ Link state routing propagates information about the status of the messaging system almost in real time to all servers in the organization. This has advantages in that it allows the messaging system to make the best decision before sending a message, it removes the chances of message looping from the messaging infrastructure, and it ensures that messages no longer bounce back and forth between servers because of out-of-date routing information.

◻ Link state routing information is communicated within a routing group on TCP port 691. Between routing groups, link state information is communicated on port 25.

◻ In Exchange Server 2003, link state routing was improved for scenarios in which no alternate path is available within the routing topology and for situations that involved intermittent network connectivity.

◻ When mail is sent externally, Exchange Server 2003 routes the message through the connector that handles the address space that most closely matches the destination recipient address.

8

KEY TERMS

bridgehead server — A server that provides a single point for delivery of e-mail and link state information between routing groups within an Exchange Server 2003 organization. It also serves as a central source for the delivery of messages inside and outside of the organization.

link state algorithm — An algorithm, which is based on the OSPF algorithm, that operates over TCP port 691 in a routing group to propagate routing status information to all of the Exchange Server 2003 servers in the organization through the routing group master. This routing status, or link state, information is used by Exchange Server 2003 to determine the best path to send messages to other servers.

Multipurpose Internet Mail Extensions (MIME) — A set of message headers, which describe what sort of content is in a message (plain text, HTML, graphics, and so on) and how it's encoded. Some of the content types are multipart, meaning that they define a complex message structure with more than one part, each of which has headers of its own. Each part has its own set of MIME headers, in addition to the headers at the beginning of the message.

routing group connector — A connector that establishes the mechanism for delivering messages between routing groups. The routing group connector connects to the defined target server in the remote site and delivers the message on behalf of servers within the routing group that hosts the connector.

routing group master — The server that keeps track of the link state data and propagates that data to the rest of the servers in the routing group. When a nonmaster server receives new link state information, the nonmaster server immediately transfers the link state information to the master, so that other servers can receive the information about the routing change.

Simple Mail Transfer Protocol (SMTP) — A protocol used to send e-mail on the Internet. SMTP is a set of rules regarding the interaction between a program sending e-mail and a program receiving e-mail.

SMTP connector — A connector that is designed to route mail to external e-mail systems, such as Internet mail hosts, or to another Exchange organization.

X.400 connector — A connector that is designed to connect Exchange servers with legacy X.400 systems or two low-bandwidth Exchange servers to each other.

REVIEW QUESTIONS

1. How does the link state algorithm reference connectors?

   a. the GUID (globally unique identifier)

   b. the SID (security identifier)

   c. the connector's name

   d. the SMTP address of the connector

2. Which connector allows delivery of messages to be scheduled based on message size?

   a. routing group connector

   b. SMTP connector

   c. X.400 connector

   d. none of the above

3. Which of the following commands is not an SMTP command? (Choose all that apply.)

   a. HELO

   b. QUIT

   c. DATA

   d. FROM

4. What features does the SMTP connector provide that the routing group connector does not provide? (Choose all that apply.)

   a. message encryption

   b. stricter authentication

   c. virus scanning

   d. address rewrites

5. The SMTP virtual server that is installed with Windows 2000/Windows 2003 comes standard with link state routing built in. True or False?

6. Which connector is not included with the Standard Edition of Exchange Server 2003?

   a. SMTP connector

   b. routing group connector

   c. X.400 connector

   d. None of the above. All of the connectors are included.

7. What did MIME introduce to facilitate the transfer of attachments with SMTP messages?

   a. additional headers

   b. a new encoding scheme

   c. compression

   d. none of the above

8. Which of the following extensions were added to the existing Windows 2000/2003 SMTP service as part of an Exchange Server 2003 installation?

   a. enhanced message categorization

   b. link state routing

   c. Installable File System

   d. all of the above

9. Which of the following network scenarios is considered a valid routing group?

   a. servers connected over a high-speed subnet

   b. servers connected over a low-bandwidth WAN

   c. servers connected over a mixed low-bandwidth WAN and high-bandwidth LAN

   d. servers connected via a wireless network

10. Which protocol does the routing group connector use?

    a. SMTP

    b. X.400

    c. proprietary

    d. MAPI

    e. TLS

11. Which component of the messaging infrastructure is responsible for distribution list expansion?

    a. categorizer

    b. advanced queuing engine

    c. System Attendant

    d. the Event service

12. How are destination message queues created by the advanced queuing engine?

    a. They are created dynamically.

    b. They are preconfigured as part of installation.

    c. Message queues are not utilized.

    d. none of the above

13. What are the benefits of using a link state algorithm?

    a. Message looping is eliminated.

    b. There is no chance of messages bouncing back and forth between servers because of invalid routes.

    c. Routing decisions are optimized.

    d. Memory requirements on the server are reduced.

14. What is the purpose of the routing group master?

    a. to distribute routing updates throughout the routing group

    b. to provide routing decisions for messaging servers

    c. to elect which server will act as the bridgehead within the routing group

    d. none of the above

15. What enhancements were added to the link state algorithm in Exchange Server 2003?

    a. Link state propagation was improved for scenarios in which no alternate path exists within the routing topology.

    b. Link state propagation has been improved for intermittent connections or connections that oscillate between being available and unavailable.

    c. Reduction in the amount of information that is transferred to keep routing tables up to date was provided.

    d. all of the above

16. What happens if you have two connectors defined with both of them assigned the same cost?

    a. Nothing, the second connector defined is only used if the first goes down.

    b. This is not a valid configuration.

    c. Messages are load-balanced across the connectors.

    d. none of the above

17. Given an environment with two connectors, the first one serving a specific domain, with the second one serving the more general domain of *, messages will be routed through the second connector if the first one fails. True or False?

18. Configuring an SMTP virtual server to accept connections only from a specific domain can cause performance degradation for your Exchange Server 2003 server. True or False?

19. If all routes to a destination routing group are down, what will be the cost assigned to that destination?

    a. infinite

    b. zero

    c. the number of hops to the destination plus one

    d. It does not mark the cost; instead, the route is removed from the routing table.

20. Which connector allows you to do open relaying?

    a. X.400 connector

    b. routing group connector

    c. SMTP connector

    d. Lotus Notes connector

8

CASE PROJECTS

Case Project 8-1: High Network Utilization

Bob Jones, an Arts professor, has written an e-mail message to the head of Network Operations complaining about the speed of the network between the remote campus that houses the Arts Department and the central campus. Network Operations investigates the bandwidth usage and discovers that the high utilization is a result of SMTP traffic and refers the matter to you. Write an e-mail response to Bob explaining the likely cause of the problem and what you can do to correct it.

Case Project 8-2: Choosing a Method of Connectivity to the Internet

As part of the planning process, you are meeting with the rest of the IT Department to brainstorm how you want to configure your e-mail servers to connect to the Internet. Make a list of the various methods for connecting your Exchange Server 2003 servers to the Internet and describe the advantages and disadvantages of each method.

Case Project 8-3: Choosing a Connector

As the person in charge of implementing e-mail services for Arctic University, you are responsible for implementing connectivity within your e-mail infrastructure. To decide which connector to implement, you are meeting with the Network Operations people to understand their requirements. Create a document describing each of the connectors and when each is appropriate to use. You can distribute this document to each faculty head before the meeting.

Chapter 8

Case Project 8-4: Implementing Redundancy in Your Internet Connection

The Accounting Department has been complaining for some time that messages being sent to external auditors have failed to be delivered. Your supervisor has asked you to look into the problem. He thinks that funding could be made available to help resolve the issue, but he needs to make the case to the university governors. Produce a report outlining the issue and the methods that can be taken to resolve the issue so that your supervisor can make his case to the university governors.

9

MANAGING DATA STORAGE AND HARDWARE RESOURCES

<hr>

After reading this chapter, you will be able to:

- ♦ Understand the data storage architecture and how to configure storage in an Exchange Server 2003 environment
- ♦ Describe the Extensible Storage Engine's use of transaction logs
- ♦ Understand content indexing and how it is used to speed up searching within Exchange Server 2003
- ♦ Understand disk subsystem configurations in different Exchange Server 2003 environments

<hr>

E-mail has seen an explosive growth within organizations and an increasing richness of messages and attachments. The growth in storage requirements to accommodate this volume required the rethinking of previous versions of the Microsoft Exchange storage architecture. The primary issue was how long it would take to recover a database in the event that the server needed to be recovered. Because databases were of such large sizes, recovery times equated to long times as well. This generally resulted in organizations not being able to meet or establish service level agreements that could be met in a reasonable amount of time.

Exchange Server 2003 helps to resolve these issues by taking a different approach to storage. Exchange Server 2003 uses several types of message stores, or storage databases, to hold the messages that make up its information architecture. The first type of store is the mailbox store, which holds the actual messages that are delivered by the mail system. The second type of store is the public folder store, which contains message information that is accessible to more than one user. Public folder stores are the preferred choice for making information available to a large number of users over a wide area.

The reason for the separation between the public folder store and the mailbox store lies in the way Exchange Server 2003 treats the information in the public folder store. Because everyone in what could be a widely distributed organization can access public folders, Exchange Server 2003 allows you to set up automatic replication of the contents of public folders. Exchange Server 2003 handles the replication of documents in public folders with no intervention on the part of an administrator after the replication is defined. Users who request a document in a public folder retrieve it from the closest copy of the public folder, rather than having all users access the requested document from a single location.

This chapter focuses on the storage architecture used in Exchange Server 2003 and the differences between the types of stores used in Exchange Server 2003. It describes what storage groups are and when and why you should create additional storage groups. The chapter looks at public folder stores, and how they can be configured. It also presents the steps necessary to configure and administer storage within your organization.

DATA STORAGE CONCEPTS

The Exchange Server 2003 information storage architecture is composed of multiple storage groups. Each **storage group** can hold up to five data stores and there can be a maximum of five storage groups. Four storage groups are used to hold data while the fifth storage group is called the Recovery Storage Group and is used for data store recovery operations. This provides a maximum of 20 data stores that can be used for storage purposes. Each data store can be either mounted or dismounted independently of each other.

Having multiple data stores in multiple storage groups has the following benefits:

- It allows organizations to host more users per server than was possible in previous versions of the software. This, in turn, provides organizations with the ability to consolidate servers and thereby reduce the costs associated with managing their e-mail infrastructure. By hosting multiple data stores per server, the sizes of individual data stores are reduced, allowing more users to be allocated per data store. For instance, it is easier to manage five data stores each having 1,000 users, than it is to manage one data store that hosts 5,000 users. If a data store becomes corrupt, it affects only 1,000 users as opposed to all 5,000 users, thereby minimizing the impact to end users due to downtime caused by data store issues.

- It reduces the potential impact of a data store going offline. By spreading users across multiple data stores, the number of users who are affected by a data store going down is some subset of the entire number of users on the server. This increases overall end-user availability.

- It provides improved recoverability. By allowing individual data stores to be restored while other data stores are running, there are shorter downtimes as it takes less time to recover a data store that houses a subset of users than it does to recover a data store that houses all users.

Storage groups allow you to group data stores logically, providing you with greater flexibility regarding how you manage your users and data stores. For example, you can group users by department, line of business, or their level of importance within the organization. Executives tend to have service level agreements that are more stringent than the other users within the organization. Having multiple data stores per storage group allows you to control the user-to-data-store ratio, so that if your organization grows, you can keep your data store at a predetermined size and simply create another data store for new users when necessary.

When you first install Exchange Server 2003, a single storage group is created called the First Storage Group. As your requirements warrant, additional storage groups can be created.

Activity 9-1: Creating an Additional Storage Group

Time Required: 10 to 20 minutes

Objective: Create an additional storage group on a server.

Description: In this activity, you create an additional storage group on your Exchange 2003 server. This storage group is named VIP Storage Group and houses the data stores for the VIP users within the organization. To create an additional storage group, complete the following steps:

1. Log on to the back-end server using the user name **Administrator** and the password **Password!**.

2. From the Windows desktop, click **Start**, point to **All Programs**, point to **Microsoft Exchange**, and then click **System Manager**.

3. Click the **plus sign (+)** next to Administrative Groups, click the **plus sign (+)** next to First Administrative Group, and then click the **plus sign (+)** next to the Servers container.

4. Click **SERVERXX**, where *XX* is the number assigned to your back-end server, and then right-click it to open the appropriate shortcut menu. On the shortcut menu, point to **New**, and then click **Storage Group**. The Properties dialog box for creating new storage groups opens, as shown in Figure 9-1.

5. In the Name text box, type **VIP Storage Group** for the storage group name.

6. Click **Browse** to the right of the Transaction log location text box, and then type **c:\temp** in the Folder text box as the location to store your transaction logs. Note that you cannot store files for additional storage groups in the same directory in which you have an existing storage group. Click **OK** in the Transaction Log dialog box.

7. Click **Browse** to the right of the System path location text box, and then type **c:\temp** in the Folder text box as the location for the system files that the storage group will use. Click **OK** in the System Path dialog box.

8. Click **OK** to create the storage group. You can now add mailbox and public folder stores to the storage group.

9. Close **Exchange System Manager**.

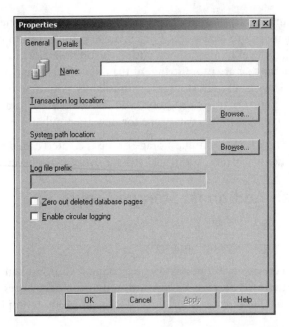

Figure 9-1   Properties dialog box for new storage group

Each storage group can contain mailbox and public folder data stores. By default, when you install Exchange Server 2003 into an organization, two data stores are created: a default mailbox store and a public folder store. Each data store consists of two database files: the rich text file (ending in .edb), which holds mail messages and **Message Application Programming Interface (MAPI)** content, and a native content file, or streaming Internet content file (ending in .stm). This file contains audio, video, and other media that are formatted as streams of Multipurpose Internet Mail Extension (MIME) data.

What happens when a client needs to read information from these stores? This depends on the client and from where the information is being read. When a MAPI client attempts to read a message from the rich text file, no conversion is necessary as clients communicate using the MAPI protocol with the back-end Exchange 2003 servers. If the client needs to read data from the native content file, the content must be converted. In this case, Exchange Server 2003 converts the message in memory on the server, and then passes the message to the MAPI client. The message is not moved from the native content file to the rich text file before being sent to the MAPI client. If the MAPI client makes a change to the message and then saves it, the message is copied from the native content file to the rich text file, and then deleted from the native content file. During the copy process, the updated message is converted from its native content to rich text before being written to the rich text file. If another client that is not MAPI-based, such as a POP/IMAP client or HTTP client, reads a message that is not in the native content file, this conversion process occurs in the opposite direction.

ACTIVITY

Activity 9-2: Creating an Additional Mailbox Store

Time Required: 10 to 20 minutes

Objective: Create an additional mailbox store on a server.

Description: In this activity, you create an additional mailbox store on your Exchange 2003 server. This mailbox store is named the Executive Data Store and houses mailbox recipients for the executives within your company. You create this store within the VIP Storage Group created in the previous activity. To create an additional data store, complete the following steps:

1. From the Windows desktop of the back-end server, click **Start**, point to **All Programs**, point to **Microsoft Exchange**, and then click **System Manager**.

2. Click the **plus sign (+)** next to Administrative Groups, click the **plus sign (+)** next to First Administrative Group, and then click the **plus sign (+)** next to the Servers container. Click the **plus sign (+)** next to SERVERXX, where XX is the student number assigned to your back-end server, and then right-click **VIP Storage Group**. On the shortcut menu, point to **New**, and then click **Mailbox Store**. The Properties dialog box for a new mailbox store opens, as shown in Figure 9-2.

9

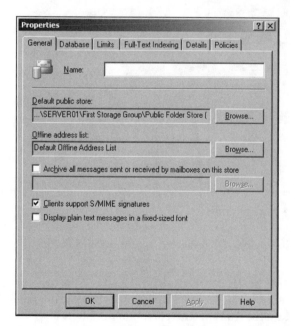

Figure 9-2   Properties dialog box for new mailbox store

3. On the General tab, type **Executive Data Store** in the Name text box.

4. Click the **Database** tab. Here, you see the default location for the Exchange database and Exchange streaming database files. There is no need to change any settings on this tab. Examine the settings to understand what they are.

5. To change the location of the database files, use the Browse buttons to the right of the related text boxes to specify new locations for these files. For this activity, note the default location of these files.

6. Changes made to Exchange Server 2003 database files can cause the files to become inconsistent over time. To correct problems that might arise, Exchange Server 2003 runs maintenance tasks on the database files daily from 1:00 a.m. to 5:00 a.m. by default. If you want to change this, click the Customize button to change the schedule. For this activity, note the default maintenance interval.

7. To specify limits within your database, click the **Limits** tab, as shown in Figure 9-3.

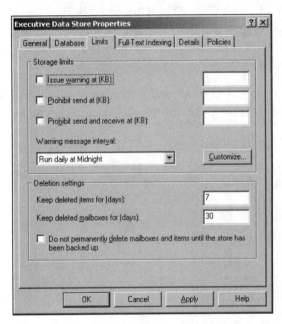

Figure 9-3 Executive Data Store storage limits

Here, you can set storage limits and deleted item retention. Configure the items as follows:

- Click the **Issue warning at (KB)** check box. This sets the size limit that a mailbox can reach before a warning is issued to the user. The warning tells the user to clear out the mailbox. Type **1024** in the corresponding text box.

- Click the **Prohibit send at (KB)** check box. This sets the size limit that a mailbox can reach before the user is prohibited from sending any new mail. The restriction ends when the user clears out the mailbox and the total mailbox size is under the limit. Type **2048** in the corresponding text box.

- Click the **Prohibit send and receive at (KB)** check box. This sets the size limit that a mailbox can reach before the user is prohibited from sending and receiving mail. The restriction ends when the user clears out the mailbox and the total mailbox size is under the limit. Type **3072** in the corresponding text box.

- Click **Run daily at 1:00 AM** in the Warning message interval drop-down list. This sets the interval for sending warning messages to users whose mailboxes exceed the designated limits. The default interval is daily at midnight.

- Keep deleted items for (Days) sets the number of days to retain deleted items. An average retention period is 14 days. If you set the retention period to 0, deleted messages aren't retained, and you can't recover them. Leave this item set at the default of 7.

- Keep deleted mailboxes for (Days) sets the number of days to retain deleted mailboxes. The default setting is 30 days. You'll want to keep most deleted mailboxes for at least 7 days to allow the administrators to extract any data that might be needed. If you set the retention period to 0, deleted mailboxes aren't retained, and you can't recover them. Leave this item set at the default.

8. Click **OK** when you are finished. Exchange Server 2003 creates the mailbox store for you. When prompted to mount the store, click **Yes** to continue. This makes the store available for use by your users.

9. Click **OK** when the store is successfully mounted.

10. Close **Exchange System Manager**.

The public folder data store, which makes up the other half of the data stores that are created by default, comprises the two database files Pub1.edb, which contains rich text data, and Pub1.stm, which contains native content data.

9

THE EXTENSIBLE STORAGE ENGINE

A storage group consists of an instance of the **Extensible Storage Engine (ESE)** transaction logging system and a set of transaction log and system files for all of the databases in the storage group.

Transaction log files include the following:

- *E##.log*—The primary transaction log files for the storage group, where ## represents the storage group prefix. The first storage group has the prefix E00, the second storage group has the prefix E01, and so on.

- *E#######.log*—The secondary transaction log files for the storage group, where the final five digits represent a hexadecimal number from 00000 to FFFFF. The first and second digits in the transaction log file name are the prefix for the related storage group. The remaining digits are numbered sequentially. For instance, the first log file for the first storage group is named E0000001.log, the first log file for the second storage group is named E0100001.log, and so on. Each log file is 5 MB in size.

- *Res1.log and Res2.log*—The reserve log files for the storage group. The reserve logs act as a buffer in the event that Exchange Server 2003 runs out of disk space. If there is a premium for disk space, Exchange Server 2003 makes use of these log files to buy time until disk space can be freed up. Each file is 5 MB in size.

System files include the following:

- *E##.chk*—Records which entries in the log files have already been written to disk. This **checkpoint file** can speed up recovery time by telling the ESE which log file entries need to be replayed and which do not.

- *tmp.edb*—Is used by the system as a temporary workspace for processing transactions.

The Extensible Storage Engine uses these files to manage transactions within the mail databases. It ensures that data integrity and consistency is maintained in the event of a system crash or media failure by ensuring that any modifications to data within the database are tracked in their entirety. When a complete set of modifications has been performed on an object within the database, the entire transaction is complete. If for any reason something occurs during the middle of the modifications that causes the remainder of the modifications not to be applied to the database, all previous modifications are undone.

When information is read from the database and loaded into memory, it is done in the form of a page. The pages within the database form a B-Tree data structure. Each page is 4 KB and contains data definitions, data, or pointers to other pages, indexes, checksums, flags, time stamps, and other information. The B-Tree structure is rarely more than three or four levels deep, but is wide. Theoretically, each database can hold up to 16 TB of information. However, a database is limited by hardware space, or by backup and restore considerations.

Each time Exchange Server 2003 needs to increase the size of a database, it does so by creating new data pages within the database and then fills those pages with information. Zeroing out deleted database pages (rather than removing them) allows Exchange Server 2003 to reuse previously created data pages. By zeroing out deleted pages, you can realize a slight performance enhancement in an environment in which old data is frequently being deleted and new data is frequently being stored in the database.

ACTIVITY

Activity 9-3: Enabling Zeroing Out of Database Pages

Time Required: 10 to 20 minutes

Objective: Enable the zeroing out of database pages for a storage group.

Description: In this activity, you enable the zeroing out of database pages to improve the performance of your server. Zeroing out of database pages is controlled at the storage group level so each storage group can have a different policy for zeroing out deleted database pages. To enable zeroing out, complete the following steps:

1. From the Windows desktop of the back-end server, click **Start**, point to **All Programs**, point to **Microsoft Exchange**, and then click **System Manager**.

2. Click the **plus sign (+)** next to Administrative Groups, click the **plus sign (+)** next to First Administrative Group, click the **plus sign (+)** next to the Servers container, and then click the **plus sign (+)** next to SERVERXX, where XX is the student number assigned to your back-end server. Right-click the **First Storage Group**, and then click **Properties** on the shortcut menu. The First Storage Group Properties dialog box opens, as shown in the Figure 9-4.

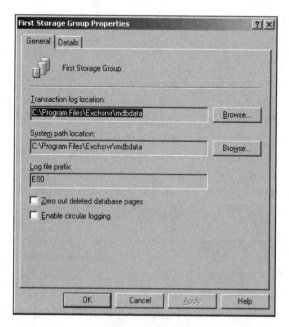

Figure 9-4   First Storage Group Properties dialog box

3. Click the **Zero out deleted database pages** check box to enable zeroing out of database pages for all the databases within this storage group.

4. When you are finished, click **OK** to save the settings and return to Exchange System Manager.

5. Close **Exchange System Manager**.

When pages from the database are read into memory, they are considered clean. After the page has been modified, it is marked dirty. At this point, additional modifications can be made to the page or the page can be written back to disk. Writing the page back to disk is done when one of the following occurs:

- The number of free pages in memory becomes too low, possibly affecting system performance. In this case, committed transactions in memory are flushed to disk to free up pages in memory for system use.

- The database service is shutting down, in which case all updated pages in memory are copied to the database file.

- The checkpoint falls too far behind in a previous transaction log file. If the number of committed transactions in the log files reaches a certain threshold, ESE flushes these changes to disk.

- Another service is requesting additional memory and the ESE needs to free up some of the memory it is currently using. ESE flushes pages from memory to the database and then updates the checkpoint file.

To actually commit a transaction to the database, the operations must be written to the transaction log buffer before being written to the transaction logs on disk. ESE uses write-ahead logging, which ensures that any changes that are intended for the database are first written to a transaction log file. Data is first written to a cached version of the log in the log buffer area in memory. The page in memory is then modified and a link is created between the data in the log buffer area and the page in memory. Before the modifications to the page in memory can be written to disk, the change recorded in the log buffer area is written to the transaction log on disk.

If power is lost to the server, it does not present a problem, as the information is recorded in the log files. Should the modifications in memory be lost, then, when the ESE service starts, the log files are replayed and the transactions are recorded to disk. Before a page is written to disk, the ESE calculates a checksum for the page and the checksum is written to the database along with the data. When the page is read from disk, the checksum is recalculated and the value is verified to be certain that it matches the requested page number. If the checksum fails or if there is a mismatch on the page number, it indicates that problems exist with the storage. This happens when the page that was written to the disk is not what was read by the ESE from disk into memory.

You might wonder why information is not written immediately to the database after it is modified in memory. The answer is that there are performance improvements obtained by not having to reread pages from the database every time they require modifications. By leaving the modified pages in memory and only recording the changes within the log buffer area and then to the transaction log, the opportunity is provided to make additional modifications to the pages in memory without having to reread the data pages from the database. This allows the modifications to be batched and written to disk at a later time.

What happens when information is written to the data store? Exchange Server 2003, like previous versions of Microsoft Exchange, continues to support a concept called Single Instance Storage. **Single Instance Storage (SIS)** works by only storing a single instance of a message when it is sent to multiple recipients, as long as the recipients are located on the same database. Single Instance Storage is not maintained if the message is sent to users who reside on different databases. Similarly, if a mailbox is moved between databases, Single Instance Storage is lost as an entire copy of the message must be moved to the alternate database, even if the original message was sent to recipients on that database. This is because Exchange Server 2003 does not preserve pointers across databases and does not re-create pointers to messages within different databases.

Here is an example. Suppose you have an Exchange 2003 server with two storage groups, each having a single mailbox store and a single public folder store. A user within the organization sends a 1-MB message to a distribution list that contains 50 members. Of the 50 recipients to whom the message is sent, 40 reside on the mailbox store located in storage group 1, while the remaining 10 recipients reside on the mailbox store in storage group 2.

SIS works by storing a single copy of the message within each store and creating pointers to the original message. Therefore, in the preceding scenario, a single copy of the message would be created in the mailbox store in storage group 1 and a single copy of the message is created in the mailbox store in storage group 2, for a total size of 4 MB (a copy is created in the transaction log for each respective storage group, giving 4 MB).

Without SIS, a copy of the message would have to be created for each individual user. This would result in 41 MB being allocated in the mailbox store of the first storage group and 11 MB being allocated in the mailbox store of the second storage group, for a total of 52 MB being used. This results in over 10 times more storage being used than if SIS were available.

However, Exchange Server 2003 does not stop at optimizing performance for writes. It also looks to optimize the read side by reading pages into a cache or buffer in memory prior to using them. This is done in anticipation that the pages will need to be read or modified in subsequent operations. Reading pages from memory is always faster than reading pages from disk. Exchange Server 2003 makes use of a mechanism called Dynamic Buffer Allocation to preallocate memory for pages as they are needed.

Dynamic Buffer Allocation increases or decreases the size of the cache based on the amount of cache required and the amount of memory available. If lots of memory is available, then Exchange uses it. Those inexperienced with Exchange might think this is a performance problem and add additional memory only to find Exchange uses it all again. Exchange uses less memory if other processes require it.

Transaction Logs

A transaction is a series of operations that are either completed in entirety or not completed at all. For instance, when you send a message from one user to another, a number of operations need to be performed. First, the message is transferred to your outbox, and then it is transmitted to the server, at which time a copy of the message is placed in your Sent Items folder. Not only is the message transferred between these folders, but the various properties of the message and the folders themselves must also be updated to reflect the transfer through the system. If a failure occurs, you do not want only some of the information to be updated. To prevent such a situation from occurring, Exchange uses transactions, which ensure that all the operations involved get performed as opposed to only some of them. When processing a transaction, Exchange Server 2003 ensures that all the operations within the transaction are applied against the database. Only after this has been done is the transaction deemed complete.

In theory, the transaction log could be one ever-expanding file. However, as you know, Exchange breaks the log down into separate files, each 5 MB in size, to make them more manageable. Until the log files are backed up, Exchange continues to create these log files incrementally, each log file consuming 5 MB in space. If you have a data store that does not contain mission-critical data, you have the option to enable **circular logging** to alleviate the issue in which log files continually consume disk space. Circular logging allows Exchange Server 2003 to overwrite transaction log files after the data they contain has been committed to the database.

ACTIVITY

Activity 9-4: Enabling Circular Logging

Time Required: 10 to 20 minutes

Objective: Enable circular logging for a storage group.

Description: Circular logging reduces the amount of disk space that is required to store transaction logs, but also makes it impossible to recover databases with anything beyond the last backup. To enable circular logging, complete the following steps:

1. From the Windows desktop of the back-end server, click **Start**, point to **All Programs**, point to **Microsoft Exchange**, and then click **System Manager**.

2. Click the **plus sign (+)** next to Administrative Groups, click the **plus sign (+)** next to First Administrative Group, click the **plus sign (+)** next to the Servers container, and then click the **plus sign (+)** next to SERVERXX, where XX is the student number assigned to your back-end server. Right-click the **VIP Storage Group**, and then click **Properties** on the shortcut menu. The VIP Storage Group Properties dialog box opens.

3. Click the **Enable circular logging** check box, and then click **OK** to return to Exchange System Manager.

4. You are presented with a warning message indicating that with circular logging enabled, you will only be able to restore databases to the time of the last backup. Click **Yes** to continue.

5. Close **Exchange System Manager**.

Each log file consists of a header section and a data section. The header section contains hard-coded paths to the databases that it references and a signature that is matched to the database signature. In Exchange Server 2003, multiple databases use the same log file because the log files service the entire storage group. This simplifies recovery because, no matter which database in a storage group you are restoring, you reference the same log files for that group. The signature ensures that the log file is matched to an identically named database.

When a database is modified, Exchange Server 2003 performs several steps. First, the page is read into the database cache, and then the time stamp on the page is updated. This time stamp is incremented on a per-database basis. Next, the log record is created, stating what is about to be done to the database. This occurs in the log cache buffer. The page is then modified and a connection is created between these two entries so that the page cannot be written to disk without the log file entry being written to disk first. This ensures that a modification to the database is first written to the log file on disk prior to it being written to the database.

In the event of a crash, Exchange Server 2003 uses the transaction logs to recover the database to a consistent state. It does so by replaying the transaction log files against the database. This replaying means that, for each log record, the page is read out of the database that the record references, and the time stamp on the page is compared to the time stamp of the log entry that references that page. If the time stamps do not match, Exchange Server 2003 knows that the modification in the log file has not been written to disk and subsequently writes the log entry to the database. If the server fails after the transaction is committed, the entire transaction is persisted, and the changes are made to the database.

If the server failed before a transaction was committed, the entire transaction is rolled back and it is as if the transaction never occurred. This rollback process occurs during the second phase of the recovery process. The version store keeps track of any operations that were performed but not finished because the transaction could not be committed. The version store provides the mechanism to track multiple operations to the same database page and ensures that each transaction sees the correct database pages. If these operations are not completed and are rolled back, the various operations that make up the transaction are undone. For instance, if a piece of mail was transferred, it is moved back to the original location. If a message was deleted, it is restored.

9

CONTENT INDEXING

Messages within a database are uniquely identified using a unique identifier called the message transfer service ID or (MTS-ID). Having a unique identifier for each message allows messages to be retrieved efficiently from a database in which volumes of messages can exist. Retrieving messages based on this unique index might be efficient for Exchange Server 2003, but it is not very practical for end users.

Users typically use some other property to order and retrieve their messages. These other properties provide an index into the database that allows Exchange to retrieve a message from the server. These types of indexes are known as secondary indexes. These indexes map the property being indexed to the primary key (which is the MTS-ID).

Exchange Server 2003 automatically implements and manages standard indexing within an Exchange Server 2003 database. Standard indexing is used with searches for common key fields such as message subjects. Users take advantage of standard indexing every time they use the Find feature within Microsoft Outlook. Standard indexing is used to quickly search To, Cc, and Subject fields.

What about searching other fields, such as the time the message was sent or the time a message was received? Or, perhaps you want to retrieve all messages that contain attachments of Microsoft Word documents that have been authored by your company's business partner, ABC Consulting? This is possible within Exchange Server 2003, but every message would have to be checked in every folder. This means that, as Exchange mailboxes grow on a server, so too does the time it takes to complete an advanced search. To accommodate these types of searches, Exchange Server 2003 makes use of two facilities to help achieve them. The first is full-text indexing, which causes properties other than those covered by standard indexing to be indexed, and the second is called property promotion. The following sections discuss both of these facilities, beginning with property promotion.

Property Promotion

Property promotion allows for advanced searches on any document or attachment property, such as Author, Lines, or Document Subject. When Exchange Server 2003 stores a document or attachment in a supported file type, the document's properties are automatically parsed and promoted to the Information Store. These properties then become a part of the messages record in the database and searches can subsequently be performed on them through the Advanced Find feature of Outlook. Not all file types are indexed. The following file types are the only types whose properties are promoted to the Information Store:

- Microsoft Word documents (*.doc)
- Microsoft Excel documents (*.xls)
- Microsoft PowerPoint documents (*.ppt)
- HTML documents (*.html, *.htm, *.asp)
- Text files (*.txt)
- Embedded MIME messages (*.eml)

Full-Text Indexing

With **full-text indexing**, Exchange Server 2003 builds an index of all searchable text in a particular mailbox or public folder store before users try to search it. Full-text indexing searches are faster than character-based searches because users are searching through the index instead of searching through the e-mail messages themselves. Full-text searches are also more comprehensive than character-based searches because attachments are indexed in addition to e-mail messages.

Full-text searches differ from character-based searches in a number of different ways, including the following:

- Searches are performed faster over large amounts of content.
- Search results include attachments in addition to messages.
- Searches for commonly used words are faster and less costly.
- Noise words (word fragments or articles such as "the") are removed from queries. As an example, a query for "sarah m" searches for "sarah" because "m" is a noise word. A search for "the plaintiff" removes "the" and only searches for "plaintiff."

■ Commas are interpreted as an OR query. For instance, a search for "Morrison, jim" finds all documents with either "Morrison" or "jim" in the document. To search for the whole phrase "Morrison, jim," put the query in quotation marks.

Full-text indexing is provided by the Microsoft Search service. It builds the initial index by processing the entire store one folder at a time. The search process identifies and logs searchable text. After the index is created, any change to a folder within the store causes a notification to be sent to the Search service to synchronize the searchable content within the folder. Depending on how you have configured the Search service to run, it either waits for the scheduled time to regenerate the index so that the new changes are included, or it updates the index shortly after the change is made.

ACTIVITY

Activity 9-5: Creating Full-Text Indexes

Time Required: 10 to 20 minutes

Objective: Create a full-text index on a data store.

9

Description: In this activity, create a full-text index for a mailbox store. For mailbox stores, the full-text index is based on all text in message bodies, message subject fields, message sender and recipient fields, as well as attachments. To create a full-text index, complete the following steps:

1. From the Windows desktop of the back-end server, click **Start**, point to **All Programs**, point to **Microsoft Exchange**, and then click **System Manager**.

2. Click the **plus sign (+)** next to Administrative Groups, click the **plus sign (+)** next to First Administrative Group, click the **plus sign (+)** next to the Servers container, and then click the **plus sign (+)** next to SERVERXX, where XX is the student number assigned to your back-end server. Click the **plus sign (+)** next to First Storage Group. Right-click **Mailbox Store (SERVERXX)**, where XX is the student number assigned to your back-end server. On the shortcut menu, click **Create Full-Text Index**. The Mailbox Store (SERVERXX) dialog box opens. Here, you can specify the path for your full-text indexes.

3. If necessary, type **C:\Program Files\Exchsrvr\ExchangeServer_SERVERXX\ Projects** in the Select the location to create the catalog text box, being certain to replace XX with the number assigned to your back-end server.

4. Click **OK** to return to Exchange System Manager. Exchange Server 2003 creates the index. The index will be about one-fifth of the size of the original data store, so you will need to use a folder on a drive with plenty of free space.

5. Close **Exchange System Manager**.

Both the Information Store service and the Search service must be running for the index to be created, updated, or deleted. Depending on the size of your store, completing a full index could take hours. Not only do indexes take up CPU cycles when they are initially created, they also take up additional disk space. Expect indexing to consume about 20 percent of the disk space of your database. As such, it is best to have this activity occur at a time when your server is underutilized.

Scheduling updates provides you with the ability to schedule updates at whatever time you feel is satisfactory to the business. The advantage of scheduling the index update is that it can be planned for off-peak hours when the server is not heavily accessed by users. The disadvantage is that indexes can become out of date.

ACTIVITY

Activity 9-6: Scheduling Index Updates and Allowing Index Searching

Time Required: 10 to 20 minutes

Objective: Set a schedule for index updates.

Description: In this activity, you configure Exchange Server 2003 to update full-text indexes automatically and to allow clients to search using the indexes. You configure these processes separately for each data store by completing the following steps:

1. From the Windows desktop of the back-end server, click **Start**, point to **All Programs**, point to **Microsoft Exchange**, and then click **System Manager**.

2. Click the **plus sign (+)** next to Administrative Groups, click the **plus sign (+)** next to First Administrative Group, click the **plus sign (+)** next to the Servers container, and then click the **plus sign (+)** next to SERVERXX, where XX is the student number assigned to your back-end server. Click the **plus sign (+)** next to First Storage Group. Right-click **Mailbox Store (SERVERXX)**, where XX is the student number assigned to your back-end server. On the shortcut menu, click **Properties**. The Mailbox Store (SERVERXX) Properties dialog box opens, where you can specify the path for your full-text indexes.

3. Click the **Full-Text Indexing** tab, as shown in Figure 9-5.

4. Use the Update interval drop-down list to choose how often the indexes should be updated. You have the following two options, but for this activity click **Run daily at 1:00 AM** in the drop-down list.

   - Specify to run the update at various hours throughout the day. Typically, you will need to update the index daily at a specific time rather than updating the index every hour or continuously as changes are made.

   - Create a custom schedule to run your updates. To do this, select Use a custom schedule, click the Customize button, and then use the Schedule dialog box to set the times when Exchange Server 2003 should make updates.

5. Click the **This index is currently available for searching by clients** check box, and then click **OK**.

6. You are prompted with a warning dialog box indicating that to make the index available, you must verify that the index has been fully populated and is not out of date. Click **OK** to continue.

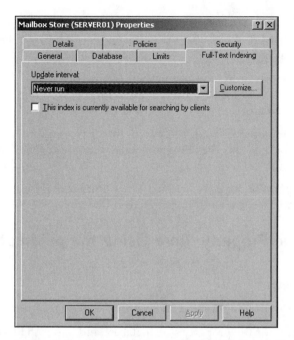

Figure 9-5   Mailbox Store (SERVERXX) Properties dialog box, Full-Text Indexing tab

7. Close **Exchange System Manager**.

Five major file types are created as part of implementing full-text indexing:

- *Catalog*— The main index for the store. Each mailbox store or public folder store has one catalog when it is indexed.

- *Property store*— File containing information about the items that have been indexed. Each Exchange 2003 server has one property store when it is indexed.

- *Property store logs*—Transaction logs created for the property store.

- *Temporary files*—Files created and deleted by the Search service as a temporary workspace.

- *Gather logs*—Transaction logs created for the catalogs. One set of logs exists for each index.

What happens if the location where you keep your indexes starts to run out of disk space? By default, index files are stored on the system drive, which typically does not have the throughput of a high-performance disk subsystem as those offered by various RAID solutions. Adding more room for expansion is one option to consider, or you could move the indexes to a different location. Unfortunately, Exchange Server 2003 does not allow you to change the index file locations easily.

Microsoft does not leave you high and dry, however. They do provide utilities that assist in this effort. These utilities can be used to move full-text indexing files to different locations from their default installation locations.

- Pstoreutl moves the property store and the property store logs to the drive you specify. The Pstoreutl tool is located in the Program Files\Common Files\System\MSSearch\Bin directory.

- SetTempPath moves the temporary directory to the drive you specify. The SetTempPath tool is located in the Program Files\Common Files\System\MSSearch\Bin directory.

- Catutil moves the index to the drive you specify. The Catutil tool is located in the Program Files\Common Files\System\MSSearch\Bin directory.

ACTIVITY

Activity 9-7: Moving the Property Store Using the pstoreutl.exe Utility

Time Required: 10 to 20 minutes

Objective: Move the property store files to a different location.

Description: The default location for the property store database and logs is the Exchange system drive. Typically, the path is C:\Program Files\exchsrvr\ExchangeServer_*ServerName*, where *ServerName* is the name of the Exchange server. One property store is shared by all full-text indexes on an Exchange server.

To increase disk performance, you might want to move the property store and logs to a different physical disk. This can be done with the Pstoreutl tool.

In this activity, you move the property store and logs to a new location. To do this, complete the following steps on SERVERXX, where XX is the number assigned to your back-end server. This activity is dependent on a full-text index being created in previous activities.

1. From the Windows desktop of the back-end server, click **Start**, and then click **Run**. The Run dialog box opens. In the Open text box, type **cmd**, and then click **OK**.

2. Type **CD \Program Files\Common Files\System\MSSearch\Bin** at the prompt, and then press **Enter**.

3. Type **pstoreutl ExchangeServer_ServerXX –M "c:\temp\ExchangeServer_ServerXX.edb"**, where XX is the student number assigned to your back-end server, and then press **Enter**.

4. Type **pstoreutl ExchangeServer_ServerXX –L "c:\temp"**, where XX is the student number assigned to your back-end server, and then press **Enter**.

5. Type **CD \temp** and then press **Enter**. Verify that the files for the property store have been moved to this location.

6. Close the **command prompt** window.

DISK STORAGE CONFIGURATION

Because of the way Exchange Server 2003 implements storage, it is necessary to examine how disk space will be used by your Exchange 2003 servers. When designing your storage subsystem for Exchange, you should consider some general factors to help guide your implementation:

- Implementing a specialized hardware solution for your storage needs and allocating your files strategically can help you decrease the CPU requirements on your server. Files that are accessed randomly should be stored separately from files that are accessed sequentially because it's faster to locate data in sequentially accessed files.

- Using a large disk to store data might not be as efficient as using multiple smaller disks. Arranged appropriately, smaller disks perform better than a single large disk because this arrangement allows information to be written in parallel across all the disks. Depending on the type of array, this could improve performance by the number of disks in your configuration. How long it takes to back up your solution plays a role in determining how you allocate your storage. If all your storage is allocated to a few databases and your backup solution is unable to back up the information within a window of time that your backup jobs run, you can severely impact the performance of your Exchange servers.

- Some Exchange servers, such as connector servers, do not require redundancy in disk storage because they hold messages for a very short period of time. However, if they are busy they can benefit from the performance advantage of RAID-0.

Taking these factors into consideration when designing your storage solution helps to optimize the performance for your Exchange environment. As mentioned, two areas that should be addressed specifically are the type of storage solution you will consider and the placement of files on that storage solution.

RAID Technologies

Storage solutions typically incorporate some type of redundant array of independent, or inexpensive, disks (RAID) configuration to optimize performance. When considering RAID configurations for your Exchange environment, you should consider four primary implementations, including RAID-0, RAID-1, RAID-0+1, and RAID-5.

RAID-0

Also known as data striping, RAID-0 functionality divides data into blocks and distributes the blocks across multiple disks in a disk array. Distributing the disk I/O load across disks and controllers improves disk I/O performance. However, striping decreases availability because one disk failure makes the entire disk array unavailable. An example of a RAID-0 configuration is provided in Figure 9-6.

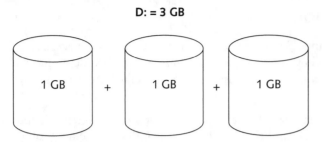

D: = 3 GB

Figure 9-6   RAID-0 configuration

RAID-1

Also known as data mirroring, RAID-1 functionality maintains identical copies of data on different disks in an array. Duplicating data provides high data availability. In addition, RAID-1 improves disk read performance because data can be read from two locations. However, RAID-1 decreases disk write performance because data must be written twice. Mirroring disks requires double the number of disks. Figure 9-7 shows an example of a RAID-1 configuration.

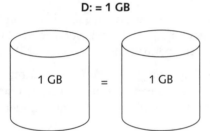

D: = 1 GB

Figure 9-7   RAID-1 configuration

RAID-0+1

This configuration combines RAID-0 striping and RAID-1 mirroring. Two RAID-0 arrays are mirrored. RAID-0+1 is fast because each RAID-0 array can write to disk quickly. It is reliable because there are two copies of all data through mirroring. Fifty percent of disk space is lost to parity information in this configuration. Figure 9-8 shows an example of a RAID-0+1 configuration.

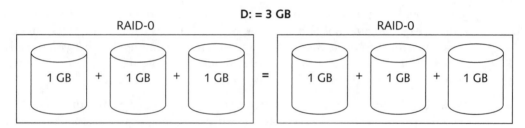

Figure 9-8   RAID-0+1 configuration

RAID-5

RAID-5 provides a fault-tolerant hard disk drive configuration in which data is spread across at least three physical disk drives. Data is divided into blocks, with two volumes containing a data block and the third volume containing a parity block. These blocks are also written so that not all of the parity blocks are on one volume. If a physical disk drive fails, the data is still available from the other two volumes. Software-based RAID-5 volumes can only be created on Dynamic Disks in Windows 2000 and higher. If a hardware RAID card is used, disks can be Basic Disks or Dynamic Disks. Figure 9-9 shows an example of a RAID-5 configuration.

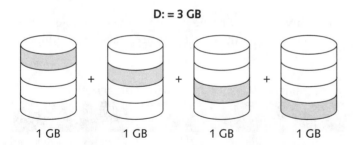

Figure 9-9   RAID-5 configuration

Placement of Files

The placement of files that make up your storage solution contributes significantly to the performance that can be obtained from your system. Exchange Server 2003 stores data in three main locations:

- SMTP queue directory
- .edb and .stm files
- Transaction log files

The SMTP queue stores SMTP messages until they are written to either a public data store, a mailbox store, or transferred to another mail system. As such, these messages only reside within the queue for a short period of time. Because of these characteristics, the SMTP queue should be optimized for performance. However, you shouldn't discount the reliability of the drive configurations that store the message queues because messages might back up in the queue due to outages of remote systems. It is recommended that you use a RAID-1 configuration for them. A RAID-1 configuration provides reliability in case of hard drive failure, but yet provides the high throughput required for messages in transit.

As discussed previously, .edb files store rich-text data, whereas .stm files store native multimedia content. Because access to these files is generally random, they can be placed on the same disk volume. Keep in mind these files store messaging data that is accessed quite frequently, so they require a high degree of reliability. To maximize performance and ensure reliability, you should use RAID-1 or RAID-0+1 for these files.

Typically, public folders are used in scenarios in which many people are accessing data, but only a few are changing it. Consequently, read performance is more important than write performance. RAID-5 is preferred in this situation because it offers excellent read performance and good write performance.

Each storage group generates its own set of transaction log files. Because of the importance of these files, you should ensure that they are stored on a highly reliable and fast storage medium such as a RAID-0+1 disk configuration. To improve the overall performance of your Exchange 2003 server, you should consider storing these files on their own separate drives.

If you configure the data files for your server properly, they can help to scale your Exchange organization efficiently while ensuring optimal performance. Table 9-1 outlines scenarios for configuring your Exchange organization.

Table 9-1 Configuration recommendations for an Exchange organization

Organization Size	Performance Needs	Storage Groups	Recommendation
Small	Low	1	Place all data files on the same drive. Consider using RAID-1 or RAID-5 to protect the data.
	High	1	Place all databases on a single drive. Place all transaction logs and system files on a different drive. Consider using RAID-5 for databases and RAID-1 for transaction logs.
Medium	Low	1	Place all databases on a single drive, using RAID-5 to protect the drive in case of failure. Place all transaction logs and system files on a different drive, using RAID-1 to protect the drive in case of failure.

Table 9-1 Configuration recommendations for an Exchange organization (continued)

Organization Size	Performance Needs	Storage Groups	Recommendation
	High	Multiple	Place all databases on a single drive, using RAID-5 to protect the drive in case of failure. Place all transaction logs on a different drive, using RAID-1 to protect the drive in case of failure. Place all system files on a third drive.
Large	Low	Multiple	Organize data according to storage groups, placing all the data for each storage group on separate drives. Use RAID-1 or RAID-5 to protect the drives.
	Medium	Multiple	Each storage group should have its own database drive. RAID-5 can be used to protect the database drives in case of failure. Place the log files and system files on different drives and use RAID-1 to protect the drives in case of failure.
	High	Multiple	Use RAID-5 to protect the drive in case of failure and allocate each database to a separate drive. Place the transaction logs on separate drives and use RAID-1 to protect the drive in case of failure. Place system files for each storage group on separate drives.

9

CHAPTER SUMMARY

- Exchange Server 2003 allows you to have up to five storage groups per server. Each storage group can have up to five databases. Four storage groups are used to hold data, while the fifth is used for recovery purposes.

- Each storage group maintains separate transaction logs for all databases located within the storage group.

- Having multiple stores per server offers benefits in terms of reduced impact to total users, faster recoverability of data, and increased scalability.

❑ Each data store consists of two database files, a rich text file (ending in .edb), which holds mail messages and MAPI content, and a native content file, or streaming Internet content file (ending in .stm), that holds audio, video, and other media that are formatted as streams of MIME data.

❑ Information is stored in its respective database in its native format. That is, MAPI information and rich text information is stored in the .edb file, whereas MIME data is stored in the .stm file. Information is converted on demand between stores as required.

❑ Zeroing out deleted database pages (rather than removing them) allows Exchange Server 2003 to reuse previously created data pages. By zeroing out deleted pages, you can realize a slight performance enhancement in an environment in which old data is frequently being deleted and new data is frequently being stored in the database.

❑ SIS works by storing only a single instance of a message when it is sent to multiple recipients as long as the recipients are located on the same database. SIS is not maintained if the message is sent to users who reside on different databases.

❑ Circular logging allows you to control transaction logs from consuming large amounts of disk space. The trade-off is that when you have circular logging enabled, you can only recover the database up to the point it was last backed up.

❑ Property promotion automatically parses and promotes document or attachment properties to the Information Store. These properties then become a part of the message record in the database, and searches can subsequently be performed on them through the Advanced Find feature of Outlook.

❑ Full-text indexing builds an index of all searchable text in a particular mailbox or public folder store before users try to search it. This facilitates improved performance as the information has already been indexed prior to it being searched.

❑ Moving the content indexing files involves making use of several utilities. These utilities include Pstoreutl, SetTempPath, and Catutil.

❑ Storage solutions typically incorporate some type of RAID configuration to optimize performance. When considering RAID configurations for your Exchange environment, you should consider four primary implementations, including RAID-0, RAID-1, RAID-0+1, and RAID-5.

Key Terms

checkpoint file — A file that records which entries in the log files have already been written to disk.

circular logging — A feature that limits the amount of disk space that is used by transaction logs. When circular logging is on, Exchange writes transaction logs as usual; however, after the checkpoint file (E##.chk) has been advanced, the inactive portion of the transaction log is discarded and overwritten.

Dynamic Buffer Allocation — A mechanism that Exchange uses to increase or decrease the size of the cache based on the amount of cache required and the amount of memory available.

Extensible Storage Engine (ESE) — The primary database used within Exchange 2003. It is a multiuser database that allows applications to store, retrieve, and index semistructured data. It is optimized for very fast storage and retrieval.

full-text indexing — A process in which Exchange builds an index of all searchable text in a particular mailbox or public folder store before users try to search it. This allows for faster and more comprehensive searches.

Message Application Programming Interface (MAPI) — A set of callable functions that provides connectivity and operational procedures against a messaging system on the back end.

property promotion — A process whereby the properties of a document or attachment of a supported file type are parsed and promoted to the Information Store to allow for advanced searches.

Single Instance Storage (SIS) — A system that stores only a single instance of a message when it is sent to multiple recipients as long as the recipients are located on the same database. SIS is not maintained if the message is sent to users who reside on different databases.

storage group — A set of up to five databases that uses the same transaction log.

REVIEW QUESTIONS

1. You go through the motions of creating an additional storage group on your Exchange 2003 server. However, when you attempt to specify the location of the files for your storage group, it does not allow you to create the files in the same location as the files for your first storage group. Why?

   a. The additional storage group makes use of existing files.

   b. The additional storage group requires that you use the system directory to store your files.

   c. The additional storage group requires that you specify different file locations for each storage group.

   d. none of the above

2. What are the benefits of having multiple storage groups? (Choose all that apply.)

   a. allows organizations to host more users per server

   b. improves memory utilization

   c. reduces recovery time

   d. reduces cache utilization

3. The disk space where you store your transaction logs is close to running out of space. What will Exchange Server 2003 do to accommodate this situation?

    a. Commit all transactions and shut down the store.

    b. Alert the administrator by sending a mail message.

    c. Make use of the res1.log and res2.log files.

    d. Dynamically allocate log files to other storage connected to your server.

4. What is the size of a page within the Exchange Server 2003 store?

    a. 4 MB

    b. 4 KB

    c. 3 KB

    d. 5 KB

5. Messages are converted dynamically from the rich text store to the native content store as required. True or False?

6. As the network administrator, you have profiled the usage of your Exchange environment. You discover that users read messages and then delete them right away. What can you do to improve the performance of your system given this situation? (Choose all that apply.)

    a. Enable zeroing out of your database pages.

    b. Enable circular logging.

    c. Move the transaction logs to separate drives.

    d. Configure multiple databases for your system.

7. What is the size of transaction logs?

    a. 4 MB

    b. 2 MB

    c. 5 MB

    d. unlimited

8. Which of the following utilities does not assist in the moving of content indexing components to new locations?

    a. Pstoreutl

    b. SetTempPath

    c. MoveCat

    d. CatMove

9. Your Exchange 2003 server has run out of disk space. Upon investigation, you discover that the directory containing your transaction logs is full of transaction logs that are consuming all of the disk space. These logs are dated over several days. What could be the problem?

a. Nothing is wrong; the problem is you require more disk space.

b. Circular logging is not enabled.

c. The server has not been backed up.

d. The server is configured not to delete transaction logs.

10. When are modified pages written back to disk? (Choose all that apply.)

a. when the number of pages in memory becomes too low

b. when the database service is shutting down

c. when the number of committed transactions in the log files reaches a certain threshold

d. all of the above

11. Why are modified pages not written to disk immediately? (Choose all that apply.)

a. because the pages first need to be written to the log buffer area

b. because the pages might be modified in the near future

c. because the time to commit counter has not reached its threshold

d. all of the above

12. You have two databases within your storage group. A 1-MB message is sent to five people, two in the first database and three in the second. What is the total disk space consumed?

a. 5 MB

b. 2 MB

c. 1 MB

d. 4 MB

13. What is Dynamic Buffer Allocation?

a. a mechanism for preallocating memory for transactions that are to be committed to the database

b. a mechanism for preallocating memory for pages that are read in as needed

c. a mechanism for optimizing the performance of SMTP queues

d. a mechanism for optimizing the performance of the MTA

14. How does Dynamic Buffer Allocation govern how large or small the cache should be? (Choose all that apply.)

a. by the amount of memory that is available

b. by the amount of cache memory that is available

    c. by the load on memory

    d. all of the above

15. How are messages uniquely identified within the database?

    a. by using a GUID

    b. by using an MTS-ID

    c. by using a SID

    d. by using a hash of the message header

16. What is a secondary index?

    a. Secondary indexes are composed of MTS-IDs.

    b. Secondary indexes are composed of properties that make up a message.

    c. Exchange Server 2003 does not make use of secondary indexes.

    d. Secondary indexes are composed of checksums for each message.

17. Single Instance Storage is maintained when mailboxes are moved between servers. True or False?

18. Outlook directly stores information in both the .edb file and the .stm file. True or False?

19. Which of the following file types has its properties promoted to the Information Store? (Choose all that apply.)

    a. *.doc files

    b. *.zip files

    c. *.txt files

    d. *.pdf files

20. Which service builds the indexes for full-text indexing?

    a. the System Attendant service

    b. the Information Store service

    c. the Message Transfer service

    d. the Microsoft Search service

21. Which services must be running for indexes to be created? (Choose all that apply.)

    a. the Microsoft Search service

    b. the System Attendant

    c. the Event service

    d. the Information Store service

22. Which of the following file types are created by full-text indexing? (Choose all that apply.)

   a. catalogs

   b. property stores

   c. gather logs

   d. cache files

   e. all of the above

23. Which of the following are valid RAID implementations? (Choose all that apply.)

   a. RAID-0

   b. RAID-1

   c. RAID-5

   d. RAID-0+5

   e. all of the above

9

CASE PROJECTS

Case Project 9-1: Planning Data Storage

As the person in charge of implementing e-mail services for Blather Consulting, you are responsible for planning the data storage on your system. After interviewing the business managers to determine the requirements of your business users, you identify that VIP users require faster recovery times for data than non-VIP users. How can you design the storage on your Exchange Server 2003 system to accommodate these requirements?

Case Project 9-2: Choosing a Disk Configuration

As an e-mail consultant with Blather Consulting, you are contracted to organizations to develop e-mail solutions for their organizations. You are called upon to make recommendations about e-mail implementations and the different components that make up an e-mail solution. Part of this involves identifying the hardware that is required to run an e-mail system. Make a list of the different types of RAID systems that can be used within an e-mail solution and what they are best used for.

Case Project 9-3: Optimizing Performance

As the IT administrator of a small organization, you have been monitoring the disk utilization on your e-mail servers for some time and noticed that the I/O utilization has become quite high. List steps you can take to reduce the I/O utilization on your server.

Case Project 9-4: Managing Disk Usage

As the technical architect for your organization, you are in the process of designing your Exchange Server 2003 system. You are considering a dedicated public folder server for your organization. Identify what you can do to minimize issues with disk space usage on your public folder server. (In your answer, make use of circular logging because it is generally a read-only configuration.)

10

SECURING EXCHANGE
SERVER 2003

After reading this chapter, you will be able to:

- Understand how to administer permissions within Exchange Server 2003
- Understand the process of delegating authority within an Exchange Server 2003 organization
- Understand the concepts behind a Public Key Infrastructure
- Describe how to install and configure a Windows 2000/2003 Public Key Infrastructure
- Describe the use of SSL/TLS for securing communication between two computers
- Understand how to make use of certificates to encrypt and sign e-mail

W hen considering security in Exchange Server 2003, you must also consider the security features provided by Windows 2000/2003. Indeed, most of the security features provided by Exchange Server 2003 are really provided by Windows Server 2003. Understanding how the two products work together is critical to properly securing Exchange. This chapter discusses security by exploring the features provided in both the Windows operating system that enable a secure messaging environment and the features provided by Exchange Server 2003 itself.

The discussion of Windows operating system security features focuses on the mechanisms provided to address authentication and access control and the Public Key Infrastructure (PKI) provided by the operating system. Because Exchange mailboxes are actually associated with user accounts within Windows 2000/2003, Exchange Server 2003 relies on the user and permission data stored in Active Directory to control access to mail-related objects. Having an understanding of Certificate Services, and the PKI provided by the underlying operating system, provides a firm foundation upon which you can design, deploy, and maintain a PKI that can be used to secure messaging traffic to and from your organization.

From an Exchange Server 2003 perspective, this chapter explores the mechanisms used to secure message delivery such as the Secure Sockets Layer/Transport Layer Security (SSL/TLS) infrastructure used to secure the SMTP traffic that traverses Internet communications between two servers.

Finally, the chapter looks at S/MIME (Secure Multipurpose Internet Mail Extensions), which makes use of the underlying PKI provided by the operating system to send encrypted and/or signed messages from client to client.

ADMINISTERING PERMISSIONS WITHIN EXCHANGE SERVER 2003

Within Exchange Server 2003, you manage security by assigning permissions in Active Directory. Exchange Server 2003 makes use of the security model of Windows 2000/2003. All Exchange Server 2003 objects are secured with a discretionary access control list (DACL) and individual access control entries (ACEs) that give users and groups permission to administer an object. Permissions for an object are configured using the Security tab of the object in Exchange System Manager. You have the ability to explicitly grant or deny permissions. A permission that is denied overrides all other instances of permissions being allowed to the user or group.

Permissions assigned to an object can be applied directly to the object or they can be inherited from their parent object. A parent object is an object that is above an object in the object hierarchy. In Exchange Server 2003, permissions are inherited through the organizational hierarchy. At the top is the organization itself. All other nodes in the tree inherit the Exchange permissions of this node. In practice, this means you will normally apply permissions to container objects like the administrative groups. In some situations, you might want to apply permissions directly to the objects themselves. This is done in Exchange System Manager.

There are two types of permissions: standard and extended. Standard permissions are part of the default permissions for Active Directory and should be familiar to anyone who has administered Windows 2000/2003 servers. An example of a standard permission is the ability to specify which users are in the server's Administrators group. Extended permissions are added when Exchange Server 2003 is installed. Extended permissions are used to gain more specific administrative control. For example, the Server object has the Administer Information Store extended permission that enables you to specify which users or groups can make changes to the Information Store objects.

Table 10-1 summarizes common object permissions, what they do, and where they are applied.

Table 10-1 Common Exchange Server 2003 permissions

Permission	Description	Where It Is Applied
Add PF to admin group	Add an existing public folder to an existing administrative group.	Administrative Groups
Administer Information Store	View and modify properties of the Information Store and its subordinate objects.	Information Store
Associated external account	Allow an account in a trusted domain to be associated with the mailbox and allowed access. Because the mailbox is the account in Exchange Server 2003, this provides the parallel to the linkage between an Exchange Server 5.5 mailbox and its corresponding Windows account.	Mailboxes
Change permissions	Change the permissions on an object, including adding or removing permissions.	Mailboxes
Create named properties in the Information Store	Create new properties in the store, including those associated with messages, public folder posts, and Information Store objects.	Folders
Create public folder	Create new public folders beneath existing public folders in any hierarchy to which they have access.	Folder hierarchy
Create top-level public folder	Create new top-level public folders at the top level of any hierarchy to which they have access.	Organization
Delete mailbox storage	Delete mailboxes from the Information Store.	Mailboxes
Full mailbox access	Grant full control for the holder on the specified mailbox. The holder can do literally anything with the mailbox.	Mailboxes
Full store access	Open or modify any property of the Information Store. Mount and dismount databases.	Mailbox store, storage group
Mail-enable public folder	Enable a public folder to receive mail at its associated SMTP address.	Public folders
Modify public folder admin ACL	Change the contents of the access control list for a public folder.	Public folders
Modify public folder item retention	Change the deleted item retention settings for an existing folder.	Public folders
Modify public folder expiry	Change the expiration settings for an existing folder.	Public folders
Modify public folder quotas	Add, remove, or change storage limits for a folder.	Public folders
Modify public folder replica list	Modify the list of public folder replicas on a particular server. It must be set on the public folder store and administrative group where replicas are to be added.	Public folders
Open mail send queue	Open the queue of outbound mail to inspect or modify it. This is normally granted only to the Exchange Servers group.	Information Store
Read metabase properties	Read properties pertaining to Internet protocol handling from the IIS-owned sections of the metabase. This is normally granted only to services.	IIS metabase
Read permissions	Read permissions and ACL entries from the selected mailbox.	Mailboxes

10

Table 10-1   Common Exchange Server 2003 permissions (continued)

Permission	Description	Where It Is Applied
Receive As	Receive mail addressed to another user. When this permission is granted along with the Send as permission, the holder effectively has full control over the mailbox.	Mailbox stores, mailboxes
Remove PF from admin group	Remove a public folder from an administrative group.	Administrative group
Send As	Send messages with another user's return address. For example, you can grant a user the Send As permission so that he can send mail that appears to be from you. Users always have this permission on their own mailbox.	Mailboxes
Take ownership	Take ownership of a mailbox. This leaves an audit trail in the systems security log.	Mailboxes
View Information Store status	View health, status, and performance information about instances of the Information Store.	Information Store

There are two extended permissions that you should use with caution: the Send As permission and the Receive As permission. Send As gives a user or group permission to impersonate another user. Receive As gives a user or group the capability to open another user's mailbox.

The permissions outlined in Table 10-1 are used to control the administration and use of Exchange Server 2003 at different levels. They can be used to globally set the permissions at the organization level, where, through inheritance, these permissions are then applied to all objects within the Exchange organization. They can be used to set the permissions at the server level, where inheritance will then apply the permissions to all child nodes on the server being permissioned. They can be used to set the permissions at the storage group level, where the permissions are then applied to all mailbox and public folder stores within the storage group. Finally, they can be applied on an individual node itself.

Before looking at the example of how to apply permissions using Exchange System Manager in Activity 10-2, you must configure Exchange System Manager to display the Security tab for all objects. By default, the Security tab is displayed only on address lists, global address lists, database (both mailbox and public folder stores), and top-level public folders.

ACTIVITY

Activity 10-1: Configuring the Security Tab Within Exchange System Manager

Time Required: 10 to 20 minutes

Objective: Enable the Security tab for all objects within Exchange System Manager.

Description: In this activity, you configure Exchange System Manager to display the Security tab for all objects within the organization. Exchange System Manager should be configured to display the Security tab on each system in your organization. Because you have already done this on your back-end server in Chapter 5, "Managing Addresses," you complete the following steps on your front-end server:

1. Log on to the front-end server using the user name **Administrator** and the password **Password!**.

2. From the Windows desktop of your front-end server, click **Start**, and then click **Run**. The Run dialog box opens. Type **REGEDT32** in the Open text box, and then click **OK**. The Registry Editor opens.

3. Click the **plus sign (+)** next to HKEY_CURRENT_USER, click the **plus sign (+)** next to Software, click the **plus sign (+)** next to Microsoft, and then click the **plus sign (+)** next to Exchange.

4. Right-click the **EXAdmin** key, point to **New**, and then click **DWORD Value**.

5. Type **ShowSecurityPage** for the name of the new entry, and then press **Enter**.

6. Right-click the **ShowSecurityPage** entry, and then click **Modify** on the shortcut menu. The Edit DWORD Value dialog box opens.

7. In the Value data text box, type the value **1**, and then click **OK**.

8. Click the **File** menu and then click **Exit** to quit the Registry Editor. The changes take effect immediately and only affect the currently logged-on user.

Activity 10-2: Assigning Permissions

Time Required: 10 to 20 minutes

Objective: Set the permissions within Exchange System Manager.

Description: In this activity, you create the Helpdesk global group and then set the permissions on the First Administrative Group to grant the Helpdesk global group permissions to administer the First Administrative Group. The permissions are then inherited by all objects beneath the First Administrative Group, including the First Routing Group.

1. First create the global group on the front-end server: From the Windows desktop of the front-end server, click **Start**, point to **All Programs**, point to **Microsoft Exchange**, and then click **Active Directory Users and Computers**.

2. In the Active Directory Users and Computers window, click the **plus sign (+)** next to secureYY.local to expand it, where *YY* is the number assigned to the front-end server.

3. Right-click the **Users** container, point to **New**, and then click **Group**.

4. Type **Helpdesk** in the Group name text box. If necessary, click the **Global** option button under Group scope, and then click the **Security** option button under Group type. Click **Next**.

5. This will not be a mail-enabled group. Click **Next** and then click **Finish**.

6. Close **Active Directory Users and Computers**. After the Helpdesk global group is created, set the permissions on the back-end server.

7. If necessary, log on to the back-end server using the user name **Administrator** and the password **Password!**.

8. From the Windows desktop of the back-end server, click **Start**, point to **All Programs**, point to **Microsoft Exchange**, and then click **System Manager**.

9. Click the **plus sign (+)** next to the Administrative Groups container, and then right-click **First Administrative Group**. Click **Properties** on the shortcut menu. The First Administrative Group Properties dialog box opens.

10. Click the **Security** tab. The First Administrative Group Properties Security tab is displayed, as shown in Figure 10-1.

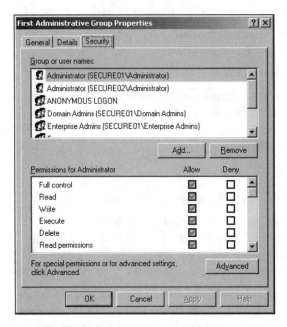

Figure 10-1   First Administrative Group Properties Security tab

11. Users or groups that already have access to the First Administrative Group are listed in the Group or user names list box. To change permissions for these users and groups, click the user or group you want to change, and then use the Permissions list box to grant or deny access permissions. If the permissions are inherited for that user or group, they will be shown in gray. To override the inherited permission, click the opposite permission.

12. To the Helpdesk group, click the **Add** button. The Select Users, Computers, or Groups dialog box opens. Use this dialog box to select users, computers, or groups that you want to add to the existing set of permissions.

13. To access accounts from other domains, click **Locations**. You will see a list that shows the current domain, trusted domains, and other resources that you are able to access. For this activity, click **Entire Directory** to view all the accounts created on both the back-end and front-end servers. Click **OK**.

14. In the Enter the object names to select text box, type **Helpdesk**. Click **OK** to add the group to the list of users and resources that have permissions to the First Administrative Group.

15. If necessary, click **Helpdesk** in the Groups or user names list box. By default, the group is granted full control. To restrict this, uncheck all the permissions with the exception of the following:

   - Read
   - Execute
   - Read permissions
   - List contents
   - Read properties
   - View information store status

 NOTE If you cannot uncheck a particular permission, move on. Some permissions cannot be removed until others are removed first. For example, you can't remove the Write permission without first removing the Write properties permission. Leave the permissions you cannot uncheck for last.

16. After you have finished modifying the permissions, click **OK** to return to Exchange System Manager.

17. Close **Exchange System Manager**.

As mentioned, objects under the parent object inherit the permissions assigned to the parent object by default. In some cases, you should block this inheritance. For example, a security group has full permissions on a parent object, but should not have any permissions on a child object. To prevent the parent's permissions from automatically propagating down to the child object, you block inheritance. You block inheritance in the following activity.

10

Activity 10-3: Blocking Inheritance

Time Required: 10 to 20 minutes

Objective: Block permission inheritance on an object.

Description: In this activity, you override or stop inheriting permissions from the First Administrative Group container. After creating a new global group, you set the permissions on the First Routing Group to disallow inheritance, set the permissions on the First Administrative Group, and then look at the permissions on the First Routing Group to determine if any are inherited. To do this, complete the following on the back-end server:

1. From the Windows desktop of the back-end server, click **Start**, point to **All Programs**, point to **Microsoft Exchange**, and then click **Active Directory Users and Computers**.

2. In the Active Directory Users and Computers window, click the **plus sign (+)** next to secureXX.local to expand it, where *XX* is the number assigned to the back-end server.

3. Right-click the **Users** container, point to **New**, and then click **Group**.

4. Type **First Administrative Group Test** in the Group name text box. If necessary, click the **Global** option button under Group scope, and then click the **Security** option button under Group type. Click **Next**.

5. This will not be a mail-enabled group. Click **Next** and then click **Finish**.

6. Close **Active Directory Users and Computers**. With the First Administrative Group Test global group created, you will set the permissions on the First Routing Group to disallow inheritance.

7. Click **Start**, point to **All Programs**, point to **Microsoft Exchange**, and then click **System Manager**.

8. Click the **plus sign (+)** next to Administrative Groups, click the **plus sign (+)** next to First Administrative Group, and then click the **plus sign (+)** next to the Routing Groups container.

9. Right-click the **First Routing Group**, and then click **Properties** on the shortcut menu. The First Routing Group Properties dialog box opens.

10. Click the **Security** tab. The First Routing Group Properties Security tab is displayed, as shown in Figure 10-2.

11. Click the **Advanced** button to open the Advanced Security Settings for First Routing Group dialog box.

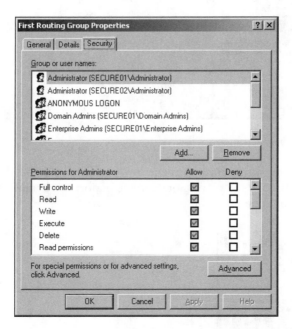

Figure 10-2   First Routing Group Properties Security tab

12. Click the **Allow inheritable permissions from the parent to propagate to this object and all child objects** check box to clear it. You are prompted with the dialog box shown in Figure 10-3.

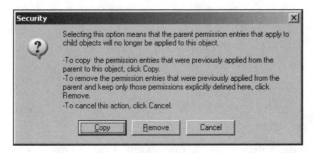

Figure 10-3   Security dialog box

13. Because the permissions have been inherited from the parent object, there are no explicit permissions on the First Routing Group object. Click **Copy** to copy the parent object permissions to this object explicitly.

14. Click **OK** in the Advanced Security Settings for First Routing Group dialog box. You are prompted with a warning indicating that you are setting deny permissions, as shown in Figure 10-4. Deny permissions take precedence over allow permissions. Click **Yes** to continue.

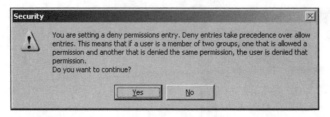

Figure 10-4   Security warning

15. You are then prompted with the Permissions warning, shown in Figure 10-5, indicating that you are about to explicitly copy the permissions and the performance implications this will incur. Click **Yes** to continue.

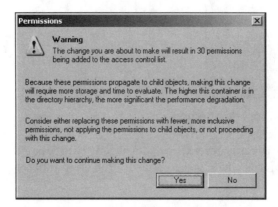

Figure 10-5   Permissions warning

The number of permissions indicated in your Permissions Warning dialog box might differ from the number shown in Figure 10-5.

NOTE

16. Click **OK** to return to Exchange System Manager.

    Next, you set the permissions on the First Administrative Group.

17. Right-click the **First Administrative Group**, and then click **Properties** on the shortcut menu.

18. Click the **Security** tab, and then click **Add**. The Select Users, Computers, or Groups dialog box opens.

19. Type **First Administrative Group Test** in the Enter the object names to select text box, and then click **Check Names**. After the name is resolved (indicated by the underline), click **OK**.

20. Click **OK** to return to Exchange System Manager. Finally, you view the permissions on the First Routing Group to see if the permissions have been inherited.

21. Right-click the **First Routing Group**, and then click **Properties** on the shortcut menu. The First Routing Group Properties dialog box opens.

22. Click the **Security** tab. Scroll through the Group or user names list box. Notice that the First Administrative Group Test global group has not been assigned to the First Routing Group. Click **Cancel** to return to Exchange System Manager.

23. Close **Exchange System Manager**.

DELEGATING AUTHORITY

When designing and implementing your Exchange Server 2003 infrastructure, you typically need to consider an administrative model for your organization. Your company might require a centralized model, one in which one group maintains control over all of the Exchange server, a decentralized model, one in which separate administrative groups are created for each group of Exchange administrators, or a mixed model, which is a combination of the two.

To facilitate any of these types of administrative models, Exchange Server 2003 provides an Exchange Administration Delegation Wizard that grants different types of permissions to different users or groups within your organization. The Exchange Administration Delegation Wizard enables you to select a user or a group, and give them a specific administrative role within the organization. (To simplify administration, you should always assign permissions to a group rather than to individual users.) The Exchange Administration Delegation Wizard supports the following three roles:

Exchange Full Administrator—In this role, users can fully administer Exchange system information (for example, add, delete, and rename objects) and modify permissions. You should delegate this role to administrators who need to configure and control access to your mail system.

Exchange Administrator—In this role, users can fully administer Exchange system information. However, they cannot modify permissions. You should delegate this role to users or groups responsible for the day-to-day administration of Exchange (for example, add, delete, and rename objects).

Exchange View Only Administrator—In this role, users can view Exchange configuration information. You should delegate this role to administrators of other administrative groups who need access to your organization's information.

When setting permissions using the Exchange Administration Delegation Wizard, the location from which you start the wizard determines the scope of objects on which the user or group will have permissions. For example, if you start the wizard from the organization object, the permissions assigned are propagated down the hierarchy to all objects in the organization. If you start the wizard from an administrative group object, permissions

10

propagate to all objects in that administrative group; however, read-only permissions are also granted from the administrative group object up the hierarchy so that the administrator can view the hierarchy.

When Exchange Full Administrator role permissions are applied to an organization container, the permissions listed in Table 10-2 are granted to objects within Exchange.

Table 10-2   Exchange Full Administrator role permissions

Container	Permissions	Do Permissions Apply to Subcontainers?
Microsoft Exchange	Full Control	Yes
Organization	Send As and Receive As denied	Yes
Administrative Groups	All permissions inherited; Send As and Receive As inherited as denied	Yes

When Exchange Administrator role permissions are applied to an organization container, permissions are granted to objects within Exchange (see Table 10-3).

Table 10-3   Exchange Administrator role permissions

Container	Permissions	Do Permissions Apply to Subcontainers?
Microsoft Exchange	All permissions except Full Control	Yes
Organization	Send As and Receive As denied	Yes
Administrative Groups	All permissions inherited except Full Control and Change; Send As and Receive As inherited as denied	Yes

Table 10-4 lists the permissions granted to objects within Exchange when Exchange View Only Administrator role permissions are applied to an organization container.

Table 10-4   Exchange View Only Administrator role permissions

Container	Permissions	Do Permissions Apply to Subcontainers?
Microsoft Exchange	Read, List object, and List content permissions allowed	Yes
Organization	Read, List object, and List contents permissions inherited; View information store status permission allowed	Yes
Administrative Groups	Read, List object, List contents, and View information store status permissions inherited	Yes

PUBLIC KEY INFRASTRUCTURES

To enable secure messaging, Exchange relies upon a set of digital certificates and certification authorities to verify the identity of all sending and receiving parties on the network. This system of entities used for authentication is known as a **Public Key Infrastructure (PKI)**. With Exchange 2000 Server, Microsoft provided their own PKI through the Key Management Service (KMS), which works with Windows 2000/2003 Certificate Services to create a PKI for performing secure messaging. With a PKI in place, users and/or servers were able to send signed and encrypted messages to each other. The KMS included with Exchange 2000 Server provided a mechanism for enrolling users in Advanced Security, and handled key archival and recovery functions. With the introduction of Exchange Server 2003, the KMS has been removed, and Exchange Server 2003 passes the duties of key archival and recovery tasks off to the operating system itself. As such, this section provides a basic introduction to Windows 2000/2003 PKI, which is then used in subsequent discussions of secure e-mail.

10

Key-Based Cryptography

A brief discussion of key-based cryptography will help explain the purpose and structure of the PKI used by Exchange and Windows Server 2003. In general, cryptographic algorithms fall into one of two categories: **symmetric (secret key) cryptography** or **asymmetric (public key) cryptography**. In symmetric cryptography, the sender and receiver share a single, predetermined key, which they use to encrypt and decrypt the transmitted message(s). The term "symmetric" derives from the fact that the same key is used on both ends of the transmission. Although this method is useful and appropriate for certain situations, it has at least one inherent flaw: The sender and receiver need to decide upon and transmit (perhaps insecurely) the shared key *before* they can send any encrypted messages. If Alice needs to send Bob the shared key before they can communicate securely, there is always the possibility that Eve may intercept this shared key and gain the ability to decrypt all encrypted messages thereafter. Public key cryptography solves this problem by eliminating the need for an insecure transmission of a single key that can be used to both encrypt and decrypt messages. Instead, public key cryptography uses asymmetric keys. For example, the key used for encryption, and the key used for decryption, are different. Moreover, there is no need for the encryption key to be kept secret (hence the term "public key"). This scheme works because it employs a so-called "trapdoor one-way" mathematical function on the plaintext message to create the encrypted message. This type of function gets its name from the fact that it is relatively easy to compute in one direction (encrypt the message) but extremely difficult to compute in the other direction (decrypt the message)—unless you have the private key. So, if Alice wants to send a message to Bob, she uses his public key to encrypt the message and transmits the encrypted message; when Bob receives the message, he uses his private key to decrypt it. Only Bob's private key will decrypt the message and this private key is never transmitted, so Eve has no way of intercepting it.

Certificates, Certificate Authorities, and Trust

To encrypt messages using a public key encryption system, senders need to be able to access the public keys of the intended recipients. This requires the use of a third party to act as a repository for users' public keys and to verify that public keys are associated with the appropriate users. As noted previously, Exchange Server 2003 relies on Windows Server 2003's built-in PKI to perform these tasks.

The Windows Server 2003 PKI is composed of several different but related features. Two of the most important for the present discussion are certificates (digital certificates) and certification authorities. A **certificate** is a digital declaration that contains a given user's public key and that states that the user is in fact who he claims to be. A CA (certification authority) is an entity that issues the certificate and attests to the fact that the certificate is valid and that the user is authentic.

Because it performs this issuing and validation of certificates, it's imperative that senders and receivers trust the certification authority implicitly. This CA can either be a third-party company, such as Thawte or VeriSign, or a Windows 2003 server configured as a CA within the organization. There may, in fact, be several CAs involved in the transmission of a message from a sender to a recipient. If, for example, Bob receives an encrypted message from Alice, he needs to verify that the public key used to encrypt the message does, in fact, belong to Alice. He does so by referencing a certificate issued by a CA, which he trusts. (Of course, all of these steps are done automatically via software; Bob doesn't need to manually check anything.) As with the message, Bob's trust of the CA is based on verifying the public key of the CA. This can be done via a certificate issued by another CA, which vouches for the authenticity of the first CA. This certification process goes on, creating a series of certificates, or a certificate chain, each trusting a certificate higher up in the chain. At the top level of this chain is the trusted root certificate. By trusting this root, Bob implicitly trusts all the certificates issued by this CA and any other CAs in the hierarchy that are certified by the root.

WINDOWS 2003 PUBLIC KEY INFRASTRUCTURES

Windows 2000/2003 certificates form the core of the Windows 2000/2003 PKI. Active Directory maintains information that a CA needs, such as user account names, group memberships, and certificate templates, as well as information about each CA installed in the domain. Active Directory also maintains certificate mappings to user accounts for authenticating clients and controlling access to network resources. You can install Windows 2000/2003 Certificate Services to create a **certificate authority (CA)** that issues and manages digital certificates in either an enterprise situation or a stand-alone situation.

Enterprise certificate servers are very Active Directory integrated. All information is stored within Active Directory, and Certificate Services is highly integrated with Windows 2000/2003 security. Alternatively, stand-alone CAs can be members of a domain or stand-alone servers in a workgroup. The stand-alone CA differs from the Enterprise CA because all data is stored in a local database and the stand-alone CA does not make use of certificate templates.

Finally, a Windows 2000/2003 PKI provides you with the capability to establish either a rooted hierarchy or cross-certification hierarchy of servers. Let's explore each of these types of hierarchies.

A **rooted hierarchy** is the most common CA structure. This type of hierarchy defines either an enterprise root CA or a stand-alone root CA. The root CA is unique in that it issues itself a certificate. This certificate is known as a self-signed certificate. Below the root CA are one or more Enterprise or stand-alone subordinate CAs. The root CA issues certificates to the subordinate CAs with the subject matching the name of the subordinate CA. Figure 10-6 provides an example of a rooted CA hierarchy.

Additional levels of CAs might exist below a subordinate CA. These CAs are often referred to as issuing CAs. Rooted CA hierarchies enable the highest form of security because you can remove the root CA from the network, thus protecting it from attack.

10

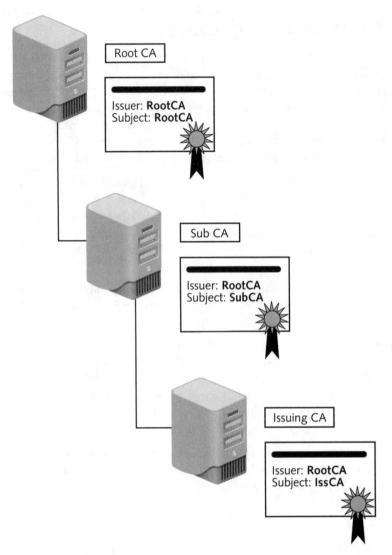

Figure 10-6   A rooted CA hierarchy

In a **cross-certification hierarchy**, a CA acts as both a root CA and a subordinate CA. This structure is used when two organizations want to establish a certificate trust between themselves. Cross-certification is commonly deployed in business-to-business scenarios when the participating organizations have existing CA hierarchies. Cross-certification allows existing hierarchies to be maintained while allowing additional CAs to exist in the hierarchy. Figure 10-7 provides an example of a cross-certification hierarchy.

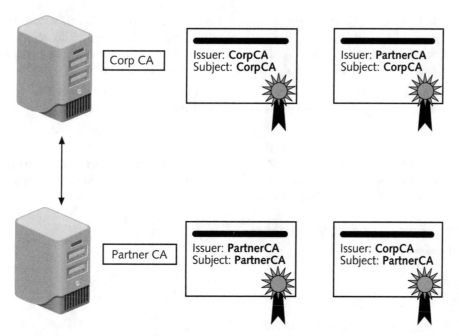

Figure 10-7   Cross-certification CA hierarchy

In this hierarchy, the Corp CA is the root CA for the corporation. In addition to the self-signed certificate signifying that the Corp CA is a root CA, the Corp CA also has a subordinate CA certificate issued by the Partner CA. This certificate indicates that the root CA is a subordinate CA of the Partner CA. Following the same logic, the Partner CA is a subordinate CA of the Corp CA.

Activity 10-4: Installing Certificate Services

Time Required: 10 to 20 minutes

Objective: Install Certificate Services into a domain.

Description: In this activity, you install Certificate Services on your back-end server. You install an enterprise CA for the forest as you will need to subsequently issue certificates to other entities in future activities.

1. From the Windows desktop of the back-end server, click **Start**, point to **Control Panel**, and then click **Add or Remove Programs**. The Add or Remove Programs dialog box opens.

2. Click **Add/Remove Windows Components**. The Windows Components Wizard starts.

3. Click the **Certificate Services** check box. You are prompted with a warning dialog box indicating that if you change the name of the machine or the domain membership, the certificates issued by the CA installed on this machine will be invalidated. Click **Yes** to continue. On the Windows Components screen, click **Next**.

4. You are prompted to specify the type of CA that you want to set up. For this particular activity, click **Enterprise root CA**, if necessary, and then click **Next** to continue.

5. At the CA Identifying Information screen, type **BLATHERCONSULTINGZZCA**, where *ZZ* is the number assigned to your group, in the Common name for this CA text box. Your screen should look similar to Figure 10-8. Click **Next** to continue.

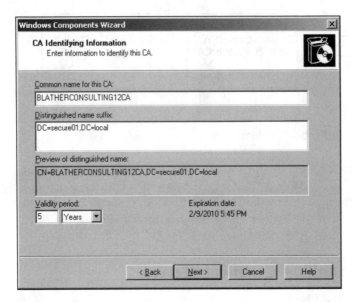

Figure 10-8   Windows Components Wizard CA Identifying Information screen

6. The Certificate Database Settings screen defines the locations of the certificate database and certificate database log. Click **Next** to accept the default locations.

7. You are prompted with a warning dialog box indicating that IIS must be temporarily stopped while Certificate Services is installed. Click **Yes** to continue.

8. If necessary, insert your Windows Server 2003 CD when prompted, and then click **OK**. Certificate Services is installed. Click **Finish** when the installation is complete.

9. Close **Add or Remove Programs**.

By default, when Windows 2003 Certificate Services is installed, Web enrollment support is also installed on the server. Users can access the Web enrollment pages via the URL *http://servername/certsrv*.

The following sections make use of Certificate Services to enable a secure messaging infrastructure.

Now that you've installed Certificate Services on the back-end server, you'll use certificates issued by your CA to enable clients and servers in your organization to communicate securely. This includes a method to implement secure messaging between servers (or between clients and servers) during message transport only, as well as a way to establish end-to-end security.

SECURING COMMUNICATIONS

By default, the SMTP protocol sends e-mail between servers in plain text format. As a result, every message you send has the potential to be exposed to any malicious user who wants to listen to communication on the SMTP port, port 25, of your mail server. One potential way to solve this problem is to require the use of SSL/TLS for SMTP connections.

SSL was developed by Netscape Communications Corporation in 1994 to secure transactions over the World Wide Web. Soon after, the Internet Engineering Task Force (IETF) began work to develop a standard protocol to provide the same functionality. SSL 3.0 was used as the basis for that work, which is known as the Transport Layer Security protocol (TLS) 1.0. Although there are some slight differences between SSL 3.0 and TLS 1.0, the differences are not dramatic and are typically referred to as **SSL/TLS**. Although SSL 3.0 and TLS 1.0 do not interoperate, TLS 1.0 does incorporate a mechanism that allows a TLS implementation to back down to SSL 3.0 should the other side not support TLS 1.0.

SSL/TLS can be used to secure both client-to-server traffic and server-to-server traffic. In a client-to-server scenario, it is used to typically secure POP/IMAP and OWA traffic between the client and back-end server. In a server-to-server scenario, SSL/TLS is used to secure traffic between two back-end SMTP servers. Securing client-to-server traffic is relatively simple. Configuring server-to-server traffic is a little more difficult than securing client-to-server traffic.

Because SMTP servers use port 25 by default for SMTP communication, using SSL/TLS on this port introduces a problem: Servers that are not using SSL/TLS cannot communicate using this port. Although another port could be assigned to SSL/TLS instead, only those clients and servers that are configured to use that port will know to do so. The solution to this and other similar problems lies in a set of extensions to SMTP called the Extended SMTP protocol (ESMTP), which allows clients to query servers to determine what features they support. In particular, the ESMTP keyword STARTTLS is used by two computers to determine if SSL/TLS is available over a particular port. If so, the computers can then use each other's digital certificates to authenticate each other and then transmit information securely. This allows for secure communication, when available, without precluding insecure communication via nodes that don't support SSL/TLS.

10

As mentioned, securing client-to-server traffic is a little simpler than securing server-to-server traffic. All that is required is that you install certificates on the default virtual servers involved and then enable the servers to require TLS encryption.

To do this, you need to acquire a digital certificate for your POP3 and SMTP virtual servers. If your SMTP bridgehead is running on the same machine as an SSL-protected OWA server, you can use the same certificate to provide secure communication with your POP/IMAP clients as with your OWA users.

ACTIVITY

Activity 10-5: Configuring a POP3 Server SSL/TLS Encryption

Time Required: 20 to 40 minutes

Objective: Configure POP3 and SMTP for SSL/TLS encryption with a POP3 client.

Description: In this activity, you configure your back-end server to force the POP3 client to negotiate an SSL/TLS connection before user credentials are sent to the server. This ensures that the user credentials that are passed by the client in clear text are encrypted using SSL/TLS. A certificate request is then generated on the POP3 virtual server so that it can encrypt traffic using SSL/TLS.

Encrypting traffic using POP3 is only one-half of the process. You also need to encrypt the client traffic being sent. To do this, you need to request and install a certificate on the back-end server's default SMTP virtual server.

To force the SSL/TLS connection, complete the following on the back-end server:

1. From the Windows desktop of the back-end server, click **Start**, point to **All Programs**, point to **Microsoft Exchange**, and then click **System Manager**.

2. Click the **plus sign (+)** next to Administrative Groups, click the **plus sign (+)** next to First Administrative Group, click the **plus sign (+)** next to the Servers container, and then click the **plus sign (+)** next to SERVERXX, where XX is the number assigned to the back-end server.

3. Click the **plus sign (+)** next to Protocols, and then click the **plus sign (+)** next to POP3.

4. Right-click the **Default POP3 Virtual Server**, and then click **Properties** on the shortcut menu. The Default POP3 Virtual Server Properties dialog box opens.

5. Click the **Access** tab and then click the **Authentication** button. The Authentication dialog box opens, as shown in Figure 10-9.

6. Check the **Requires SSL/TLS encryption** check box, and then click **OK** to return to the Default POP3 Virtual Server Properties dialog box.

7. Next, you generate the certificate request on the default POP3 virtual server. Click the **Certificate** button. The Web Server Certificate Wizard starts. Click **Next** to continue.

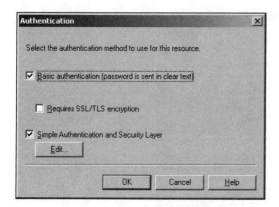

Figure 10-9   Authentication dialog box

8. When prompted to select the method you want to use for this Web site, click **Create a new certificate**, if necessary, and then click **Next** to continue.

9. At the Delayed or Immediate Request screen, click **Send the request immediately to an online certification authority**, and then click **Next**.

10. At the Name and Security Settings screen, type **SERVERXX SSL/TLS Certificate**, where *XX* is the number assigned to the back-end server, in the Name text box, and then click **Next** to continue.

11. At the Organization Information screen, if necessary, type **Blather Consulting** in the Organization text box, and **North America** in the Organizational unit text box. Click **Next** to continue.

12. You are prompted for the site's common name. In the Common name text box, type **serverXX.secureXX.local**, where *XX* is the number assigned to the back-end server, and then click **Next** to continue.

13. At the Geographical Information screen, if necessary, type **CA** for the Country/Region, type **Ontario** for the State/province, and type **Toronto** for the City/locality. Click **Next** to continue.

14. At the Choose a Certification Authority screen, ensure **serverXX.secureXX.local\BLATHERCONSULTINGZZCA**, where *XX* is the number assigned to the back-end server and *ZZ* is the number assigned to your group, is selected in the Certification authorities drop-down list, and then click **Next**.

15. The Certificate Request Submission screen displays a summary of the choices selected, as shown in Figure 10-10. Click **Next** to submit the certificate request.

16. The Completing the Web Server Certificate Wizard screen indicates that the certificate is now installed on the POP3 virtual server. To close the wizard, click **Finish**.

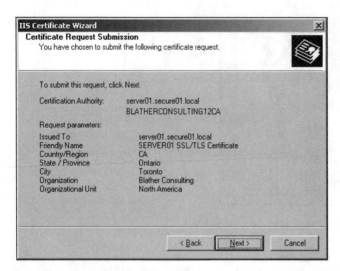

Figure 10-10   IIS Certificate Wizard Certificate Request Submission screen

17. Click **OK** in the Default POP3 Virtual Server Properties dialog box.

    Finally, to secure outbound communications from your client, you need to request and install a certificate on your default SMTP virtual server.

18. In Exchange System Manager, if necessary, click the **plus sign (+)** next to Administrative Groups, click the **plus sign (+)** next to First Administrative Group, click the **plus sign (+)** next to the Servers container, click the **plus sign (+)** next to SERVERXX, where *XX* is the number assigned to the back-end server, and then click the **plus sign (+)** next to the Protocols container.

19. Click the **plus sign (+)** next to SMTP. Right-click the **Default SMTP Virtual Server**, and then click **Properties** on the shortcut menu. The Default SMTP Virtual Server Properties dialog box opens.

20. Click the **Access** tab and then click the **Certificate** button to start the certificate request. At the Welcome to the Web Server Certificate Wizard screen, click **Next** to continue.

21. At the Server Certificate screen, click **Create a new certificate**, if necessary, and then click **Next**.

22. At the Delayed or Immediate Request screen, click **Send the request immediately to an online certification authority**, and then click **Next**.

23. In the Name text box, type **SERVERXX SMTP SSL/TLS Certificate**, where *XX* is the number assigned to the back-end server, and then click **Next**.

24. At the Organization Information screen, if necessary, type **Blather Consulting** in the Organization text box, and **North America** in the Organizational unit text box. Click **Next** to continue.

25. In the Common name text box, type **serverXX.secureXX.local**, where *XX* is the number assigned to the back-end server, and then click **Next** to continue.

26. At the Geographical Information screen, if necessary, type **CA** for the Country/Region, type **Ontario** for the State/province, and type **Toronto** for the City/locality. Click **Next** to continue.

27. At the Choose a Certification Authority screen, ensure **serverXX.secureXX.local\BLATHERCONSULTINGZZCA**, where *XX* is the number assigned to the back-end server and *ZZ* is the number assigned to your group, is selected in the Certification authorities drop-down list, and then click **Next**.

28. At the Certificate Request Submission screen, click **Next** to submit the request.

29. Click **Finish** when the certificate is successfully installed.

30. Click the **Authentication** button. In the Authentication dialog box, click the **Requires TLS encryption** check box, and then click **OK** to return to the Default SMTP Virtual Server Properties dialog box.

31. Click **OK** in the Default SMTP Virtual Server Properties dialog box to return to Exchange System Manager.

32. Close **Exchange System Manager**.

After the back-end server has been configured, you need to configure the client to connect securely to the server.

ACTIVITY

Activity 10-6: Configuring a POP3 Client for Access to a Secure POP3 Server

Time Required: 20 to 40 minutes

Objective: Configure Outlook Express for communication with a secure POP3 server.

Description: In this activity, your front-end server acts as the client. On the front-end server, you configure Outlook Express to support SSL/TLS encryption with the back-end server. To support communication with the back-end, the client must trust the certificate authority that issued the certificate to the POP3 server. To do so, a root certificate will be installed on the front-end server establishing this trust.

This activity assumes Outlook is installed and configured on the back-end server for the Administrator (installed and configured in Chapter 4, "Configuring Outlook and Outlook Web Access"), and Outlook Express is configured on the front-end server for Mike Jones (configured in Chapter 7, "Configuring and Managing Exchange Server").

Prior to configuring your client, you need to download the root certificate to establish a trust with the certificate that was installed on the back-end server. To do so, complete the following:

1. On the front-end server, click **Start**, point to **All Programs**, and then click **Internet Explorer**.

2. In the Address Bar, type **http://SERVERXX/CertSrv**, where *XX* is the number assigned to the back-end server, and then click the **Go** button.

If this does not resolve, in the Address Bar, type **http://192.168.0.XX/CertSrv**, where *XX* is the number assigned to the back-end server, and then click the **Go** button.

3. When prompted for a user name and password, type **Administrator** in the User name text box and **Password!** in the Password text box, and then click **OK**. The Welcome page for Certificate Services on your back-end server opens, as shown in Figure 10-11.

Figure 10-11 Certificate Services Welcome page

If you receive a "The page cannot be displayed" error in Internet Explorer, click the **Refresh** button on the toolbar.

4. Click the **Download a CA certificate, certificate chain, or CRL** link. The Download a CA Certificate, Certificate Chain, or CRL page opens.

5. Click the **install this CA certificate chain** link to install the necessary root certificate to allow your client to connect to the server.

6. The Potential Scripting Violation dialog box opens, warning you that untrusted certificates could be installed. Click **Yes** to install the certificates.

7. When the certificate chain is successfully installed, close **Internet Explorer**.

Next, you configure the connection in Outlook Express.

8. Click **Start**, point to **All Programs**, and then click **Outlook Express**.

9. If the Logon dialog box opens, click **Cancel**.

10. If the Outlook Express dialog box opens indicating a connection error, click **Hide**.

11. Click **Tools** on the menu bar, and then click **Accounts**.

12. Click the **Mail** tab. Ensure the mail account is selected, and then click **Properties**.

13. In the Properties dialog box, click the **Servers** tab.

14. In the Outgoing Mail Server section, click the **My server requires authentication** check box, and then click the **Settings** button. Ensure the **Use same settings as my incoming mail server** option button is selected, and then click **OK**.

15. Click the **Advanced** tab. Check the two **This server requires a secure connection (SSL)** check boxes in the Server Port Numbers section, and then click **OK**.

16. Click **Close** in the Internet Accounts dialog box. Outlook Express can now securely send and receive mail.

17. Test this secure connection by sending an e-mail to and receiving an e-mail from the Administrator.

18. If necessary, expand the **Local Folders** node, and click **Inbox**.

19. Click the **Create Mail** button on the toolbar.

20. In the New Message window, type **Administrator@blatherconsultingXX.com** in the To text box, where *XX* is the number assigned to the back-end server, **Message to test secure account settings** in the Subject text box, and **This is a test message** in the body. When finished, click the **Send** button. Leave Outlook Express open.

21. Switch to the back-end server. Click **Start**, point to **All Programs**, point to **Microsoft Office**, and then click **Microsoft Office Outlook 2003**. Outlook opens to the Administrator's Inbox. You should see the new message sent from Mike Jones.

NOTE   If you do not see the new message, press **F9** to start the Send/Receive process.

22. If necessary, select the new message from Mike Jones in the Inbox, and then click the **Reply** button on the toolbar.

23. Type **I successfully received your message** in the body, and then click **Send**. Close **Outlook** on the back-end server.

24. Switch back to the front-end server. Click the **Send/Recv** button on the toolbar. You should see the Administrator's reply in the Inbox. This indicates the testing is successful. Close **Outlook Express**.

As mentioned, setting up TLS for use with connector-based SMTP traffic is slightly more complicated. You can select one of the following three scenarios when enabling SSL/TLS:

- *Force SSL/TLS for all e-mail traffic*—This scenario effectively restricts Exchange Server 2003 to communicating only with other hosts that support SSL/TLS by turning on SSL/TLS for all outbound e-mail. If the destination host does not support SSL/TLS, the mail will be returned as nondeliverable.

- *Enabling SSL/TLS for specific domains*—This scenario restricts outbound SSL/TLS to domains that support SSL/TLS encryption. Presumably, these are domains that you know support this option. To find out, telnet to port 25 on the destination server, and type EHLO. If the response from the server includes a STARTTLS command, the destination server supports SSL/TLS. To restrict to specific domains requires that you set up separate SMTP connectors that are dedicated to handling traffic for these domains.

- *Enabling SSL/TLS for inbound e-mail*—This scenario requires that the connecting server transfer all e-mail using SSL/TLS.

Typically, organizations do not force all mail traffic to make use of SSL/TLS, but rather enable SSL/TLS for specific domains that are known to support SSL/TLS and create separate SMTP connectors in their Exchange Server 2003 organization to support communication with those domains.

E-Mail Encryption

The **S/MIME** protocol allows users to send secure e-mail by digitally signing or encrypting e-mail messages. Unlike SSL/TLS, which secures messages only during transit between computers, S/MIME, an updated version of the MIME encoding standard, ensures so-called "end-to-end" security by allowing users to encrypt messages when they are created and by allowing recipients to decrypt messages upon receipt. Using the certificates issued and authenticated by a CA, recipients can decrypt messages using their private keys and verify the identity of the sender(s). The CAs used to issue certificates and validate messages do not have to be within the same organization; the S/MIME standard is designed to enable compatibility and authentication between different organizations and among different vendors.

To configure Outlook 2003 for secure messaging, you first need to obtain a certificate for your client.

Activity 10-7: Configuring Outlook 2003 for S/MIME

Time Required: 20 to 40 minutes

Objective: Obtain a digital certificate for your Outlook client.

Description: In this activity, you obtain a digital certificate for your Outlook clients to enable secure transfer of e-mail between them. Each client will obtain a certificate from the CA.

For this activity, the back-end server acts as one client and a Windows XP machine acts as the other. Please keep in mind that in a real-world situation you would complete this activity on two client machines; the back-end server would not act as a client. You must have Outlook installed and configured for the Administrator on the back-end server (this was installed and configured in Chapter 4), and Outlook installed and configured for the user Test1 on the Windows XP machine (this was installed and configured in Chapter 5). If you do not have access to a Windows XP client machine, you cannot complete this activity or Activity 10-8.

1. From the Windows desktop of the client machine, click **Start**, point to **All Programs**, and then click **Internet Explorer**.

2. In the Address Bar, type **http://SERVERXX/CertSrv**, where *XX* is the number assigned to the back-end server, and then click the **Go** button.

> If this does not resolve, type **http://192.168.0.XX/CertSrv** in the Address Bar, where *XX* is the number assigned to the back-end server, and then click the **Go** button.

NOTE

3. When prompted for a user name and password, type **Test1**, in the User name text box and **Password!** in the Password text box, and then click **OK**.

4. The Welcome page for Certificate Services on your back-end server opens. Click the **Request a certificate** link.

> If you receive a "The page cannot be displayed" error in Internet Explorer, click the **Refresh** button on the toolbar.

NOTE

5. At the Request a Certificate page, click the **User Certificate** link.

6. At the User Certificate – Identifying Information page, click the **Submit** button.

7. Click **Yes** in the Potential Scripting Violation Warning dialog box to request the certificate now.

8. At the Certificate Issued page, click the **Install this certificate** link.

9. The Potential Scripting Violation dialog box opens, warning you that untrusted certificates could be installed. Click **Yes** to install the certificates.

10

10. If the Security Warning dialog box opens asking for verification to install the certificate, click **Yes**.

11. When the certificate chain is successfully installed, close **Internet Explorer**.

12. Open Outlook, by clicking **Start**, pointing to **All Programs**, pointing to **Microsoft Office**, and then clicking **Microsoft Office Outlook 2003**.

13. In the Choose Profile dialog box, click **TEST User 1** in the Profile Name drop-down list, if necessary, and then click **OK**.

14. When prompted for a user name and password, type **Test1**, in the User name text box and **Password!** in the Password text box, and then click **OK**.

15. Click **Tools** on the menu bar, and then click **Options**. The Options dialog box opens.

16. Click the **Security** tab.

17. If necessary, click the **Send clear text signed message when sending signed messages** check box. Click the **Settings** button. The Change Security Settings dialog box opens, as shown in Figure 10-12.

Figure 10-12   Change Security Settings dialog box

18. In the Security Settings Name text box, type **My S/MIME Settings (test1@secureXX.local)**, where *XX* is the number assigned to the back-end server.

19. Click the **Default Security Setting for this cryptographic message format** check box, and then click the **Default Security Setting for all cryptographic messages** check box.

20. Click the **Choose** button next to the Signing Certificate text box. In the Select Certificate dialog box, ensure the certificate issued to **Test1** is selected, and then click **OK**. Click the **Choose** button next to the Encryption Certificate text box. Again, in the Select Certificate dialog box, ensure the certificate issued to Test1 is selected, and then click **OK**.

21. Click **OK** in the Change Security Settings dialog box. Click **OK** again to return to Outlook. Leave Outlook open on the client machine for the next activity.

22. Repeat Steps 1 to 11 on the back-end server to install the appropriate user certificate for the Administrator. Be certain to use the user name **Administrator** and password **Password!** in Step 3.

23. On the back-end server, open Outlook, by clicking **Start**, pointing to **All Programs**, pointing to **Microsoft Office**, and then clicking **Microsoft Office Outlook 2003**.

24. Click **Tools** on the menu bar, and then click **Options**. The Options dialog box opens. Click the **Security** tab.

25. If necessary, click the **Send clear text signed message when sending signed messages** check box. Click the **Settings** button.

26. In the Security Settings Name text box, if necessary, type **My S/MIME Settings (Administrator@blatherconsultingXX.com)**, where *XX* is the number assigned to the back-end server. If necessary, click the **Default Security Setting for this cryptographic message format** check box, and then click the **Default Security Setting for all cryptographic messages** check box.

27. Click the **Choose** button next to the Signing Certificate text box. In the Select Certificate dialog box, ensure the certificate issued to Administrator is selected, and then click **OK**. Click the **Choose** button next to the Encryption Certificate text box. Again, in the Select Certificate dialog box, ensure the certificate issued to Administrator is selected, and then click **OK**.

28. Click **OK** in the Change Security Settings dialog box. Click **OK** again to return to Outlook. Leave Outlook open on the back-end server for the next activity.

After you have configured your clients, you can then create and send encrypted and/or digitally signed messages between them.

Activity 10-8: Sending Encrypted and Signed E-Mail

Time Required: 10 to 20 minutes

Objective: Send encrypted and signed e-mail between two Outlook clients.

Description: In this activity, you send an encrypted and digitally signed e-mail between two Outlook e-mail clients and reply to the e-mail that was sent. This activity makes use of the Administrator and Test1 accounts on the back-end server and Windows XP client machine. You must successfully complete Activity 10-7 before completing this activity.

1. If necessary, open **Microsoft Outlook** on the back-end server.

2. Click the **New** button on the toolbar to compose a new message. In the Untitled – Message window, type **Test1** in the To text box, **S/MIME test** in the Subject text box, and **This is a test** in the body.

3. Click **View** on the menu bar, and then click **Options**. The Message Options dialog box opens.

4. Click the **Security Settings** button. The Security Properties dialog box opens.

5. Click both the **Encrypt message contents and attachments** and the **Add digital signature to this message** check boxes. When finished, click **OK**. Click **Close** in the Message Options dialog box.

6. Click the **Send** button to deliver the message to Test1. Leave Outlook open.

7. Switch to the **Windows XP** client machine. If necessary, open **Outlook** and log on as **Test1**.

8. You should see the new message from the Administrator. The message icon indicates that it contains a digital signature and the contents cannot be read in the Reading Pane, as shown in Figure 10-13.

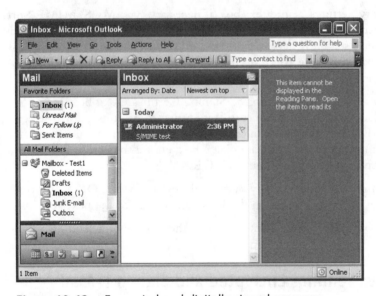

Figure 10-13   Encrypted and digitally signed message

 If you do not see the new message, press **F9** to start the Send/Receive process.

NOTE

9. Double-click the message in the Inbox to view its contents. Click the **Reply** button, and then type **This is a reply** in the body of the message. Click the **Send** button.

10. Close the **S/MIME test** message, and then close **Outlook** on the Windows XP client machine.

11. Return to the back-end server. You should have an encrypted reply from Test1.

 If you do not see the new message, press **F9** to start the Send/Receive process.

NOTE

12. Close **Outlook**.

CHAPTER SUMMARY

- Permissions that are assigned to an object within Exchange Server 2003 can be applied directly to the object itself, or they can be inherited from their parent object.

- There are two types of permissions: standard and extended. Standard permissions are part of the default permissions for Active Directory. Extended permissions are added when Exchange Server 2003 is installed.

- The Exchange Administration Delegation Wizard enables you to select a user or a group and give them a specific administrative role within the organization.

- A Microsoft Windows PKI provides an integrated set of services and administrative tools for creating, deploying, and managing public key–based applications using public key cryptography.

- In symmetric key cryptography, the encryption and decryption keys are identical. Parties wanting to secure their communication using secret keys must, under symmetric key cryptography, exchange their encryption/decryption keys securely before they can exchange encrypted data.

- Public key cryptography uses asymmetric keys (that is, the keys used for encryption and for decryption are different). Moreover, there is no need for the encryption key to be kept secret.

- Certificates are used to verify the identities of senders and receivers. A certificate is a digital declaration that contains a given user's public key and that states that the user is in fact who she claims to be.

- A CA is an entity that issues a digital certificate and attests to the fact that the certificate is valid and that the user is authentic.

- A certificate chain associates a certificate with a list of issuing CAs that ultimately leads to a certificate that the receiver implicitly trusts.

10

◻ A root certificate forms the root of a certificate hierarchy that the receiver accepts as authentic.

◻ SSL/TLS can be used to encrypt and secure both client-to-server traffic and server-to-server traffic.

◻ Server-to-server SSL/TLS is best handled using a separate dedicated SMTP connector.

◻ The S/MIME protocol allows users to send secure e-mail by digitally signing or encrypting e-mail messages.

◻ S/MIME is an updated version of the MIME encoding standard that ensures so-called "end-to-end" security by allowing users to encrypt messages when they are created and by allowing recipients to decrypt messages upon receipt.

KEY TERMS

asymmetric (public-key) cryptography — A method of encrypting and decrypting messages in which the key used for encryption and the key used for decryption are different. This method assumes that the encryption key will be made public rather than be kept secret.

certificate — An attachment to an electronic message used to verify that a user sending a message is who he claims to be, and to provide the receiver with the means to encode a reply.

certificate authority (CA) — An entity that issues (digital) certificates containing users' public keys and other identifying information.

cross-certification hierarchy — A configuration in which a CA acts as both a root CA and a subordinate CA (to another root CA in a different organization).

Public Key Infrastructure (PKI) — A system of digital certificates and certification authorities used to authenticate the identity of all parties in a secure messaging environment.

rooted hierarchy — A configuration in which all of the CAs in an organization are arranged below a common root CA.

S/MIME — A specification for formatting non-ASCII messages so that they can be sent over the Internet in an encrypted format.

SSL/TLS — An acronym for Secure Sockets Layer/Transport Layer Security, a protocol that guarantees privacy and data integrity between client/server applications and between server-to-server communication.

symmetric (secret-key) cryptography — A method of encrypting and decrypting messages in which encryption and decryption is achieved using a single, shared key that is known only to the sender and receiver.

REVIEW QUESTIONS

1. You request and install certificates for two servers that will be used to communicate securely using TLS. Prior to installing the certificates and configuring TLS, communication between the two servers was successful. However, after implementing the secure channel, you find that the communication fails when you send messages. What might the problem be?

   a. The certificates were not obtained from the same organizations.

   b. The certificates have expired.

   c. The certificates are not trusted because the root certificates have not been installed.

   d. There is a problem with the configuration.

2. Which of the following are extended permissions? (Choose all that apply.)

   a. add public folder to admin group

   b. modify public folder admin ACL

   c. modify public folder replica list

   d. all of the above

3. Which of the following is a valid role that can be delegated with the Exchange Administration Delegation Wizard? (Choose all that apply.)

   a. Exchange Full Administrator

   b. Exchange Administrator

   c. Exchange View Only Administrator

   d. all of the above

4. What are the key characteristics of a digital signature? (Choose all that apply.)

   a. Only someone possessing the private key could have created the digital signature.

   b. Anyone with access to the public key can verify the digital signature.

   c. Any modification of the signed data invalidates the digital signature.

   d. The digital signature can be used to encrypt the data.

5. TLS allows both server-to-server and client-to-server encryption. True or False?

6. Which of the following is required by the receiver to trust that they really have the sender's public key? (Choose all that apply.)

   a. The CA has provided a certificate that can be guaranteed to not be tampered with.

   b. The receiver trusts the CA that issued the certificate.

   c. The receiver has received messages from the sender previously.

   d. The receiver is ensured that the sending server is valid.

10

7. What are the choices available when setting up connector-based SSL/TLS encryption? (Choose all that apply.)

    a. Force SSL/TLS for all e-mail traffic.

    b. Force SSL/TLS for selected incoming traffic within the same domain.

    c. Force SSL/TLS for selected incoming traffic within specific domains.

    d. Enable SSL/TLS for inbound e-mail.

8. Which of the following security mechanisms provides end-to-end security?

    a. S/MIME

    b. TLS

    c. SSL

    d. none of the above

9. Which of the following encryption techniques requires the exchange of encryption keys?

    a. public key encryption

    b. symmetric encryption

    c. S/MIME

    d. none of the above

10. Which of the following mechanisms establishes trust between a public key and the owner of the corresponding private key?

    a. digital signature

    b. digital certificate

    c. certificate authority

    d. certificate chain

11. What is the difference between standard and extended permissions?

    a. Standard permissions are only available when Exchange Server 2003 is installed.

    b. Standard permissions are only available after a schema upgrade.

    c. Standard permissions are part of the default permissions for Active Directory.

    d. There is no difference.

12. Which of the following encryption techniques involve different encryption and decryption keys?

    a. symmetric encryption

    b. public key encryption

    c. round robin encryption

    d. none of the above

13. What must the receiver trust implicitly before certificates can be trusted?

    a. the certificate authority

    b. the root certificate

    c. the sending server

    d. the issuing organization

14. Why should you use caution with the Send As permission?

    a. Send as gives the user or group access to another person's mailbox.

    b. Send as gives the user or group permission to impersonate another user.

    c. Send as gives the user or group permission to administer the Administration group.

    d. none of the above

15. Why should you use caution with the Receive As permission?

    a. Receive as gives the user or group access to another person's mailbox.

    b. Receive as gives the user or group permission to impersonate another user.

    c. Receive as gives the user or group permission to administer the Administration group.

    d. none of the above

16. How do you enable the Security tab for all objects within Exchange System Manager?

    a. Enable the Security tab option on the properties of the organization.

    b. Enable the Security tab option on the properties of the Admin Group.

    c. Set the ShowSecurityPage registry entry.

    d. none of the above

17. S/MIME security requires that the corresponding parties involved in the communication have certificates issued from the same CA. True or False?

18. S/MIME security requires that you establish a Windows Public Key Infrastructure. True or False?

19. Which type of certificate server is Active Directory integrated?

    a. enterprise certificate server

    b. stand-alone certificate server

    c. both A and B

    d. neither A and B

10

20. What defines a root CA?

    a. It is a CA that issues certificates for the organization.

    b. It is Active Directory integrated.

    c. It is the only CA that issues itself a certificate.

    d. none of the above

21. Where is a cross-certification hierarchy typically used?

    a. in a delegated certificate environment

    b. in a small enterprise in which there is typically one server

    c. in a business-to-business scenario that requires trust between CAs in different organizations

    d. in a business-to-consumer scenario that requires trust between the organization and their clients

22. Which of the following ESMTP commands are related to TLS encryption? (Choose all that apply.)

    a. STOPTLS

    b. STARTTLS

    c. TLSENCRYPT

    d. TLSDECRYPT

23. Which clients typically use SSL/TLS encryption to secure the communications channel between themselves and the server? (Choose all that apply.)

    a. POP clients

    b. IMAP clients

    c. Outlook clients

    d. OWA clients

24. Implementing a separate SMTP connector for secure server-to-server TLS communication is the best approach to implementing TLS security between two organizations. True or False?

Case Projects

CASE
PROJECTS

Case Project 10-1: Choosing an Approach to Implementing Secure E-Mail Between Two Organizations

As the person in charge of implementing e-mail services within your company, you are considering the best approach to implementing a secure channel between two organizations. Describe the different approaches that can be used to implement security between two organizations and the benefits and drawbacks to each.

Case Project 10-2: Choosing Roles to Delegate

As part of the planning process, you are meeting with your administrators to identify who should have access to each of the administrative groups within your Exchange Server 2003 organization. Your organization consists of multiple administrative groups and you have a decentralized administrative model. You have a requirement to be able to view each administrative group but make changes only to your own administrative group. How would you go about setting this up and what roles would you use to implement this type of model within your e-mail organization?

Case Project 10-3: Choosing a Certificate Provider

As part of implementing S/MIME within your organization, you are considering whether you should implement your own PKI or use certificates from a third-party vendor. What are some of the items you need to take into consideration when considering your options?

Case Project 10-4: Implementing Client-to-Server Encryption

As the head of e-mail services within your organization, you have been requested by the Security Department to set up secure communications between your POP clients and your back-end servers. What are the steps needed to make this happen?

10

11

BACKUP AND RECOVERY OF EXCHANGE SERVER 2003

> **After reading this chapter, you will be able to:**
>
> ♦ Mitigate the risk of Exchange Server 2003 disasters
>
> ♦ Plan for disaster recovery
>
> ♦ Back up Exchange Server 2003
>
> ♦ Restore a failed Exchange 2003 server
>
> ♦ Restore a corrupted Exchange Server 2003 store
>
> ♦ Restore an Exchange mailbox or message
>
> ♦ Understand how to replace a clustered Exchange 2003 server that has failed

No one ever expects their Exchange 2003 server to fail, but there is always a risk of it happening. To guarantee that you can recover from a failure, you must plan ahead to ensure you have the necessary information to perform a restore. This chapter leads you through the planning process.

The first step in preparing for disaster recovery is performing a backup of your Exchange 2003 server. After the information in Exchange is backed up, you can restore whatever part of that information you require. This chapter shows you how to back up Exchange properly so that it can be recovered. In addition, you learn how to restore a completely failed server, a corrupted Information Store, or accidentally deleted mailboxes and messages. Finally, you see how to replace a clustered Exchange 2003 server that has failed.

PREVENTING DISASTERS

In computing terms, a disaster is when your hardware fails, software becomes unstable, or data becomes corrupt. Essentially, when your server stops functioning, and a simple reboot doesn't fix the situation, you have a disaster.

The prudent thing for an Exchange administrator to do is prevent a disaster whenever possible. Some of the things you can do to prevent a disaster include the following:

- Implement redundant hardware
- Implement redundant services
- Use clustering

Redundant Hardware

To prevent data loss from disk failure, you can implement RAID. RAID is a system in which multiple disks are combined into a single logical unit in which the failure of a single disk does not result in data loss. The two most common RAID configurations are RAID-1 and RAID-5.

RAID-1 is a system that uses two disks. Each disk is an exact copy of the other. If one disk fails, the server continues to operate using the remaining good disk. This is also referred to as mirroring or duplexing.

RAID-5 is a system that uses three or more disks. When information is saved to a RAID-5 set, the information is spread evenly among the disks. In addition, parity information (also called a checksum) is generated and stored on the disks. The parity information allows the system to tolerate the failure of a single disk and keep functioning without any data loss.

Servers can be purchased with many other redundant hardware components. The two most common are power supplies and network cards. Power supplies are one of the most failure-prone components in a server. Buying a server with redundant power supplies allows a failed power supply to be replaced even while the server is still up and running. Redundant network cards ensure that connectivity to the network and service to clients are maintained when a network card fails.

Redundant Services

Keeping Exchange Server 2003 running properly is not limited to the functionality of a single server. Exchange Server 2003 relies on network services to function properly. Specifically, Exchange Server 2003 uses both DNS and Active Directory. These services can be made fault tolerant to prevent outages.

If DNS is unavailable on the network, an Exchange server is unable to deliver mail to external sites, and perhaps internally, depending on the configuration of your Exchange system. DNS is made fault tolerant by having at least two DNS servers available on the network and configuring the Exchange server to use both DNS servers. DNS is also used to find domain controllers for authentication. If Active Directory is unavailable to an Exchange server, users are not able to authenticate. When users cannot authenticate, they are not able to send or receive messages. To ensure Active Directory is fault tolerant, you should have at least two domain controllers for each domain.

Clustering

Clustering is a high-availability solution in which multiple servers work together to provide services. Exchange Server 2003 can be one of those services. Windows Server 2003 allows for two types of clustering: active/active or active/passive. Both methods of clustering require that the Exchange databases and log files be stored on external storage, such as an external SCSI enclosure or storage area network (SAN). All servers in the cluster are connected to the external storage so that they can all access the same data.

Active/active clustering is a system in which Exchange Server 2003 is installed and running on two servers. Each server, or node, actively responds to user requests and manages messages. When one server fails, the other takes over its tasks. After a failover, the level of usage might overwhelm a single server. However, it is cost effective because all hardware is being utilized. This system supports two servers.

11

Active/passive clustering is a system in which Exchange Server 2003 is installed on up to eight servers, but running on up to only seven servers. When an active server fails, one of the inactive servers takes over its tasks. This system is more scalable because it supports up to seven active servers and does not suffer from performance degradation when a server fails. However, this system can be more expensive because at least one server is sitting idle.

PLANNING FOR DISASTER RECOVERY

Properly planning for disaster recovery is essential to successful disaster recovery. Without the right information, even a complete backup of the Exchange Server 2003 databases is not enough to bring your Exchange 2003 server back to life.

The following tasks should be part of your disaster recovery planning:

- Document your existing Exchange 2003 server configuration
- Choose a logging method
- Separate log files and databases
- Have a consistent backup schedule
- Ensure enough free disk space
- Prepare detailed written instructions on recovery

Documentation

It is essential to document the configuration of your Exchange 2003 server so that it can be replicated if a server fails. It is equally important to ensure that this documentation remains timely and up to date as software and hardware configurations change frequently. Documentation should include the following:

- Server operating system version and service packs
- Server network configuration, including IP address and DNS servers
- Exchange Server 2003 service packs
- Name of the Exchange organization
- Name of the administrative group in which the server is located
- Names of storage groups on the server
- Names of logical databases in the storage groups on the server

Logging

A set of log files is maintained for each storage group on an Exchange 2003 server. All database changes for a storage group are written to the log files before the database is updated. These log files are used by Exchange Server 2003 to keep track of partially completed transactions if there is a problem such as a power failure. By default, Exchange Server 2003 keeps all transactions in the log files until a full backup is performed. This is important because these log files, when combined with the last backup of the database files, allow recovery of messages up to the point of failure. Without the log files, recovery is limited to the time of the last backup.

Exchange Server 2003 has a setting called circular logging. Circular logging removes information from the log files after it is committed to the database. This significantly reduces disk space requirements and backup capacity requirements because the log files typically do not grow beyond 15–20 MB. If circular logging is used, however, the system only can be restored to the point of the last backup. Microsoft recommends that circular logging not be used, but it can be appropriate when there is a shortage of disk space or backup capacity.

To illustrate the difference between standard logging and circular logging, think of an Exchange server with a corrupted database. Assume that the Exchange system was backed up at 1:00 a.m. the previous morning. If the database becomes corrupt at 3:00 p.m. the next day with circular logging enabled, it can be restored to the state it was in at 1:00 a.m. when the last backup was performed. All information, such as mail messages and appointments, added to the system since 1:00 a.m. is lost. If standard logging is used, the database can be restored, the transaction logs replayed, and the system restored to the state it was in at 3:00 p.m. just before the database became corrupted. No messages are lost with standard logging.

Log File Location

Log files should be stored on physically different drives from databases to aid recovery. If both log files and the Exchange databases are stored on the same drive when a failure occurs, it is recoverable to the most recent backup. If the log files and databases are stored on separate drives, and a drive storing databases fails, the most recent copy of the databases can be restored to another drive and the transaction logs replayed to restore the state of the databases to the point just before the failure.

Backup Scheduling

It is important to keep a consistent backup schedule so that recovery is faster and more reliable. Ideally, a full backup of the Exchange 2003 server is performed every night. Backups should be an automatic process, not a manual one. If Exchange backups are a manual process initiated only by administrators, it is likely that the backups are often not performed. When the backup process is automated, it is important that an administrator be responsible for confirming it was completed successfully and logging which day's backup is stored on which tape. Monitoring and logging backups ensures that they are available when required.

Backup logs should be checked to ensure that the backup was successful. On a monthly basis, backups should be tested to ensure they work properly. This has the added benefit of testing your written restore procedures.

Available Disk Space

Repairing databases and the recovery storage group require extra disk space. Repairing databases requires free disk space equivalent to the database plus about 10 percent extra for working space on the drive. The recovery storage group requires free disk space equivalent to the storage group being restored.

A good rule of thumb is to keep free disk space on each Exchange 2003 server equivalent to the largest storage group on the server. If this is not possible, an external disk drive that is large enough can be added for recovery purposes when required.

Written Instructions

When faced with a failed Exchange 2003 server, the most seasoned administrator is likely to be nervous. Nervous or anxious people seldom have the clear thinking processes required to rebuild an Exchange 2003 server quickly and properly. To make this task easier, have detailed written instructions on how to perform restores of servers, storage groups, databases, and mailboxes. Written instructions limit the amount of thinking required to perform a recovery. When written instructions are created, however, be sure to test them. If they are not tested, they may contain errors. Instructions with errors can be worse than having no instructions at all.

BACKING UP EXCHANGE SERVER 2003

Backing up Exchange Server 2003 is an essential step in disaster recovery. The information copied during the backup is used to restore missing or corrupt information. Without a good backup, recovery is not possible.

To perform backups of Exchange Server 2003 effectively, you must understand the following:

- How database backups are different from file backups
- Differences in backup software
- What needs to be backed up
- Offline backups
- Full-text indexes

Database Backups

Many administrators are very familiar with file system backups but not database backups. Backing up a database is fundamentally different than backing up the file system. Exchange Server 2003 uses databases and needs to be thought of as a database when backups are performed.

File system backups use the archive attribute to track files and perform different backup types. The most common backup types are full, differential, and incremental. Full backups take a copy of all files. Differential backups take a copy of all files that have changed since the last full backup. Incremental backups take a copy of all files that have changed since the last incremental or full backup.

Database backups do not follow the same logic as file system backups because databases are composed of only a few files that constantly change. In addition, log files must be taken into account. The terms full, differential, and incremental backup are still used, however.

Full Backup

A **full backup** of Exchange takes a copy of the database files and the transaction logs. It also clears the transaction logs off of the hard drive. Clearing the transaction logs is essential to prevent disk space shortages. If the transaction logs are not cleared, the number of transaction logs grows until no disk space remains and Exchange Server 2003 is forced to shut down.

With a full backup, databases and storage groups can be restored. No other backups are required with a full backup.

Differential Backup

A **differential backup** of Exchange does not take a copy of the database files. It only takes a copy of the transaction logs. It does not remove transaction logs from the hard drive.

When Exchange databases are very large, a differential backup can be smaller and faster than a full backup. Differential backups also can be used to perform a backup quickly several times partway through the day to allow greater recoverability.

Like file system backups, differential backups of Exchange must always be used in conjunction with full backups. Only the most recent differential backup and the full backup are required to restore Exchange successfully.

Incremental Backup

An **incremental backup** of Exchange also does not take a copy of the database files. It takes a copy of the transaction logs and then removes the transaction logs from the hard drive.

Similar to a differential backup, an incremental backup is smaller and faster than a full backup. It also can be used partway through the day to supplement a daily full backup. Note that incremental backups must be used in conjunction with a full backup. To restore Exchange successfully, the full backup and all incremental backups performed since the full backup are required.

Backup Software

11

The standard version of NT Backup that is included with Windows 2000 Server or Windows Server 2003 is not able to back up Exchange properly. This is also true of standard third-party backup software. They cannot back up Exchange without stopping Exchange. They also do not properly track and delete transaction logs.

An updated version of NT Backup is installed when the Exchange Administrative Tools are installed. The updated version of NT Backup is able to back up Exchange databases and transaction logs while Exchange is running and properly track the transaction logs. For third-party backup tools, an Exchange agent must be purchased.

The updated version of NT Backup uses the **Exchange backup API** to perform a backup of Exchange. This is what allows online backups to be taken while Exchange is running. Exchange performance will slow noticeably on a busy server during backups with this API, however. This method of backup checks for database errors as part of the backup process.

The major benefit of using NT Backup to perform backups is the price. There is no cost because it is included with Exchange Server 2003. Unfortunately, it is unable to perform backups of Exchange across the network. As a result, you must have a backup device such as a tape drive attached to the Exchange server. Larger organizations often prefer to have one central backup server and use third-party backup software to back up Exchange across the network.

To simulate a network backup, some organizations use NT Backup to back up Exchange to a file instead of tape. Then, the file containing the Exchange backup can be backed up across the network. This saves the cost of buying an Exchange agent for third-party backup software.

NT Backup does not have the ability to restore individual mailboxes or messages directly. It backs up storage groups. Some third-party backup solutions have the ability to back up and restore individual messages. This is called **brick-level backup and restore**. It takes large amounts of backup media to perform a brick-level backup because the backup does not recognize SIS (Single Instance Storage). In addition, brick-level backups do not replace the need for storage group backups; they are an addition to them.

Some third-party backup solutions use the new **Volume Shadow Copy** service in Windows Server 2003 to perform backups. Volume Shadow Copy takes a snapshot of the databases, and then the backup is performed on the snapshot. This method of backup does not slow the performance of Exchange during backup. This method of backup does not check for database errors as part of the backup, however.

ACTIVITY

Activity 11-1: Backing Up Exchange Server 2003

Time Required: 10 to 20 minutes

Objective: Perform a full backup of an Exchange Server 2003 store.

Description: In this activity, you learn how to perform a full backup of an Exchange Server 2003 store, the First Storage Group. To ensure there is data to back up, you first create a new user, log on to OWA (Outlook Web Access) as that user, and then create a new message. This backup is used to perform restores in later activities in this chapter. To create the backup, complete the following:

1. Log on to the back-end server using the user name **Administrator** and password **Password!**.

2. Click **Start**, point to **Administrative Tools**, and then click **Active Directory Users and Computers**. The Active Directory Users and Computers window opens.

3. If necessary, click the **plus sign (+)** next to secureXX.local to expand its contents, where XX is the number assigned to the back-end server, and then click **Users** in the left pane.

4. Right-click **Users**, point to **New**, and then click **User**. The New Object – User dialog box opens.

5. In the First name text box, type **Demitri**; in the Last name text box, type **Santos**; in the User logon name text box, type **dsantos**; and then click **Next**.

6. In the Password text box, type **Password!**; in the Confirm password text box, type **Password!**. Uncheck the **User must change password at next logon** check box, and then click **Next**.

7. To accept the default values for the Exchange mailbox, click **Next**, and then click **Finish**.

8. Close **Active Directory Users and Computers**.

9. Click **Start**, point to **All Programs**, and then click **Internet Explorer**.

10. In the Address Bar, type **https://serverXX.secureXX.local/Exchange**, where XX is the number assigned to the back-end server, and then click the **Go** button.

11. If a Security Alert opens warning you that you are about to view pages over a secure connection, click the **In the future, do not show this warning** check box, and then click **OK**.

12. If a Security Alert opens warning you that revocation information for the security certificate is not available, click **Yes** to continue.

13. If a Security Alert opens warning you about the certificate information, click **Yes** to continue.

14. When prompted to log on, type **SECUREXX\dsantos** in the Domain\user name text box, where XX is the number assigned to the back-end server, type **Password!** in the Password text box, and then click **Log On**. The Microsoft Outlook Web Access page for Demitri Santos opens.

15. To ensure there is data to back up, create a new item in the Inbox for Demitri. Click **New** to create a new message.

16. In the **To** text box, type **dsantos**; in the Subject text box, type **Test Message**; and then click **Send**.

17. Click the **Check for New Messages** button to view the message Demitri sent to himself.

18. Close **Internet Explorer**.

19. Finally, you initiate the backup. Click **Start**, point to **All Programs**, point to **Accessories**, point to **System Tools**, and then click **Backup**.

20. Click **Next** to begin the Backup or Restore Wizard.

21. If necessary, click the **Back up files and settings** option button, and then click **Next**.

22. At the What to Back Up screen, click the **Let me choose what to back up** option button, and then click **Next**.

23. At the Items to Back Up screen, click the **plus sign (+)** next to Microsoft Exchange Server, click the **plus sign (+)** next to SERVERXX, where XX is the number assigned to the back-end server, click the **plus sign (+)** next to **Microsoft Information Store**, and then check the **First Storage Group** check box, as shown in Figure 11-1. Click **Next**.

24. At the Backup Type, Destination, and Name screen, click the **Browse** button, click **My Computer**, double-click **Local Disk (C:)**, and then click the **Save** button. The completed screen is shown in Figure 11-2. Click **Next**.

25. Click **Finish**. The backup you are performing is very small and should finish in less than one minute.

26. When the backup is finished, click the **Close** button. The backup is saved as the file C:\Backup.bkf.

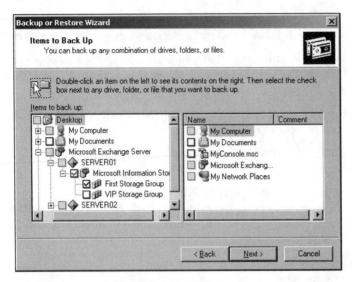

Figure 11-1   Items to Back Up screen

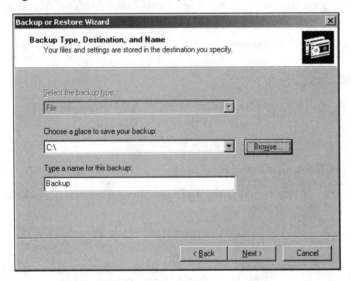

Figure 11-2   Backup Type, Destination, and Name screen

What to Backup

Backing up the Exchange databases is not enough to ensure successful recovery when an entire server has failed. Important Exchange configuration information is stored in Active Directory and the IIS metabase as well. To ensure you can recover an entire Exchange 2003 server, back up the following:

- Operating system directories
- System state
- Exchange Server 2003 folders (except the databases and log files)
- Exchange databases and log files
- Cluster quorum (if in a cluster)
- Cluster disk signatures (if in a cluster)

The **system state** is a set of data residing within several important but disparate components that are required for recovery. The actual components that comprise the system state vary depending on the configuration of the server. If the server is a domain controller, Active Directory is included. If Certificate Services is installed, it too is included. The registry that contains configuration information is included, as is the IIS metabase, which is important for OWA and Certificate Services.

Offline Backups

An **offline backup** is performed by taking a copy of the Exchange database and transaction logs when the Exchange services are stopped. The important thing to note is that the Exchange services must be stopped and users cannot access the system while those services are stopped. An offline backup also does not remove transaction logs.

An offline backup can be used if third-party backup software does not support the Exchange backup API. The version of NT Backup included with Exchange Server 2003 supports online backups, however, and should be used instead. If network backups are required, use NT Backup to back up the file and then back up the file across the network.

Some database errors prevent an online backup from being performed. In this case, you can perform an offline backup before performing repairs with the Eseutil command (a utility included with Exchange used for maintenance and repair functions).

Full-Text Indexes

Exchange uses full-text indexes to make searches of Information Stores faster. It is not necessary to back up indexes because they contain redundant information that is already contained in the databases. In fact, it is not possible to restore them. To recover full-text indexes, they must be re-created.

Activity 11-2: Recovering from a Lost Full-Text Index

Time Required: 5 to 10 minutes

Objective: Re-create a full-text index.

Description: A full-text index is used to speed up searching through Information Stores. Full-text indexes are not backed up as part of an Exchange backup because they easily can be re-created. In this activity, you learn how to re-create the full-text index created in Chapter 9, "Managing Data Storage and Hardware Resources."

1. From the Windows desktop of your back-end server, click **Start**, point to **All Programs**, point to **Microsoft Exchange**, and then click **System Manager**. The Exchange System Manager opens.

2. In Exchange System Manager, click the **plus sign (+)** next to Administrative Groups, click the **plus sign (+)** next to First Administrative Group, click the **plus sign (+)** next to Servers, and then click the **plus sign (+)** next to SERVERXX, where XX is the number assigned to the back-end server.

3. Click the **First Storage Group**, as shown in Figure 11-3.

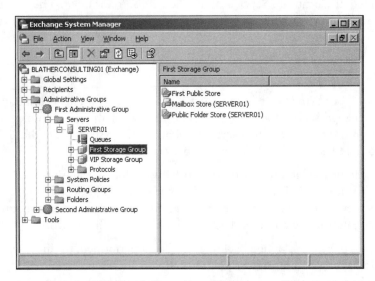

Figure 11-3   Viewing Information Stores

4. If you are concerned that an index is incorrect, you can force it to be re-created. In the right pane, right-click **Mailbox Store (SERVERXX)**, where XX is the number assigned to the back-end server, and then click **Start Full Population** on the shortcut menu.

5. Click **Yes** to start the update process immediately.

6. Click **Yes** to indicate you are sure that you want to start the full population. Exchange Server 2003 repopulates the index.

7. Close **Exchange System Manager**.

RESTORING A FAILED EXCHANGE 2003 SERVER

To require restoring an entire Exchange server, the server must experience a catastrophic failure. This can be a hardware or software failure, such as disk or operating system failures. For example, if your Exchange server is hacked and can no longer be booted, the entire server must be restored.

It is a common misconception that to restore a server you must have identical hardware. This is not true. You can restore a full backup of Windows 2000 Server or Windows Server 2003 on different hardware. NT Backup is intelligent enough to understand which device drivers should not be restored. The only requirement is that the same drive letters must exist and the operating system on the replacement server must be patched to the same level as the original.

NOTE For more information about how a restore on different hardware works, see the Microsoft knowledge base article Q249694 (*http://support.microsoft.com:80/ support/kb/articles/q249/6/94.asp*).

The recovery process is as follows:

1. Install the same version of Windows on new (or repaired) hardware with a temporary server name that is different from the failed server and not joined to a domain in the Active Directory forest.

2. Install all Windows service packs to match the failed server.

3. Restore the last operating system backup from the old server, including the system state. This changes the computer name to the same as the failed server and restores all necessary information for the server to log on as the previous computer account.

4. Install Exchange Server 2003 in disaster recovery mode. Disaster recovery mode is entered by using the switch /disasterrecovery when setup.exe is run. This switch prevents the Information Stores from being mounted after installation. The databases must be restored before the Information Stores are mounted.

   a. During the installation, ensure that you only select components that were installed on the failed server.

   b. Place the databases and log files in the same location as they were located on the failed server.

11

5. Using disaster recovery mode, install all service packs for Exchange Server 2003 to match the failed server.

6. Restore the latest version of database files and log files that are available. If you are able to save the database files and log files from the failed server, use these. If not, restore them from backup.

Activity 11-3: Recovering from a Failed Server

ACTIVITY

Time Required: 10 to 20 minutes

Objective: Research the detailed steps for recovering from a failed Exchange 2003 server.

Description: In this activity, go to the Microsoft Web site and download a book about Exchange Server 2003 disaster recovery. This book has excellent information about a number of disaster recovery scenarios. Read the section about recovering from a failed server.

1. From the Windows desktop of the back-end server, click **Start**, point to **All Programs**, and then click **Internet Explorer**.

2. In the Address Bar, type **http://www.microsoft.com/downloads/details.aspx?FamilyID=A58F49C5-1190-4FBF-AEDE-007A8F366B0E**, and then click the **Go** button. The page to download the Exchange Server 2003 Disaster Recovery Operations Guide opens.

3. On the right side of the page, click the **Download** button.

4. In the File Download dialog box, click the **Save** button.

5. If necessary, click **Desktop**, and then click the **Save** button. The download for this file takes about one minute with high-speed Internet.

6. When the download is complete, click the **Close** button.

7. Close **Internet Explorer**.

8. On the desktop, double-click **Ex2k3_Disaster-Recovery_Ops.exe**. The WinZip Self-Extractor dialog box opens.

9. In the Unzip to folder text box, type **C:**, click the **Unzip** button, click **OK**, and then click the **Close** button.

10. Click **Start**, point to **All Programs**, point to **Accessories**, and then click **Windows Explorer**.

11. Click the **plus sign (+)** next to My Computer, and then click **Local Disk (C:)**.

12. In the right pane, double-click **Exchange 2003 Disaster Recovery Operations.doc**.

13. Scroll down and read the table of contents for this book.

14. Scroll down to page 107 and read the section on Exchange Member Server Recovery.

15. Close the document.

16. Close **Windows Explorer**.

RESTORING A CORRUPTED EXCHANGE 2003 STORE

When an Exchange Server 2003 store becomes corrupted to the point at which it no longer can be accessed, it must be restored. In this situation, the current transaction logs are usually still accessible and can be used after the store is restored. The current transaction logs are replayed after the databases are restored and no information is lost. For the restore process to be successful, the Exchange 2003 Information Store service must be running. In addition, the store that is being restored must be dismounted. A mounted store cannot be restored.

NOTE

It is a best practice to rename corrupted stores and copy log files before doing a restore. This way, if the restore does not work properly, a repair on the damaged store can be attempted.

11

The process performed during a restore of an Exchange Server 2003 is as follows:

1. The database files from backup are copied back to disk. If the existing database files are not renamed or copied elsewhere, they are lost.

2. The log files from backup are copied to a temporary directory.

3. A restore.env file is created in the same temporary directory as the log files. This file is used to control the restore process and applies to only a single store. If you restore multiple stores at one time, the restore.env file for the last store overwrites the restore.env file for any previous stores. Exchange Server 2003 stores must be restored one at a time.

4. A hard recovery is performed. A **hard recovery** replays the transaction logs that were restored. This process is triggered during the restore process by checking the Last Restore Set check box. If additional incremental or differential restores of transaction logs are not required, this option should not be checked. It should only be checked for the last incremental restore or the differential restore.

5. A **soft recovery** is performed. This process replays the current transaction logs and makes the store information current to the point of failure.

6. The temporary directory with transaction log files is removed.

Multiple stores can be restored before performing hard recovery. To function properly, each store must be restored individually using a separate temporary directory for each. When each is restored, the Last Restore Set check box must be unchecked. After all stores and log files have been restored, a hard recovery can be triggered for each store individually by running eseutil /cc from a command prompt in the temporary directory for each store.

Activity 11-4: Restoring an Exchange Server 2003 Store

Time Required: 20 to 30 minutes

Objective: Restore an Exchange Server 2003 store from backup.

Description: If an Exchange Server 2003 store becomes corrupted, restoring it is often the fastest way to get it up and running again. In this activity, you restore the First Storage Group on your back-end server using the Backup utility and the backup file created in Activity 11-1. To do this, complete the following:

1. From the Windows desktop of the back-end server, click **Start**, point to **All Programs**, point to **Microsoft Exchange**, and then click **System Manager**.

2. In Exchange System Manager, click the **plus sign (+)** next to Administrative Groups, click the **plus sign (+)** next to First Administrative Group, click the **plus sign (+)** next to Servers, and then click the **plus sign (+)** next to SERVERXX, where XX is the number assigned to the back-end server.

3. Click the **plus sign (+)** next to First Storage Group.

4. Right-click the **First Public Store**, and then click **Dismount Store** on the shortcut menu.

5. A dialog box indicates that the store will be inaccessible to users while dismounted, as shown in Figure 11-4. Click **Yes** to confirm that you want to continue. The store must be dismounted to be restored. The Exchange services must be running, however.

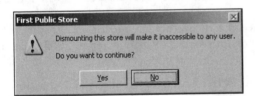

Figure 11-4 Dismount warning

6. Right-click **Mailbox Store (SERVERXX)**, where XX is the number assigned to the back-end server, and then click **Dismount Store** on the shortcut menu.

7. Click **Yes** to confirm you want to continue.

8. Right-click **Public Folder Store (SERVERXX)**, where XX is the number assigned to the back-end server, and then click **Dismount Store** on the shortcut menu.

9. Click **Yes** to confirm you want to continue.

10. Close **Exchange System Manager**.

11. Click **Start**, point to **All Programs**, point to **Accessories**, point to **System Tools**, and then click **Backup**.

12. At the Welcome to the Backup or Restore Wizard screen, click **Next**.

13. At the Backup or Restore screen, click the **Restore files and settings** option button, and then click **Next**.

14. In the left pane of the What to Restore screen, click the **plus sign (+)** next to File, click the **plus sign (+)** next to Backup.bkf, and then check the **SERVERXX\Microsoft Information Store\First Storage Group** check box, where XX is the number assigned to the back-end server, as shown in Figure 11-5. Click **Next**.

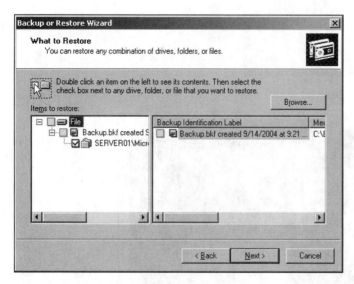

Figure 11-5   What to Restore screen

15. At the Restore Database Server screen, your server name is automatically filled in the Restore To text box. In the Temporary location for log and patch file text box, type **C:\templog**.

16. Leave the **Last Restore Set (Log file replay will start after this restore completes)** check box unchecked. This allows you to restore additional incremental or differential backups after the full backup is complete. Click **Next**.

17. At the Completing the Backup or Restore Wizard screen, click **Finish**. The Restore Progress dialog box opens showing you the progress of the restore.

18. When the restore is complete, as shown in Figure 11-6, click **Close**.

19. Click **Start**, click **Run**, type **cmd** in the Open text box, and then click **OK**.

20. Type **cd \templog\First Storage Group** and then press **Enter**.

21. Type **dir** and then press **Enter**. You can see the restored log file and restore.env, as shown in Figure 11-7.

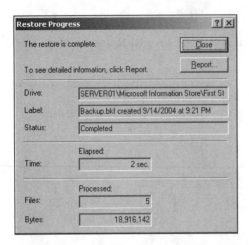

Figure 11-6   Restore Progress dialog box

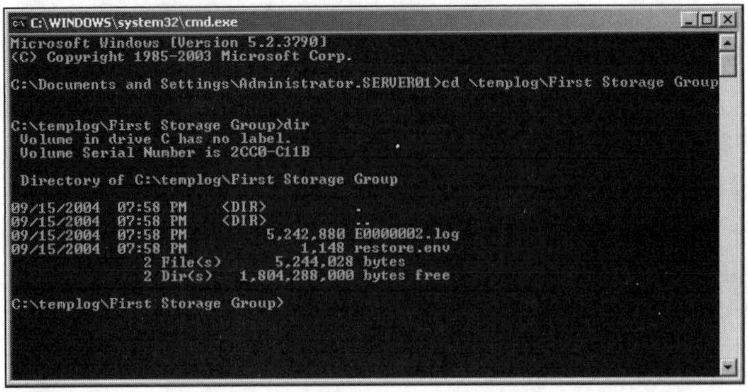

Figure 11-7   Restored files

22. To force the hard recovery, type **"C:\Program Files\Exchsrvr\bin\eseutil"** /cc (including the quotation marks), and then press **Enter**.

23. When the restore is finished, close the **Command Prompt** window.

24. Click **Start**, point to **All Programs**, point to **Microsoft Exchange**, and then click **System Manager**.

25. In Exchange System Manager, click the **plus sign (+)** next to Administrative Groups, click the **plus sign (+)** next to First Administrative Group, click the **plus sign (+)** next to Servers, click the **plus sign (+)** next to SERVERXX, where XX is the number assigned to the back-end server, and then click the **plus sign (+)** next to First Storage Group.

26. Right-click **First Public Store**, and then click **Mount Store** on the shortcut menu. Click **OK** when the store is successfully mounted.

27. Right-click **Mailbox Store (SERVERXX)**, where XX is the number assigned to the back-end server, and then click **Mount Store** on the shortcut menu. Click **OK** when the store is successfully mounted.

28. Right-click **Public Folder Store (SERVERXX)**, where XX is the number assigned to the back-end server, and then click **Mount Store** on the shortcut menu. Click **OK** when the store is successfully mounted.

29. Close **Exchange System Manager**.

RESTORING AN EXCHANGE MAILBOX OR MESSAGE

Far more common than needing to restore an entire Exchange server or store is the need to recover a single mailbox or message. Some of the reasons you might need to recover a mailbox or message include the following:

- Reviewing deleted messages as part of a legal action

- Retrieving accidentally deleted messages

- Allowing a manager to review the mail of a terminated employee

The following four methods can be used to restore missing messages or mailboxes:

- Recover deleted items in Outlook or OWA.

- Reattach a mailbox to a user.

- Use an alternate recovery forest.

- Use the recovery storage group.

Recovering Deleted Items in Outlook or OWA

When a message is deleted from the Inbox or another folder in Outlook, the item is placed in the Deleted Items folder. When a message is deleted from the Deleted Items folder, it is no longer visible to the user, but the message is still available to be restored by using the Recover Deleted Items option in Outlook or OWA.

As you might imagine, messages cannot be restored in this way forever. At some point, they must be purged to limit the size of the Exchange stores. The length of time deleted items are retained is configurable by the Exchange administrator.

Activity 11-5: Modifying the Deleted Item Retention Time

Time Required: 5 to 10 minutes

Objective: Modify the deleted item retention time.

11

Description: By default, deleted messages are recoverable for seven days. As an administrator, you can modify how long the messages are recoverable. In this activity, you extend the deleted item retention time to 14 days and ensure that no items are purged until they have been backed up at least once.

1. From the Windows desktop of the back-end server, click **Start**, point to **All Programs**, point to **Microsoft Exchange**, and then click **System Manager**.

2. In Exchange System Manager, click the **plus sign (+)** next to Administrative Groups, click the **plus sign (+)** next to First Administrative Group, click the **plus sign (+)** next to Servers, click the **plus sign (+)** next to SERVERXX, where XX is the number assigned to the back-end server, and then click the **plus sign (+)** next to First Storage Group.

3. Right-click **Mailbox Store (SERVERXX)**, where XX is the number assigned to the back-end server, and then click **Properties**. The Mailbox Store (SERVERXX) Properties dialog box opens.

4. Click the **Limits** tab.

5. In the Keep deleted items for (days) text box, change the default value of 7 to **14**. This ensures that deleted items are recoverable for 14 days.

6. Check the **Do not permanently delete mailboxes and items until the store has been backed up** check box. This ensures all deleted items are recoverable from a backup.

7. Click **OK**.

8. Close **Exchange System Manager**.

Having changed the deleted item retention time, you now recover a deleted message via Outlook Web Access.

ACTIVITY

Activity 11-6: Recovering Deleted Items in Outlook Web Access

Time Required: 10 to 20 minutes

Objective: Recover a deleted item in Outlook Web Access.

Description: Exchange Server 2003 allows deleted items to be recovered in Outlook Web Access. Previous versions of Exchange only allowed deleted items to be recovered in the full Outlook Client. In this activity, you delete a message in Outlook Web Access and then recover it.

1. From the Windows desktop of the back-end server, click **Start**, point to **All Programs**, and then click **Internet Explorer**.

2. In the Address Bar, type **https://serverXX.secureXX.local/Exchange**, where XX is the number assigned to the back-end server, and then click the **Go** button.

3. If a Security Alert opens warning you that revocation information for the security certificate is not available, click **Yes** to continue.

4. If a Security Alert opens warning you about the certificate information, click **Yes** to continue.

5. When prompted to log on, type **SECUREXX\dsantos** in the Domain\user name text box, where XX is the number assigned to the back-end server, type **Password!** in the Password text box, and then click **Log On**. The Microsoft Outlook Web Access page for Demitri Santos opens.

6. In the Inbox, right-click the **Test Message** received in Activity 11-1, and then click **Delete**.

7. In the Folders pane, click **Deleted Items**.

8. Right-click **Test Message**, and then click **Delete**.

9. Click **OK** to confirm the deletion.

10. In the left pane, click the **Options** button.

11. Scroll down to the bottom of the page, as shown in Figure 11-8.

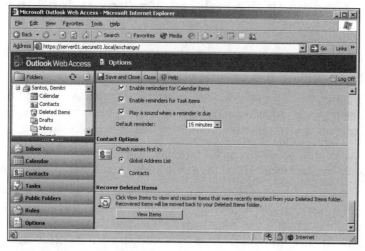

Figure 11-8   OWA options

12. Click the **View Items** button.

13. Click to select **Test Message**, if necessary, and then click the **Recover** button.

14. Close the **Recover Deleted Items** window.

15. In the Folders pane, click **Delete Items**. Notice that the deleted message is recovered.

16. Click and drag **Test Message** to the **Inbox**.

17. Click **Inbox** and confirm that test message is there.

18. Close **Internet Explorer**.

Reattaching Mailboxes

Technology workers are used to hearing stories about the mistakes made by users in their organizations. What they do not hear about as often is the mistakes made by their coworkers. One of the worst mistakes that can happen is a user account being deleted. One way to fix this is restoring the user object in Active Directory. However, it is relatively difficult to restore a single object in Active Directory and most of the time administrators re-create the user account instead.

By default, deleted mailboxes are retained for 30 days before they are purged. As long as the deleted mailbox has not been purged, it can be reattached to the new user account using Exchange System Manager. A mailbox also can be attached to a different account if a manager needs to review the contents after a user is dismissed. A single user account can only have a single mailbox attached to it. Because of this, it is often a good idea to create a temporary user object specifically for attaching mailboxes temporarily. This way, the user you are reviewing can still read his own mail.

ACTIVITY

Activity 11-7: Modifying the Deleted Mailbox Retention Time

Time Required: 5 to 10 minutes

Objective: Increase the mailbox retention period to reduce the risk of deleted mailboxes being purged before they can be reattached.

Description: By default, deleted mailboxes are recoverable for 30 days. As administrator, you can modify how long the mailboxes are recoverable. In this activity, you extend the deleted mailbox retention time to 60 days. To do this, complete the following:

1. From the Windows desktop of the back-end server, click **Start**, point to **All Programs**, point to **Microsoft Exchange**, and then click **System Manager**.

2. In Exchange System Manager, click the **plus sign (+)** next to Administrative Groups, click the **plus sign (+)** next to First Administrative Group, click the **plus sign (+)** next to Servers, click the **plus sign (+)** next to SERVERXX, where XX is the number assigned to the back-end server, and then click the **plus sign (+)** next to First Storage Group.

3. Right-click **Mailbox Store (SERVERXX)**, where XX is the number assigned to the back-end server, and then click **Properties**. The Mailbox Store (SERVERXX) Properties dialog box opens.

4. Click the **Limits** tab.

5. In the Keep deleted mailboxes for (days) text box, change the default value of 30 to **60**. This ensures that deleted mailboxes are recoverable for 60 days.

6. Click **OK**.

7. Close **Exchange System Manager**.

Should you need to reattach a deleted mailbox, and assuming the mailbox has not yet been purged, you can use the Mailbox Recovery Center to reattach the mailbox to the appropriate user. Before doing this, you can use the Cleanup Agent to ensure that the mailbox is disconnected from the user and marked for deletion.

Activity 11-8: Reattaching a Deleted Mailbox

Time Required: 20 to 40 minutes

Objective: Reattach a deleted mailbox to a new user.

Description: After a user is deleted, the mailbox is still recoverable. In this activity, you attach the mailbox of a deleted user to a new user. You first create a new user, create a mailbox for that user by logging on to OWA, delete that user, and then create a second new user, which is the user to which you attach the deleted mailbox.

1. From the Windows desktop of the back-end server, click **Start**, point to **Administrative Tools**, and then click **Active Directory Users and Computers**. The Active Directory Users and Computers window opens.

2. If necessary, click the **plus sign (+)** next to secureXX.local, where XX is the number assigned to the back-end server, and then click **Users** in the left pane.

3. Right-click **Users**, point to **New**, and then click **User**. The New Object – User dialog box opens.

4. In the First name text box, type **Sheila**; in the Last name text box, type **Wright**; in the User logon name text box, type **swright**; and then click **Next**.

5. In the Password text box, type **Password!**; in the Confirm password text box, type **Password!**. Uncheck the **User must change password at next logon** check box, and then click **Next**.

6. To accept the default values for the Exchange mailbox, click **Next**, and then click **Finish**.

7. Close **Active Directory Users and Computers**.

8. Click **Start**, point to **All Programs**, and then click **Internet Explorer**.

9. In the Address Bar, type **https://serverXX.secureXX.local/Exchange**, where XX is the number assigned to the back-end server, and then click the **Go** button.

10. If a Security Alert opens warning you that revocation information for the security certificate is not available, click **Yes** to continue. If a Security Alert opens warning you about the certificate information, click **Yes** to continue.

11. When prompted to log on, type **SECUREXX\swright** in the Domain\user name text box, where XX is the number assigned to the back-end server, type **Password!** in the Password text box, and then click **Log On**. The Microsoft Outlook Web Access page for Sheila Wright opens.

12. Click **New** to create a new message.

11

13. In the **To** text box, type **swright**; in the Subject text box, type **Message for Recovery**; and then click **Send**.

14. Click the **Check for New Messages** button to view the message Sheila sent to herself.

15. Close **Internet Explorer**.

16. Click **Start**, point to **Administrative Tools**, and then click **Active Directory Users and Computers**.

17. If necessary, click the **plus sign (+)** next to secureXX.local, where XX is the number assigned to the back-end server, and then click **Users** in the left pane.

18. In the right pane, right-click **Wright, Sheila**, and then click **Delete**.

19. The Active Directory dialog box opens, as shown in Figure 11-9. Click **Yes**.

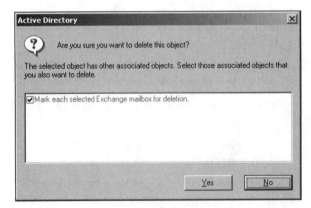

Figure 11-9   Confirm deleting the mailbox

20. Right-click **Users**, point to **New**, and then click **User**. The New Object – User dialog box opens.

21. In the First name text box, type **NewSheila**. In the Last name text box, type **Wright**. In the User logon name text box, type **nwright**, and then click **Next**.

22. In the Password text box, type **Password!**; in the Confirm password text box, type **Password!**. Uncheck the **User must change password at next logon** check box, and then click **Next**.

23. Uncheck the **Create an Exchange mailbox** check box, click **Next**, and then click **Finish**.

24. Close **Active Directory Users and Computers**.

25. Click **Start**, point to **All Programs**, point to **Microsoft Exchange**, and then click **System Manager**.

26. In Exchange System Manager, click the **plus sign (+)** next to Administrative Groups, click the **plus sign (+)** next to First Administrative Group, click the **plus sign (+)** next to Servers, click the **plus sign (+)** next to SERVERXX, where XX is the number assigned to the back-end server, click the **plus sign (+)** next to First Storage Group, click the **plus sign (+)** next to Mailbox Store (SERVERXX), where XX is the number assigned to the back-end server, and then click **Mailboxes**.

27. Notice that the mailbox for Sheila Wright is still listed. Right-click **Mailboxes** and click **Run Cleanup Agent**. This process runs automatically by Exchange Server 2003 and disconnects mailboxes from deleted users marking the mailboxes for deletion. This process runs periodically, but you forced the process to happen because you want to work with the disconnected mailbox right away. The mailbox for Sheila Wright now has a red X to indicate it is disconnected and marked for deletion.

28. Right-click **Wright, Sheila** and notice that the available options are Reconnect and Purge. The Reconnect option lets you join this mailbox to another user object. Click any area off the shortcut menu to close it.

29. In the left pane, under the organization level, click the **plus sign (+)** next to Tools, and then click **Mailbox Recovery Center**.

30. Right-click **Mailbox Recovery Center**, and then click **Add Mailbox Store**. The Add mailbox store(s) dialog box opens.

31. In the Enter the object names to select text box, type **Mailbox Store**, and then click **Check Names**.

32. In the Multiple Names Found dialog box, click **Mailbox Store (SERVERXX)**, where XX is the number assigned to the back-end server, and then click **OK**. Click **OK** in the Add mailbox store(s) dialog box. The Mailbox Recovery Center now shows the disconnected mailbox of Sheila Wright, as shown in Figure 11-10.

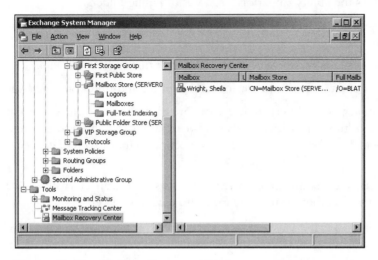

Figure 11-10   Mailbox Recovery Center

33. Right-click **Wright, Sheila**, and then click **Find Match**. The Exchange Mailbox Matching Wizard starts.

34. Click **Next** to find a match. You get a message that there is a conflict and it cannot be matched. Click **Finish**.

35. Right-click **Wright, Sheila**, and then click **Resolve Conflicts**. The Exchange Mailbox Conflict Resolution Wizard starts. Click **Next**.

36. At the User matching screen, click **Browse**, type **nwright** in the Enter the object name to select text box, click **Check Names**, and then click **OK**.

37. Click **Next** and then click **Finish**.

38. Right-click **Wright, Sheila** and then click **Reconnect**. The Exchange Mailbox Reconnect Wizard starts. Click **Next**.

39. At the Ready to proceed screen, read the warning, and then click **Next**.

40. When complete, click **Finish**.

41. Close **Exchange System Manager**.

Using an Alternate Recovery Forest

An **alternate recovery forest** is, at minimum, a single server that has a copy of your Exchange organization. In the following activity, you increase the mailbox retention period to reduce the risk of deleted mailboxes being purged before they can be reattached. It is completely separate from the production environment and is used only for testing and recovery purposes.

Advantages of an alternate recovery forest include the following:

- It provides the ability to perform restores of public folders.
- It allows testing of backup integrity without affecting the production environment.
- It allows mailbox recovery even after the retention period has expired.
- It can act as a test environment for service packs and third-party add-ons.

The major disadvantage of an alternate recovery forest is the cost and hassle of maintaining separate hardware. Although such redundancy is certainly expensive and inefficient, these disadvantages are often offset by the increased protection against disaster afforded by such a configuration.

The following sections cover how to prepare a recovery server in an alternate recovery forest and how to recover a mailbox or message from the recovery server.

Preparing the Recovery Server

The server hosting Exchange Server 2003 in the alternate recovery forest must be installed with the same organization name, administrative group name, storage group name, and database name. If this is done properly, the **LegacyExchangeDN attribute** of the recovery server will match the server that was the source of the backups.

The LegacyExchangeDN attribute is retained in Exchange Server 2003 for backward compatibility with Exchange Server 5.5. However, even if Exchange Server 5.5 does not exist in an Exchange organization, the LegacyExchangeDN attribute is present. If the attribute does not match the source server, the Information Store cannot be mounted.

In a large organization with many servers and administrative groups, the requirement for many servers with different values for the LegacyExchangeDN attribute would be onerous. In Exchange 2000 Server, the only ways to change the value of the attribute were by either removing and reinstalling Exchange 2000 Server or editing the value of the attribute on every affected object. Both methods were time consuming. Exchange Server 2003 includes a utility, legacydn.exe, which is able to change the value of the LegacyExchangeDN attribute on all necessary objects.

11

NOTE   You can find out more about legacydn.exe in the Microsoft knowledge base article 324606 (*http://support.microsoft.com/?id=324606*).

NOTE   You can find detailed information about the LegacyExchangeDN attribute in the Microsoft Product Support Services white paper Exchange 2000 Server Database Recovery (*http://www.microsoft.com/technet/prodtechnol/exchange/2000/support/dbrecovr.mspx*). Read the section Alternate Server Recovery under the heading Information Store Recovery Scenarios.

Recovering a Mailbox from the Recovery Server

After Exchange Server 2003 has been installed on the recovery server, a store must be created with the same name as the store that is about to be restored. The new store is empty without any messages in it. Restore the source store from backup over the empty new store just as you would if you were recovering from a corrupt store.

After the restore completes and the store is mounted, messages in mailboxes can be recovered by copying them to a .pst file. Follow these steps to do so:

1. Create a user object in Active Directory.

2. Connect the user object to a recovered mailbox.

3. Copy the mailbox to a .pst file. For a single mailbox, this can be done in Outlook. For many mailboxes, you can use the Exmerge utility.

4. Log on to the original mailbox and copy the required messages from the .pst file to original mailbox using Outlook.

Using the Recovery Storage Group

The **recovery storage group** is a new feature in Exchange Server 2003. It allows administrators to restore an Exchange store to a recovery storage group on an existing server instead of creating an alternate recovery forest.

Exchange Server 2003, Enterprise Edition is limited to four storage groups on a single server. Exchange Server 2003, Standard Edition is limited to one storage group on a single server. The recovery storage group does not count against these limits.

The major advantage of using the recovery storage group is its simplicity. It does not require any extra hardware to be implemented. There are some limitations, however, including the following:

- The recovery storage group must be in the same administrative group as the server the backup is from.
- The user account associated with the mailbox must still exist in Active Directory.
- The mailbox must not have been purged from the store.
- Public folders cannot be restored.
- Messages must be recovered using exmerge.exe from Exchange Server 2003.

Overall, using the recovery storage group is fairly simple and uses the following steps:

1. Create a recovery storage group.
2. Add the mailbox store being recovered to the recovery storage group.
3. Restore the mailbox store to the recovery storage group.
4. Use exmerge.exe to extract mailboxes from the recovery storage group to .pst files or directly to user mailboxes.

NOTE If messages extracted from the recovery storage group are written directly to the user mailboxes, the user account running exmerge.exe must have Receive As permissions to the user mailboxes being recovered. By default, members of the Administrators group are denied this right. This right is not required when copying the contents of the recovery storage group to .pst files.

NOTE For detailed information about using the recovery storage group, read the electronic book *Using Exchange Server 2003 Recovery Storage Groups*, available from Microsoft (*http://go.microsoft.com/fwlink/?LinkId=23233*).

Activity 11-9: Using the Recovery Storage Group

Time Required: 20 to 40 minutes

Objective: Use the recovery storage group to restore a mailbox.

Description: The recovery storage group allows you to restore individual mailboxes from an Information Store without using an alternate recovery forest. In this activity, you create a recovery storage group; restore the First Storage Group backup, created in Activity 11-1, to the new recovery storage group; and then recover Demitri Santos's messages to a .pst file using ExMerge. To do this, complete the following:

1. From the Windows desktop of the back-end server, click **Start**, point to **All Programs**, point to **Microsoft Exchange**, and then click **System Manager**. The Exchange System Manager opens.

2. Click the **plus sign (+)** next to Administrative Groups, click the **plus sign (+)** next to First Administrative Group, click the **plus sign (+)** next to Servers, and then click SERVERXX, where XX is the number assigned to the back-end server.

3. To create the new recovery storage group, right-click SERVERXX, where XX is the number assigned to the back-end server, point to **New**, and then click **Recovery Storage Group**. The Recovery Storage Group Properties dialog box opens.

4. To accept the default locations for the transaction log and system path, click **OK**. The recovery storage group is created and displayed in Exchange System Manager, as shown in Figure 11-11.

11

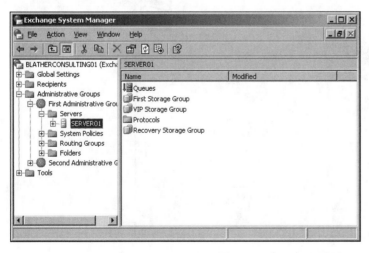

Figure 11-11   Recovery storage group

5. Right-click **Recovery Storage Group**, and then click **Add Database to Recover**. The Select database to recover dialog box opens.

6. In the Search results list, click **Mailbox Store (SERVERXX)**, where XX is the number assigned to the back-end server, and then click **OK**. The Mailbox Store (SERVERXX) Properties dialog box opens.

7. Click **OK** to close the Mailbox Store (SERVERXX) Properties dialog box.

8. Minimize **Exchange System Manager**.

9. Now to recover messages, click **Start**, point to **All Programs**, point to **Accessories**, point to **System Tools**, and then click **Backup**.

10. Click **Next** to begin the Backup or Restore Wizard.

11. Click the **Restore files and settings** option button, and then click **Next**.

12. In the left pane of the What to Restore screen, click the **plus sign (+)** next to File, click the **plus sign (+)** next to **Backup.bkf**, and then click the label **SERVERXX\ Microsoft Information Store\First Storage Group**, where XX is the number assigned to the back-end server. Do not click the check box.

13. In the right pane, check the **Log Files** and **Mailbox Store (SERVERXX)** check boxes, where XX is the number assigned to the back-end server, as shown in Figure 11-12. Click **Next**.

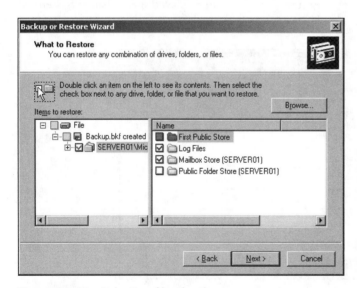

Figure 11-12   Selecting files for the recovery storage group

14. At the Restore Database Server screen, your server name is automatically filled in the Restore To text box. In the Temporary location for log and patch files text box, type **C:\templog**.

15. Check the **Last Restore Set (Log file replay will start after this restore completes)** check box, and then click **Next**.

16. At the Completing the Backup or Restore Wizard screen, click **Finish**.

17. When the restore is complete, click **Close** in the Restore Progress dialog box.

18. Click **Exchange System Manager** on the taskbar to reactivate the window.

19. If necessary, click the **plus sign (+)** next to SERVERXX, where XX is the number assigned to the back-end server, and then click the **plus sign (+)** next to the recovery storage group. Right-click **Mailbox Store (SERVERXX)**, where XX is the number assigned to the back-end server, and then click **Mount Store** on the shortcut menu.

20. Click **Yes** to clear the warning shown in Figure 11-13. This warning always appears and does not indicate that there is a problem.

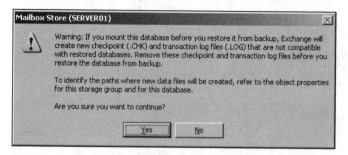

Figure 11-13   Recovery storage group warning

21. When the store is successfully mounted, click **OK**.

22. Close **Exchange System Manager**.

23. Now, you will download ExMerge. Click **Start**, point to **All Programs**, and then click **Internet Explorer**.

24. In the Address Bar, type **http://www.microsoft.com/downloads/details.aspx?FamilyId=429163EC-DCDF-47DC-96DA-1C12D67327D5**, and then click the **Go** button. This opens the Web page for downloading ExMerge.

25. Click the **Download** button on the right side of the page.

26. In the File Download dialog box, click **Open**. If a Security Warning opens, click **Yes** to continue.

27. In the Choose Directory For Extracted Files text box, type **C:**, and then click **OK**. ExMerge should be placed in this location because .dll files it requires are located here. When the extraction is complete, click **OK**.

28. Close **Internet Explorer**.

29. You will now use ExMerge to extract Demitri's messages to a .pst file. Click **Start**, click **Run**, type **cmd** in the Open text box, and then click **OK**.

30. Type **cd \Program Files\exchsrvr\bin**, and then press **Enter**. To copy the exmerge.exe file to this location, type **copy C:\exmerge\exmerge.exe**, and then press **Enter**.

31. Type **exmerge.exe** and press **Enter**. The Microsoft Exchange Mailbox Merge Wizard starts. Click **Next**.

32. At the Procedure Selection screen, if necessary, click the **Extract or Import (Two Step Procedure)** option button, as shown in Figure 11-14. Click **Next** to continue.

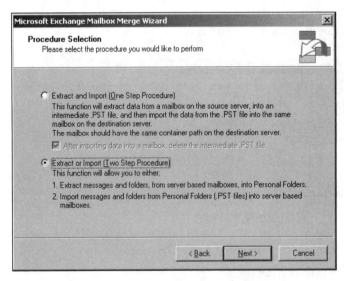

Figure 11-14   Procedure Selection screen

33. At the Two Step Procedure screen, if necessary, click the **Step 1: Extract data from an Exchange Server Mailbox** option button, and then click **Next**.

34. At the Source Server screen, type **SERVERXX** in the Microsoft Exchange Server Name text box, where XX is the number assigned to the back-end server, and then click **Next**.

35. At the Database Selection screen, check the **RECOVERY STORAGE GROUP/ MAILBOX STORE (SERVERXX)** check box, where XX is the number assigned to the back-end server, as shown in Figure 11-15, and then click **Next**.

36. At the Mailbox Selection screen, click **Santos, Demitri**, and then click **Next**.

37. At the Locale Selection screen, click **Next** to accept the default locale of English(US).

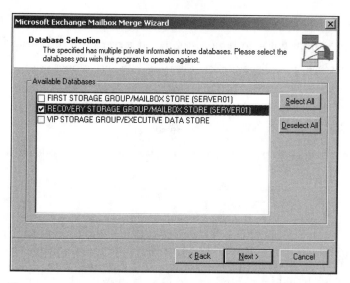

Figure 11-15   Database Selection screen

38. At the Target Directory screen, click the **Change Folder** button, click **Local Disk (C:)**, click **OK**, and then click **Next**.

39. At the Save Settings screen, click **Next** to accept the default settings.

40. When the operations are successfully completed, click **Finish**. The messages from the mailbox for Demitri Santos have been extracted to C:\DSANTOS.PST.

41. Close all open windows.

Restoring Clustered Exchange Servers

The process for restoring clustered Exchange 2003 servers varies depending on the error. A corrupted database in a cluster is restored in the same way as a nonclustered server. It is restored and the transaction logs are replayed to bring the database back to its current state. The only potential complication is ensuring that the database is restored to the proper server in the cluster.

A failed server is actually a faster process to fix. When one Exchange 2003 server in a cluster fails, the storage groups and services hosted by that server start on another server in the cluster. The users whose mailboxes were failed over will notice a short interruption while the services are starting on the new server.

If the server has failed due to hardware problems or a corrupt operating system, there is no need to restore the server in exactly the same state because the cluster operates properly without it. All that needs to be done is remove the failed server from the cluster and add a new server to replace the failed one.

The steps for replacing a failed Exchange 2003 server in a cluster are as follows:

1. Use Cluster Administrator to remove the failed server from the cluster.

2. Build a new server to replace the failed server. This server does not need to have the same name as the failed server.

3. Join the new server to the cluster.

4. Install Exchange Server 2003 on the new server.

5. Move resources back to the new server or leave it as a passive node in the cluster.

CHAPTER SUMMARY

- Disasters with Exchange Server 2003 can be prevented by using redundant hardware, redundant services, and clustering. Redundant hardware often used includes hard drives configured as RAID-1 or RAID-5, power supplies, and network cards. The two most important services that should be redundant are DNS and Active Directory. Clustering limits service outages for failed servers to only a few minutes. Clusters can be configured as active/active or active/passive.

- It is important to plan properly for disaster recovery. Proper planning includes configuration documentation, choosing a logging method, separating log files and databases, having a consistent backup schedule, ensuring enough free disk space for disaster recovery, and preparing detailed written instructions for disaster recovery.

- By default, Exchange Server 2003 keeps transaction logs until a full backup is performed. Circular logging deletes transaction log files after their contents have been committed to the database.

- A full backup of Exchange Server 2003 takes a copy of the databases and the transaction logs, and then deletes the transaction logs from disk. A differential backup takes a copy of only the transaction logs and does not delete the transaction logs from disk. An incremental backup takes a copy of only the transaction logs, and then deletes the transaction logs from disk.

- Exchange Server 2003 includes an updated version of NT Backup that is able to back up Exchange stores while Exchange services are running by using the Exchange backup API. Third-party backup solutions can perform brick-level backups and Volume Shadow Copy backups.

- Backups of Exchange 2003 servers should include the operating system directories, system state, Exchange Server 2003 folders (without databases and logs), and Exchange stores. If in a cluster, the cluster quorum and cluster disk signatures also should be backed up.

- An offline backup is a copy of the Exchange databases taken when the Exchange services are stopped. These can be used if third-party backup software does not support the Exchange backup API.

❑ A failed Exchange server can be restored by reinstalling Windows and Exchange Server 2003. When installing Exchange Server 2003, you must use the /disasterrecovery switch.

❑ A corrupted Exchange Server 2003 store can be restored with NT Backup. A hard recovery that replays the restored transaction logs is performed automatically unless the Last Recovery Set check box is unchecked during the restore. A soft recovery, which replays the current transaction logs, is performed automatically after the hard recovery.

❑ Messages and mailboxes can be restored by recovering deleted items in Outlook, reattaching a mailbox to a user account, using an alternate recovery forest, or using the recovery storage group.

❑ An alternate recovery forest is a copy of the Exchange organization that is completely separate from the production environment. It allows restores of public folders, testing of backup integrity, mailbox recovery after the retention period has expired, and can act as a test environment for service packs.

❑ The recovery storage group is a new feature in Exchange Server 2003. It is a storage group that can be added to any existing Exchange 2003 server regardless of storage group limitations. The only utility that can retrieve messages from the recovery storage group is ExMerge.

❑ Clustered Exchange servers are restored by rebuilding them as a new cluster server. There is no need for them to have exactly the same configuration or name as the failed server.

KEY TERMS

active/active clustering — A cluster in which services are running on all nodes in the cluster. Windows Server 2003 and Exchange Server 2003 support only two-node active/active clusters.

active/passive clustering — A cluster in which at least one server sits idle with no services running. The passive server waits to take over from a failed server. Windows Server 2003 and Exchange Server 2003 support up to an eight-node active/passive cluster.

alternate recovery forest — A copy of the Exchange organization that is completely separate from the production environment and is used to restore Exchange stores and recover messages.

brick-level backup and restore — A type of backup performed by some third-party backup software that takes a copy of each message in user mailboxes, allowing individual messages to be restored.

differential backup — A backup that takes a copy of only the transaction logs and does not delete the transaction logs from the disk.

Exchange backup API — An interface used by backup programs to back up Exchange stores while the Exchange server is up and running.

full backup — A backup that takes a copy of the databases and transaction logs, and then deletes transaction logs from the disk.

hard recovery — The replaying of restored transaction logs that occurs after a database has been restored.

incremental backup — A backup that takes a copy of only the transaction logs and deletes the transaction logs from the disk.

LegacyExchangeDN attribute — An attribute of objects in Active Directory that is required for backward compatibility with Exchange Server 5.5. If this attribute is not correctly configured during a restore, the store is unable to mount.

offline backup — A backup that requires the Exchange services to be stopped while a copy of the stores is taken.

recovery storage group — A new feature in Exchange Server 2003 that lets administrators restore a store and recover messages on an existing Exchange 2003 server rather than using an alternate recovery forest.

soft recovery — The replaying of the current transaction logs that occurs after a hard recovery.

system state — The configuration information on a Windows server that includes the registry and Active Directory that can be backed up as a unit.

Volume Shadow Copy — A service that takes a snapshot of files for backup even while they are open.

REVIEW QUESTIONS

1. Which type of RAID requires at least three disks and can survive a single disk failure without data loss?

   a. RAID-0

   b. RAID-1

   c. RAID-5

   d. mirroring

2. Which service is required for authentication to Exchange Server 2003?

3. How many active servers are supported in an active/active cluster?

   a. two

   b. three

   c. four

   d. seven

4. An active/passive cluster supports up to seven active nodes. True or False?

5. Which of the following should be included in planning for disaster recovery planning? (Choose all that apply.)

   a. Exchange configuration documentation

   b. ensuring enough free disk space

   c. detailed written recovery instructions

   d. separate log files and databases

6. By default, transaction logs are never deleted until a full backup is taken. True or False?

7. How much free disk space should be available for disaster recovery?

8. An Exchange 2003 server configured to use circular logging has a full backup at 2:00 a.m. and a differential backup at noon. If an Exchange database becomes corrupt at 3:00 p.m., at what time can the server database be recovered to?

9. Which tasks does a differential backup of Exchange Server 2003 perform? (Choose all that apply.)

   a. copy the database files

   b. copy the transaction logs

   c. reset the archive attribute on the database files

   d. delete the transaction logs from disk

10. Which tasks does an incremental backup of Exchange Server 2003 perform? (Choose all that apply.)

    a. copy the database files

    b. copy the transaction logs

    c. reset the archive attribute on the database files

    d. delete the transaction logs from disk

11. Which feature of Exchange Server 2003 is used by NT Backup and allows stores to be backed up while the Exchange services are running?

    a. LegacyExchangeDN

    b. circular logging

    c. brick-level backup

    d. Exchange backup API

12. Which type of backup is performed if the backup software does not support the Exchange backup API?

    a. full

    b. differential

    c. incremental

    d. offline

13. Which part of Exchange Server 2003 is not restored from backup?

    a. full-text indexes

    b. system state

    c. transaction logs

    d. databases

11

14. To restore a failed Exchange 2003 server, you must have identical hardware. True or False?

15. Which switch must be used when reinstalling a failed Exchange 2003 server?

16. When an Exchange store is restored, a soft recovery takes place before a hard recovery. True or False?

17. Which events can trigger a hard recovery? (Choose all that apply.)

    a. perform a restore with the check box Last Recovery Set checked

    b. run eseutil.exe /hard

    c. run eseutil.exe /cc

    d. restart the Exchange services

18. Which is the easiest way to recover a deleted message?

    a. the Recover Deleted Items option in Outlook

    b. attach the mailbox to a new user

    c. an alternate recovery forest

    d. the recovery storage group

19. By default, for how many days can a recovery storage group be used to recover a deleted mailbox?

20. An alternate recovery forest is required to restore messages from a public folder. True or False?

CASE PROJECTS

CASE
PROJECTS

Case Project 11-1: Preventing Exchange Server Failure

Gigantic Life Insurance has 4,000 users and availability of Exchange is critical to productivity. If an Exchange server is down for even half an hour, thousands of dollars in staff time are lost. What would you suggest to prevent server failure and minimize downtime in the event of a server failure?

CASE
PROJECTS

Case Project 11-2: Recovering a Lost Mail Message

Hyperactive Media Sales has 10 roaming salespeople using OWA to access their mail. The administrator used an alternate recovery forest to recover deleted messages when they were using Exchange 2000 Server. What other options are available for restoring a single message in Exchange Server 2003? Which do you recommend?

Case Project 11-3: Enhancing Recoverability

Helping Hand Social Services has a single Exchange 2003 server supporting 150 users. A full backup is taken at 1:00 a.m.

E-mail and calendaring have become a critical part of fulfilling their organizational goals. At the last board meeting, concerns were raised about how much information would be lost if the Exchange server were to fail at the end of the business day. What do you suggest to minimize the amount of data that would be lost if the server failed at 3:00 p.m.?

Case Project 11-4: Adjusting for Low Disk Space

Buddy's Machine Shop has Exchange Server 2003 installed on a server with limited disk space. The backup tape unit in their server malfunctions occasionally and the nightly full backup fails approximately 20 percent of the time.

Recently, the Exchange services stopped because the disk holding the transaction logs ran out of space. What do you suggest so that this does not happen in the future?

12

TROUBLESHOOTING CONNECTIVITY

After reading this chapter, you will be able to:

♦ Understand the tools available for troubleshooting transport issues and when they should be used

♦ Understand nondelivery reports and NDR codes

♦ Understand the types of issues that can contribute to transport errors

A simple click and an e-mail message is magically sent to a colleague's computer in another state or country. To the user, it seems like a simple process. But the administrators who handle the e-mail for an Exchange Server 2003 organization know that a lot of behind-the-scenes work is required to move mail between desktops. Even when the administrator has taken every precaution to ensure that mail flows without interruption within the Exchange organization, there is still the possibility that mail flow issues will arise. As an Exchange administrator, you have to prepare yourself and know what actions to take should message flow–related problems occur. That is the purpose of this chapter.

This chapter looks at some of the common problems that can arise when mail is transported within your organization and outside your organization. Typically, issues arise from the improper configuration of your e-mail system. By verifying configuration settings, you should be able to ensure that your installation of Exchange Server 2003 is properly configured for sending and receiving Internet e-mail. You should also be able to significantly reduce the amount of time it takes to manage any message flow issues you might experience.

If the configuration of your system seems in order, and you are still having problems, you'll need to investigate the problem more closely. To help you do so, Exchange Server 2003 and Windows Server 2003 provide a number of tools that, along with your knowledge of messaging systems, can assist you in troubleshooting the problem. Some of these tools have been enhanced in Exchange Server 2003 to allow for more advanced troubleshooting techniques. This chapter looks at each of these tools, pointing out enhancements where appropriate, and walks you through their use to provide a basic understanding of how they work.

Finally, when messages are not delivered, Exchange Server 2003 assists by providing NDRs (nondelivery reports), which can be used to understand why the system could not deliver a message. The chapter looks at these NDR codes and helps you understand what they mean.

TOOLS FOR TROUBLESHOOTING

Where do you go for troubleshooting information? What tools can you use? Your tools and resources include the Windows Server 2003 event log, the SMTP protocol log, the SMTP and X.400 Queue Viewer, diagnostics logging, and message tracking. You examine each of these tools to see how each can be used to help troubleshoot messaging within your Exchange Server 2003 organization.

Diagnostics Logging

Exchange Server 2003 assists in troubleshooting by allowing you to enable **diagnostics logging** on the transport server. This is done on the Diagnostics Logging tab of the server's Properties dialog box. By increasing the logging levels related to the MSExchangeTransport service, you can increase the amount of information that is written to the application log by the transport. The more events logged, the more transport-related events you can view in the application log. This provides more information to help you diagnose issues with the transportation of messages by your server. Table 12-1 provides a description of each event category. In general, you should increase the event-logging level of the category associated with the type of problem you are having. For example, you should increase the logging level of the Categorizer category if you experience problems with address resolution or distribution list expansion.

Table 12-1   MSExchangeTransport event-logging categories

Category	Description
Routing Engine/Service	Used to troubleshoot routing issues
Categorizer	Used to troubleshoot problems with the categorizer, which handles such tasks as resolving sender and recipient addresses and building membership lists for distribution groups
Connection Manager	Used to troubleshoot issues involving Connection Manager, such as dial-up and virtual private networking

Table 12-1   MSExchangeTransport event-logging categories (continued)

Category	Description
Queuing Engine	Used to troubleshoot problems with the queuing engine, which handles the assignment of messages to various message delivery queues
Exchange Store Driver	Used to troubleshoot issues with the Exchange store driver, which is responsible for communication between the SMTP service and the Exchange Information Store service
SMTP Protocol	Used to troubleshoot general SMTP issues
NTFS Store Driver	Used to troubleshoot issues with the NTFS store driver, which handles message transport to (and from) the message store

Exchange Server 2003 supports the following four levels of diagnostics logging:

- *None*—Provides the default level of diagnostics logging. At this level, Exchange Server 2003 records one entry for events with a logging level of zero.

- *Minimum*—Writes summary entries in the event logs. At this level, Exchange Server 2003 records one entry for events with a logging level of 1 or lower. You can use minimum logging to help identify where a problem might be occurring but not to pinpoint the exact problem.

- *Medium*—Writes both summary and detailed entries in the event logs. At this level, Exchange Server 2003 records entries for events with a logging level of 3 or lower. Use this logging level when you have identified where a problem is occurring and need to get more information to resolve it.

- *Maximum*—Provides a complete audit trail of every action that a service performs. At this level, Exchange Server 2003 records entries for event with a logging level of five or lower, which is essentially everything it is doing. As a result, server performance is affected severely. You need to watch the log files closely when you use this level. If you don't, they might run out of space.

Activity 12-1: Configuring Transport Diagnostics Logging

Time Required: 10 to 20 minutes

Objective: Configure diagnostics logging on a server.

Description: In this activity, you configure diagnostics logging on a server. You configure diagnostics logging separately for each Exchange 2003 server in the organization. For the purposes of this activity, you configure diagnostics logging only on the back-end server. You look at how the diagnostics logging is enabled on the MSExchangeTransport service. To do this, configure logging on the back-end server as follows:

1. Log on to the back-end server using the user name **Administrator** and password **Password!**.

2. From the Windows desktop of the back-end server, click **Start**, point to **All Programs**, point to **Microsoft Exchange**, and then click **System Manager**.

3. Click the **plus sign (+)** next to Administrative Groups, click the **plus sign (+)** next to First Administrative Group, and then click the **plus sign (+)** next to the Servers container. Right-click **SERVERXX**, where XX is the student number assigned to the back-end server, and then click **Properties** on the shortcut menu. The SERVERXX Properties dialog box opens.

4. Click the **Diagnostics Logging** tab. The Diagnostics Logging tab is displayed, as shown in Figure 12-1.

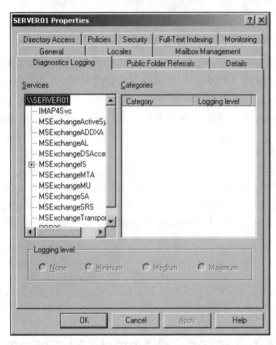

Figure 12-1   SERVERXX Properties Diagnostics Logging tab

5. The Services list box includes all of the services that you can track. Click the **MSExchangeTransport** service. The Categories list displays the major activities that you can track, such as Routing Engine/Service, Categorizer, Queuing Engine, and so on.

6. In the Categories list, click **Routing Engine/Service**, and then click the **Maximum** option button. Repeat this step for each category in the Categories list box.

7. When finished, click **OK** to return to Exchange System Manager.

8. Close **Exchange System Manager**.

Event Logging

Events generated by diagnostics logging are recorded in the Windows event logs, in particular, the application and system event logs. The primary log that you need to check is the application log. In the application log, you will find the key events recorded by the Exchange services. Other logs should also be checked to determine if there are problems that might be contributing to a transport problem, such as system or DNS problems. Figure 12-2 shows an example of an application log.

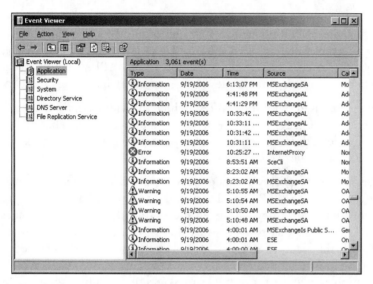

Figure 12-2   Application log

Each event in the event log can be further investigated by opening its properties page. Double-click an event to open the Event Properties dialog box. Information contained in the Event Properties dialog box includes the following:

- *Source*—The application, service, or component that logged the event

- *Category*—The category of the event, which is sometimes used to further describe the related action

- *Event ID*—An identifier for the specific event

- *User*—The user account that was logged on when the event occurred

- *Computer*—The name of the computer on which the event occurred

- *Description*—A text description of the event (shown in the detailed entries)

- *Data*—Any data or error code output created by the event (shown in the detailed entries)

Queue Viewer

Queues in Exchange Server 2003 provide a mechanism to hold messages while they are being processed for routing and delivery inside and outside the Exchange organization. Exchange Server 2003 supports link queues and transport queues and provides the **Queue Viewer** tool to allow you to examine the various queues and the messages they contain.

Link queues are created by Exchange Server 2003 when multiple messages are bound for the same destination. These queues are accessible only when they have messages waiting to be routed.

Transport queues include SMTP queues, X.400 queues, and MAPI queues. MAPI clients and other mail connectors (such as Microsoft Exchange Connector for Lotus Notes and Microsoft Exchange Connector for Novell GroupWise) use MAPI queues to transport mail to the clients and between heterogeneous messaging systems such as Notes and GroupWise.

The X.400 queues are used with the MTA, which provides addressing and routing information for sending messages from one server to another. MTA relies on the X.400 transfer stacks to provide additional details for message transfer, and these stacks are similar in purpose to the Exchange virtual servers.

The SMTP queues act as temporary holding areas for internal and external mail. When messages are sent through an SMTP virtual server, they remain in an SMTP queue until delivery is complete. Only when they have been successfully delivered are messages cleared from each queue. This means that messages that do not complete delivery remain in the queue associated with the stage of delivery at which the problem(s) occurred. In other words, by determining in which queue messages are "stuck," you can deduce which stage of the transmission is problematic. So, for example, messages that accumulate in the "Messages waiting to be routed" SMTP queue suggest that there is some type of routing problem in your Exchange system.

For clues to help you determine which events to look for in the event logs, examine the text of messages in the properties of the SMTP queues. As noted previously, you can adjust the logging level of various event-logging categories based on the information you find when examining the SMTP queues.

Table 12-2 lists the main SMTP queues along with descriptions of each.

Table 12-2   SMTP queues

SMTP Queue	Description
Messages awaiting directory lookup	Contains messages to recipients awaiting address resolution in Active Directory. Message accumulation in this queue usually indicates problems with the categorizer.
Messages waiting to be routed	Contains messages waiting to be routed to a destination server. Suspect routing problems if messages accumulate in this queue.

Table 12-2   SMTP queues (continued)

SMTP Queue	Description
Remote delivery [Connector name | Server name | Remote domain]	Holds messages that are destined for the remote domain. The name of the queue matches the remote domain to which the message is being delivered. Message accumulation in this queue also indicates routing problems.
Final destination currently unreachable	Holds messages whose destination server cannot be reached; may indicate that there is no valid route to the intended destination.
Pre-submission	Holds messages that have been accepted by the SMTP service but have not yet been sent to the categorizer. If messages accumulate in this queue, it might be because the categorizer is not processing messages quickly enough.
DSN messages pending submission	Contains delivery status notifications that have been acknowledged and accepted by the SMTP service but have not yet been delivered to the recipient. Messages in this queue might indicate problems with the Exchange Information Store.
Failed message retry queue	Contains messages that can't be routed because the destination server is unreachable. Messages can accumulate here for a variety of reasons, including performance-related problems, message corruption, or insufficient system resources.

12

Exchange Server 2003 has enhanced the Queue Viewer to improve the monitoring of message queues. Now, you can view X.400 and SMTP queues in Queue Viewer rather than from their respective protocol nodes. You can also set the refresh rate of the queues using the Settings option. You can view additional information about a particular queue by clicking the queue. Queue Viewer also includes new options such as Disable Outbound Mail, which lets you disable the outbound mail from all SMTP queues.

ACTIVITY

Activity 12-2: Accessing the Queue Viewer

Time Required: 5 to 10 minutes

Objective: Access the Queue Viewer within Exchange System Manager.

Description: In this activity, you access the Queue Viewer within Exchange System Manager on the back-end server. To access the Queue Viewer, complete the following steps on the back-end server:

1. From the Windows desktop of the back-end server, click **Start**, point to **All Programs**, point to **Microsoft Exchange**, and then click **System Manager**. Exchange System Manager opens.

2. Click the **plus sign (+)** next to Administrative Groups, click the **plus sign (+)** next to First Administrative Group, click the **plus sign (+)** next to the Servers container, and then click the **plus sign (+)** next to **SERVERXX**, where XX is the number assigned to the back-end server.

3. Click the **Queues** container. In the details pane, a list of available queues is displayed, as shown in Figure 12-3. Examine your list of queues.

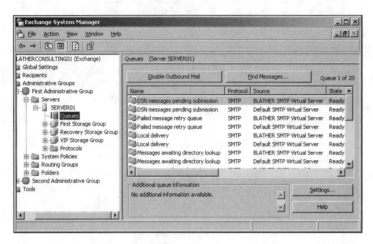

Figure 12-3   Queue Viewer

4. When finished, close **Exchange System Manager**.

Typically, when you access the Queue Viewer you won't see messages in any of the queues. This is because Exchange Server 2003 processes them and routes them before the viewer has a chance to update its display. If messages remain in a queue, there is likely some sort of problem. If you see a consistent or growing number of messages, you need to investigate the problem further.

When you click the Queues node in System Manager, you get a summary of the currently available queues for the selected node. These queues can include both transport and link queues. Although queue summaries provide important details for troubleshooting message flow problems, you do have to know what to look for. The connection state is the key information to look at first. This value tells you the state of the queue. You can find a queue's state in the State column or by noting the icon used for the queue. States you will see include the following:

- *Active*—An active queue is needed to allow messages to be transported out of a link queue. This state is indicated by an open folder icon.

- *Ready*—A ready queue is needed to allow messages to be transported out of a transport queue. When link queues are ready, they can have a connection allocated to them. This state is indicated by a folder icon with a white check mark in a green circle.

- *Scheduled*—The server is waiting for a scheduled connection time. This state is indicated by a folder icon with a clock.

- *Frozen*—The queue is frozen, and none of its messages can be processed for routing. Messages can enter the queue, however, as long as the Exchange routing categorizer is running. You must unfreeze the queue to resume normal queue operations. This state is indicated by a folder icon with a circled red square.

- *Retry*—The server is waiting to retry after a connection attempt failed. This state is indicated by a folder icon with a circled arrow.

- *Remote*—The server is waiting for a remote command to dequeue.

- *Warning*—The queue is either not available or an error occurred. This state is indicated by a folder icon with a circled red exclamation point.

When trying to troubleshoot issues with connectivity, the first step typically is to freeze the queue to see if messages are entering the queue as expected. When you freeze a queue, all message transfer out of that queue stops. This means that messages continue to enter the queue but no messages leave it. After you have frozen the queue, you can use the following information provided by the Queue Viewer to assist in troubleshooting:

- *Time oldest message submitted*—Tells you when the oldest message was sent by a client. Any time the oldest message has been in the queue for several days, you have a problem with message delivery.

- *Time next connection retry*—When the connection state is Retry, tells you when another connection attempt will be made. You can use Force Connection on the queue's shortcut menu to attempt a connection immediately.

- *Total message size (KB)*—Tells you the total size of all messages in the queue. If you see a large message size waiting in the queue, you could have a connectivity or routing issue.

- *Number of messages*—Provides information on the total number of messages waiting in the queue. If a large number of messages are waiting in the queue, you could have a connectivity or routing problem.

- *Additional queue information*—Provides additional information that can be used to troubleshoot issues. Information on errors returned from Exchange to the SMTP service, such as remote server connectivity issues or being unable to find the destination via DNS, will be displayed.

12

Activity 12-3: Freezing and Unfreezing Queues

Time Required: 5 to 10 minutes

Objective: Freeze a queue using the Queue Viewer.

Description: In this activity, you freeze a queue using the Queue Viewer on the back-end server. To do this, complete the following steps:

1. From the Windows desktop on the back-end server, click **Start**, point to **All Programs**, point to **Microsoft Exchange**, and then click **System Manager**. Exchange System Manager opens.

2. Click the **plus sign (+)** next to Administrative Groups, click the **plus sign (+)** next to First Administrative Group, click the **plus sign (+)** next to the Servers container, and then click the **plus sign (+)** next to **SERVERXX**, where XX is the number assigned to the back-end server.

3. Click the **Queues** container.

4. In the details pane, right-click the **Local delivery** queue for the Default SMTP Virtual Server, and then click **Freeze** on the shortcut menu to freeze the queue. The queue is frozen, as indicated by the queue's icon, shown in Figure 12-4.

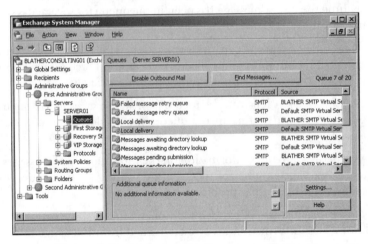

Figure 12-4   Local delivery queue frozen

5. To unfreeze the queue, right-click the **Local delivery** queue for the Default SMTP Virtual Server, and then click **Unfreeze** on the shortcut menu.

6. Close **Exchange System Manager**.

After you have frozen a queue, you might find that the number of messages start to build up significantly depending on the size of your organization. You can make use of the Find Message option to search for messages by specifying search criteria such as the sender or recipient, and the message state (such as frozen). You can also specify the number of messages you want your search to return.

ACTIVITY

Activity 12-4: Using Find Within the Queue Viewer

Time Required: 10 to 20 minutes

Objective: Use the Find feature to find messages in Queue Viewer.

Description: In this activity, you use the Find feature within the Queue Viewer. You freeze the Messages pending submission queue, use Microsoft Outlook to send yourself a message, and then make use of the Find feature within the Queue Viewer to view the message. To do this, complete the following steps on the back-end server:

1. From the Windows desktop of the back-end server, click **Start**, point to **All Programs**, point to **Microsoft Exchange**, and then click **System Manager**. Exchange System Manager opens.

2. Click the **plus sign (+)** next to Administrative Groups, click the **plus sign (+)** next to First Administrative Group, click the **plus sign (+)** next to the Servers container, and then click the **plus sign (+)** next to **SERVERXX**, where XX is the number assigned to the back-end server.

3. Click the **Queues** container. In the details pane, right-click the **Messages pending submission** queue for the Default SMTP Virtual Server (scroll if necessary), and then click **Freeze** on the shortcut menu. The Messages pending submission queue is frozen, as indicated by its icon.

4. Minimize **Exchange System Manager**.

5. To start Outlook, click **Start**, point to **All Programs**, point to **Microsoft Office**, and then click **Microsoft Office Outlook 2003**. Outlook opens connected to the Administrator's account.

6. To send a message to yourself, click **New**, type **Administrator** in the To text box, type **Test Message** in the Subject text box, type **Testing** in the body, and then click **Send**. When finished and your message is sent, close **Outlook**.

7. Click the **Exchange System Manager** button on the taskbar.

8. In the Queue Viewer, double-click the **Messages pending submission** queue for the Default SMTP Virtual Server. The Find Messages - Messages pending submission dialog box opens, as shown in Figure 12-5.

12

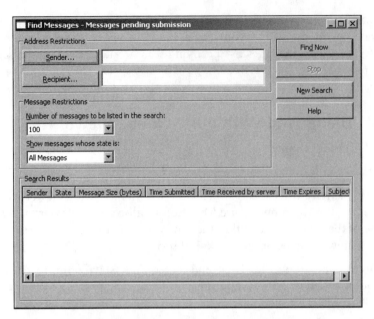

Figure 12-5   Find Messages - Messages pending submission dialog box

9. To return all messages currently in the queue, click **Find Now**. If there are a large number of messages, you can narrow the search by specifying who sent the message, or for whom the message was destined.

10. One result is returned—the message you sent to yourself. Double-click the **message** in the Search Results list box. The Message Properties dialog box opens, as shown in Figure 12-6.

    The Message Properties dialog box displays information about the message, including the sender, subject, priority, size, recipients, and so on. When finished viewing the message's information, click **OK**.

11. Close the **Find Messages** dialog box. You are returned to Exchange System Manager.

12. In the details pane, right-click the **Messages pending submission** queue for the Default SMTP Virtual Server, and then click **Unfreeze** on the shortcut menu.

13. To see that the message has been sent, double-click the **Messages pending submission** queue for the Default SMTP Virtual Server. In the Find Messages - Message pending submission dialog box, click the **Find Now** button. No messages are found. This indicates your message has been sent. Close the **Find Messages** dialog box.

14. Close **Exchange System Manager**.

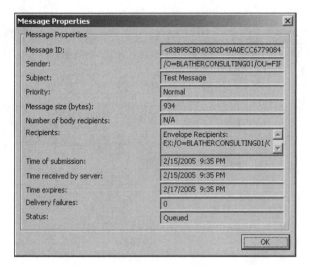

Figure 12-6   Message Properties dialog box

Protocol Logging

Protocol logging allows you to track conversations that occur between virtual servers and external clients or hosts. Protocol logging can be used to troubleshoot issues with SMTP and HTTP. You can use log information to identify issues such as the following:

- Whether a client is able to connect to a specified virtual server or whether there were issues with sending and receiving protocol commands or data

- How long it took to send information between the client and server, how long it took to establish a connection, or how long it took to send or receive a command between the server and client

- What errors might have occurred, and whether they are Windows related or related to the protocol itself

- Whether there are issues with authentication while connecting to the server

When you enable protocol logging, you specify the properties that you want to track. Table 12-3 lists some of the key properties that you need to track when troubleshooting issues using protocol logging.

Table 12-3   Key protocol logging properties and fields

Property Name	Log Field	Description
Date	date	Connection date
Time	time	Connection time
Client IP	c-ip	IP address of the client issuing the command
User Name	cs-username	Account name of an authenticated user

Table 12-3   Key protocol logging properties and fields (continued)

Property Name	Log Field	Description
Service Name	s-sitename	Name of the service processing the command
Server Name	s-computername	Name of the server receiving the command
Server IP Address	s-ip	IP address of the server receiving the command
Method	cs-method	Protocol command sent by the client
Protocol Status	sc-status	Protocol reply code
Win32 Status	sc-win32-status	Windows status or error code
Bytes Sent	sc-bytes	Number of bytes sent by the server
Bytes Received	cs-bytes	Number of bytes received by the server
Time Taken	time-taken	Length of time the command took to complete in milliseconds

Other attributes might or might not be supported depending on the protocol that is being logged. If the particular attribute is not supported, the field for that attribute is recorded with a "0" (zero) or a "−" (dash).

Using protocol logging to troubleshoot issues with connectivity isn't recommended unless it is performed for short durations of time. The primary reason for this is because protocol logging is process and resource intensive. Exchange Server 2003 must perform a lot of work to log activity related to a particular protocol. As you track more and more properties, the more system resources protocol logging requires.

Protocol logging is accomplished through Internet Information Services and can be recorded in one of the four following formats:

- *W3C Extended Log File Format*—This format writes the log in ASCII text using the World Wide Web Consortium extended log file format. Each entry is written on a new line, and fields are space delimited. This is the default style that is used when logging information.

- *NCSA Common Log File Format*—This format writes the log in ASCII text using the National Center for Supercomputing Applications (NCSA) common format. Each entry is written on a new line and fields are space delimited.

- *ODBC Logging*—This format writes the log entries to a database that supports Open Database Connectivity (ODBC).

- *Microsoft IIS Log File Format*—This format writes the log in ASCII text fusing the IIS log file format. Each entry is written on a new line and fields are tab delimited.

By default, these protocol log files are written to a subdirectory of %SystemRoot%\System32\Logfiles. ASCII log files begin with a header that identifies the protocol or service used to create the file, the protocol that is being logged, a date and time stamp, and a delimited list of fields contained in the body of the log file.

Protocol logging must be enabled separately on each virtual server that you have created.

ACTIVITY

Activity 12-5: Enabling Protocol Logging

Time Required: 5 to 10 minutes

Objective: Enable SMTP protocol logging on an Exchange Server 2003 SMTP virtual server.

Description: In this activity, you enable protocol logging on the default SMTP virtual server on your back-end server. You enable protocol logging on each virtual server separately; however, in this activity, you enable protocol logging on the default SMTP virtual server only. To enable logging, complete the following steps:

1. From the Windows desktop of the back-end server, click **Start**, point to **All Programs**, point to **Microsoft Exchange**, and then click **System Manager**.

2. Click the **plus sign (+)** next to Administrative Groups, click the **plus sign (+)** next to First Administrative Group, click the **plus sign (+)** next to the Servers container, click the **plus sign (+)** next to **SERVERXX**, where XX is the number assigned to the back-end server, and then click the **plus sign (+)** next to the **Protocols** container.

3. Click **SMTP**, right-click **Default SMTP Virtual Server**, and then click **Properties** on the shortcut menu. The Default SMTP Virtual Server Properties dialog box opens.

4. On the General tab, click the **Enable logging** check box.

5. In the Active log format drop-down list, click **W3C Extended Log File Format**, if necessary, and then click the **Properties** button. The Logging Properties dialog box opens, as shown in Figure 12-7.

6. On the General tab, click **Daily**, if necessary, for the New log schedule.

7. Click the **Advanced** tab. Click the **Date** and **Time** check boxes. Repeat this for every remaining property in the Extended logging options list box until they are all checked. When finished, click **OK** to return to the Default SMTP Virtual Server Properties dialog box. Click **OK** to return to Exchange System Manager.

8. Close **Exchange System Manager**.

12

Message Tracking

To help administrators track down messages when needed—if, for example, an important message was never received—Exchange provides the ability to create logs containing information about all messages sent throughout the organization. The logs contain many important details about each message, including the time the message was sent and/or received, sender and recipient information, message size, header information, and so on. Enabling **message tracking** on a server is as simple as checking one or two check boxes.

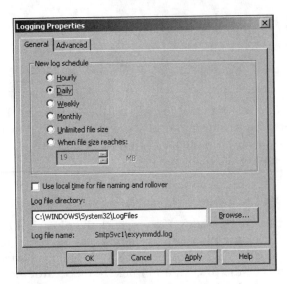

Figure 12-7   Logging Properties dialog box

Doing so tracks all types of messages, including those on public folders and system messages. To find information about a message in the logs, you use the **Message Tracking Center**, which allows you to search for messages using the logged details as criteria for the search.

Message tracking is enabled on each server individually within your organization. Because you can differentiate between standard and extended logging, you have the option of tailoring logging to your environment. For servers such as bridgehead servers that act as intermediates in the paths messages traverse, you might want to enable extended logging to provide more information on which to search. For servers such as mailbox servers, you might not be interested in as much information but might want to try to minimize the amount of information that is maintained by only enabling standard logging.

ACTIVITY

Activity 12-6: Enabling Message Tracking

Time Required: 10 to 20 minutes

Objective: Enable message tracking on an Exchange 2003 server.

Description: In Chapter 2, "Installing and Configuring Exchange Server 2003," you enabled message tracking on the back-end server through the use of a policy. In this activity, you enable message tracking on your front-end server. When considering enabling message tracking, you need to ensure that you have adequate disk space not only for the services and applications that use the disk, but for the log files as well. On servers that process large quantities of mail, the tracking logs grow quickly, so you must ensure you have enough space in place to handle the anticipated volumes. To enable message tracking on your front-end server, complete the following steps:

1. If necessary, log on to the front-end server using the user name **Administrator** and password **Password!**.

2. From the Windows desktop of the front-end server, click **Start**, point to **All Programs**, point to **Microsoft Exchange**, and then click **System Manager**. The Exchange System Manager opens.

3. Click the **plus sign (+)** next to Administrative Groups, click the **plus sign (+)** next to the Second Administrative Group, and then click the **plus sign (+)** next to the Servers container.

4. Right-click **SERVERYY**, where YY is the number assigned to the front-end server, and then click **Properties** on the shortcut menu. The SERVERYY Properties dialog box opens.

5. On the General tab, click the **Enable message tracking** check box. This enables standard logging on the front-end server. A message appears informing you to grant the appropriate users access to the \\SERVERYY\SERVERYY.log directory, where YY is the number assigned to the front-end server. Click **OK** to continue.

6. To also enable extended logging, click the **Enable subject logging and display** check box.

7. To help manage the disk space that log files utilize, click the **Remove log files** check box, and then type **14** in the Remove files older than (days) text box. This setting retains two weeks worth of log files.

8. Click **OK** to return to Exchange System Manager.

9. Close **Exchange System Manager**.

After you have enabled message tracking on your server, Exchange Server 2003 maintains message logs in the C:\Program Files\Exchsrvr\ServerName.log directory, where *ServerName* is the name of your server. Within this directory, each log file is named by the date the file was created, using the format YYYYMMDD.log. Log files take the same format as protocol log files. They are written as tab-delimited text and begin with a header that records the following:

- Information that identifies the file as a message tracking log file

- The version of the Exchange System Attendant that created the file

- A tab-delimited list of fields contained in the body of the log file

Because log files are standard text, you can use any text editor to view the log files. Also, because the text is written in tab-delimited format, you can import the file into a word processor such as Microsoft Word.

Rummaging through the log files themselves can be time consuming. Fortunately, Exchange Server 2003 provides the Message Tracking Center to assist you with searching for message information in your logs.

12

ACTIVITY

Activity 12-7: Using the Message Tracking Center

Time Required: 10 to 20 minutes

Objective: Use the Message Tracking Center in Exchange System Manager.

Description: You use the Message Tracking Center in Exchange System Manager to track a message. Remember, message tracking was enabled on the back-end server in Chapter 2 through the use of a policy. In this activity, you send a message to yourself, and then track that message using the Message Tracking Center. To do this, complete the following steps on the back-end server:

1. From the Windows desktop of the back-end server, click **Start**, point to **All Programs**, point to **Microsoft Office**, and then click **Microsoft Office Outlook 2003**. Outlook opens connected to the Administrator's account.

2. To send yourself a message to track, click the **New** button, type **Administrator** in the To text box, type **Message To Track** in the Subject text box, type **Message** in the body, and then click the **Send** button.

3. When the message is sent, close **Outlook**.

4. Click **Start**, point to **All Programs**, point to **Microsoft Exchange**, and then click **System Manager**. The Exchange System Manager opens.

5. Click the **plus sign (+)** next to Tools, and then click **Message Tracking Center**. The Message Tracking Center opens, as shown in Figure 12-8.

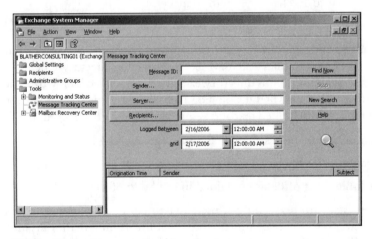

Figure 12-8   Message Tracking Center

6. To search for messages, you need to at least provide a server name. Click the **Server** button. The Select the server(s) to search for this message dialog box opens. In the Enter the object names to select text box, type **SERVERXX**, where XX is the number assigned to the back-end server, click the **Check Names** button, and then click **OK**.

7. By default, messages logged between 12:00 a.m. today and 12:00 a.m. tomorrow are tracked. To track messages in a different time period, use the "Logged Between" and "and" drop-down lists to select the correct dates. For this activity, you leave the default values. Click the **Find Now** button to find all message tracked in this period.

8. In the messages list, find and click the **Message To Track** message sent by the Administrator. The Message History window opens, as shown in Figure 12-9.

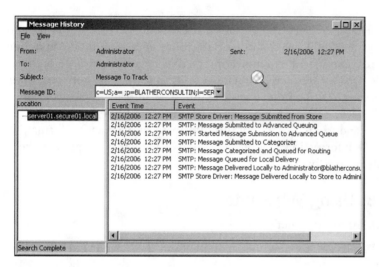

Figure 12-9 Message History window

9. Examine the event information for this message. Take note of all of the events occurring between message submission and message delivery. If there were a problem with the messaging system, you could most likely track it here. When finished, close the **Message History** window.

10. Close **Exchange System Manager**.

Exchange Server 2003 enhances the message tracking capabilities that were provided in Exchange 2000 Server. In Exchange 2000 Server, messages were never tracked past the categorization stage during the transport of the message. Therefore, when you looked at the message history for a particular tracked message, you never saw any tracking information. Exchange Server 2003 now tracks subsequent phases of the transport process when the recipient address is verified against Active Directory and the route is determined. Specifically, the following new categories are available as part of the message history:

- Messages categorized and queued for routing

- Messages routed and queued for local delivery

- Messages routed and queued for remote delivery

- Messages queued for categorization

- Messages queued for local delivery retry
- Messages queued for routing retry

Tracking this additional information can provide more insight into what might be causing the transport failures if you are having issues with message delivery.

WinRoute

WinRoute is an Exchange Server 2003 tool that extracts the current routing information that Exchange Server 2003 makes use of to route messages inside and outside the organization. WinRoute works by connecting to Exchange Server 2003 on port 691, the same port that is used to transfer link state routing information between servers. After connecting to a server, WinRoute extracts the link state information for the organization. The information that is extracted comes in the form of GUIDS that identify connectors, bridgehead servers, and so on. To present this information in a readable format, WinRoute matches the GUID information to objects in Active Directory to present the link state information in a readable format.

ACTIVITY

Activity 12-8: Using WinRoute

Time Required: 10 to 20 minutes

Objective: Use WinRoute to view information about the current Exchange Server 2003 routing environment.

Description: In this activity, you view the current Exchange Server 2003 routing information through WinRoute. You learn how to use the utility and the information within it. WinRoute is not available as part of an Exchange Server 2003 installation, so you first download and install the tool on your back-end server. You must download the tool and install it separately. To download WinRoute, visit the URL provided in Step 2 of this activity. This activity assumes you install the utility in C:\Temp\WinRoute. After downloading and installing the tool, complete the following on your back-end server, to view message routing information:

1. From the Windows desktop, click **Start**, point to **All Programs**, and then click **Internet Explorer**. Internet Explorer opens.

2. In the Address Bar, type **http://www.microsoft.com/exchange/**, and then click the **Go** button to navigate to the Microsoft Exchange Server Home page.

3. Click the **Downloads** link in the navigation bar on the left side of the page. On the Downloads for Exchange 2003 page, scroll down to the WinRoute link under Tools. Click the **WinRoute** link.

4. On the Exchange Server WinRoute page, click the **Download** button on the right side. In the File Download dialog box, click **Open**. If a Security Warning appears, click **Yes** to continue.

5. In the Choose Directory For Extracted Files dialog box, type **C:\Temp**, and then click **Ok**. When the extraction is complete, click **OK** and then close **Internet Explorer**.

6. To start WinRoute, click **Start**, and then click **Run**. The Run dialog box opens. Type **C:\Temp\WinRoute\WinRoute.exe** in the Open text box, and then click **OK**. WinRoute starts.

7. Click **File** on the menu bar, and then click **New Server Query**. The Query Server dialog box opens. Type **SERVERXX** in the Enter the server name text box, where XX is the number assigned to the back-end server, and then click **OK**.

8. The serverXX window opens, where XX is the number assigned to the back-end server. Maximize this window within the WinRoute interface, if necessary. This window displays the current routing information in three panes, as shown in Figure 12-10. Navigate through and examine the information available in the three panes.

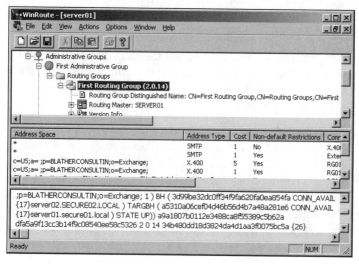

Figure 12-10   WinRoute interface

9. When finished, click **File** on the menu bar, and then click **Exit**.

The interface contains three window panes. The middle pane is the most useful pane to investigate routing issues. The middle pane, or address space pane, contains all the address spaces known to the server, along with their associated type, cost, restrictions, connector, source routing group, and administrative group. This pane shows all address spaces known to the Exchange Server 2003 organization. When investigating routing issues, identify the connector that would be used to transport the message by matching the recipient's address to the address space associated with the connector. There might be more than one connector that can deliver the message, in which case you need to examine the cost associated with the connector to further clarify which route the message will take. Cost is typically not an issue unless two connectors use the exact same address space.

As you are investigating issues within the address space pane, you might require additional information about an object being referenced. This is when the top pane, or tree view pane, comes into play. This pane contains a hierarchical representation of the organizational routing table. The organization is broken into two nodes, a General Info node and an Administrative Groups node.

The General Info node displays general information about routing within your organization, such as the routing engine version and a digest number, which is used to evaluate whether routing information is synchronized. Each time a change in the routing topology occurs, this digest number is incremented. The General Info node also presents the organization's distinguished name.

The organization's administrative groups are listed under the Administrative Groups node. Each routing group in the organization is represented as a separate node within the appropriate administrative group. For each routing group node, WinRoute displays the routing group distinguished name, routing master, version information about the routing group, routing group addresses used internally by Exchange Server 2003, members, and connectors used within the routing group.

For each routing group member, WinRoute displays the distinguished name of the server, whether the routing service on the member server is in communication with the master, the server version, which is modified as the member server is moved between routing groups, and the build version of Exchange running on the member server.

Connector information is probably the most important information presented in this pane. Connector information presents the different connectors configured within the routing group. For each connector, WinRoute displays the distinguished name, type, legacy distinguished name, and local and remote bridgehead server addresses. For MTAs, the name of the bridgehead server is specified. For SMTP and routing group connectors, the address fields are either blank (if DNS is used) or contain the FQDN (fully qualified domain name) of the smart host that is being used for relaying. Finally, information regarding any restrictions on the connector, address spaces hosted by the connector, and status of the connector is provided.

The last pane in the WinRoute interface is the bottom pane, or raw routing data table pane. This pane contains the routing information that Exchange actually makes use of. Typically, this pane is presented for information purposes only because of the cryptic nature of the information contained within it. As objects are highlighted in the tree view pane, the corresponding section within the raw routing data table are highlighted.

Telnet

One tool that is useful for testing SMTP connectivity is the Telnet tool. Telnet is a terminal emulation program that can be used to verify that SMTP is installed and configured properly by allowing you to type SMTP commands directly to deliver messages to end users. You can use Telnet to verify that the server is available over the Internet and troubleshoot issues with connectivity behind firewalls and issues regarding mail flow.

ACTIVITY

Activity 12-9: Using Telnet to Test SMTP Connectivity

Time Required: 10 to 20 minutes

Objective: Use Telnet to test connectivity with a remote server.

Description: In this activity, you use the Telnet utility to connect to your Exchange 2003 server to test that you can send an SMTP message to a recipient within your Exchange Server 2003 organization. This activity tests SMTP connectivity between the two computers within your workgroup. For this activity, use your front-end and back-end servers. First, you need to start the Telnet service on the back-end server, and then you can start a Telnet session on the front-end server.

1. From the Windows desktop of the back-end server, click **Start**, and then click **Run**. In the Open text box, type **services.msc**, and then click **OK**. The Services console opens.

2. In the Services console, scroll down to the **Telnet** service. Right-click **Telnet**, and then click **Properties**.

3. In the Telnet Properties (Local Computer) dialog box, click **Automatic** in the Startup type drop-down list. Click the **Start** button to start the service. When the service is started, click **OK**.

4. Close the **Services** console.

5. Switch to the front-end server. From the Windows desktop of the front-end server, click **Start**, and then click **Run**. The Run dialog box opens. Type **telnet** in the Open text box, and then click **OK**. The Telnet utility starts in a command window.

6. Type **SET LOCALECHO** and then press **Enter**. This allows you to view the responses to the commands you enter.

7. Type **SET ?** and then press **Enter**. You are presented with a list of available telnet commands.

8. Type **open SERVERXX 25** and then press **Enter**, where XX is the number assigned to the back-end server. This opens a connection to the back-end server on port 25.

9. Type **EHLO** and then press **Enter**.

10. Type **MAIL FROM: dsantos@blatherconsultingXX.com**, where XX is the number assigned to the back-end server, and then press **Enter** to continue. You are prompted with a message indicating that the sender is okay. If the machine you are sending from is not part of the same Active Directory forest, the SMTP server responds with an error. By default, Exchange Server 2003 requires that all clients be authenticated against Active Directory.

12

If you receive an error such as Invalid Address or Unrecognized command, type the command again.

NOTE

11. Type **RCPT TO: administrator@blatherconsultingXX.com**, where XX is the number assigned to the back-end server, and then press **Enter** to continue. The Administrator's address is echoed back to you. If the recipient is not a valid recipient or the server does not accept mail from the domain entered, the SMTP server returns an error.

If you receive an error such as Invalid Address or Unrecognized command, type the command again.

NOTE

12. Type **DATA** and then press **Enter**. This allows you to start entering the text for the body of your message.

13. Type **Subject: This is a test using Telnet**, and then press **Enter**.

14. Type **Hello** and then press **Enter**.

15. Type a **period (.)** and then press **Enter**. A period by itself indicates that you are terminating entering text for your message. If mail is working properly, a response appears indicating that the mail has been queued for delivery to the end user.

16. To exit Telnet, type **quit**, press **Enter**, and then press **Enter** again. At the Microsoft Telnet prompt, type **quit**, and then press **Enter**.

17. Switch to the back-end server. Click **Start**, point to **All Programs**, point to **Microsoft Office**, and then click **Microsoft Office Outlook 2003**. Outlook opens connected to the Administrator's account.

18. There will be a new message from Demitri Santos in the Inbox. Open this **message** to view it. When finished, close the **message**, and then close **Outlook**.

NONDELIVERY REPORTS

What happens when a message is undeliverable? As a sender of a message, you want to be notified when a delivery error occurs. Fortunately, Exchange Server 2003 assists with this by implementing delivery status notifications (DSN). DSNs can be broken into the following three categories:

- Messages indicating success
- Messages indicating a persistent, transient failure
- Messages indicating a permanent failure

Messages indicating some type of failure are more formally known as **NDRs (nondelivery reports)**. Figure 12-11 provides an example of an NDR.

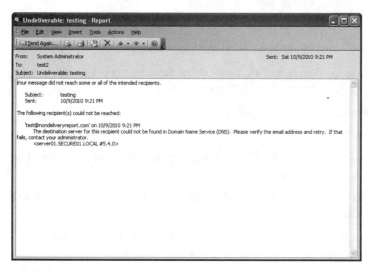

Figure 12-11   Nondelivery report

In this particular example, the NDR was generated by Exchange Server 2003, because the destination server for the domain specified in the recipient address could not be found in DNS. The NDR specifies the subject of the message, the time it was generated, the text describing the problem, and a status code preceded by the name of the server that generated the status code. In Figure 12-11, the status code is 5.4.0, and the server that generated the code was server01.SECURE01.LOCAL. The following activity gives you some insight on the NDR status, or diagnostic, codes, including possible causes and troubleshooting solutions.

Activity 12-10: Researching NDR Diagnostic Codes

Time Required: 10 to 20 minutes

Objective: Research NDR diagnostic codes.

Description: In this activity, you download a book about Exchange Server 2003 transport and routing from Microsoft TechNet. This book has excellent information on troubleshooting transport and routing issues in your organization, including a detailed chapter on NDRs. You are going to look specifically at this chapter. Complete the following steps:

1. From the Windows desktop of the back-end server, click **Start**, point to **All Programs**, and then click **Internet Explorer**.

2. In the Address Bar, type **http://www.microsoft.com/technet/prodtechnol/ exchange/2003/library/extransrout.mspx**, and then click the **Go** button. The Microsoft TechNet Exchange Server 2003 Transport and Routing Guide page opens.

3. In the Summary section, click the **Download the Exchange Server 2003 Transport and Routing Guide** link. The Microsoft Download Center Exchange Server 2003 Transport and Routing Guide page opens.

4. On the right side of the page, click the **Download** button.

5. In the File Download dialog box, click the **Save** button.

6. If necessary, click **Desktop**, and then click the **Save** button. The download for this file takes about one minute with high-speed Internet.

7. When the download is complete, click the **Close** button.

8. Close **Internet Explorer**.

9. On the desktop, double-click **Ex2K3_Transport_Routing_Guide.exe**. The WinZip Self-Extractor dialog box opens.

10. In the Unzip to folder text box, type **C:**, click the **Unzip** button, click **OK**, and then click the **Close** button.

11. Click **Start**, point to **All Programs**, point to **Accessories**, and then click **Windows Explorer**.

12. Click the **plus sign (+)** next to My Computer, and then click **Local Disk (C:)**.

13. In the details pane, double-click **Exchange Server 2003 Transport and Routing Guide.doc**.

14. Scroll down and read the table of contents for this book. Notice Chapters 11, 12, and 13 discuss troubleshooting.

15. Scroll down to the beginning of **Chapter 13** on **page 199**. Read this entire chapter, paying special attention to the NDR codes, causes, and troubleshooting solutions presented in Table 13-2.

16. When finished, close the document.

17. Close **Windows Explorer**.

IDENTIFYING TRANSPORT ISSUES

Typically, issues arise from the improper configuration of your e-mail system. When troubleshooting transport issues, you need to perform a primary task of verifying configuration settings. The following sections outline issues that might arise and cause message transportation problems within your environment.

Active Directory Issues

Microsoft Exchange Server 2003 relies significantly on Active Directory to provide it with information regarding the various objects that the Exchange back-end must work with, such as connectors, message stores, recipients, contacts, and groups. If these objects do not contain required information for a variety of reasons, it can cause issues within the e-mail environment.

Attributes might be missing from Active Directory objects for a number of reasons, including accidental error, global catalog issues, Active Directory Connector (ADC) replication issues, move mailbox issues, and so on. A major component of an Exchange 2003 server is the message categorizer. The message categorizer performs a number of tests on a message to come to a decision about how to process and route the message within the messaging infrastructure. To perform these tests, it relies heavily on information provided by Active Directory, such as recipient information, contact information, Exchange Server 5.5 recipient information, connector information, and so on. If any of these objects is missing any of the required attributes or if they are incorrect, the message might remain stuck in the categorizer, or it generates an NDR. Table 12-4 outlines different attributes that you should inspect to ensure that they are populated properly for Exchange Server 2003 to process messages correctly.

Note that different objects have different attribute requirements. For instance, Exchange Server 5.5 recipients only require the legacyExchangeDN, homeMDB, and homeMTA attributes for the categorizer to determine where the message should be routed. Other objects require different attributes.

Table 12-4 E-mail objects and their required attributes

Attribute	Example
homeMDB	CN=Mailbox Store (SERVER01),CN=First Storage Group,CN=InformationStore,CN=SERVER01, CN=Servers,CN=First Administrative Group,CN=Administrative Groups,CN=BLATHERCONSULTING01,CN=Microsoft Exchange,CN=Services,CN=Configuration, DC=SECURE01,DC=LOCAL
homeMTA	CN=Microsoft MTA,CN=SERVER01,CN=Servers,CN=First Administrative Group,CN=Administrative Groups,CN=BLATHERCONSULTING01,CN=Microsoft Exchange,CN=Services,CN=Configuration, DC=SECURE01,DC=LOCAL
legacyDN	/o=Blatherconsulting01/ou=First Administrative Group/ cn=Recipients/cn=dsantos
mail	dsantos@blatherconsulting01.com
mailNickname	dsantos
msExchHomeServerName	/o=BLATHERCONSULTING01/ou=First Administrative Group/ cn=Configuration/cn=Servers/cn=SERVER01

Table 12-4   E-mail objects and their required attributes (continued)

Attribute	Example
msExchMailboxGuid	0x06 0x4f 0x69 0xcc 0x5e 0xfe 0x79 0x4f 0x8c 0x6e 0x7b 0x67 0x57 0x92 0x51 0xd2
msExchMailboxSecurityDescriptor	This is a binary blob that does not display a value in ADSI Edit or LDP
proxyAddresses	SMTP: dsantos@blatherconsulting01.com smtp: dsantos@blatherconsultingdir12.com smtp: dsantos@blatherconsultinggroup12.com SMTP: dsantos@blatherconsultingsrv01.com SMTP: dsantos@SECURE01.LOCAL X400:c=us;a= ;p=BLATHERCONSULTING;o=Exchange; s=dsantos
targetAddress	SMTP: info@gwl.ca

If attributes are missing, you need to investigate whether they are missing for one object or multiple objects and whether the objects were migrated using the Active Directory Connector or created using the Move Mailbox tool. Investigate each of these to determine if they are the source of the missing attributes.

One of the purposes of the RUS (Recipient Update Service) is to correct any omissions to attributes that might occur when an object is created. The RUS has three default system policies that cover mail-enabled recipients, mailbox-enabled users, and hidden distribution group membership. These recipient policies attempt to correct required object attributes whose values are missing. Each policy configures attributes as follows:

- The Mail-Enabled Recipient Policy tries to create and populate the legacyExchangeDN or displayName attributes if the mailNickname attribute is set.

- The Mailbox-Enabled Recipient Policy populates the msExchHomeServerName, homeMDB, homeMTA, legacyExchangeDN, displayName, and msExchMailboxGUID attributes, if it finds the mailNickname and one of either msExchHomeServerName, homeMDB, or homeMTA populated.

- For the hidden distribution group membership policy, depending on how the hideDLMembership attribute is set, the RUS modifies the security descriptor for the group either to allow or disallow the membership for the group to be viewed.

To correct missing attribute issues, use Exchange System Manager and execute the Update Now action on a specific RUS to update the missing attributes on the recipient object that is experiencing this issue. Alternatively, execute the Rebuild action on the selected RUS to rebuild all recipient objects. For further information on how to update or rebuild the RUS, refer to Chapter 5, "Managing Addresses."

Addressing Issues

If you are planning to perform a mail migration to consolidate multiple organizations into one, or migrate an Exchange Server 5.5 organization to a separate Exchange 2000 Server organization, you need to communicate some issues to the users who are being migrated. One of these issues is that any messages in their premigrated mailbox, and any entries that currently exist in their personal address book or contact list, are no longer valid. This does not apply to entries that are SMTP, X.400, or GroupWise based, as long as the routing infrastructure is still in place to route these mail types.

This is because the address entries refer to the previous organization, which is no longer valid in the consolidated organization world. To resolve this issue, in your Outlook client ensure that you always select addresses from the GAL (Global Address List). Users who have been migrated need to delete their existing personal address books and contact lists, and then re-create them.

Routing Issues

Routing information is maintained within a routing group by the routing group master. The routing group master is responsible for updating information on all member servers within the routing group. Between routing groups, routing group bridgehead servers are responsible for communicating routing information between themselves. When issues arise with any of these components, or the underlying network, problems with routing in your environment can occur. Some of the problems that could arise include the following:

12

- Disconnection between routing group member and master. Member servers are unable to connect to the master server for routing updates.

- Conflicts between routing group masters. Sometimes, two or more servers mistake the wrong server as the routing group master. This can result in conflicting information being propagated, which can result in routing issues materializing.

- Problems that are caused by deleted routing groups. Deleted routing groups can cause a malfunction in routing as well as mail loops. Exchange routing cannot automatically remove deleted routing groups, member servers, or member connectors from the link state table. Resolve this issue by shutting down all servers within the organization to purge the routing cache information.

- Connectors that are not marked as down. There are situations in which a connector's link state might be marked as up when it is in fact down. For routing to mark a connector as down, all source bridgehead servers have to be down.

- Oscillating connections. Connectors that are on an unreliable network and are marked as up and then down repeatedly cause excessive link state updates between servers and can result in connectors being marked as down when in fact they are up, or vice versa.

Your most important tool for troubleshooting these types of messages is WinRoute. Use this tool along with the others mentioned in this chapter to investigate issues with routing in your organization, and outside of your organization. Also, you should check the underlying network infrastructure to determine if there are any components contributing to the problem such as firewalls that may be blocking the ports required to transmit routing information or if there are any underlying DNS issues with name resolution. Finally, always try for the easy solution by verifying that Exchange Server 2003 services are up and running.

CHAPTER SUMMARY

- Diagnostics logging provides an invaluable tool for determining what is happening with the current Exchange Server 2003 transport environment. By increasing the logging levels related to the MSExchangeTransport service, you can increase the amount of information that is written to the application log and further your understanding of what is occurring during troubleshooting situations.

- Event logs provide valuable insight into error and warning conditions that may be occurring with the transfer of messages in your e-mail system.

- The Queue Viewer allows messages within Exchange 2003 server queues to be examined and controlled. The Queue Viewer provides the ability to freeze and unfreeze the queues so that you can monitor message flow into queues and between queues.

- Protocol logging allows you to track conversations that occur between virtual servers and external clients or hosts. It allows you to track the exact conversations that occur between two hosts.

- Message tracking maintains log files that record information about messages traversing your system. You can use the logs to determine the status of a message, such as whether a message was sent, received, or is waiting in the queue to be delivered.

- WinRoute is an Exchange Server 2003 tool that extracts the current routing information that Exchange Server 2003 makes use of to route messages inside and outside the organization. This allows you to see the information that Exchange Server 2003 uses to decide how to route messages and allows you to troubleshoot issues with routing.

- Telnet can be used to verify that SMTP is installed and configured properly and allows you to type SMTP commands directly to deliver messages to end users. You can use Telnet to verify that the server is available over the Internet and troubleshoot issues with connectivity behind firewalls, and to troubleshoot issues regarding mail flow.

- Nondelivery reports or NDRs are a form of delivery status notifications, which indicate some form of failure when transmitting messages. NDRs provide valuable information about why a message is not delivered to its destination.

- When troubleshooting issues with message routing, ensure that issues are not related to missing attributes within Active Directory. If objects such as recipients, contacts, or groups do not have required attributes, errors can result in the delivery of your message to its final destination.

❑ If you are migrating Exchange users from one organization to another organization, and users experience issues with message delivery, ensure that they are making use of addresses out of the GAL as opposed to addresses from personal address books. Address entries within personal address books will be invalid in the new organization. This also applies to addresses that exist in migrated messages, meaning that you will not be able to reply to messages that have been migrated.

❑ Routing issues can arise for a number of reasons, including member servers not being able to communicate with the routing group master, conflicts between routing group masters, problems with deleted routing groups, and oscillating connections. When troubleshooting these types of issues, use WinRoute to understand what Exchange Server 2003 is using to decide how to route messages.

KEY TERMS

diagnostics logging — A facility for increasing the level of information that is logged by the messaging system. Diagnostics logging allows you to track what the system is doing for each message being processed.

message tracking — A facility with Exchange Server 2003 that tracks all messages being transported through a messaging system. Message tracking maintains information about the various states the message passes through on its way to its destination.

Message Tracking Center — An Exchange tool that allows you to search message tracking logs for messages based on specified criteria, such as sender, recipient, time sent/delivered, server, message size, and so on.

nondelivery report (NDR) — A message indicating that the delivery has failed. This report returns a code and information as to why the message could not be delivered to its final destination. NDRs are a valuable source of information when trying to troubleshoot message routing issues.

protocol logging — A tool to log conversations between servers or between clients and servers. Each command that is used within the conversation is tracked.

Queue Viewer — A tool used to examine queues used within Exchange Server 2003. This tool can be used to view queues and the messages they contain to help determine why messages are not being properly delivered.

WinRoute — An Exchange tool that extracts and displays the routing information that Exchange is using to route messages throughout the network.

12

REVIEW QUESTIONS

1. Your users indicate that they are receiving NDR messages indicating that the destination host could not be found. What tool would you use to determine if the destination host is available? (Choose all that apply.)

    a. NSLookup

    b. WinRoute

    c. message tracking

    d. Telnet

2. You have an organization with two mail servers. Both act as mailbox servers. Users complain that they cannot send mail to users who are not located on their own server. Which tool would you use to identify where these messages are located in the transport process? (Choose all that apply.)

    a. message tracking

    b. Queue Viewer

    c. event logging

    d. Telnet

3. Which of the following is not an event category that can be tracked by diagnostics logging?

    a. Routing Engine/Service

    b. Categorizer

    c. Queuing Engine

    d. HTTP Store Driver

4. Which of the following event services is used to troubleshoot routing issues within an Exchange Server 2003 organization? (Choose all that apply.)

    a. MSExchangeMU

    b. MSExchangeIS

    c. MSExchangeTransport

    d. MSExchangeDSAccess

5. Enabling protocol logging helps to identify authentication issues with clients connecting to the server to transfer messages. True or False?

6. Which is the primary event log for troubleshooting Exchange Server 2003 issues?

    a. system

    b. security

    c. application

    d. all of the above

7. Which of the following is not an SMTP queue?

    a. Messages awaiting directory lookup

    b. Final destination currently unreachable

    c. Pre-submission

    d. Categorizer queue

    e. Failed message retry queue

8. Which of the following are valid states for a queue in Exchange Server 2003?

    a. Active

    b. Ready

    c. Retry

    d. Frozen

    e. all of the above

9. After you have frozen a queue, what information can you obtain through the Queue Viewer? (Choose all that apply.)

    a. Time oldest message submitted

    b. Time Next Connection Retry

    c. Number of Messages

    d. Categorizer state

10. What are some of the issues that can be resolved using protocol logging? (Choose all that apply.)

    a. whether there is a delay in transmitting a specific message

    b. whether the problem might be Windows related or protocol related

    c. whether a client is able to connect with a specified virtual server

    d. whether the name can be resolved to a specific IP address

    e. TDI

11. You have a user who insists he did not receive a message that was sent to him. What tool can you use to determine if the message was actually delivered?

    a. WinRoute

    b. message tracking

    c. Queue Viewer

    d. protocol logging

12. Which of the following categories is available as part of the message history tracked within the Message Tracking Center?

    a. messages categorized and queued for routing

    b. messages routed and queued for local delivery

    c. messages queued for routing retry

    d. all of the above

12

13. Which of the following WinRoute panes is the most useful for troubleshooting?

    a. Address Space Pane

    b. Treeview Pane

    c. Raw routing data table pane

    d. none of the above

14. Which of the following attributes is not a required attribute that Exchange makes use of in routing messages?

    a. mail

    b. mailNickname

    c. company

    d. msExchMailboxGuid

15. Which of the following is not a supported level of diagnostics logging?

    a. None

    b. Maximum

    c. High

    d. Minimum

16. Which of the following logging levels provides a complete audit of every action that a service performs?

    a. Maximum

    b. Medium

    c. None

    d. Minimum

17. Nondelivery reports are a subset of delivery status notifications. True or False?

18. The MTA queue handles processing of SMTP traffic. True or False?

19. What are the different transport queues available within Exchange Server 2003? (Choose all that apply.)

    a. SMTP queues

    b. X.400 queues

    c. MAPI queues

    d. all of the above

20. Which queue holds messages prior to them being sent off to categorization?

    a. Messages waiting to be routed

    b. Messages awaiting directory lookup

    c. Pre-submission

    d. DSN messages pending submission

CASE PROJECTS

CASE PROJECTS

Case Project 12-1: Troubleshooting Transport Issues Between Organizations

Your users are indicating that they are having issues sending messages to companies outside of your organization. Messages sent internally seem to work fine. As the administrator of your e-mail infrastructure, identify the steps that you would use to troubleshoot these issues.

CASE PROJECTS

Case Project 12-2: Strategy for Troubleshooting Transport Issues

As the head of your organization's help desk, you have the responsibility of training your staff on how to troubleshoot technical issues within your organization. Come up with an approach to troubleshooting mail delivery issues that identifies the steps you would take to identify the nature of the problem and the tools you might use for each step.

CASE PROJECTS

Case Project 12-3: Troubleshooting Migration Issues

As the project manager for the e-mail migration project within your company, you are tasked with coming up with a communication to end users about the impacts that will be felt as a result of migrating their mailboxes to the new organization. Identify what should be included in the communication.

12

13

MONITORING AND TROUBLESHOOTING THE SERVER

After reading this chapter, you will be able to:

♦ Understand the tools available for monitoring the health of the Exchange Server 2003 environment

♦ Understand the different steps used by nightly online maintenance to maintain server Information Stores

♦ Describe the maintenance tools used for maintaining, troubleshooting, and fixing an Exchange 2003 server

♦ Understand the process involved in troubleshooting server issues

One key to running a successful e-mail infrastructure is keeping a watchful eye on its operation. By closely monitoring your organization and its components, you can spot potential problems before they occur and can quickly respond to the problems that do occur. Monitoring also allows you to identify trends in usage patterns that signal opportunities for optimization and future planning. As an Exchange administrator, you should routinely monitor connections, services, servers, and resource usage. These elements are the keys to ensuring that your organization is running smoothly. Because you can't be on-site 24 hours a day, you can set alerts as part of implementing your monitors to notify you when problems occur.

Ideally, you want to prevent problems from occurring so you are never notified. No one likes to wake up early in the morning to a pager beeping frantically because the server is down. To help avoid this type of problem, you should take a proactive approach to preventing problems. Exchange Server 2003 provides tools that can be run on your system to ensure the integrity of and help prevent problems with your Exchange organization. This chapter looks at those tools and how they can be used to help prevent those nasty pages late in the evening.

Of course, even the most well-designed systems are not perfect. Despite your best planning and efforts, it is likely that, at some point, you will have problems with your Exchange Server 2003 system. So what do you do when problems arise? Troubleshooting Exchange Server 2003 is a skill that you will develop as you solve real problems on your network. Obviously, one chapter alone cannot teach you all you need to know about every type of issue that might arise in your organization. This chapter does, however, provide insight into some of the troubleshooting tools available to help you solve problems when they occur.

MONITORING

Having a tool that checks over the status of your servers and connectors can be a valuable asset to your organization. Exchange Server 2003 provides server and link monitors that assist you in keeping an eye on your organization. **Server monitors** check the status of designated services, as well as the usage of various resources on a particular Exchange Server 2003. **Link monitors**, or connection status monitors, check the status of a connector between two servers. You configure and view the status of monitoring of both types of objects using Exchange System Manager.

ACTIVITY

Activity 13-1: Viewing Monitors

Time Required: 10 to 15 minutes

Objective: View the status of existing monitors.

Description: In this activity, you view the list of servers within the organization and determine their current status to ensure that they are operating. In addition, you also verify that the connectors you have established between servers are available to transmit messages. Complete the following steps on the back-end server:

1. Log on to the back-end server using the user name **Administrator** and password **Password!**.

2. From the Windows desktop of the back-end server, click **Start**, point to **All Programs**, point to **Microsoft Exchange**, and then click **System Manager**.

3. Click the **plus sign (+)** next to the Tools folder, click the **plus sign (+)** next to the Monitoring and Status folder, and then click the **Status** folder.

4. In the details pane, you will see the existing connectors and servers in your organization, as shown in Figure 13-1. Each of the servers and connectors within the organization are identified along with the administrative group they belong to and the status of each. If the server or connector is online, the status is set to Available. Examine your list of servers and connectors.

NOTE The status for your front-end server might show as critical. This is okay. If you are performing the activities in the accompanying lab manual, you stopped a critical service (unnecessary for front-end servers) on the front-end server in Chapter 7, "Configuring and Managing Exchange Server."

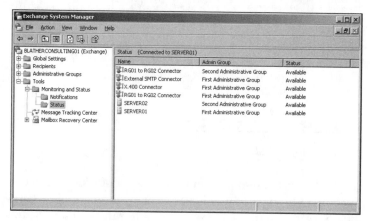

Figure 13-1 Server and connector status

5. Switch to the front-end server. If necessary, log on to the front-end server using the user name **Administrator** and password **Password!**. Click **Start** and then click **Shut Down**. The Shut Down Windows dialog box opens.

6. Ensure **Shut down** is selected in the "What do you want the computer to do?" drop down list. In the Option drop-down list, click **Application: Maintenance (Planned)**, and then click **OK**. This shuts down the server.

7. When the front-end server is completely shut down, switch to the back-end server. In Exchange System Manager, right-click the **Status** folder, and then click **Refresh** on the shortcut menu. Notice that the status of the front-end server has changed to Unreachable, as shown in Figure 13-2.

NOTE If the status of your front-end server does not change, or if you receive any warnings, confirm any warning messages, and then move on to Step 8.

8. Close **Exchange System Manager** on the back-end server.

9. Restart the front-end server. Log on using the user name **Administrator** and the password **Password!**.

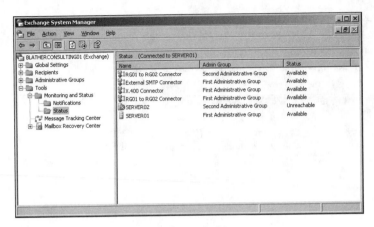

Figure 13-2 Server status unreachable

A server monitor checks designated resources and Windows 2000/2003 services on a server to detect critical situations. This type of monitor is created automatically when you install Exchange Server 2003. Server monitors allow you to monitor the status of the following six types of resources:

- Windows 2000 service
- SMTP queue growth
- X.400 queue growth
- CPU utilization
- Free disk space
- Available virtual memory

If a service you've configured for monitoring is stopped, Exchange Server 2003 generates a warning or a critical event. When you install Exchange Server 2003, a set of preconfigured services are installed by default for monitoring. These services include the following:

- Microsoft Exchange Information Store
- Microsoft Exchange MTA Stacks
- Microsoft Exchange Routing Engine
- Microsoft Exchange System Attendant
- Simple Mail Transport Protocol (SMTP)
- World Wide Web Publishing Service

NOTE

If you are performing the activities in the accompanying lab manual, you disabled the Microsoft Exchange MTA Stacks service on the front-end server. This is why you may have received a critical status for the front-end server in Activity 13-1.

In addition to these services, you might want to add additional services, such as an antivirus service or a backup agent so that you are monitoring not only Exchange Server 2003 but also those services related to the overall functionality of your server.

Activity 13-2: Configuring Service Monitoring

Time Required: 15 to 20 minutes

Objective: Configure service monitoring on your server.

Description: In this activity, you add and configure services to be monitored on your back-end server. You also configure notifications that allow you to be notified when problems occur on any server in your organization. You can configure two types of notifications: an e-mail notification or a script notification. With an e-mail notification, an e-mail is sent to the mailbox that is specified when a server or connector enters a "warning" or "critical" state. With a script notification, a script is executed when a server or connector enters a warning or critical state. To set up service monitoring and associated notifications, complete the following steps:

1. From the Windows desktop of the back-end server, click **Start**, point to **All Programs**, point to **Microsoft Exchange**, and then click **System Manager**.

2. Click the **plus sign (+)** next to Administrative Groups, click the **plus sign (+)** next to First Administrative Group, click the **plus sign (+)** next to Servers, and then right-click **SERVERXX**, where XX is the number assigned to the back-end server. On the shortcut menu, click **Properties**. The SERVERXX Properties dialog box opens.

3. Click the **Monitoring** tab. After a few moments, the Monitoring tab is displayed, as shown in Figure 13-3.

4. Click the **Add** button. The Add Resource dialog box opens, as shown in Figure 13-4. Click **Windows 2000 service** and then click **OK**. The Services dialog box opens.

5. In the Services dialog box, click the **Add** button. The Add Service dialog box opens. Scroll down and click **Microsoft Exchange Management**. Click **OK** to return to the Services dialog box. Type **Exchange Management Service** in the Name text box, click **Critical** in the When service is not running change state to drop-down list, and then click **OK** to return to the SERVERXX Properties dialog box, where XX is the number assigned to the back-end server.

6. Click **OK** to return to Exchange System Manager.

7. Click the **plus sign (+)** next to Tools, and then click the **plus sign (+)** next to Monitoring and Status. Right-click the **Notifications** folder, point to **New**, and then click **E-mail notification**. The Properties dialog box for e-mail notifications opens, as shown in Figure 13-5.

13

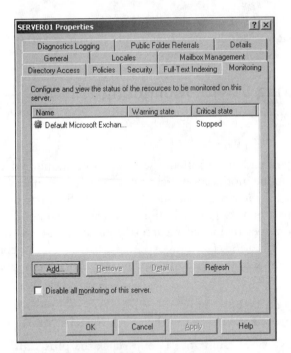

Figure 13-3   Monitoring tab

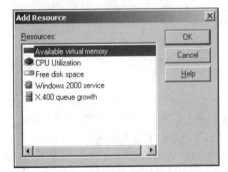

Figure 13-4   Add Resource dialog box

8. Click the **Select** button. The Select Exchange Server dialog box opens. Type **SERVERXX** in the Enter the object name to select text box, where **XX** is the number assigned to the back-end server. Click **OK** to return to the notification Properties dialog box.

9. Click **All servers** in the Servers and connectors to monitor drop-down list.

10. Click **Warning state** in the Notify when monitored items are in drop-down list.

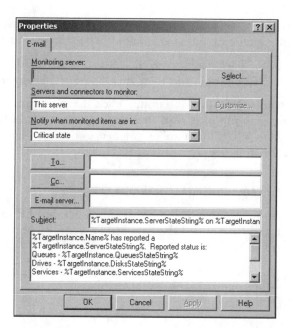

Figure 13-5 Notification Properties dialog box

11. Click the **To** button. The Select Recipient dialog box opens. Type **Administrator**. Notifications will be sent to the Administrator. Click **OK** to return to the notification Properties dialog box. Click **OK** to return to Exchange System Manager.

12. Close **Exchange System Manager**.

You should keep a close eye on the growth of queues, as continued queue growth is an important indicator of potential issues within your e-mail system. When monitoring the queues, monitoring for a certain number of messages is not important. What is important is whether the queue continually grows over time. If a messaging queue grows continuously, it means that messages are not leaving the queue and are not being delivered as fast as new messages arrive. This can be an indicator of network or system problems that might require attention. When you configure queue monitoring, you can specify the number of minutes of continual queue growth that will cause the server to enter a warning or critical state. Exchange Server 2003 provides two types of server monitors to assist with monitoring queues: the X.400 and SMTP queue monitors.

Activity 13-3: Configuring SMTP Queue Monitoring

Time Required: 10 to 20 minutes

Objective: Configure queue monitoring to monitor for sustained queue growth.

Description: In this activity, you configure message queue monitoring on the server to watch for sustained queue growth for extended periods of time. If a messaging queue grows continuously, it means that messages aren't leaving the queue and aren't being delivered as fast as new messages arrive. This can be an indicator of network or system problems that might need attention. To configure queue monitoring, complete the following steps:

1. From the Windows desktop of the back-end server, click **Start**, point to **All Programs**, point to **Microsoft Exchange**, and then click **System Manager**.

2. Click the **plus sign (+)** next to Administrative Groups, click the **plus sign (+)** next to First Administrative Group, click the **plus sign (+)** next to Servers, and then right-click **SERVERXX**, where XX is the number assigned to the back-end server. On the shortcut menu, click **Properties**. The SERVERXX Properties dialog box opens.

3. Click the **Monitoring** tab. The Monitoring tab is displayed.

4. Click the **Add** button. The Add Resource dialog box opens. Click **SMTP queue growth** in the Resources list, and then click **OK**. The SMTP Queue Thresholds dialog box opens, as shown in Figure 13-6.

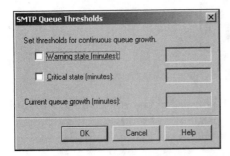

Figure 13-6   SMTP Queue Thresholds dialog box

5. Click the **Warning state (minutes)** check box, and then type **10** in the corresponding text box. A queue that's growing continuously for more than 10 minutes is usually an indicator of a potential problem.

6. Click the **Critical state (minutes)** check box, and then type **30** in the corresponding text box. If the queue is growing continuously for more than 30 minutes, it indicates a serious problem with the network or the server.

7. Click **OK** to return to the SERVERXX Properties dialog box, and then click **OK** to return to Exchange System Manager.

8. Close **Exchange System Manager**.

As powerful as hardware is these days, servers can still be brought to their knees if overtaxed. Your job as an administrator is to make sure this doesn't happen. Monitoring the CPU utilization can help you to identify issues related to insufficient processing power on the server. If CPU utilization runs at 100% for an extended period of time, you typically need to reboot the server.

High CPU utilization can also indicate that too many services are running on the machine and that you might need to consider offloading services to another machine. Using CPU monitoring, you can specify how long the CPU should run above a certain utilization level before the server's state changes to Warning or Critical.

Activity 13-4: Configuring CPU Utilization Monitoring

Time Required: 10 to 20 minutes

Objective: Configure CPU utilization monitoring to monitor for sustained high CPU usage on a server.

Description: In this activity, you configure CPU utilization monitoring on the server to monitor the CPU usage on the back-end server. When CPU utilization is too high, the server is unable to process messages effectively or manage other critical functions. As a result, queues can grow or internal data structures might back up, resulting in the server becoming too bogged down with work. To configure CPU utilization monitoring, complete the following steps:

1. From the Windows desktop of the back-end server, click **Start**, point to **All Programs**, point to **Microsoft Exchange**, and then click **System Manager**.

2. Click the **plus sign (+)** next to Administrative Groups, click the **plus sign (+)** next to First Administrative Group, click the **plus sign (+)** next to Servers, and then right-click **SERVERXX**, where XX is the number assigned to the back-end server. On the shortcut menu, click **Properties**. The SERVERXX Properties dialog box opens.

3. Click the **Monitoring** tab. The Monitoring tab is displayed.

4. Click the **Add** button. The Add Resource dialog box opens. Click **CPU Utilization** in the Resources list, and then click **OK**. The CPU Utilization Thresholds dialog box opens, as shown in Figure 13-7.

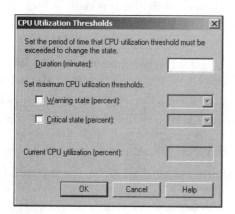

Figure 13-7   CPU Utilization Thresholds dialog box

13

5. In the Duration (minutes) text box, type **5**.

6. Click the **Warning state (percent)** check box, and then click **80** in the corresponding drop-down list. When CPU utilization is 80% or greater for an extended period of time, you should be aware of it so that you can begin investigating the problem and monitoring it more closely.

7. Click the **Critical state (percent)** check box, and then click **100** in the corresponding drop-down list. When CPU utilization is at 100% or greater for an extended period of time, you need to issue a critical state alert to act on the problems that might be causing the utilization to max out.

8. Click **OK** to return to the SERVERXX Properties dialog box, and then click **OK** to return to Exchange System Manager.

9. Close **Exchange System Manager**.

Disk space is another resource that should be closely monitored. Exchange Server 2003 makes use of disk space for data storage, logging, tracking, and also for virtual memory. When Exchange Server 2003 runs out of disk space, adverse effects can be experienced and, typically, Exchange Server 2003 begins to shut down services. This is why it is important to monitor your server's free disk space and be notified when you need to take action by replacing undersized disk drives, freeing up space on existing drives, investigating log usage, or taking other measures.

ACTIVITY

Activity 13-5: Configuring Free Disk Space Monitoring

Time Required: 10 to 20 minutes

Objective: Configure disk space monitoring to monitor the free space on your server.

Description: In this activity, you configure disk space monitoring on the back-end server to monitor the disk space usage on the server. When disk space runs out, the server can begin to malfunction because it has no place to store the information. To prevent serious issues, you should monitor free disk space closely on all your servers. To configure disk space monitoring on the back-end server, complete the following steps:

1. From the Windows desktop of the back-end server, click **Start**, point to **All Programs**, point to **Microsoft Exchange**, and then click **System Manager**.

2. Click the **plus sign (+)** next to Administrative Groups, click the **plus sign (+)** next to First Administrative Group, click the **plus sign (+)** next to Servers, and then right-click **SERVERXX**, where XX is the number assigned to the back-end server. On the shortcut menu, click **Properties**. The SERVERXX Properties dialog box opens.

3. Click the **Monitoring** tab. The Monitoring tab is displayed. Click the **Add** button. The Add Resource dialog box opens. Click **Free disk space** in the Resources list, and then click **OK**. The Disk Space Thresholds dialog box opens, as shown in Figure 13-8.

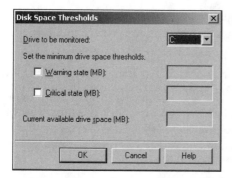

Figure 13-8   Disk Space Thresholds dialog box

4. Click the **Warning state (MB)** check box, and then type **100** in the corresponding text box. When disk space is below this value, you need to ensure you are notified of the problem so that you can begin investigating the problem and monitoring it closer.

5. Click the **Critical state (MB)** check box, and then type **25** in the corresponding text box. When disk space is below this value, you need to issue a critical state alert so you can immediately look at ways of alleviating the free space issue.

6. Click **OK** to return to the SERVERXX Properties dialog box, and then click **OK** to return to Exchange System Manager.

7. Close **Exchange System Manager**.

If you are running out of disk space, chances are you might be encountering memory issues as well. Windows 2000/2003 makes use of virtual memory, in which the server uses as memory not only the physical memory installed in the computer, but also disk space, which is configured to appear to the operating system as additional physical memory. This "virtual" memory takes the form of a page file, or swap file, which is an area on disk that is used as a temporary storage location to "swap" information in and out of physical memory.

It is important to get an idea of how much memory is available, whether in RAM or on disk. As with CPU utilization, you need to know not only whether the server dips below a certain usage threshold for memory, but also whether it remains below that threshold over a period of time. You can specify how long the server's available virtual memory should remain below the specified thresholds before the monitor changes the state of the machine to Warning or Critical.

Activity 13-6: Configuring Virtual Memory Monitoring

Time Required: 10 to 20 minutes

Objective: Configure virtual memory monitoring to monitor the available virtual memory on your server.

Description: In this activity, you configure virtual memory monitoring on the back-end server to monitor the virtual memory usage on the server. Because Exchange is extremely memory intensive, it is a good idea to keep an eye on available virtual memory. This helps you see if the server is using memory efficiently. To configure virtual memory monitoring, complete the following steps:

1. From the Windows desktop, click **Start**, point to **All Programs**, point to **Microsoft Exchange**, and then click **System Manager**.

2. Click the **plus sign (+)** next to Administrative Groups, click the **plus sign (+)** next to First Administrative Group, click the **plus sign (+)** next to Servers, and then right-click **SERVERXX**, where XX is the number assigned to the back-end server. On the shortcut menu, click **Properties**. The SERVERXX Properties dialog box opens.

3. Click the **Monitoring** tab. The Monitoring tab is displayed. Click the **Add** button to open the Add Resource dialog box. Click **Available virtual memory** in the Resources list, if necessary, and then click **OK**. The Virtual Memory Thresholds dialog box opens, as shown in Figure 13-9.

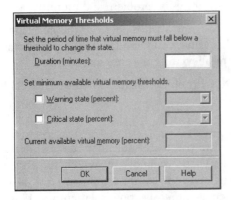

Figure 13-9 Virtual Memory Thresholds dialog box

4. In the Duration (minutes) text box, type **5**.

5. Click the **Warning state (percent)** check box, and then click **10** in the corresponding drop-down list. When virtual memory is below 10% for an extended period of time, you need to ensure you are notified of the problem so that you can investigate the problem or monitor the situation more closely.

6. Click the **Critical state (percent)** check box, and then click **5** in the corresponding drop-down list, if necessary. When virtual memory is below 5%, you need to issue a critical state alert so you can immediately look at ways of alleviating your memory issue.

7. Click **OK** to return to the SERVERXX Properties dialog box, and then click **OK** to return to Exchange System Manager.

8. Close **Exchange System Manager**.

The final type of resource that you can monitor within your system is the link monitor. Link monitors are automatically created for each connector present on a server. The status of each link monitor is listed as either available or unavailable. Unlike server monitors, you don't need to configure anything special for a link monitor.

PREVENTIVE MAINTENANCE

In addition to monitoring certain key aspects of the Exchange environment, you can also run regular maintenance tasks to reduce the likelihood of any problems occurring. For instance, Exchange Server 2003 runs regular maintenance activities to ensure that your databases are consistent with what is expected and to clean up the databases. These maintenance tasks are run automatically by the server on a nightly basis. This is done to validate that the Information Store is free from corruption and to ensure that items no longer needed by the system are removed from the database.

ACTIVITY

Activity 13-7: Configuring the Maintenance Interval for Exchange Databases

Time Required: 5 to 10 minutes

Objective: Configure the maintenance interval for the Exchange databases on your server.

13

Description: In this activity, you configure the time at which the maintenance routines run against the databases on your back-end server. By default, Exchange Server 2003 runs maintenance tasks daily from 1:00 a.m. until 5:00 a.m. This activity changes the interval to 11:00 p.m. until 3:00 a.m. To configure the maintenance interval, complete the following steps:

1. From the Windows desktop of your back-end server, click **Start**, point to **All Programs**, point to **Microsoft Exchange**, and then click **System Manager**.

2. Click the **plus sign (+)** next to Administrative Groups, click the **plus sign (+)** next to First Administrative Group, click the **plus sign (+)** next to Servers, and then click the **plus sign (+)** next to SERVERXX, where XX is the number assigned to the back-end server.

3. Click the **plus sign (+)** next to First Storage Group, and then right-click **Mailbox Store (SERVERXX)**, where XX is the number assigned to the back-end server. On the shortcut menu, click **Properties**. The Mailbox Store (SERVERXX) Properties dialog box opens.

4. Click the **Database** tab, and then click **Run daily from 11:00 PM to 3:00 AM** in the Maintenance interval drop-down list.

5. Click **OK** to return to Exchange System Manager.

6. Close **Exchange System Manager**.

Information Store Maintenance

As discussed, nightly Information Store maintenance can be configured to run at a time determined by the administrator. If maintenance ends before all of the tasks have been completed, the last task running is recorded and allowed to run until completion. If the last task isn't the last task in the set of tasks that are performed, then the next time the maintenance procedures are run, the next maintenance task in the list is run. The maintenance picks up where it left off. The types of tasks that are performed by this nightly maintenance activity are discussed in the following sections.

Purge Indexes

Indexes are used within a database to reduce the time it takes to locate information within the store. The Exchange Server 2003 Information Store creates indexes dynamically as the Information Store is used. For instance, when information is re-sorted or requested in a different sort order, the Information Store service creates an index to accommodate this new sort order. During the course of operation, thousands of indexes can be created on a table. To clean up these indexes, the Information Store assigns an expiry time to them. If the index is not used within this expiry time, typically it is no longer required. During the online maintenance process, these expiry times are compared to the current time and the index is deleted if it has expired. By default, Exchange Server 2003 removes indexes that are older than 40 days.

Tombstone Cleanup

Each mailbox has a folder structure that contains the various mailbox items and provides a way of organizing these different items. This folder structure is created automatically as part of the creation of each mailbox. When a message is deleted within a folder, the message is deactivated and marked for deletion from the Exchange store and a **tombstone** is created for the message. This tombstone, or marker, is then propagated to all other stores in the organization where the local copy of the object is tombstoned, or marked for deletion. By default, the tombstone for each object is set to 60 days. This setting ensures that deletions for the objects have replicated across all the stores, so that the object is deleted off each server that has a replicated copy. During the Information Store maintenance cycle, each tombstone is examined to determine if it has exceeded the 60 days that was set for it. If the tombstone has expired, the object is permanently deleted from the store by the maintenance cycle.

Deleted Item Retention Cleanup

When messages are deleted, they are placed in deleted item retention. As part of the nightly maintenance process, the deleted item retention for every user is examined to determine if any of the messages that are contained within the dumpster, or deleted item retention store, have exceeded the deleted item retention period set on the store. If so, the object is permanently deleted and cleaned out of the dumpster.

Public Folder Expiry

As part of nightly maintenance, Exchange Server 2003 goes through each message within the public folders to determine if it has expired according to values set through the Limits tab on the public Information Store container. If so, the message is removed from the public folder store.

Activity 13-8: Setting the Age Limit on Public Information Stores

Time Required: 5 to 10 minutes

Objective: Configure the age limit for public folders on the public folder store.

Description: Age limits are used to control the amount of information that users can post to public folders. Users who exceed the designated limits receive warning messages and are subject to restrictions, such as the inability to post messages. To configure the age limit on public folders, complete the following steps:

1. From the Windows desktop of the back-end server, click **Start**, point to **All Programs**, point to **Microsoft Exchange**, and then click **System Manager**.

2. Click the **plus sign (+)** next to Administrative Groups, click the **plus sign (+)** next to First Administrative Group, click the **plus sign (+)** next to Servers, and then click the **plus sign (+)** next to SERVERXX, where XX is the number assigned to the back-end server.

3. Click the **plus sign (+)** next to First Storage Group, and then right-click **Public Folder Store (SERVERXX)**, where XX is the number assigned to the back-end server. On the shortcut menu, click **Properties**. The Public Folder Store (SERVERXX) Properties dialog box opens.

4. Click the **Limits** tab. The Limits tab is displayed, as shown in Figure 13-10.

5. Click the **Age limit for all folders in this store (days)** check box, and then type **90** in the corresponding text box.

6. Click **OK** to set this limit and return to Exchange System Manager.

7. Close **Exchange System Manager**.

Folder Tombstoning

When public folders are deleted, the same process occurs as with any other object. A tombstone object is created for the public folder and it is replicated throughout the organization. By default, the tombstone for each public folder is set to 180 days. During the Information Store maintenance cycle, each tombstone is examined to determine if it has expired. If so, the public folder is permanently deleted from the store.

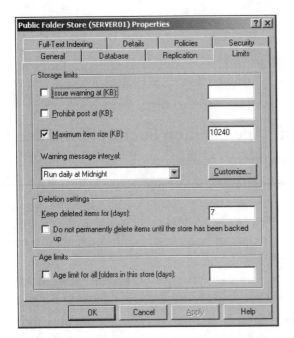

Figure 13-10 Public Folder Store (SERVERXX) Limits tab

Conflict Aging

When an item is modified on a public folder by two individuals, it is possible for a conflict to occur. That is, one user can overwrite the change made by another user, because both users modified and saved the same message in a public folder at the same time. This is an undesirable situation, but does occur on occasion. During nightly maintenance, Exchange Server 2003 determines if the conflict has been resolved by the participants in question. If not, this process determines if the conflict age limit has been exceeded. If so, it takes action to help resolve the conflict on the users' behalf. This is known as **conflict aging**.

Site Folder Check and Version Information Update

Every public folder database that contains a replica of the system configuration folder and system folders for the administrative group is checked to ensure that duplicate system folders do not exist and that the version information is up to date. If duplicate folders exist, they are removed from the administrative group. If the version information is out of date, it is updated with the latest information.

Mailbox Cleanup

When accounts are deleted from Active Directory, the mailbox is not deleted immediately. Rather, the mailbox still resides in the Information Store for another 30 days. This is done to provide administrators with the opportunity to re-create the user account within Active Directory and then attach the Exchange Server 2003 mailbox. This is valid for situations in which an employee might leave a company and then return within the 30-day window. The nightly maintenance activities look for mailboxes whose associated Active Directory accounts have been deleted and have exceeded the 30-day retention period. If any are found, these mailboxes are deleted from the Information Store.

Message Table Check

To ensure that folder information maintained within the database is consistent with message information within the database, nightly maintenance checks the reference count for each message and determines if it is zero. If the reference count is zero, this indicates that the message currently is not referenced by any folder and as such will never be displayed. If any such message is encountered, it is deleted as the Information Store has no way of knowing to which folder the message belongs.

Online Defragmentation

The final, and perhaps most important, task of nightly maintenance is the online defragmentation process. This task is performed when at least one of the previous maintenance tasks was able to complete within the defined maintenance schedule. When started, the Information Store service performs a full pass over the database to free up pages by compacting records into the fewest number of pages possible. Database objects that are no longer being used are deleted and mailbox store and public folder store data are reorganized so as to make more efficient use of the available storage space. This reorganization, in turn, helps to reduce the amount of I/O that is required to store and retrieve information from the database.

If the online defragmentation process does not complete before the maintenance window ends, it is suspended. Then, when the next online defragmentation maintenance window opens, the process continues where it left off. This ensures that the defragmentation process, which is very I/O-intensive, does not continue during working hours and cause sluggishness or other performance problems.

MAINTENANCE UTILITIES

In most cases, nightly maintenance is enough to keep your server running smoothly. However, there may be occasions when you might want to perform additional preventive maintenance tasks. In this case, some utilities are provided by Microsoft to assist with these tasks. Some of the more important tools include the following:

- ESEUTIL
- ISINTEG
- RPC Ping
- MTA Check utility

The following sections outline the use of each of these utilities.

13

ESEUTIL

The **ESEUTIL** utility is used to perform maintenance and repair operations on Exchange Server 2003 Information Stores. This utility comes with a number of options for performing maintenance tasks against a database and for viewing information about the database. This section looks at some of the more useful and common options that will assist you with maintaining your databases and salvaging the data within it. The options that are explored in this section include performing an integrity check, performing an offline defragmentation, and the options available for repairing a database.

Before you perform any operations with ESEUTIL, it is recommended that you try to restore your database from a verified backup. This is the first step you should perform prior to using any of the ESEUTIL features. If this is unsuccessful, you should then make a copy of the database on which you will be performing operations. This allows you to at least have the original database to work with if something goes wrong with the ESEUTIL utility. It never hurts to have a whole range of options if something goes wrong. After you have made a copy of your database, run the ESEUTIL utility with the integrity checker option to determine the extent of any issues with your database. The integrity checker option examines the database signatures, examines the signatures on each page, and ensures that the .edb file has an associated .stm file. Ideally, after running ESEUTIL with the integrity checker option, it should return no errors. However, if it does identify issues with your database, it is still useful to know what the extent of the issues are and the likelihood of a successful repair operation using the ESEUTIL utility.

ACTIVITY

Activity 13-9: Using ESEUTIL to Check the Integrity of Your Database

Time Required: 10 to 20 minutes

Objective: Run the ESEUTIL utility to check the integrity of mailbox store on your server.

Description: In this activity, you check the integrity of the Mailbox Store (SERVERXX), where XX is the number assigned to the back-end server, by running the ESEUTIL utility. When checking the integrity of the database, ESEUTIL does not make any changes, rather it checks the database tables, rebuilds all indexes on a temporary database (TEMPTINTEG. edb), and compares the indexes to the original.

1. From the Windows desktop of the back-end server, click **Start**, point to **All Programs**, point to **Microsoft Exchange**, and then click **System Manager**.

2. Click the **plus sign (+)** next to Administrative Groups, click the **plus sign (+)** next to First Administrative Group, click the **plus sign (+)** next to Servers, and then click the **plus sign (+)** next to SERVERXX, where XX is the number assigned to the back-end server.

3. Click the **plus sign (+)** next to First Storage Group, and then right-click **Mailbox Store (SERVERXX)**, where XX is the number assigned to the back-end server. On the shortcut menu, click **Dismount Store**. This dismounts the database in preparation for the run of an integrity check.

4. A warning message box indicating that dismounting the store will make it inaccessible to users appears. Click **Yes** to continue.

5. Minimize **Exchange System Manager**.

6. Click **Start** and then click **Command Prompt**. The command prompt window opens.

7. Type **cd \Program Files\Exchsrvr\bin** in the command prompt window. Press **Enter** when finished.

8. Type **eseutil /g "c:\Program Files\Exchsrvr\mdbdata\priv1.edb"** (including the quotes), and then press **Enter**.

9. When the utility completes, you are either notified of the success, as shown in Figure 13-11, or you are presented with a list of issues that the utility has uncovered.

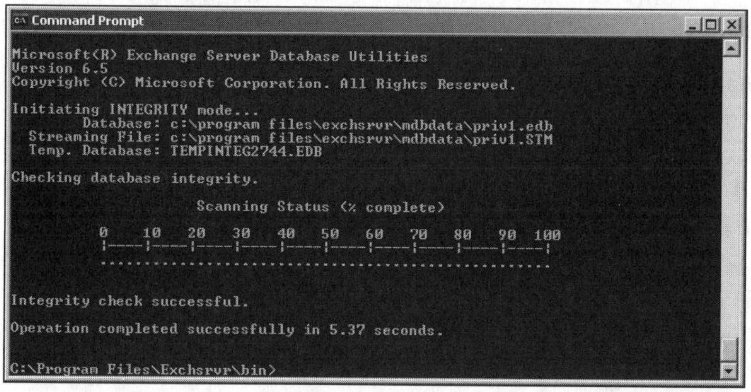

```
Command Prompt                                              _ □ X

Microsoft(R) Exchange Server Database Utilities
Version 6.5
Copyright (C) Microsoft Corporation. All Rights Reserved.

Initiating INTEGRITY mode...
         Database: c:\program files\exchsrvr\mdbdata\priv1.edb
   Streaming File: c:\program files\exchsrvr\mdbdata\priv1.STM
   Temp. Database: TEMPINTEG2744.EDB

Checking database integrity.

                Scanning Status (% complete)

     0    10   20   30   40   50   60   70   80   90   100
     !----!----!----!----!----!----!----!----!----!----!
     ..................................................

Integrity check successful.

Operation completed successfully in 5.37 seconds.

C:\Program Files\Exchsrvr\bin>
```

Figure 13-11   ESEUTIL utility integrity check results

10. Close the **command prompt** window.

11. Click the **Exchange System Manager** button on the taskbar. Within Exchange System Manager, right-click **Mailbox Store (SERVERXX)**, where XX is the number assigned to the back-end server. On the shortcut menu, click **Mount Store** to remount the database.

12. When the operation is complete, you are presented with a message box indicating that it was successfully mounted. Click **OK**.

13. Close **Exchange System Manager**.

The public folder store and the mailbox store on an Exchange server begin as empty database files. As information is stored within these databases, they begin to grow. Unfortunately, the reverse is not the case. As information is deleted from the databases, the databases do not shrink. Rather, the emptied space is simply marked as available for use during routine garbage collection performed during the nightly maintenance activity. When new information is written to the database, it is written into any available free space within the database before the database is enlarged to hold additional information. This method of using free space before the database is enlarged can result in single items actually being broken up and stored in several physical places within the database, a process known as **fragmentation**.

As noted previously, during the nightly maintenance tasks that are performed on the Information Store, Exchange Server 2003 defragments the databases and also checks for database inconsistencies. These inconsistency checks are also performed by Exchange Server 2003 every time the server is shut down and started. Because of this routine maintenance, fragmentation and inconsistency within the database is not much of a problem on an Exchange 2003 server. However, online defragmentation routines do nothing about the size of the databases themselves. To compact the databases, you must turn to an offline utility. Exchange's ESEUTIL utility can also perform database defragmentation while the Information Store service is stopped.

Offline defragmentation can be useful in situations in which you move many mailboxes off an Information Store or you archive a large number of attachments to a Hierarchical Storage Management solution and want to reclaim the disk space freed up within the database. If you are simply reclaiming the free disk space that gets created on a day-to-day basis because of regular deletions from the store, it is something that should be addressed on a case-by-case basis. Typically, shrinking a database that is used in a typical day-to-day environment is pointless if the database will just grow back to its original size.

ACTIVITY

Activity 13-10: Using ESEUTIL to Perform an Offline Defragmentation

Time Required: 10 to 20 minutes

Objective: Perform an offline defragmentation of the mailbox store on your server.

Description: In this activity, you perform an offline defragmentation of the mailbox database on your Exchange 2003 server. ESEUTIL defragments the database by moving the used pages in the database into contiguous blocks in a new database. Unused pages are discarded, which is the only way to recover empty space inside the database for other uses. By default, ESEUTIL writes the contents of the database file to a temporary file, tempdfrg. edb. When this process is complete, the temporary database becomes the new database and replaces the original database. After this new database is created, a new signature is written to the database. As a result, previous transaction logs can no longer be played into the database nor can transactions created after the defragmentation process has been run be played into the old database.

1. From the Windows desktop on the back-end server, click **Start**, point to **Administrative Tools**, and then click **Services**.

2. Scroll down the list of services, and then right-click **Microsoft Exchange Information Store**. On the shortcut menu, click **Stop**. This stops the databases and places them in an offline state in preparation for recovery and repair.

3. Minimize the **Services** window.

4. Click **Start** and then click **Command Prompt**. The command prompt window opens.

5. Type **cd \Program Files\Exchsrvr\bin** in the command prompt window, and then press **Enter**.

6. Type **eseutil /d "c:\Program Files\Exchsrvr\mdbdata\priv1.edb"** (including the quotes), and then press **Enter**. When the operation completes, you are presented with a message indicating success, as shown in Figure 13-12.

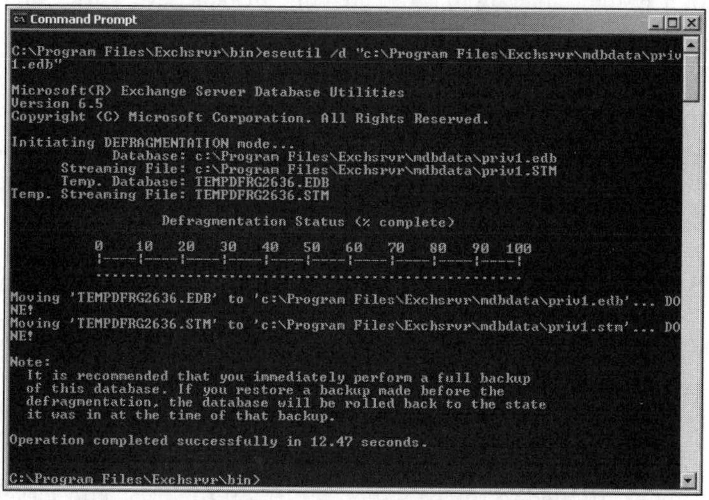

Figure 13-12   ESEUTIL utility defragmentation results

7. Type **eseutil /r "c:\Program Files\Exchsrvr\mdbdata\priv1.edb"** (including the quotes), and then press **Enter** when finished.

8. Close the **command prompt** window.

9. Click the **Services** button on the taskbar, and then right-click **Microsoft Exchange Information Store**. Click **Start** on the shortcut menu. This starts the Information Store service.

10. Close the **Services** window.

Although ESEUTIL is useful for recovering disk space, it is rare to perform such an operation. ESEUTIL really helps in situations in which the database is corrupt and you don't have a valid backup. In this situation, you can make use of recovery and repair modes that ESEUTIL provides to help restore a database.

Recovery mode works by applying records within transaction stores against the database—similar to what occurs when your Information Store starts. This helps to ensure that the database has all the transactions committed to the database and that ESEUTIL is working with all the data, including those transactions that were processed but not yet committed to the database. This should always be run prior to performing the other modes.

You use repair mode to try to resurrect your database. Repair mode goes through the database and checks and repairs critical structures inside the database, such as system tables, attachment tables, and so on, and checks for damaged pages in the database. If a damaged, or corrupt, page is encountered, ESEUTIL repairs the page by truncating or modifying it, and, as such, it is possible that there might be data loss after the repair is finished. This data might be part of an e-mail message, a calendar appointment, a note, an attachment, or, in the worst case, part of a system table.

If the data is part of a system table, such as the attachment table, every user on the server might lose the attachments to their messages. This is only one possible scenario. If the data is part of another system table, the damage can be just as severe.

In repair mode, the ESEUTIL utility fixes individual tables and the pages within them. However, it does nothing to maintain the relationships between the tables. As you will see, these types of issues are resolved using the ISINTEG utility. For now though, you explore the use of the ESEUTIL utility to repair a database in the following activity.

ACTIVITY

Activity 13-11: Using ESEUTIL to Recover and Repair a Database

Time Required: 10 to 20 minutes

Objective: Perform a recovery and repair of a mailbox store on your server using ESEUTIL.

Description: In this activity, you perform a repair of the Mailbox Store (SERVERXX), where XX is the number assigned to the back-end server, on the back-end server. Prior to repairing a database, it is highly recommended that you perform a recovery operation before attempting any repairs. This is to ensure that all transactions have been committed to the database prior to running the repair. Without performing a recovery operation, there is a good possibility that you can lose information within your database. To perform a recovery and repair operation, complete the following steps:

1. From the Windows desktop, click **Start**, point to **Administrative Tools**, and then click **Services**.

2. Scroll down the list of services, and then right-click **Microsoft Exchange Information Store**. On the shortcut menu, click **Stop**. This stops the databases and places them in an offline state in preparation for recovery and repair.

3. Minimize the **Services** window.

4. Click **Start** and then click **Command Prompt**. The command prompt window opens.

5. Type **cd \Program Files\Exchsrvr\bin** in the command prompt window, and then press **Enter**.

6. Type **eseutil /r E00 /s "c:\Program Files\Exchsrvr\mdbdata" /l "c:\Program Files\Exchsrvr\mdbdata" /d "c:\Program Files\ Exchsrvr\mdbdata"** (including the quotes), and then press **Enter**. The switch /s is used to indicated the location of the system files, and the switch /l is used to indicate the location of the log files. When the operation completes, you are presented with a message indicating success, as shown in Figure 13-13.

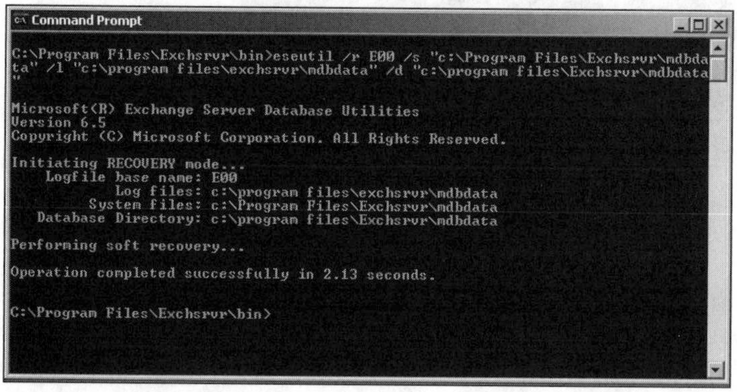

Figure 13-13   ESEUTIL utility recovery results

7. Type **eseutil /p "c:\Program Files\Exchsrvr\mdbdata\priv1.edb"** (including the quotes), and then press **Enter**.

8. You are prompted with a warning box indicating that you should only run repair on damaged or corrupted databases and that information in the transaction log files will not be applied to the database and could be lost. Click **OK** to continue. When the database repair operation completes, you are presented with a success message, as shown in Figure 13-14.

9. Close the **command prompt** window.

10. Click the **Services** button on the taskbar.

11. In the Services window, right-click **Microsoft Exchange Information Store**, and then click **Start** on the shortcut menu. This starts the Information Store service.

12. Close the **Services** window.

ISINTEG

As mentioned in the preceding section, the ESEUTIL utility does nothing to resolve issues with relationships between tables. This is the responsibility of the **Information Store Integrity Checker (ISINTEG)** utility. For example, if the ESEUTIL utility is run and

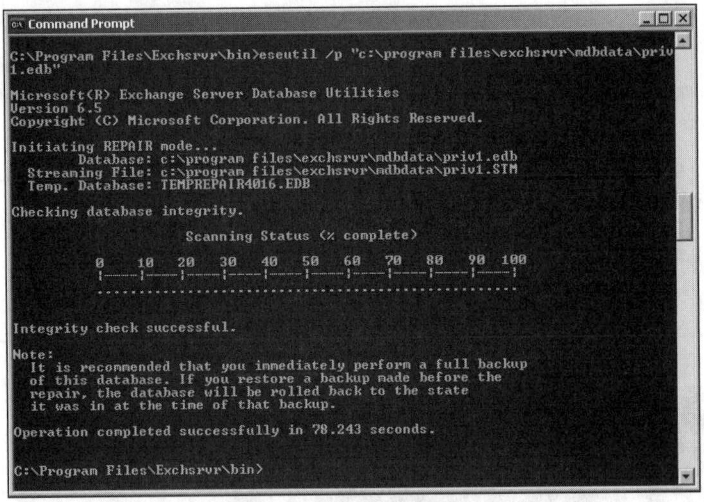

Figure 13-14 ESEUTIL utility repair results

discards some unreadable messages in the Msgs table (which contains all the messages for each mailbox contained on the database), a folder in your mailbox may end up with references to those deleted messages. To resolve this issue, you use the ISINTEG utility in conjunction with the ESEUTIL utility. The ISINTEG utility maintains relationships between the tables, and in this scenario, removes any references to a message if the message information was deleted.

The ISINTEG utility finds and eliminates common errors from the Microsoft Exchange Server public and private Information Store databases and has two modes of operation: a check mode and a check and fix mode.

In check mode, ISINTEG searches the Information Store databases for table errors, incorrect reference counts, and unreferenced objects. It performs various tests for logical errors. It verifies the integrity of information in the database, not of the database itself—that is the job of ESEUTIL. It does this by cross-checking information within the different tables in the store looking for table errors, incorrect reference counts, and orphaned objects—none of which should exist in a consistent database. Table 13-1 outlines the tests and the categories into which these tests fall.

Table 13-1 Categories of ISINTEG tests

Category	Specific Tests
Folder/message tests	folder, message, aclitem, delfld, acllist, timedev, rowcounts, attach, morefld, global, searchq, dlvrto, search, dumpster-props, namedprop
Private IS only	rcvfld, mailbox, oofhist
Public IS only	peruser, artidx, newsfeed

Table 13-1   Categories of ISINTEG tests (continued)

Category	Specific Tests
Reference count tests	msfsoftref, attachref, acllistref, aclitemref, newsfeedref, fldrcv, fldsub, dumpsterref
Group tests	allfoldertests, allacltests
Special tests	deleteextracolumns

In check mode, the ISINTEG utility only reports on the errors that are encountered; it does nothing to repair them—this is the responsibility of the check and fix mode.

ACTIVITY

Activity 13-12: Using ISINTEG to Check on the Integrity of a Database

Time Required: 10 to 20 minutes

Objective: Check the integrity of a mailbox store on the server using ISINTEG.

Description: In this activity, you perform an integrity check of the Mailbox Store (SERVERXX), where XX is the number assigned to the back-end server. If you were to make use of the ESEUTIL utility to recover and repair your database, it is highly recommended that you also make use of the ISINTEG utility to perform a fix of the database. This is because the ESEUTIL utility only checks the physical well-being of the database. It does nothing to check the integrity of the relationships or information within the database.

1. From the Windows desktop of the back-end server, click **Start**, point to **All Programs**, point to **Microsoft Exchange**, and then click **System Manager**.

2. Click the **plus sign (+)** next to Administrative Groups, click the **plus sign (+)** next to First Administrative Group, click the **plus sign (+)** next to Servers, and then click the **plus sign (+)** next to SERVERXX, where XX is the number assigned to the back-end server.

3. Click the **plus sign (+)** next to First Storage Group, and then right-click **Mailbox Store (SERVERXX)**, where XX is the student number assigned to your back-end server. On the shortcut menu, click **Dismount Store**. This dismounts the database in preparation for an integrity check being run.

4. You are provided with a warning message box indicating that dismounting the store will make it inaccessible to users. Click **Yes** to continue.

5. Minimize the **Exchange System Manager**.

6. Click **Start** and then click **Command Prompt**. The command prompt window opens.

7. Type **cd \Program Files\Exchsrvr\bin** in the command prompt window, and then press **Enter**.

8. Type **isinteg –s SERVERXX –fix –test allfoldertests**, where XX is the number assigned to the back-end server. Press **Enter** when finished.

13

9. ISINTEG can only check databases that are offline. When prompted, type **2**, and then press **Enter** to initiate a check on the Mailbox Store (SERVERXX), where XX is the number assigned to the back-end server.

NOTE   If your Mailbox Store (SERVERXX) does not correspond with number 2, type the appropriate number.

10. Type **Y** and then press **Enter** to confirm your database selection.

11. When the operation completes, close the **command prompt** window.

12. Click the **Exchange System Manager** button on the taskbar, and then right-click **Mailbox Store (SERVERXX)**, where XX is the number assigned to the back-end server. Click **Mount Store** on the shortcut menu.

13. Click **OK** when the store is successfully mounted.

14. Close **Exchange System Manager**.

RPC Ping

Many of the connections among computers in an Exchange organization rely on **RPCs (remote procedure calls)**. An RPC allows a program on one computer to execute a program on another computer. Exchange servers in a routing group rely on RPCs to communicate with one another. For example, when an Exchange Server MTA needs to open an RPC link with a remote Exchange Server MTA, it does the following:

1. Perform TCP handshaking to establish a TCP connection with the remote server.

2. Establish an RPC connection with the remote server's endpoint mapper (the service that manages the mappings between RPC services and ports).

3. Request (from the remote server) the port number on which the remote server's MTA is listening.

4. Perform a two-way handshake with the remote server to establish a bidirectional conversation between the two MTAs. (The handshake is called "two-way" because the calling server must verify the name and password of the remote server and the remote server must verify the name and password of the calling server.)

Similarly, Exchange clients connect to Exchange servers by using RPCs. When a user starts Exchange System Manager on a client workstation, the client connects to remote Exchange servers via RPCs in a similar manner as two MTAs connecting to each other. Often, connectivity problems in an Exchange organization are the result of bad RPC connectivity.

You can use the **RPC Ping** utility to confirm the RPC connectivity between two systems as well as to make sure that Exchange services are responding to requests from clients and other servers. RPC Ping has two components: a server component and a client component.

The server component of RPC Ping is a file named rpings.exe, which you must start on the server before using the client component. By default, RPC can make use of a number of underlying transport protocols, depending on the ones that have been configured on your server. The following protocols are tested by default if they are available:

- IPX/SPX
- Named Pipes
- NetBIOS
- TCP/IP
- VINES

You can restrict the server component to only using a single protocol sequence, instead of them all, if you are sure of the protocol that will be used.

After the server component has been launched, you use the RPC Ping client, on another computer, to test RPC connectivity. Table 13-2 lists the options that can be specified.

Table 13-2   RPC Ping client options

Option	Description
Exchange server	Specifies the NetBIOS name or IP address of the server running the RPC Ping server.
Protocol sequence	Specifies the RPC mechanism that will be used in the test. Options include Any (all protocol sequences are tested), Named Pipes, IPX/SPX, TCP/IP, NetBIOS, and VINES. Set the protocol that is being used to the protocol setting on the RPC server.
Endpoint	Specifies protocol-specific ports that the RPC client uses to communicate with the server. Choose RPing to collect information about RPC Ping client to server communication itself. You can choose Store to simulate communications with the Information Store service on the Exchange server, and choose Admin to simulate communications with the Exchange server.
Number of pings	Specifies whether to ping the server continuously or a certain number of times. This option is available only if you choose Ping Only mode.
Mode	Specifies the mode. Ping Only means that the ping is returned directly by the RPC Ping server. Endpoint Search returns Pings from detected endpoints.
Run with security	Verifies authenticated RPCs.

If the RPC Ping from the client is successful with a particular protocol, you need to move that protocol to first in the binding order so that the client system will not have any problems connecting to the Exchange server. If the RPC Ping is not successful, you might want to use a packet analyzer such as Network Monitor in Windows 2000/2003 to further analyze the packets and RPC traffic.

Activity 13-13: Using RPC Ping to Test Connectivity

Time Required: 10 to 20 minutes

Objective: Test RPC connectivity with the Exchange 2003 server using RPC Ping.

Description: In this activity, you make use of the RPC Ping utility to test RPC connectivity between a client workstation and an Exchange 2003 server. The RPC Ping utility is part of the Windows 2003 Resource Kit Tools. As such, you first need to download and install this kit on both the client and server. For the purpose of this activity, the front-end server acts as the client machine. Complete the following steps to test RPC connectivity between your client workstation and the Exchange 2003 server.

1. From the Windows desktop of the back-end server, click **Start**, point to **All Programs**, and then click **Internet Explorer**. Internet Explorer opens.

2. In the Address Bar, type **http://www.microsoft.com/windowsserver2003**, and then click the **Go** button to navigate to the Microsoft Windows Server 2003 Home page.

3. Point to **Downloads** in the navigation bar on the left side of the page, and then click the **Tools** link. On the Windows Server 2003 Tools page, scroll down and click the **Windows Server 2003 Resource Kit Tools** link.

4. On the Windows Server 2003 Resource Kit Tools page, click the **Download** button on the right side. In the File Download dialog box, click **Open**. If a Security Warning appears, click **Yes** to continue.

5. The Windows Resource Kit Tools Setup Wizard starts. At the Welcome to the Windows Resource Kit Tools Setup Wizard, click **Next** to continue.

6. At the End-User License Agreement screen, click the **I Agree** option button, and then click **Next** to continue.

7. At the User Information screen, accept the default information by clicking **Next** to continue.

8. At the Destination Directory screen, click **Install Now**.

9. When the installation is complete, click **Finish**, and then close **Internet Explorer**.

10. Repeat Steps 1 to 9 on the front-end server.

11. On the back-end server, click **Start**, and then click **Command Prompt**. The command prompt window opens.

12. Type **cd \Program Files\Windows Resource Kits\Tools** in the command prompt window, and then press **Enter**.

13. Type **rpings** and then press **Enter**. The RPC Ping server component of the RPC Ping test starts, as shown in Figure 13-15.

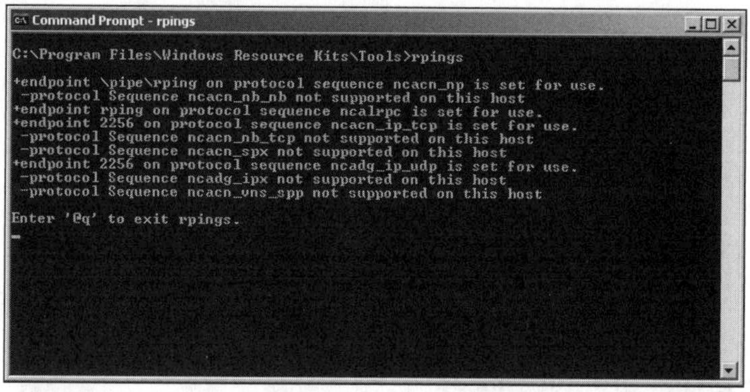

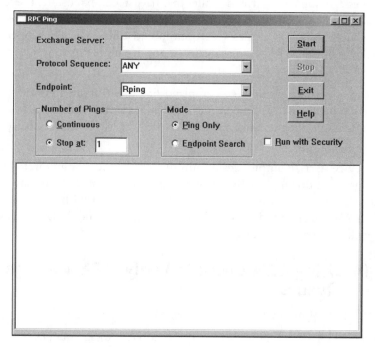

Figure 13-15   RPC Ping server-side component

14. Leave the command prompt open and switch to the front-end server. On the front-end server, click **Start**, and then click **Run**. The Run dialog box opens. Type **"c:\Program Files\Windows Resource Kits\Tools\rpingc"** (including the quotes) in the Open text box, and then click **OK**. The RPC Ping client-side component interface opens, as shown in Figure 13-16.

13

Figure 13-16   RPC Ping client-side component

15. In the Exchange Server text box, type **SERVERXX**, where XX is the number of the back-end server. Click the **Continuous** option button, and then click the **Start** button. The client (front-end server) begins to ping the server (back-end server) continuously.

16. After a few seconds, click the **Stop** button to stop the RPC Ping client-side component.

17. Click the **Exit** button to close the RPC Ping client-side component window.

18. Switch to the back-end server. In the command prompt window, type **@q** to stop the server-side component.

19. Close the **command prompt** window.

MTA Check

The MTA (Message Transfer Agent) was responsible for the transfer of all messages outside Exchange Server 5.5. Now, the MTA's use is limited to handling message transfer for the X.400 connector. The MTA maintains a separate message queue for each X.400 connector to which it routes messages.

All of the MTA's message queues are stored in files that have a .dat extension. These files are located in the \Exchsrvr\Mtadata directory on the Exchange 2003 server. These files can become corrupted, just like any other files. Corruption of .dat files typically happens during an improper shutdown of the MTA, such as during a power failure. It can result in message delivery problems and MTA startup problems.

The **MTA Check** utility (mtacheck.exe) is a command-line tool that attempts to fix all MTA message queues and the messages that those queues contain. It automatically discards all corrupt messages from the queues, backing up those messages in the \Exchsrvr\Mtadata\Mtacheck.out directory.

When the MTA service starts, it automatically runs the MTA Check utility if it determines that the MTA was not shut down properly. During an automatic check, events are logged to the Windows 2000/2003 application log, and an MTACHECK.LOG file is created in the \Exchsrvr\Mtadata\Mtacheck.out directory. You can also run the MTA Check utility manually by using the mtacheck command.

ACTIVITY

Activity 13-14: Using MTA Check to Verify MTA Message Queues

Time Required: 10 to 20 minutes

Objective: Use the MTA Check utility to verify the MTA message queues.

Description: In this activity, you make use of the MTA Check utility to verify the MTA database, clean up messages, and repair the MTA database, if necessary. To use MTA Check, you first download it from the Microsoft Web site. Complete the following steps to verify the MTA message queue database:

1. From the Windows desktop of the back-end server, click **Start**, point to **All Programs**, and then click **Internet Explorer**. Internet Explorer opens.

2. In the Address Bar, type **http://www.microsoft.com/exchange/**, and then click the **Go** button to navigate to the Microsoft Exchange Server Home page.

3. Click the **Downloads** link in the navigation bar on the left side of the page. On the Downloads for Exchange 2003 page, scroll down to the MTA Check (English Only) link under Tools. Click the **MTA Check (English Only)** link.

4. On the Exchange Server MTA Check page, click the **Download** button on the right side. In the File Download dialog box, click **Open**. If a Security Warning appears, click **Yes** to continue.

5. In the Choose Directory For Extracted Files dialog box, click **Ok**. When the extraction is complete, click **OK**, and then close **Internet Explorer**.

6. To run the MTA Check utility, you need to copy the Mtacheck.exe file to the C:\Program Files\Exchsrvr\bin directory. To do this, double-click the **MtaCheck** folder on the desktop. Right-click **Mtacheck.exe**, and then click **Copy** on the shortcut menu. Click the **Up** button on the toolbar. Double-click **My Computer**, double-click **Local Disk (C:)**, double-click **Program Files**, double-click **Exchsrvr**, and then double-click **bin**. In the bin directory, click **Edit** on the menu bar, and then click **Paste**. Close the **C:\Program Files\Exchsrvr\bin** window.

7. Click **Start**, point to **Administrative Tools**, and then click **Services**. The Services window opens.

8. Scroll down the list of services, and then right-click **Microsoft Exchange MTA Stacks**. Click **Stop** on the shortcut menu. You must stop the MTA Service prior to running the MTA Check utility.

9. Minimize the **Services** window.

10. Click **Start** and then click **Command Prompt**. The command prompt window opens.

11. Type **cd \Program Files\Exchsrvr\bin** in the command prompt window, and then press **Enter**.

12. Type **mtacheck /v** and then press **Enter**. The verification of the MTA queues starts. When the check is complete, your results will look similar to Figure 13-17.

13. Close the **command prompt** window.

14. Click the **Services** button on the taskbar, and then right-click **Microsoft Exchange MTA Stacks**. Click **Start** on the shortcut menu. The MTA service restarts.

15. Close the **Services** window.

13

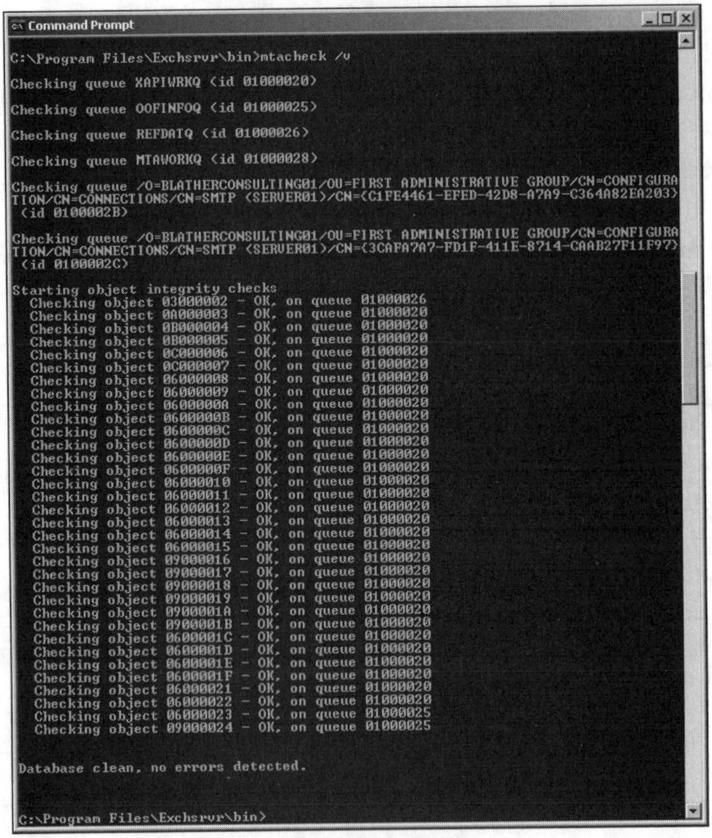

Figure 13-17 MTA Check integrity check results

RESOLVING SERVER ISSUES

Even with monitoring tools to help you identify issues early on and tools to assist with preventing issues before they arise, you can still run into problems. Typically, problematic issues arise out of new installations or migrations; after the infrastructure has become stable, such issues tend to subside and administrators can tend to other day-to-day activities. However, until such time, you will likely have to deal with a whole range of problems that may arise. This section looks at some of the areas that may require troubleshooting and presents strategies for investigating them.

When troubleshooting problems, you should always take a top-down approach to your investigation and use the tools provided to help diagnose the issue. At first, you may not have a complete understanding of the problem and may be struggling to determine exactly where the problem is. For most problems, the key to finding a solution is to learn as much as you can about the problem. Combining this with the knowledge you have about how the e-mail infrastructure should operate—and how it should interact with the underlying directory environment and with other external e-mail systems—goes a long way in helping you to resolve problems within your environment.

The following provides a set of guidelines you can follow when investigating issues to help you learn more about the problem:

1. Is the issue client related, or does it appear to be server related?

2. Are clients experiencing sluggish performance, or have they stopped responding?

3. Can the problem be duplicated, or is it random? What is the frequency of the problem?

4. Do all clients experience the problem, or is it confined to an individual or select set of individuals? What is common about the problem?

5. Review event logs. Look at the system log for general service problems, and look at the application log for Exchange-specific problems. If there are problems with the infrastructure, the software running on that infrastructure will, ideally, notify you that it is having problems. Investigate the logs to look for clues to these problems.

6. Investigate the queues. Determine if mail is backing up anywhere within the e-mail infrastructure. This can be an indicator of whether the problem is related to a connector, remote host connectivity, DNS resolution issues, and so on.

7. Monitor performance counters. If your system looks sluggish or you are receiving complaints of slowness, examining the performance counters, and specifically the Exchange-related performance counters, can provide insight into the problems.

8. Check that DNS is configured properly. The majority of Exchange Server 2003 directory access problems are caused by DNS and name resolution problems. You should investigate DNS if you suspect a directory access issue. Symptoms of DNS trouble include failures in starting Exchange Server 2003 services and setup failures.

9. Verify the configuration of Active Directory and the correct operation of the domains and the Active Directory servers within it. For instance, if Exchange Server 2003 cannot determine which site it belongs to, directory access will fail. The most common problem occurs when the Active Directory administrator renames the "Default-First-Site-Name" and forgets to create subnets. Determine if you can access domain controllers within your domain. If domain controllers are not accessible, Exchange Server 2003 cannot gain access to configuration information or information about recipients to whom messages are to be delivered. As such, this causes problems for your servers and the delivery of messages on your server or between servers.

10. Investigate permissions issues to determine if they are related to the problem at hand. Permissions issues tend to be the cause of a significant number of problems.

11. If you are troubleshooting front-end/back-end server configurations in which a firewall is involved, ensure that the firewall rules are configured properly so that the servers can communicate as expected.

13

Although these guidelines are very general in nature, they provide a basis to start investigating issues. When troubleshooting a problem, the trick is to try to narrow the scope of the problem. Understanding how to fix specific problems is useful only if you can match your specific problem to the corresponding solution. Unfortunately, there are usually no easy answers to problems unless they have been encountered before. If the problem is new, be prepared to do some investigating.

CHAPTER SUMMARY

- ❑ Service monitoring allows you to configure a utility that will monitor the up or down status of services on your computer. By default, a server monitor checks various Exchange Server 2003 services that affect the operation and performance of your server.

- ❑ Queue monitoring allows you to configure a utility that will monitor the queue growth over time. When you configure queue monitoring, you can specify the number of minutes of continual queue growth that will cause the server to enter a warning or critical state.

- ❑ CPU monitoring allows you to configure a utility that will monitor the CPU utilization on your system. Using CPU monitoring, you can specify how long the CPU can run above a certain utilization level before the server's state changes to Warning or Critical.

- ❑ Disk monitoring allows you to configure a utility that will monitor the disk utilization on your system. Using disk monitoring, you can specify the threshold that your free disk space can fall below before the server's state changes to Warning or Critical.

- ❑ Virtual memory monitoring allows you to configure a utility that will monitor the memory usage on your server. Using virtual memory monitoring, you can configure memory thresholds so that, if your server falls below a specific threshold, the monitor changes the state of the server to Warning or Critical.

- ❑ Nightly Information Store maintenance performs routine tasks on the Information Store to ensure the store is consistent and without error. It also performs cleanup of various objects within the database to make sure that the database does not contain extraneous information that is no longer required.

- ❑ The ESEUTIL utility is used to perform operations on Exchange Server 2003 Information Stores. It is used to check that the database is syntactically correct. It does nothing to verify that the data contained within the database is contextually correct.

- ❑ The ISINTEG utility is used to perform operations on Exchange Server 2003 Information Stores. It is used to check that the information within a database is contextually correct and that the relationships between tables within the database are correct.

- ❑ The RPC Ping utility is used to confirm RPC connectivity between two systems, as well as to make sure that Exchange services are responding to requests from clients and other servers. RPC Ping has two components: a server component and a client component.

- The MTA Check utility is a command-line tool that attempts to fix all MTA message queues and the messages that those queues contain. It automatically discards all corrupt messages from the queues, but not before backing them up.

- When troubleshooting problems, you should always take a top-down approach to investigating an issue and use the tools provided to help diagnose the issue. The key to helping resolve any issue is to learn as much as you can about the problem and combine it with the knowledge you have about how your e-mail infrastructure should operate.

KEY TERMS

conflict aging — A process that identifies whether the issue of a public folder item modified by two different users has been resolved by the users themselves. If not, and the conflict age limit has been exceeded, the conflict is resolved by the system.

ESEUTIL — A utility used to perform maintenance and repair options—including defragmentation, integrity checking, and database repair—on Exchange Server 2003 Information Stores.

fragmentation — A state that occurs within a database when information is not written to the database contiguously. The inefficiency of writing and reading noncontiguous data to and from the disk increases disk I/O, resulting in lower performance.

Information Store Integrity Checker (ISINTEG) — A utility that finds and eliminates common errors from the Microsoft Exchange Server public and private Information Store databases.

link monitor — One of two types of monitors created by default during the Exchange Server 2003 installation. This monitor, also known as a connection status monitor, checks the status of a connector between servers to determine if it is available. A connection status monitor is created automatically for each connector on the server.

MTA Check — A command-line tool that attempts to fix all MTA message queues and the messages that those queues contain.

remote procedure call (RPC) — A protocol that allows a program on one computer to execute a program on another computer. This is based on the client/server model, in which the requesting program is considered the client and the executing program is considered the server. Exchange servers in a routing group rely on this protocol to communicate with one another. Similarly, Exchange clients rely on this protocol to connect to Exchange servers.

RPC Ping — A utility used to confirm the connectivity between two RPC systems.

server monitor — One of two types of monitors created by default during the Exchange Server 2003 installation. This monitor checks designated resources and Windows 2000/2003 services on a server to detect critical situations.

tombstone — A marker designating an Information Store item to be deleted in Exchange Server 2003. During the Information Store nightly maintenance cycle, these markers are examined, and if found to be past a default expiration date, the corresponding item is permanently deleted.

13

Review Questions

1. What are the types of resources that can be monitored using Exchange Server 2003 server monitors? (Choose all that apply.)

   a. Windows 2000/2003 services

   b. security auditing

   c. virtual memory

   d. event log notifications

2. What are the types of notifications that you can configure for server monitoring? (Choose all that apply.)

   a. script

   b. page

   c. event log

   d. e-mail

3. What types of queue monitors are available? (Choose all that apply.)

   a. MTA queue

   b. SMTP queue

   c. X.400 queue

   d. all of the above

4. When will an SMTP queue monitor send a notification for a warning or critical state?

   a. when the SMTP queue is detected as being down

   b. when the SMTP queue has breached a preset threshold

   c. when the SMTP queue breaches a threshold for a predetermined amount of time

   d. none of the above

5. When performing integrity checks using the ESEUTIL utility, you should always run the ISINTEG utility as well. True or False?

6. Which of the following is not performed by the nightly maintenance activities?

   a. folder tombstoning

   b. conflict aging

   c. offline defragmentation

   d. message table check

7. Offline defragmentation should be performed after which of the following scenarios?

   a. when the Information Store is backed up every evening

   b. when the database has been repaired using the ESEUTIL utility and the ISINTEG utility

    c. when SMTP queue thresholds have been exceeded

    d. after a migration of mailboxes from one server to another

8. What does the ISINTEG utility do?

    a. checks the physical consistency of the database

    b. checks the logical consistency of the database

    c. checks both the logical and physical consistency of the database

    d. none of the above

9. Which of the following is not a category of ISINTEG testing?

    a. reference count tests

    b. defragmentation tests

    c. folder/message tests

    d. public IS tests

    e. private IS tests

10. What are the protocols RPC Ping uses for communication if available? (Choose all that apply.)

    a. MAPI

    b. IPX/SPX

    c. TCP/IP

    d. VINES

    e. NETBIOS

13

11. Where are MTA queues located?

    a. within their own .edb database

    b. within .dat files located on your server

    c. within .que files located on your server

    d. within the IIS metabase

12. How does the ESEUTIL utility deal with damaged pages in a corrupt database when the repair option has been selected?

    a. It truncates or modifies the page.

    b. It bypasses the page.

    c. It moves the page to the bottom of the database and removes any references.

    d. It appends information to the page and writes it back to the database.

13. What are the modes under which ISINTEG runs? (Choose all that apply.)

    a. check mode

    b. fix mode

    c. check and fix mode

    d. optimize mode

14. Which of the following is not a service that is monitored by default in Exchange Server 2003?

    a. Microsoft Exchange Event service

    b. Microsoft Exchange MTA Stacks

    c. Microsoft Exchange Information Store

    d. Simple Mail Transport Protocol (SMTP)

15. What is the purpose of the ESEUTIL utility's recovery mode option?

    a. to check the integrity of the database

    b. to apply the current transaction logs against the database

    c. to recover the database before transaction logs are applied

    d. to recover the transaction logs prior to applying them to the database

16. By default, the ESEUTIL utility writes the contents of the database file to a temporary file and then replaces the existing database with the temporary database. True or False?

17. When repairing an Exchange Server 2003 database, the recovery option should be run before the repair option. True or False?

18. What does the ESEUTIL utility do?

    a. checks the physical consistency of the database

    b. checks the logical consistency of the database

    c. checks both the logical and physical consistency of the database

    d. none of the above

19. The ESEUTIL and ISINTEG utilities can be run on an Information Store when it is still mounted by the Information Store service. True or False?

CASE PROJECTS

CASE PROJECTS

Case Project 13-1: Choosing a Tool for Troubleshooting

You are the e-mail administrator for Blather Consulting Inc. and are responsible for maintaining and troubleshooting the Exchange 2003 servers in your company. You receive a help desk ticket identifying an issue with a client not being able to connect to an Exchange 2003 server. You investigate the problem and connect to the user's mailbox from another workstation in your environment. What other tools can you use to determine what the problem might be between the client and the server?

Case Project 13-2: Performing Preventive Maintenance on Your Information Stores

You are the technical specialist within your company responsible for implementing the technical procedures for projects involving e-mail. Your current project is tasked with implementing a new Exchange 2003 server and migrating mailboxes to it from another Exchange 2003 server as part of alleviating performance issues on the current server. What are the steps you would go through to complete the job?

Case Project 13-3: Troubleshooting Your Environment

You are receiving calls from account services indicating that some users are having issues when they try to address messages. When they click the To button in Outlook to bring up the Global Address List, it takes an extended period of time to come up. For some users, it does not come up at all. Furthermore, you are receiving complaints about messages not reaching their target destinations. What are the steps you could use to help troubleshoot the problem?

13

14

UPGRADING TO EXCHANGE SERVER 2003

> **After reading this chapter, you will be able to:**
> ♦ Upgrade Exchange 2000 Server to Exchange Server 2003
> ♦ Upgrade a cluster from Exchange 2000 Server to Exchange Server 2003
> ♦ Upgrade Exchange Server 5.5 within an Exchange organization
> ♦ Migrate Exchange Server 5.5 to a new Exchange organization

This chapter covers four different scenarios for upgrading to Exchange Server 2003. The first scenario, upgrading from Exchange 2000 Server, is for organizations that have already migrated from Exchange Server 5.5 to Exchange 2000 Server. Upgrading a cluster from Exchange 2000 Server is covered in the second scenario.

A large number of organizations still using Exchange Server 5.5 are upgrading to Exchange Server 2003. Exchange Server 5.5 cannot be upgraded directly to Exchange Server 2003, as Exchange 2000 Server can be. You first have to upgrade Exchange Server 5.5 to Exchange 2000 Server, and then upgrade the new Exchange 2000 Server to Exchange Server 2003. An easier upgrade method is to migrate your Exchange Server 5.5 information to a new Exchange 2003 server. This involves installing a new Exchange 2003 server into the current environment, either in the current organization or in a new organization, and then moving all of the Exchange Server 5.5 mailboxes over to the new Exchange 2003 server.

The strategy used to perform this type of upgrade varies depending on the size of the organization. Companies that want to keep the existing Exchange organization structure can migrate to Exchange Server 2003 within the same organization. This strategy is covered in the third scenario. Companies that want to create a new Exchange organization structure or consolidate multiple Exchange organizations can migrate Exchange Server 5.5 to a new Exchange organization. This strategy is covered in the fourth scenario.

UPGRADING EXCHANGE 2000 SERVER TO EXCHANGE SERVER 2003

Many organizations upgrade to Exchange Server 2003 because of new features, such as improved remote access. These features were discussed in Chapter 1, "Introduction to Exchange Server 2003." However, the upgrade can also be performed because of a decision to standardize servers to Windows Server 2003. Exchange 2000 Server cannot run on Windows Server 2003, so if an organization decides to upgrade all servers to Windows Server 2003, Exchange also has to be upgraded.

The upgrade from Exchange 2000 Server to Exchange Server 2003 is an easy one because both products share the same overall infrastructure and can coexist in the same Exchange organization without the complexity of connectors. However, some services that are available in Exchange 2000 Server are not available or supported in Exchange Server 2003. Before upgrading to Exchange Server 2003, the unsupported services must be removed. You can remove these services through the Exchange 2000 Server Setup Wizard. The services that must be removed are as follows:

- Key Management Service
- Exchange 2000 Conferencing Server
- Exchange Chat service
- Instant Messaging service
- cc: Mail connector
- MS Mail connector
- Microsoft Mobile Information Server

After unsupported services are removed, the upgrade process can begin. Except for front-end/back-end servers, the servers in an Exchange organization can be upgraded in any order. When upgrading front-end/back-end servers, the front-end servers must be upgraded first.

The Upgrade Process

After a server to upgrade has been selected, a full backup of the server should be made. Everything on the server should be backed up, not just Exchange 2000 Server. This backup is essential for disaster recovery if problems occur during the upgrade process. Problems are relatively rare, but you should always plan for them.

After the server is backed up, complete the following:

1. Close all Exchange 2000 Server utilities such as Exchange System Manager.
2. Run ForestPrep.
3. Run DomainPrep.
4. Ensure the server is running a minimum of Exchange 2000 Service Pack 3.

5. Install Exchange Server 2003.

6. Remove Exchange 2000 Server optimizations from the registry.

Closing utilities such as Exchange System Manager on the server being upgraded is essential. If these utilities are open, the upgrade process is unable to replace them with the newer versions that are used with Exchange Server 2003. To be sure all utilities are closed, it is a best practice to exit out of all programs and utilities prior to the upgrade. To ensure that other administrators do not have any utilities open, disable Terminal Services.

If this is the first Exchange 2003 server installed in the forest, ForestPrep must be run to extend the Active Directory schema to support Exchange Server 2003. This process can take from 20 minutes on small networks to several hours on larger networks and can be performed at any time before the first Exchange 2003 server is installed. It is a best practice to run ForestPrep several days before the actual server upgrade. This ensures that there is time to replicate the changes throughout the entire forest.

DomainPrep must be run in the root domain of the forest if this is the first Exchange 2003 server. In addition, DomainPrep must be run once in each domain before the first Exchange 2003 server is installed in that domain.

Before you upgrade an Exchange 2000 Server to Exchange Server 2003, the server must be running at least Exchange 2000 Service Pack 3. This is needed to complete the upgrade process successfully through Exchange setup. Without it, the Exchange setup halts the upgrade process.

To install an upgrade of Exchange Server 2003, run setup.exe (found in the \setup\i386 directory of the Microsoft Exchange Server 2003 CD), just as if you were performing a new installation. This starts the Microsoft Exchange Installation Wizard, which finds the already installed components of Exchange 2000 Server and selects them for upgrade. At the Component Selection screen of the installation wizard, the action selected for these components is upgrade instead of install.

NOTE

An upgrade must be installed in the same language as the original Exchange 2000 server.

During the upgrade, most configuration settings from Exchange 2000 Server are carried over into Exchange Server 2003 with no changes. For example, settings for POP3, IMAP, and NNTP are not changed. Some settings that were blank in Exchange 2000 Server have default settings in Exchange Server 2003. For example, the maximum message size for Exchange 2000 Server is blank by default. In Exchange Server 2003, the default maximum message size is 10 MB. If the setting is blank on an upgraded server, the new default takes effect. If the setting was configured in Exchange 2000 Server by an administrator, the setting from Exchange 2000 Server carries over to Exchange Server 2003.

A number of registry settings are available in Exchange 2000 Server for optimizing performance. Many of these are no longer relevant in Exchange Server 2003 or can cause problems in Exchange Server 2003. These registry settings must be removed after the upgrade. For a list of these registry settings, view the Exchange Server 2003 Deployment Guide available for download at the Microsoft Web site.

Activity 14-1: Downloading the Exchange Server Deployment Guide

Time Required: 10 to 20 minutes

Objective: Download and review the Exchange Server 2003 Deployment Guide.

Description: The Exchange Server 2003 Deployment Guide is a document available from Microsoft that describes different options for installing Exchange Server 2003. One of the topics covered is the Exchange 2000 Server registry optimizations that should be removed from Exchange 2003 servers. In this activity, you read which registry keys should be removed.

1. Log on to your back-end server with the user name **Administrator** and the password **Password!**.

2. To open Internet Explorer, click **Start**, point to **All Programs**, and then click **Internet Explorer**.

3. In the Address Bar, type **http://www.microsoft.com/exchange**, and then click the **Go** button. The Microsoft Exchange Server home page opens, as shown in Figure 14-1.

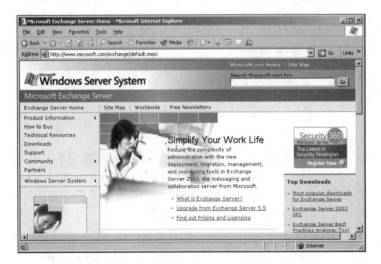

Figure 14-1 Microsoft Exchange Server home page

Web sites change frequently, so your page may appear differently.

4. Click the **Technical Resources** link on the navigation bar on the left side of the screen. The Technical Resources for Exchange Server page opens.

5. Click the **Exchange Server 2003 Technical Documentation Library** link. The Exchange Server 2003 Technical Documentation Library page opens.

6. Scroll down to the **Deployment** section, and then click the **Deployment Guide for Exchange Server 2003** link.

7. On the right side of the Exchange Server 2003 Deployment Guide page, click **English** in the Download drop-down list, if necessary, and then click the **Go** button. The Download Center's Exchange Server 2003 Deployment Guide page opens.

8. Click the **Download** button on the right side of the page.

9. In the File Download dialog box, click the **Save** button, click **Desktop**, and then click the **Save** button.

10. When the download is complete, click the **Close** button, and then close **Internet Explorer**.

11. On the Desktop, double-click the **E2k3Deploy.exe** file. The WinZip Self-Extractor opens.

12. In the Unzip to folder text box, type **C:**, as shown in Figure 14–2, and then click **Unzip**.

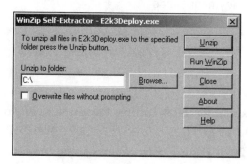

Figure 14-2   Unzipping E2k3Deploy.exe

13. When the extraction is complete, click **OK**, and then click **Close**.

14. Click **Start**, point to **All Programs**, point to **Accessories**, and then click **Windows Explorer**.

15. In the left pane, click the **plus sign (+)** next to My Computer, and then click **Local Disk (C:)**.

16. In the right pane, double-click **Exchange Server 2003 Deployment Guide.doc**. The document opens, as shown in Figure 14-3.

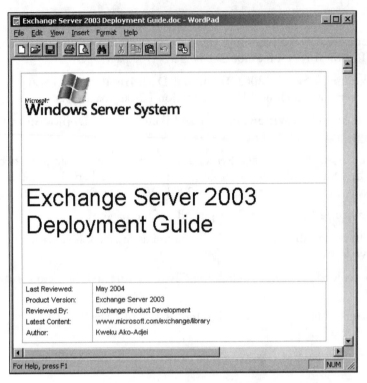

Figure 14-3 Exchange Server 2003 Deployment Guide

Your document might open in a different text editor, depending on the software installed on your server.

NOTE

17. Scroll down to the **Removing Exchange 2000 Tuning Parameters** section in Chapter 3, "Upgrading from Exchange 2000 Server." This is approximately page 42.

18. Read the **Removing Exchange 2000 Tuning Parameters** section. When you are finished, close all open windows.

UPGRADING A CLUSTER TO EXCHANGE SERVER 2003

Upgrading an Exchange 2000 Server cluster to Exchange Server 2003 is essentially the same process as upgrading stand-alone servers. In general, you must upgrade one server in the cluster at a time until the entire cluster is upgraded. To ensure proper failover during the upgrade, all Exchange 2000 servers must run a minimum of Service Pack 3. Exchange 2003 servers are able to mount Exchange 2000 Server Service Pack 3 Information Stores. An instance of Exchange running on a cluster is an **Exchange Virtual Server (EVS)**.

The process for upgrading an Exchange 2000 Server two-node active/passive cluster is as follows (node 1 refers to the active node, and node 2 refers to the passive node):

1. Run ForestPrep and DomainPrep where appropriate.

2. Ensure both nodes are running a minimum of Exchange 2000 Server Service Pack 3.

3. Perform a full backup of node 1 and node 2.

4. Fail over the EVS from node 1 to node 2.

5. Upgrade node 1.

6. Take the EVS offline.

7. Fail back the EVS from node 2 to node 1.

8. Upgrade the Exchange Virtual Server.

9. Upgrade node 2.

During this process, there are only a few minutes of downtime while services fail over between nodes. It is possible that, with appropriate warning and the consent of business units, the upgrade can be completed during production hours because of the small downtime window.

The process shown for upgrading an active/passive cluster is approximately the same one used to upgrade an active/active cluster. Exchange services are failed over to another server before each server upgrade and then failed back after the upgrade is complete. In an active/active cluster, performance might deteriorate because a single server is temporarily taking over the workload of two servers.

14

UPGRADING EXCHANGE SERVER 5.5 WITHIN AN EXCHANGE ORGANIZATION

Most companies have only a single Exchange organization for all of their users. In this situation, the simplest upgrade path from Exchange Server 5.5 to Exchange Server 2003 is to migrate the Exchange Server 5.5 information within the Exchange organization. This allows mailboxes to be migrated one at a time to reduce service outages and preserve access to existing resources.

The following steps are required to migrate Exchange Server 5.5 within an Exchange organization:

1. Migrate Windows NT accounts to Active Directory.

2. Install and configure the ADC (Active Directory Connector).

3. Install Exchange Server 2003 and migrate mailboxes.

4. Remove Exchange Server 5.5.

Migrating Windows NT Accounts

Many Exchange Server 5.5 installations are installed on Windows NT and are using Windows NT domains. Exchange Server 2003 requires user information to be present in Active Directory. Depending on organizational requirements, user accounts can be migrated either by upgrading Windows NT domains to Active Directory domains, or by using the **Active Directory Migration Tool (ADMT)**.

When Windows NT domains are upgraded to Active Directory domains, the SID for each user is retained; this preserves security rights such as mailbox rights. In addition, the domain structure remains intact. So, for example, if there were five domains before the upgrade, there are still five domains after the upgrade. Organizations that have decided to consolidate domains as part of implementing Active Directory should use ADMT instead.

ADMT copies user accounts from one domain to another. This is useful when a new domain structure is required—for example, multiple domains being consolidated into one. Users that are copied via ADMT retain their existing security settings through the **SIDHistory** attribute. When ADMT creates accounts in the new domain, the accounts have a new, unique SID. This SID does not have access to the resources of the original user object, so, to retain security settings, ADMT creates an attribute for each new user named SIDHistory. The SIDHistory attribute contains the SID of the original user account. This SID stored in SIDHistory is used to access all of the resources that were available to the original user account.

There must be a trust relationship between domains for SIDHistory to function properly.

NOTE

ACTIVITY

Activity 14-2: Researching the SIDHistory attribute

Time Required: 10 to 20 minutes

Objective: Research some information about the SIDHistory attribute.

Description: SIDHistory is an attribute of user objects that is used by Active Directory when users are copied from one domain to another. This is most commonly done with ADMT. In this activity, you learn more about how SIDHistory works.

1. From the Windows desktop of your back-end server, click **Start**, point to **All Programs**, point to **Accessories**, and then click **Windows Explorer**.

2. In the left pane, click the **plus sign (+)** next to My Computer, and then click **Local Disk (C:)**.

3. In the right pane, double-click **Exchange Server 2003 Deployment Guide.doc**. This activity assumes this document will open in WordPad. If you have a different text editor or word processor installed, such as Word, you will have to modify the steps accordingly.

4. Press **Ctrl+F** to open the Find dialog box, as shown in Figure 14-4.

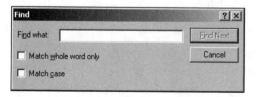

Figure 14-4   Find dialog box

NOTE

If using a text editor or word processor other than WordPad, modify Steps 4 to 6 as appropriate for your text editor's Find feature.

5. In the Find what text box, type **sidhistory**, and then click the **Find Next** button.

6. Click **Cancel**.

7. Scroll to the beginning of the **Using Active Directory Migration Tool** section, which is on approximately page 61 in Chapter 4 of the guide. Read this section.

8. When finished, close the document, and then close **Windows Explorer**.

9. To open Internet Explorer, click **Start**, point to **All Programs**, and then click **Internet Explorer**.

10. In the Address Bar, type **http://www.microsoft.com/technet/prodtechnol/ windows2000serv/deploy/cookbook/cookchp1.mspx**, and then click the **Go** button. This takes you to Chapter 1 of the Domain Migration Cookbook, as shown in Figure 14-5. This information was originally written for Windows 2000 but is also valid for Windows Server 2003.

NOTE

Web sites change frequently, so your page may appear differently.

11. Read this entire Web page to understand more about SIDHistory.

12. When finished, close **Internet Explorer**.

Now that you have learned more about the SIDHistory attribute, you install and use ADMT.

14

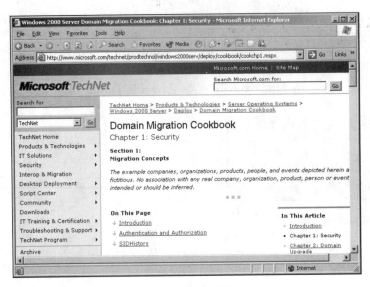

Figure 14-5   Domain Migration Cookbook

Activity 14-3: Installing ADMT

Time Required: 10 to 20 minutes

Objective: Install and run ADMT.

Description: ADMT migrates user accounts from Windows NT domains to Active Directory domains. As part of this process, the SIDhistory attribute is populated. In this activity, you download, install, and then start ADMT.

1. From the Windows desktop of the back-end server, click **Start**, point to **All Programs**, and then click **Internet Explorer**.

2. In the Address Bar, type **http://www.microsoft.com/downloads**, and then click the **Go** button.

3. In the Search for a download text box on the left side of the page, type **ADMT**, and then click the **Go** button.

4. On the Search Results page, click the **Active Directory Migration Tool v.2.0** link. The Download Center's Active Directory Migration Tool v.2.0 page is displayed, as shown in Figure 14-6.

5. Click the **Download** button on the right side of the page.

6. In the File Download dialog box, click the **Save** button.

7. In the Save As dialog box, click **Desktop**, if necessary, and then click **Save**.

8. When the download is complete, click **Close**, and then close **Internet Explorer**.

9. On the desktop, double-click **admt2.exe**. The WinZip Self-Extractor opens.

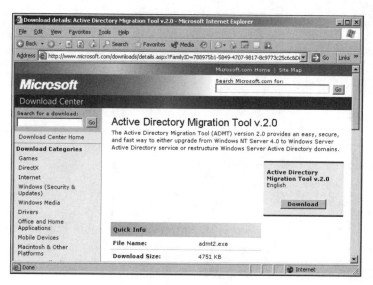

Figure 14-6   Download Center's Active Directory Migration Tool v.2.0 page

10. In the Unzip to folder text box, type **C:**, and then click **Unzip**.

11. When the extraction is complete, click **OK**, and then click **Close**.

12. To view the ADMT Readme file, click **Start**, and then click **Run**. In the Open text box, type **C:\admt\readme.doc**, and then click **OK**. This opens the document shown in Figure 14-7.

13. Scroll down and read the table of contents. Note sections you may want to review later.

14. Close the document.

15. To install ADMT, click **Start**, and then click **Run**. In the Open text box, type **C:\admt\admigration.msi**, and then click **OK**. This starts the Active Directory Migration Tool Setup Wizard, as shown in Figure 14-8. Click **Next** to continue.

16. At the License Agreement screen, click the **I accept the License Agreement** option button, and then click **Next**.

17. At the Installation Folder screen, accept the default installation path by clicking **Next**.

18. At the Start Installation screen, click **Next** to begin the installation.

19. When the installation is complete, click **Finish**.

20. To start ADMT, click **Start**, point to **Administrative Tools**, and then click **Active Directory Migration Tool**. The Active Directory Migration Tool opens.

14

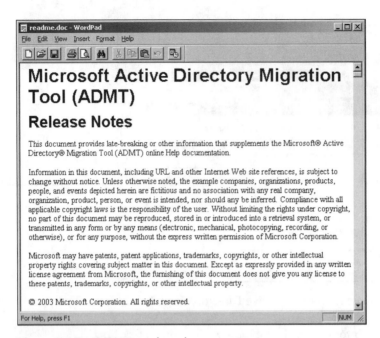

Figure 14-7   ADMT readme.doc

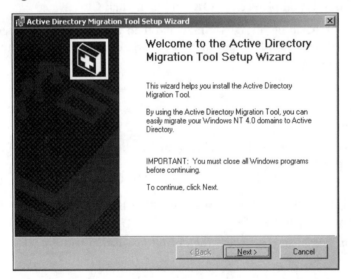

Figure 14-8   Active Directory Migration Tool Setup Wizard

21. In the left pane, right-click **Active Direction Migration Tool** to view the shortcut menu, shown in Figure 14-9. This menu shows the options available for migrating user accounts and groups.

22. Close **ADMT**.

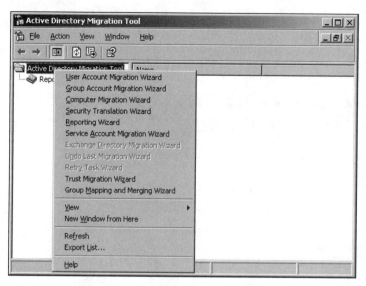

Figure 14-9   ADMT shortcut menu

Active Directory Connector

Whereas Exchange Server 5.5 uses an internal directory to manage configuration information, Exchange Server 2003 uses Active Directory. When Exchange Server 5.5 and Exchange Server 2003 coexist in the same organization, there must be ongoing synchronization between the Exchange Server 5.5 directory and Active Directory. The ADC performs this task.

After ADC is installed, the ADC Tools are used to configure ADC. Configuration tasks include setting the server and log path, collecting Exchange Server 5.5 information, identifying user accounts attached to resources, and configuring connection agreements.

ACTIVITY

Activity 14-4: Installing ADC

Time Required: 10 to 15 minutes

Objective: Install and run ADC.

Description: ADC is used to synchronize information between Active Directory and the Exchange Server 5.5 directory. In this activity, you install ADC from your Microsoft Exchange Server 2003 CD. After installation, you run ADC and view some of the available options.

1. On your back-end server, insert your Microsoft Exchange Server 2003 CD.

2. Click **Start**, point to **All Programs**, point to **Accessories**, and then click **Windows Explorer**.

14

3. In the left pane, click the **plus sign (+)** next to My Computer, click the **plus sign (+)** next to your CD-ROM drive, click the **plus sign (+)** next to **ADC**, and then click **I386**. The ADC installation files are displayed in the right pane, as shown in Figure 14-10.

Figure 14-10   ADC installation files

4. In the right pane, scroll down and double-click **SETUP.EXE**. The Microsoft Active Directory Connector Setup Wizard starts, as shown in Figure 14-11. Click **Next** to continue.

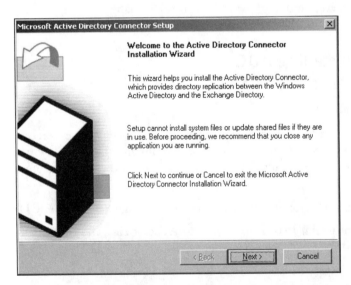

Figure 14-11   Microsoft Active Directory Connector Setup Wizard

5. At the End-User License Agreement screen, click the **I accept the terms of the license agreement** option button, and then click **Next**.

6. At the Component Selection screen, click the **Microsoft Active Directory Connector Service component** and the **Microsoft Active Directory Connector Management components** check boxes, and then click **Next**.

7. At the Install Location screen, accept the default install location by clicking **Next**.

8. At the Service Account screen, accept the default account of Administrator as the service account. Type **Password!** in the Account password text box, and then click **Next**.

9. When the installation is complete, click **Finish**.

10. Close **Windows Explorer**.

11. To start ADC, click **Start**, point to **All Programs**, point to **Microsoft Exchange**, and then click **Active Directory Connector**. The Active Directory Connector Services window opens.

12. In the left pane, click **ADC Tools**, as shown in Figure 14-12. ADC Tools requires all the steps required to configure connectors between Active Directory and the Exchange Server 5.5 directory.

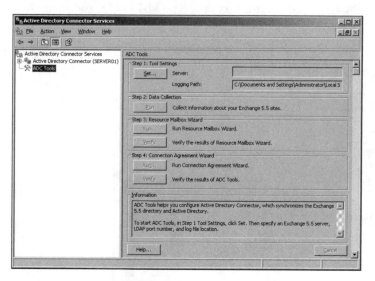

Figure 14-12   ADC Tools

13. Close **Active Directory Connector Services**.

Resource Mailbox Wizard

In Exchange Server 2003, each user can only be associated with a single mailbox; by contrast, in Exchange Server 5.5, each user can be associated with multiple mailboxes. Exchange Server 5.5 uses this ability to allow users to access and control joint resources, such as conference rooms. This difference causes extra, unwanted users to be created by ADC during synchronization for each resource mailbox. To prevent ADC from creating users for resource mailboxes, the value of Custom Attribute 10 must be set to **NTDSNoMatch**. This can be edited manually for each resource mailbox. However, that is time consuming. The **Resource Mailbox Wizard** in ADC scans user accounts, identifies those with multiple mailboxes, and assigns the NTDSNoMatch attribute to resource mailboxes.

Activity 14-5: Researching NTDSNoMatch

Time Required: 10 to 20 minutes

Objective: Research information about NTDSNoMatch.

Description: NTDSNoMatch is the value used to prevent user accounts from being created for Exchange Server 5.5 resource mailboxes. In this activity, you learn more information about NTDSNoMatch.

1. From the Windows desktop of your back-end server, click **Start**, point to **All Programs**, and then click **Internet Explorer**.

2. In the Address Bar, type **http://support.microsoft.com**, and then click the **Go** button.

3. In the Search the Knowledge Base text box, type **kb274173**, and then click the **Go** button.

4. Click the **XADM: Documentation for the NTDSNoMatch Utility** link.

5. Read the knowledge base article shown in Figure 14-13.

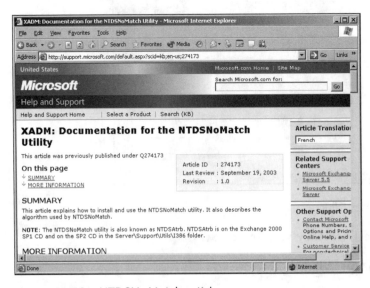

Figure 14-13   NTDSNoMatch article

6. When you are done reading the article, close **Internet Explorer**.

Connection Agreements

ADC uses connection agreements to control the replication of information between the Exchange Server 5.5 directory and Active Directory. The connection agreements can control the direction of synchronization and the synchronization schedule. There are three types of connection agreements:

- *Recipient connection agreement*—A **recipient connection agreement** controls the replication information about recipients. If ADMT or a domain upgrade is not used to create user accounts in Active Directory for Exchange Server 5.5 mailboxes, a recipient connection agreement causes them to be created.

- *Public folder connection agreement*—A **public folder connection agreement** controls the replication of public folder configuration information and can only exist if a recipient connection agreement also exists.

- *Configuration connection agreement*—A **configuration connection agreement** controls the replication of general Exchange configuration information and is required for Exchange Server 5.5 to coexist in the same Exchange organization with Exchange Server 2003.

NOTE

Recipient connection agreements and public folder connection agreements do not control the replication of messages in mailboxes or public folders.

14

Installing Exchange Server 2003 and Migrating Mailboxes

Exchange Server 2003 can be installed into an existing Exchange Server 5.5 organization. During the installation of Exchange Server 2003, at the Installation Type screen, select the Join or upgrade an existing Exchange 5.5 organization option. During the installation, all Exchange 5.5 servers must be up and running.

Placing the Exchange 2003 server in the same Exchange organization as the Exchange 5.5 server makes it easy to move mailboxes and their contents from one server to another. The process is performed with the Exchange 2003 Task Wizard, which is exactly the same as moving a mailbox from one Exchange 2003 server to another. The Exchange 2003 Task Wizard can be accessed by right-clicking a user object in Active Directory Users and Computers or by right-clicking a mailbox in Exchange System Manager.

Public folder replication from Exchange Server 5.5 to Exchange Server 2003 must be configured with the **Public Folder Migration Tool (PFMigrate)**. PFMigrate immediately migrates the hierarchy of public folders but not the contents; public folder contents are replicated over time. The time required to replicate contents varies depending on the number and size of messages to be replicated.

Removing Exchange Server 5.5

Exchange 5.5 servers can be removed after all the messages have been migrated to Exchange 2003 servers. This is done by running the setup.exe file from the Microsoft Exchange Server 5.5 CD, and selecting to remove all components.

In most cases, at least some Exchange 5.5 servers will be the first Exchange servers installed in a site. These servers perform a number of roles, including routing calculation server, and are responsible for site folders such as the Schedule+ Free Busy Information folder. The roles must be moved to a new server before the Exchange 5.5 server is removed. In addition, a number of objects can be removed when the last Exchange 5.5 server is removed from an organization.

ACTIVITY

Activity 14-6: Researching Exchange Server Removal

Time Required: 10 to 20 minutes

Objective: Research information about removing servers from Exchange organizations.

Description: Some Exchange servers perform special roles within a site or an organization. It is important to be aware of these roles and how to migrate them to other servers. In this activity, you research what needs to be done when Exchange servers are removed from an organization.

1. From the Windows desktop of the back-end server, click **Start**, point to **All Programs**, and then click **Internet Explorer**.

2. In the Address Bar, type **http://support.microsoft.com**, and then click the **Go** button.

3. In the Search the Knowledge Base text box, type **kb822450**, and then click the **Go** button.

4. On the Search Results page, click the **How to remove the last Exchange Server 5.5 computer from an Exchange Server 2003 administrative group** link.

5. This article gives a step-by-step description of how to remove the final Exchange 5.5 server from an Exchange Server 2003 administrative group. Read the article.

6. When finished, click the **Back** button to return to the English Knowledge Base page.

7. In the "For" text box, type **kb152959**, and then press **Enter**.

8. Click the **XADM: How to Remove the First Exchange Server in a Site** link.

9. Read the article.

10. When finished, close **Internet Explorer**.

Migrating Exchange Server 5.5 to a New Exchange Organization

Exchange Server 2003 and Exchange Server 5.5 do not need to coexist in the same Exchange organization to migrate information between the two. You can create a brand-new Exchange organization and migrate Exchange Server 5.5 users to it.

Migrating to a new Exchange organization allows several Exchange Server 5.5 organizations to be combined into one. This is useful when, for example, Exchange Server 5.5 was deployed on a departmental basis, but centralized management is now desired. In smaller companies, this can be a simpler migration path.

The following steps are required to migrate Exchange Server 5.5 to a new Exchange organization:

1. Install Exchange Server 2003 and migrate Windows NT accounts to Active Directory.

2. Install and configure the Active Directory Connector.

3. Migrate mailboxes.

4. Migrate public folders.

5. Retire Exchange Server 5.5.

Installing Exchange Server 2003 and Migrating Windows NT Accounts

In this migration, the process for installing Exchange Server 2003 is exactly the same as a new Exchange Server 2003 organization. No special preparations are required. After the installation, accounts are typically migrated to Active Directory from Windows NT using ADMT. Just as in the intra-organizational migration, ADMT uses SIDHistory to retain mailbox permissions when accounts are migrated to Active Directory. If permission retention is not required, ADMT is not required because the accounts are automatically created later in the process by the Exchange Server Migration Wizard or ADC.

Installing and Configuring ADC

ADC is required for inter-organizational migrations if Exchange Server 5.5 and Exchange Server 2003 will coexist. This ensures that messages are properly delivered between both organizations during the migration process. If all of the Exchange information can be migrated in a single, short process, ADC is not required.

When ADC is implemented for an inter-organizational migration, a recipient connection agreement is used but a configuration connection agreement is not used. Configuration connection agreements are used only for intra-organizational migrations because separate Exchange organizations do not share configuration information or connectors.

14

Note that concerns about resource mailboxes are still valid for inter-organizational migrations. Resource mailboxes must have Custom Attribute 10 configured with a value of NTDSNoMatch, or users are created for them by ADC. The simplest mechanism to do this is the Resource Mailbox Wizard available in ADC tools.

Migrating Mailboxes Between Exchange Organizations

The **Exchange Server Migration Wizard** is included with Exchange Server 2003 and is installed with the administrative tools. It is a flexible tool that can move mailboxes as a single step from Exchange Server 5.5 directly into Exchange Server 2003, or as a two-step process that stores Exchange Server 5.5 mailboxes in files before importing them into Exchange Server 2003. The one-step process is appropriate when network communication is fast and reliable. The two-step process is appropriate when network communication is not reliable.

No limits exist on how many times the migration can be performed. This allows you to migrate mailboxes in batches rather than all at once. It is easier to recover from a failed migration when users are migrated in small batches because you can easily discover which mailboxes have been migrated and which have not.

When mailboxes are migrated, the Exchange Server Migration Wizard attempts to match each mailbox with a user account that exists in Active Directory. If it is unable to match the mailbox with a user account, the administrator performing the migration can select accounts. This is useful if accounts have been created with a different naming convention in the new domain. If the user accounts do not already exist, the Exchange Server Migration Wizard creates them based on user information from Exchange Server 5.5.

NOTE   The Exchange Server Migration Wizard can also import information and mailboxes from Novell GroupWise, Lotus Notes, Lotus cc:Mail, Microsoft Mail, IMAP servers, and LDAP servers.

The Exchange Server Migration Wizard cannot perform a number of tasks, including the following:

- Migrating public folders
- Migrating distribution lists
- Migrating inbox rules
- Migrating .pst files (personal folders)
- Migrating .pab files (personal address books)
- Preserving access to other mailboxes
- Preserving access to public folders
- Migrating mailboxes to another server in the same Exchange organization

Exchange Server 5.5 uses custom recipients as a means to add e-mail addresses into the GAL. These are not supported in Exchange Server 2003. During the migration process, the Exchange Server Migration Wizard creates contacts to replace custom recipients.

Migrating Public Folders

In an intra-organizational migration, public folders can be replicated from the Exchange 5.5 server to Exchange 2003 servers. This is not possible in an inter-organizational migration. The **InterOrg Replication Utility** replicates public folders between two Exchange organizations. This allows meetings and appointments to be shared between organizations.

The InterOrg Replication Utility is composed of a Configuration program and the Replication Service. The Configuration program sets parameters for how often replication happens and which folders are replicated. The parameters are stored in a configuration file that is used by the Replication Service to control the replication process.

ACTIVITY

Activity 14-7: Researching the InterOrg Replication Utility

Time Required: 10 to 20 minutes

Objective: Research more information about the InterOrg Replication Utility.

Description: The InterOrg Replication Utility is used to replicate public folder contents between an Exchange 5.5 server and an Exchange 2003 server. In this activity, you learn more about the InterOrg Replication Utility.

14

1. From the Windows desktop of the back-end server, click **Start**, point to **All Programs**, and then click **Internet Explorer**.

2. In the Address Bar, type **http://support.microsoft.com/kb/238573**, and then click the **Go** button. The XADM: Installing, Configuring, and Using the InterOrg Replication Utility article is displayed.

3. Read the article.

4. When finished, close **Internet Explorer**.

Retiring Exchange Server 5.5

After all mailboxes and public folders have been migrated to Exchange Server, the Exchange 5.5 servers can be retired. The only links between the old and new Exchange organizations are domain trusts, ADC replicating directory information, and the InterOrg Replication Utility. After all three of these are removed, the old Exchange 5.5 server can be turned off. No special removal process for Exchange 5.5 servers exists after an inter-organizational migration.

Chapter Summary

- Exchange 2000 servers can be upgraded to Exchange Server 2003 with an in-place upgrade. Exchange 2000 Server services that are not supported by Exchange Server 2003 must be removed before upgrading.

- When upgrading Exchange 2000 servers to Exchange Server 2003, all Exchange 2000 Server utilities on the server must be closed. In addition, ForestPrep and DomainPrep must be run before installation. After the installation, any Exchange 2000 Server optimizations must be removed from the registry.

- Upgrading servers in an Exchange 2000 Server cluster is similar to upgrading single stand-alone servers. Exchange virtual servers should be failed over to other servers during the upgrade process. After the upgrade, the EVS should be failed back to the original server and upgraded to match the server.

- Exchange 2003 servers can be added to an Exchange Server 5.5 organization to perform an intra-organizational migration. This strategy is useful if there is no need to modify the structure of an Exchange organization.

- An intra-organizational migration requires Windows NT accounts to be migrated to Active Directory. Accounts can be migrated by upgrading Windows NT domains to Active Directory or using ADMT. ADMT uses SIDHistory to preserve security settings.

- ADC is used to provide connectivity between Active Directory and the Exchange Server 5.5 directory. ADC uses recipient connection agreements, public folder connection agreements, and configuration connection agreements.

- ADC Tools can be used to identify resource mailboxes. Custom Attribute 10 should be set to a value of NTDSNoMatch for each resource mailbox to prevent ADC from creating user accounts for them.

- During an intra-organizational migration, the Exchange Server 5.5 mailboxes can be moved individually from the Exchange 5.5 servers to Exchange 2003 servers. This allows for a phased migration. Mailboxes are moved using the Exchange 2003 Task Wizard. Public folders are replicated using PFMigrate.

- Multiple Exchange Server 5.5 organizations can be migrated to a single Exchange Server 2003 organization using an inter-organizational migration. Windows accounts are migrated to Active Directory using ADMT. ADC is required if Exchange Server 5.5 and Exchange Server 2003 are required to coexist for a period of time.

- Mailboxes are migrated between Exchange organizations using the Exchange Server Migration Wizard. If an Active Directory account does not already exist for each mailbox, one is created for each. The Exchange Server Migration Wizard is not able to migrate public folders, distribution lists, or inbox rules.

- The InterOrg Replication Utility is used to replicate public folder contents during an inter-organizational migration.

Key Terms

Active Directory Migration Tool (ADMT) — A utility that migrates accounts from one domain to another. It is commonly used to migrate accounts from Windows NT domains to Active Directory.

configuration connection agreement — The settings that are used by ADC to control the replication of configuration information between Active Directory and the Exchange Server 5.5 directory. These are only used for intra-organizational migrations.

Exchange Server Migration Wizard — A utility used to migrate mailbox contents during inter-organizational migrations.

Exchange Virtual Server (EVS) — An instance of Exchange running on a cluster. An EVS can be failed over from one cluster node to another.

InterOrg Replication Utility — A utility that replicates public folder contents during an inter-organizational migration.

NTDSNoMatch — The value that must be set in Custom Attribute 10 of resource mailboxes. When this is set, ADC does not create users for resource mailboxes.

public folder connection agreement — The settings that are used by ADC to control the replication of public folder information between Active Directory and the Exchange Server 5.5 directory. These can only be used if a recipient connection agreement is in place.

Public Folder Migration Tool (PFMigrate) — A utility that configures the replication of public folder contents during an intra-organizational migration.

recipient connection agreement — The settings that are used by ADC to control the replication of recipient information between Active Directory and the Exchange Server 5.5 directory.

Resource Mailbox Wizard — A wizard that sets the value of Custom Attribute 10 of Exchange Server 5.5 resource mailboxes to NTDSNoMatch.

SIDHistory — An attribute of a user object that is set and created by ADMT. It is used to preserve security settings when users are migrated from one domain to another.

Review Questions

1. Exchange Server 2003 can be installed in an existing Exchange Server 5.5 organization. True or False?

2. Which utility is required to upgrade an Exchange 2000 server to Exchange Server 2003?

    a. ADMT

    b. ADC

    c. NTDSNoMatch

    d. none

3. Which custom attribute must have a value of NTDSNoMatch to prevent user objects from being created for resource mailboxes?

   a. custom attribute 1

   b. custom attribute 5

   c. custom attribute 8

   d. custom attribute 10

4. Which steps are required before upgrading the first Exchange 2000 server to Exchange Server 2003? (Choose all that apply.)

   a. run DomainPrep

   b. run ForestPrep

   c. close all Exchange 2000 Server utilities

   d. remove Exchange 2000 Server optimizations from the registry

5. Which statement accurately describes how settings are affected by an upgrade from Exchange 2000 Server to Exchange Server 2003?

   a. There are no changes to settings.

   b. Exchange Server 2003 default settings are always applied.

   c. Exchange Server 2003 default settings are applied only if the Exchange 2000 Server setting is blank.

   d. Exchange Server 2003 default settings are applied only if the option is selected during installation.

6. The downtime required to upgrade an Exchange 2000 Server cluster to Exchange Server 2003 is the same as upgrading a single Exchange 2000 server. True or False?

7. Which utility moves Windows NT accounts into Active Directory?

   a. ADMT

   b. ADC

   c. MS mail connector

   d. PFMigrate

8. What does the SIDHistory attribute contain?

9. A trust must exist between two domains for SIDHistory to function properly. True or False?

10. Which attributes of a user object are used when calculating security permissions for a user object? (Choose all that apply.)

    a. logon name

    b. SID

    c. GUID

    d. SIDHistory

11. Which utility can be used to set the NTDSNoMatch attribute for Exchange Server 5.5 resource mailboxes?

12. Which type of connection agreement controls the creation of user accounts in Active Directory?

 a. recipient connection agreement

 b. public folder connection agreement

 c. user connection agreement

 d. configuration connection agreement

13. Which utility is used to migrate mailbox contents during an intra-organizational migration from Exchange Server 5.5 to Exchange Server 2003?

 a. ADMT

 b. ADC

 c. PFMigrate

 d. Exchange 2003 Task Wizard

14. Which utility is used to migrate mailbox contents during an inter-organizational migration from Exchange 2000 Server to Exchange Server 2003?

15. The Exchange Server Migration Wizard can migrate public folder contents. True or False?

16. What replaces custom recipients when the Exchange Server Migration Wizard is used to migrate them to Exchange Server 2003?

 a. contacts

 b. resource mailboxes

 c. user mailboxes

 d. nothing—they remain custom recipients

17. How is Exchange Server 5.5 removed from a server?

18. Which type of migration requires ADC to maintain synchronization of user information? (Choose all that apply.)

 a. inter-organizational migration from Exchange Server 5.5

 b. intra-organizational migration from Exchange Server 5.5

 c. moving mailboxes between Exchange 2003 servers

 d. intra-organization migration from Exchange 2000 Server

19. Which utility is required to replicate public folder contents during an inter-organizational migration?

20. All mail is migrated by the Exchange Server Migration Wizard, including mail in .pst files. True or False?

14

Case Projects

Case Project 14-1: Choosing a Migration Strategy

Exchange Server 5.5 was originally installed into Gigantic Life Insurance as a departmental e-mail solution. Eventually, five different Exchange organizations served the entire company. This structure is preventing Gigantic Life Insurance from implementing Active Directory. Describe how you would fix this.

Case Project 14-2: Migrating Mailboxes

During the migration of the first Exchange organization for Gigantic Life Insurance, a number of extra Active Directory users were created. The new users had the same name as resource mailboxes in the Exchange Server 5.5 organization. Explain why this happened and how it can be prevented for future domains.

Case Project 14-3: Migrating an Exchange Server 5.5 Organization

Helping Hand Social Services has a single Exchange 5.5 server supporting 150 users. They have bought a new server and want it to be their Exchange 2003 server. Active Directory is already installed and functioning properly for their domain. List the steps required to migrate from Exchange Server 5.5 to Exchange Server 2003.

Case Project 14-4: Upgrading an Exchange 5.5 Server

Buddy's Machine Shop has a single Exchange 5.5 server on a relatively new machine running Windows 2000 Server with Service Pack 3. Active Directory is already in use. Buddy wants to keep using the same hardware for Exchange Server 2003. What steps do you recommend?

A

EXAM OBJECTIVES FOR MCSE CERTIFICATION

EXAM #70-284: IMPLEMENTING AND MANAGING MICROSOFT EXCHANGE SERVER 2003

Installing, Configuring, and Troubleshooting Exchange Server 2003

Objective	Chapter: Section	Activities
Prepare the environment for deployment of Exchange Server 2003	Chapter 2: Installing and Configuring Exchange Server 2003	Activity 2-1 Activity 2-2 Activity 2-3
	Chapter 14: Upgrading to Exchange Server 2003	Activity 14-1
Install, configure, and troubleshoot Exchange Server 2003	Chapter 2: Installing and Configuring Exchange Server 2003	Activity 2-4 Activity 2-8 Activity 2-9 Activity 2-10 Activity 2-11 Activity 2-12
	Chapter 7: Configuring and Managing Exchange Server	Activity 7-1 Activity 7-2 Activity 7-3
Install, configure, and troubleshoot Exchange Server 2003 in a clustered environment	Chapter 11: Backup and Recovery of Exchange Server 2003	
	Chapter 14: Upgrading to Exchange Server 2003	
Upgrade from Exchange Server 5.5 to Exchange Server 2003	Chapter 14: Upgrading to Exchange Server 2003	
Migrate from other messaging systems to Exchange Server 2003 • Use the Migration Wizard to migrate from other messaging systems • Migrate from other Exchange organizations	Chapter 12: Troubleshooting Connectivity Chapter 14: Upgrading to Exchange Server 2003	Activity 14-2 Activity 14-3 Activity 14-4 Activity 14-5 Activity 14-7
Configure and troubleshoot Exchange Server 2003 for coexistence with other Exchange organizations	Chapter 8: Managing Routing and Internet Connectivity	
Configure and troubleshoot Exchange Server 2003 for coexistence with other messaging systems	Chapter 8: Managing Routing and Internet Connectivity	

A

Objective	Chapter: Section	Activities
Configure and troubleshoot Exchange Server 2003 for interoperability with other SMTP messaging systems	Chapter 8: Managing Routing and Internet Connectivity	Activity 8-1 Activity 8-2 Activity 8-7 Activity 8-8

Managing, Monitoring, and Troubleshooting Exchange Server Computers

Objective	Chapter: Section	Activities
Manage, monitor, and troubleshoot server health	Chapter 12: Troubleshooting Connectivity	Activity 12-1
	Chapter 13: Monitoring and Troubleshooting the Server	Activity 13-1 Activity 13-2 Activity 13-3 Activity 13-4 Activity 13-5 Activity 13-6 Activity 13-7 Activity 13-9 Activity 13-10 Activity 13-12 Activity 13-14
Manage, monitor, and troubleshoot data storage	Chapter 9: Managing Data Storage and Hardware Resources	Activity 9-1 Activity 9-2 Activity 9-3 Activity 9-4 Activity 9-5 Activity 9-6 Activity 9-7
	Chapter 11: Backup and Recovery of Exchange Server 2003	Activity 11-2
	Chapter 13: Monitoring and Troubleshooting the Server	Activity 13-8
Manage, monitor, and troubleshoot Exchange Server clusters	Chapter 11: Backup and Recovery of Exchange Server 2003	

Objective	Chapter: Section	Activities
Perform and troubleshoot backups and recovery	Chapter 11: Backup and Recovery of Exchange Server 2003	Activity 11-1 Activity 11-2 Activity 11-3 Activity 11-4 Activity 11-5 Activity 11-6 Activity 11-7 Activity 11-8 Activity 11-9
	Chapter 13: Monitoring and Troubleshooting the Server	Activity 13-11
Remove an Exchange Server computer from the organization	Chapter 14: Upgrading to Exchange Server 2003	Activity 14-6

Managing, Monitoring, and Troubleshooting the Exchange Organization

Objective	Chapter: Section	Activities
Manage and troubleshoot public folders	Chapter 6: Public Folders	Activity 6-1 Activity 6-2 Activity 6-3 Activity 6-4 Activity 6-5 Activity 6-6 Activity 6-7 Activity 6-8 Activity 6-9
Manage and troubleshoot virtual servers	Chapter 7: Configuring and Managing Exchange Server	Activity 7-5 Activity 7-6 Activity 7-7 Activity 7-8
	Chapter 8: Managing Routing and Internet Connectivity	Activity 8-1 Activity 8-2 Activity 8-6
Manage and troubleshoot front-end and back-end servers	Chapter 4: Configuring Outlook and Outlook Web Access	Activity 4-10
	Chapter 7: Configuring and Managing Exchange Server	Activity 7-4
	Chapter 10: Securing Exchange Server 2003	Activity 10-5 Activity 10-6

A

Objective	Chapter: Section	Activities
Manage and troubleshoot connectivity	Chapter 4: Configuring Outlook and Outlook Web Access	Activity 4-2 Activity 4-3 Activity 4-5 Activity 4-7 Activity 4-8 Activity 4-9
	Chapter 8: Managing Routing and Internet Connectivity	Activity 8-3 Activity 8-4 Activity 8-5
	Chapter 12: Troubleshooting Connectivity	Activity 12-2 Activity 12-3 Activity 12-4 Activity 12-5 Activity 12-6 Activity 12-7 Activity 12-8 Activity 12-9 Activity 12-10
	Chapter 13: Monitoring and Troubleshooting the Server	Activity 13-13
Monitor, manage, and troubleshoot infrastructure performance	Chapter 13: Monitoring and Troubleshooting the Server	Activity 13-7 Activity 13-9 Activity 13-10 Activity 13-12 Activity 13-14

Managing Security in the Exchange Environment

Objective	Chapter: Section	Activities
Manage and troubleshoot connectivity across firewalls	Chapter 4: Configuring Outlook and Outlook Web Access	Activity 4-10
Manage audit settings and audit logs	Chapter 12: Troubleshooting Connectivity	
Manage and troubleshoot permissions	Chapter 10: Securing Exchange Server 2003	Activity 10-2 Activity 10-3

Objective	Chapter: Section	Activities
Manage and troubleshoot encryption and digital signatures	Chapter 4: Configuring Outlook and Outlook Web Access	Activity 4-6
	Chapter 10: Securing Exchange Server 2003	Activity 10-4 Activity 10-5 Activity 10-6 Activity 10-7 Activity 10-8
Detect and respond to security threats	Chapter 10: Securing Exchange Server 2003	

Managing Recipient Objects and Address Lists

Objective	Chapter: Section	Activities
Manage recipient policies	Chapter 3: Managing Recipients	Activity 3-10
	Chapter 5: Managing Addresses	Activity 5-8 Activity 5-9 Activity 5-10 Activity 5-11
Manage user objects	Chapter 3: Managing Recipients	Activity 3-1 Activity 3-2 Activity 3-7 Activity 3-8 Activity 3-9
Manage distribution and security groups	Chapter 3: Managing Recipients	Activity 3-3 Activity 3-4 Activity 3-6
Manage contacts	Chapter 3: Managing Recipients	Activity 3-5
Manage address lists	Chapter 5: Managing Addresses	Activity 5-1 Activity 5-2 Activity 5-3 Activity 5-4 Activity 5-5 Activity 5-6 Activity 5-7

Managing and Monitoring Technologies that Support Exchange Server 2003

A

Objective	Chapter: Section	Activities
Diagnose problems arising from host resolution protocols	Chapter 12: Troubleshooting Connectivity	
Diagnose problems arising from Active Directory issues	Chapter 12: Troubleshooting Connectivity	
Diagnose network connectivity problems	Chapter 12: Troubleshooting Connectivity	Activity 12-9 Activity 12-10

Glossary

Active Directory — The directory service included with Windows 2000 Server and Windows Server 2003.

Active Directory Migration Tool (ADMT) — A utility that migrates accounts from one domain to another. It is commonly used to migrate accounts from Windows NT domains to Active Directory.

Active Directory Users and Computers — The primary user and group administrative tool in Active Directory environments.

active/active clustering — A cluster in which services are running on all nodes in the cluster. Windows Server 2003 and Exchange Server 2003 support only two-node active/active clusters.

active/passive clustering — A cluster in which at least one server sits idle with no services running. The passive server waits to take over from a failed server. Windows Server 2003 and Exchange Server 2003 support up to an eight-node active/passive cluster.

administrative group — A group used to define the administrative topology for your Exchange organization. It is logically defined, meaning that at a conceptual level, it can be based on geography, department, division, or function.

alternate recovery forest — A copy of the Exchange organization that is completely separate from the production environment and is used to restore Exchange stores and recover messages.

application service provider (ASP) — A company that provides outsourced access to an application running at a remote location for a subscription fee.

asymmetric (public-key) cryptography — A method of encrypting and decrypting messages in which the key used for encryption and the key used for decryption are different. This method assumes that the encryption key will be made public rather than be kept secret.

attachment blocking — A feature that automatically blocks e-mail attachments with certain file extensions such as .exe or .vbs.

back-end server — An Exchange server in a multiserver environment that stores user mailboxes and public folders. It accepts client requests through the front-end server. All interaction is with the front-end server, not with the clients directly.

backfilling — The process by which out-of-sync public folders resynchronize. Backfill can recover from the following situations: lost replication message(s), a public folder server going offline, and then coming online after an extended period of time. A public folder server being restored from a backup.

brick-level backup and restore — A type of backup performed by some third-party backup software that takes a copy of each message in user mailboxes, allowing individual messages to be restored.

bridgehead server — A server that provides a single point for delivery of e-mail and link state information between routing groups within an Exchange Server 2003 organization. It also serves as a central source for the delivery of messages inside and outside of the organization. In an Exchange 2000 Server organization, it is the server running Exchange 2000 Server that hosts routing group connectors.

Cached Exchange Mode — A new feature available when using Exchange Server 2003 with Outlook 2003 that caches a copy of the user mailbox on the client system, allowing many tasks to be carried out on the cached version rather than requiring access to the "live" Exchange server.

centralized administrative model — A model in which one group maintains complete control over all of the Exchange servers.

certificate — An attachment to an electronic message used to verify that a user sending a message is who he claims to be, and to provide the receiver with the means to encode a reply.

certificate authority (CA) — An entity that issues (digital) certificates containing users' public keys and other identifying information.

Certificate Services — The Windows 2000 Server or Windows Server 2003 service that allows an organization to issue its own certificates.

checkpoint file — A file that records which entries in the log files have already been written to disk.

circular logging — A feature that limits the amount of disk space that is used by transaction logs. When circular logging is on, Exchange writes transaction logs as usual; however, after the checkpoint file (E##.chk) has been advanced, the inactive portion of the transaction log is discarded and overwritten.

cluster — A group of independent servers (commonly referred to as nodes) that work together to ensure system availability.

clustering — A system in which a service or application is installed on two or more servers, and if the application fails on one server, another takes over its role. Clustering enhances availability of services and applications.

configuration connection agreement — The settings that are used by ADC to control the replication of configuration information between Active Directory and the Exchange Server 5.5 directory. These are only used for intra-organizational migrations.

conflict aging — A process that identifies whether the issue of a public folder item modified by two different users has been resolved by the users themselves. If not, and the conflict age limit has been exceeded, the conflict is resolved by the system.

connection filtering — A feature that restricts which servers are allowed to send messages to Exchange Server 2003. Servers can be blocked based on block lists that identify open relay servers.

contacts — The objects that represent people external to a particular company or organization.

cross-certification hierarchy — A configuration in which a CA acts as both a root CA and a subordinate CA (to another root CA in a different organization).

custom address list — An address list that has been created and customized.

database messaging system — A messaging system in which a service on the server manages the central database of messages. These messaging systems are very scalable.

decentralized administrative model — A model in which a separate administrative group is created for each group of Exchange administrators who will manage the Exchange servers and users within their own administrative jurisdiction.

default address lists — The address lists that have been installed by default during an Exchange Server 2003 installation.

diagnostics logging — A facility for increasing the level of information that is logged by the messaging system. Diagnostics logging allows you to track what the system is doing for each message being processed.

differential backup — A backup that takes a copy of only the transaction logs and does not delete the transaction logs from the disk.

distribution group — An Active Directory group used for the purpose of distributing e-mail messages to all group members.

domain controller — A Windows server that stores a copy of the Active Directory database.

Domain Name Service (DNS)—The distributed database system that provides name resolution services on TCP/IP networks.

DomainPrep—The tool used to prepare each Active Directory domain prior to the installation of Microsoft Exchange Server 2003.

Dynamic Buffer Allocation — A mechanism that Exchange uses to increase or decrease the size of the cache based on the amount of cache required and the amount of memory available.

e-mail address recipient policies — The policies that control e-mail address generation in the organization, and you can also use them to establish new default e-mail addresses on a global basis.

ESEUTIL — A utility used to perform maintenance and repair options—including defragmentation, integrity checking, and database repair—on Exchange Server 2003 Information Stores.

Exchange backup API — An interface used by backup programs to back up Exchange stores while the Exchange server is up and running.

Exchange Server Migration Wizard — A utility used to migrate mailbox contents during inter-organizational migrations.

Exchange System Manager—The primary Exchange management tool installed with Exchange Server 2003.

Exchange Virtual Server (EVS) — An instance of Exchange running on a cluster. An EVS can be failed over from one cluster node to another.

Extensible Storage Engine (ESE) — The primary database used within Exchange 2003. It is a multiuser database that allows applications to store, retrieve, and index semistructured data. It is optimized for very fast storage and retrieval.

folder edit conflict — A folder edit conflict occurs when two or more public folder contacts change a public folder design at the same time.

forest root domain — The first domain created in an Active Directory forest.

ForestPrep — The tool used to prepare an Active Directory forest prior to the installation of Microsoft Exchange Server 2003.

forms-based authentication — An Outlook Web Access feature that allows users to log on with their domain name, user name, and password, or their full user principal name (UPN).

fragmentation — A state that occurs within a database when information is not written to the database contiguously. The inefficiency of writing and reading noncontiguous data to and from the disk increases disk I/O, resulting in lower performance.

front-end server — A server that accepts requests from clients and proxies them to the appropriate back-end server for processing. Front-end servers act as an intermediary for connections to back-end servers. They do not host mailboxes or public folders directly.

full backup — A backup that takes a copy of the databases and transaction logs, and then deletes transaction logs from the disk.

full-text indexing — A process in which Exchange builds an index of all searchable text in a particular mailbox or public folder store before users try to search it. This allows for faster and more comprehensive searches.

Global Address List (GAL) — An address list generated by Exchange Server 2003 that contains, by default, an aggregation of all messaging recipients within the Exchange Server 2003 organization as well as all users within a foreign e-mail system connected by a dedicated connector, such as the Lotus Notes Connector or the GroupWise Connector. If no such connectors exist, the list contains all mail and mailbox-enabled recipients in the Exchange Server 2003 organization only.

global catalog server — A domain controller that holds a copy of all objects in an Active Directory forest and a subset of that object's attributes.

group — A collection of Active Directory objects that helps to simplify the management of objects with common requirements.

hard recovery — The replaying of restored transaction logs that occurs after a database has been restored.

incremental backup — A backup that takes a copy of only the transaction logs and deletes the transaction logs from the disk.

InetOrgPerson — A special user object with an extended set of attributes to support interactions with other directory services.

Information Store Integrity Checker (ISINTEG) — A utility that finds and eliminates common errors from the Microsoft Exchange Server public and private Information Store databases.

Installable File System — An API that allows you to access files stored on disk in formats other than FAT and HPFS, and access files that are stored on a network file server.

Internet Message Access Protocol (IMAP) — A protocol that is used by e-mail clients to retrieve messages from mail servers. It can manage multiple folders for message storage. As of this writing, the current version of the protocol is IMAP4.

InterOrg Replication Utility — A utility that replicates public folder contents during an inter-organizational migration.

junk e-mail filtering — A feature that automatically moves messages deemed likely to be junk mail to a junk mail folder.

Kerberos — The primary authentication protocol used in Active Directory environments.

LegacyExchangeDN attribute — An attribute of objects in Active Directory that is required for backward compatibility with Exchange Server 5.5. If this attribute is not correctly configured during a restore, the store is unable to mount.

Lightweight Directory Access Protocol (LDAP) — The protocol used to query the Active Directory database.

link monitor — One of two types of monitors created by default during the Exchange Server 2003 installation. This monitor, also known as a connection status monitor, checks the status of a connector between servers to determine if it is available. A connection status monitor is created automatically for each connector on the server.

link state algorithm — An algorithm, which is based on the OSPF algorithm, that operates over TCP port 691 in a routing group to propagate routing status information to all of the Exchange Server 2003 servers in the organization through the routing group master. This routing status, or link state, information is used by Exchange Server 2003 to determine the best path to send messages to other servers.

Mail Exchanger (MX) — The DNS resource record used to designate a mail server.

Mailbox Manager recipient policies — The policies that help manage user mailboxes so that users experience fewer problems. Mailbox Manager does this by helping you to keep track of mailbox usage. You can also notify users when their mailboxes have messages that should be cleaned up, or you can take action to clean up mailboxes by moving or deleting messages explicitly.

mailbox-enabled recipient — A recipient object that has a mailbox on an Exchange server, allowing it to send, receive, and store messages.

mail-enabled recipient — A recipient object that can receive e-mail messages but cannot store messages on (nor send messages via) an Exchange server.

Message Application Programming Interface (MAPI) — A set of callable functions that provides connectivity and operational procedures against a messaging system on the back end.

message edit conflict — A conflict that occurs when the content and/or properties associated with a message are modified on any server.

message tracking — A facility with Exchange Server 2003 that tracks all messages being transported through a messaging system. Message tracking maintains information about the various states the message passes through on its way to its destination.

Message Tracking Center — An Exchange tool that allows you to search message tracking logs for messages based on specified criteria, such as sender, recipient, time sent/delivered, server, message size, and so on.

messaging system — At a minimum, a method to send text messages from one computer user to another. More sophisticated systems also include features such as calendaring.

Microsoft Management Console (MMC) — The management environment into which different snap-in tools can be added for the purpose of managing system and application settings.

mixed administrative model — A model in which day-to-day administration is decentralized, however, functional administration, such as public folder trees management, policy management, and so on, is centralized into another administrative group.

mixed mode — The default Exchange Server 2003 organizational mode that supports environments running Exchange 5.5 servers.

MTA Check — A command-line tool that attempts to fix all MTA message queues and the messages that those queues contain.

multimaster replication — A replication mechanism that does not involve a centralized master copy of the information. When data is modified at each source, the changes are then automatically replicated from that source to all other replicas within the infrastructure.

Multipurpose Internet Mail Extensions (MIME) — A set of message headers, which describe what sort of content is in a message (plain text, HTML, graphics, and so on) and how it's encoded. Some of the content types are multipart, meaning that they define a complex message structure with more than one part, each of which has headers of its own. Each part has its own set of MIME headers, in addition to the headers at the beginning of the message. The headers allow the receiving client to determine which "helper" applications might be necessary to read the message or access attachments.

native mode—The primary Exchange Server 2003 organizational mode for environments that do not include Exchange 5.5 servers that makes it possible to take advantage of all Exchange Server 2003 features.

nondelivery report (NDR) — A message indicating that the delivery has failed. This report returns a code and information as to why the message could not be delivered to its final destination. NDRs are a valuable source of information when trying to troubleshoot message routing issues.

NTDSNoMatch — The value that must be set in Custom Attribute 10 of resource mailboxes. When this is set, ADC does not create users for resource mailboxes.

offline address list — A set of address lists in files that are created and stored on an offline address lists server. Users who work offline can connect to an Exchange 2003 server and download offline address lists remotely to obtain information about other users in the organization.

offline backup — A backup that requires the Exchange services to be stopped while a copy of the stores is taken.

Outlook 2003 — The primary messaging and collaboration software package used to interact with an Exchange server.

Outlook Express — The free Internet e-mail client provided with Microsoft operating systems.

Outlook Web Access (OWA) — The Exchange Server 2003 feature that allows users to access an Outlook-like environment from a Web browser. The Exchange Server 2003 version of OWA has almost the complete functionality of the standard Outlook client.

Post Office Protocol version 3 (POP3) — A protocol that is used by e-mail clients to retrieve messages from mail servers. Messages are typically downloaded to the client computer and removed from the server. POP3 can manage only a single folder, usually named Inbox, for message storage.

property promotion — A process whereby the properties of a document or attachment of a supported file type are parsed and promoted to the Information Store to allow for advanced searches.

protocol logging — A tool to log conversations between servers or between clients and servers. Each command that is used within the conversation is tracked.

public folder — A storage location in Exchange Server 2003 that facilitates the exchange of all types of information, such as e-mail messages, shared calendars, discussion groups, shared mailboxes, and messsaging applications, between groups of people in the organization.

public folder connection agreement — The settings that are used by ADC to control the replication of public folder information between Active Directory and the Exchange Server 5.5 directory. These can only be used if a recipient connection agreement is in place.

Public Folder Migration Tool (PFMigrate) — A utility that configures the replication of public folder contents during an intra-organizational migration.

public folder referral — A referral that enables you to route information requests to specific folders. Public folder referrals between routing groups are transitive and allow all referrals over the connection when enabled.

public folder replica — A replica that provides multiple, redundant information points and load balancing for accessing data.

Public Folder Replication Agent (PFRA) — The agent that monitors changes, additions, and deletions. This agent also sends change messages to other Information Stores on which replicated instances are located.

public folder store — A database for storing public folders in Exchange Server 2003.

public folder tree — An object in Active Directory that defines the folder hierarchy.

Public Key Infrastructure (PKI) — A system of digital certificates and certification authorities used to authenticate the identity of all parties in a secure messaging environment.

public root store — The default public folder store for an Exchange Server 2003 organization.

query-based distribution group — A special distribution group whose membership is defined dynamically according to the results of an LDAP query.

Queue Viewer — A tool used to examine queues used within Exchange Server 2003. This tool can be used to view queues and the messages they contain to help determine why messages are not being properly delivered.

recipient — Any Active Directory object that can receive e-mail messages in an Exchange organization. These include users, distribution groups, and public folders.

recipient connection agreement — The settings that are used by ADC to control the replication of recipient information between Active Directory and the Exchange Server 5.5 directory.

recipient policy — A policy applied to users and groups that allows the centralized configuration of e-mail address and mailbox management settings.

Recipient Update Service (RUS) — The service that builds and maintains address lists by creating and maintaining Exchange Server 2003–specific attribute values within Active Directory.

recovery storage group — A special storage group that lets administrators restore backed-up versions of Exchange databases and recover messages on an existing Exchange 2003 server rather than using an alternate recovery forest. This is a new feature in Exchange Server 2003.

remote procedure call (RPC) — A protocol that allows a program on one computer to execute a program on another computer. This is based on the client/server model, in which the requesting program is considered the client and the executing program is considered the server. Exchange servers in a routing group rely on this protocol to communicate with one another. Similarly, Exchange clients rely on this protocol to connect to Exchange servers.

remote procedure call (RPC) over Hypertext Transfer Protocol (HTTP) — A protocol that lets the full Outlook client communicate with Exchange Server 2003 over the Internet by encapsulating RPC requests within HTTP packets.

Resource Mailbox Wizard — A wizard that sets the value of Custom Attribute 10 of Exchange Server 5.5 resource mailboxes to NTDSNoMatch.

rooted hierarchy — A configuration in which all of the CAs in an organization are arranged below a common root CA.

routing group — A group that is a collection of servers that enjoy permanent, high-bandwidth connectivity. By default, Exchange Server 2003 functions as though all servers in an organization belong to a single, large routing group.

routing group connector — A connector that establishes the mechanism for delivering messages between routing groups. The routing group connector connects to the defined target server in the remote site and delivers the message on behalf of servers within the routing group that hosts the connector. This is the preferred method of connecting routing groups.

routing group master — The server that keeps track of the link state data and propagates that data to the rest of the servers in the routing group. When a nonmaster server receives new link state information, the nonmaster server immediately transfers the link state information to the master, so that other servers can receive the information about the routing change.

RPC Ping — A utility used to confirm the connectivity between two RPC systems.

scaling out — The process of installing an application on multiple servers to enhance performance.

schema — The group of all defined object classes and attributes supported by Active Directory. The Active Directory schema must be extended (via ForestPrep) to support Exchange Server 2003.

Secure Multipurpose Internet Mail Extension (S/MIME) — A protocol that is used to secure e-mail messages through the use of encryption and digital signatures.

Secure Sockets Layer (SSL) — A protocol developed to securely transmit data over the Internet in an encrypted format.

security group — An Active Directory group that is typically created for the purpose of assigning permissions or rights to group members.

server monitor — One of two types of monitors created by default during the Exchange Server 2003 installation. This monitor checks designated resources and Windows 2000/2003 services on a server to detect critical situations.

shared file messaging system — A messaging system in which client software performs the work of managing messages. These messaging systems are not very scalable.

SIDHistory — An attribute of a user object that is set and created by ADMT. It is used to preserve security settings when users are migrated from one domain to another.

Simple Mail Transfer Protocol (SMTP) — A protocol used to send e-mail on the Internet. SMTP is a set of rules regarding the interaction between a program sending e-mail and a program receiving e-mail. It was created in 1982.

Single Instance Storage (SIS) — A system that stores only a single instance of a message when it is sent to multiple recipients as long as the recipients are located on the same database. SIS is not maintained if the message is sent to users who reside on different databases.

SMTP connector — A connector that is designed to route mail to external e-mail systems, such as Internet mail hosts, or to another Exchange organization.

soft recovery — The replaying of the current transaction logs that occurs after a hard recovery.

SSL/TLS — An acronym for Secure Sockets Layer/ Transport Layer Security, a protocol that guarantees privacy and data integrity between client/server applications and between server-to-server communication.

storage group — A set of up to five databases that uses the same transaction log.

symmetric (secret-key) cryptography — A method of encrypting and decrypting messages in which encryption and decryption is achieved using a single, shared key that is known only to the sender and receiver.

system policy — The settings that simplify the administration of groups of servers, mailbox stores, and public folder stores by centralizing the configuration of multiple objects.

system state — The configuration information on a Windows server that includes the registry and Active Directory that can be backed up as a unit.

tombstone — A marker designating an Information Store item to be deleted in Exchange Server 2003. During the Information Store nightly maintenance cycle, these markers are examined, and if found to be past a default expiration date, the corresponding item is permanently deleted.

top-level public folder — Referred to as the parent folder. The top-level folder represents the top of a public folder tree. If the new public folder is a top-level folder, the contents of the new folder are on the user's public folder server.

virtual private network (VPN) — A remote access connection that encrypts information as it is transmitted across the Internet to keep it private.

Volume Shadow Copy — A service that takes a snapshot of files for backup even while they are open.

WinRoute — An Exchange tool that extracts and displays the routing information that Exchange is using to route messages throughout the network.

X.400 connector — A connector that is designed to connect Exchange servers with legacy X.400 systems or two low-bandwidth Exchange servers to each other.

Index

535

Microsoft® Windows® Server 2003
Enterprise Edition 180-Day Evaluation

The software included in this kit is intended for evaluation and deployment planning purposes only. If you plan to install the software on your primary machine, it is recommended that you back up your existing data prior to installation.

System requirements

To use Microsoft Windows Server 2003 Enterprise Edition, you need:

- Computer with 550 MHz or higher processor clock speed recommended; 133 MHz minimum required; Intel Pentium/Celeron family, or AMD K6/Athlon/Duron family, or compatible processor (Windows Server 2003 Enterprise Edition supports up to eight CPUs on one server)
- 256 MB of RAM or higher recommended; 128 MB minimum required (maximum 32 GB of RAM)
- 1.25 to 2 GB of available hard-disk space*
- CD-ROM or DVD-ROM drive
- Super VGA (800 × 600) or higher-resolution monitor recommended; VGA or hardware that supports console redirection required
- Keyboard and Microsoft Mouse or compatible pointing device, or hardware that supports console redirection

Additional items or services required to use certain Windows Server 2003 Enterprise Edition features:

- For Internet access:
  - Some Internet functionality may require Internet access, a Microsoft Passport account, and payment of a separate fee to a service provider; local and/or long-distance telephone toll charges may apply
  - High-speed modem or broadband Internet connection
- For networking:
  - Network adapter appropriate for the type of local-area, wide-area, wireless, or home network to which you wish to connect, and access to an appropriate network infrastructure; access to third-party networks may require additional charges

Note: To ensure that your applications and hardware are Windows Server 2003–ready, be sure to visit **www.microsoft.com/windowsserver2003**.

* Actual requirements will vary based on your system configuration and the applications and features you choose to install. Additional available hard-disk space may be required if you are installing over a network. For more information, please see **www.microsoft.com/windowsserver2003**.

Uninstall instructions

This time-limited release of Microsoft Windows Server 2003 Enterprise Edition will expire 180 days after installation. If you decide to discontinue the use of this software, you will need to reinstall your original operating system. You may need to reformat your drive.